W9-ASI-587

THE WORLD OF PERSONS

THE WORLD OF PERSONS

by

CHARLES WINCKELMANS DE CLÉTY, S.J.

With a Foreword by

FREDERICK C. COPLESTON, S.J.

and a Preface by

PROFESSOR JEAN LADRIÈRE

NEW YORK

SHEED & WARD

SHEED & WARD INC.
64 University Place, New York, N.Y. 10003

First published 1967

CUM PERMISSU SUPERIORUM ORDINIS

NIHIL OBSTAT: JOHN M. T. BARTON, S.T.D., L.S.S., Censor

IMPRIMATUR: ✠ PATRICK CASEY, Vicar-General
Westminster, 13 February 1967

The Nihil obstat *and* Imprimatur *are official declarations that a book or pamphlet is free of doctrinal or moral error. No implication is contained therein that those who have granted the* Nihil obstat *and* Imprimatur *agree with the opinions expressed.*

This book has been accepted by the University of Poona (India) as a thesis for the Ph.D. degree. We are grateful to the University of Poona for permission to publish it.

Library of Congress Catalog Card No.: 67-21905

Printed in Great Britain

Foreword

by Frederick C. Copleston, S.J.

Wittgenstein remarked in his *Notebooks*, under the date 12th August 1916, that the I enters into philosophy through the fact that the world is *my* world. And this idea reappears in the *Tractatus* (5. 641). Father Winckelmans de Cléty is not indeed concerned, in the first instance at least, with what Wittgenstein calls "the philosophical I" or "the metaphysical subject". At the same time his book can be regarded as being, in part at least, a study, and indeed a penetrating study, of the concept of "my world" or, rather, of the relation "I and my world". By saying this I am not trying to represent the author as in any sense a follower of Wittgenstein. He stands in the tradition of continental phenomenology, not in that of the so-called analytic movement. And his philosophical idiom is certainly not that of Professor Gilbert Ryle or the late J. L. Austin. But as the language of this book is somewhat different from that to which recent British and American philosophizing has accustomed us, it may be useful to draw attention to the connection between one of the main themes of the book and a concept mentioned by Ludwig Wittgenstein. With Wittgenstein the concept, which seems to derive originally from Schopenhauer's doctrine of the world as "my idea", is developed linguistically. "*The limits of my language* mean the limits of my world" (*Tractatus*, 5. 6). With Father Winckelmans de Cléty the concept seems to me to be developed on the lines of existentialist phenomenology. "My own life ('I live') constitutes the meaning of the universe: the world of which I have experience is essentially the field of my existence; in other words, my existence *is* the existence of the world-for-me" (pp. 30–1).

According to the author my world is constituted "by the life-act which I am" (p. 350), while our world, the common human world, is a plurality of mutually involved personal worlds. On this interpretation of the concept of "the world" the question obviously arises whether it makes any sense to speak of a world existing before men, before human persons. The author grasps the bull by the horns and solves the problem in terms of a metaphysical theory which is in some respects reminiscent of the philosophy of Berkeley but which is likely to cause some eyebrow-raising. However, if philosophers always sedulously avoided propounding any theory which might cause surprise, we should be without the philosophies of Leibniz, Kant and Wittgenstein, to name only three celebrated philosophers. After all, Wittgenstein said some pretty odd things. And a measure of intrepidity in metaphysical speculation doubtless comes as a refreshing change from a diet of glimpses of the obvious. In any case, if the conclusion seems unacceptable to the reader, he should devote his attention to the premiss.

The writer of this Foreword finds himself unable to go all the way with Father Winckelmans de Cléty. But philosophers are not noted for seeing eye to eye with one another. And it is by no means necessary to agree with all that an author says in order to derive stimulus from his writing. Paradoxically, perhaps one can sometimes derive special enlightenment and stimulus from thinkers with whom one is inclined to disagree fairly strongly. In any case this is a serious and indeed remarkable work. It can hardly be said to represent the fashionable style of philosophizing in this country. But we badly need some variety. The word "metaphysics" is indeed no longer a term of abuse. We are told that we can say what we like, provided that we give some reason for saying it. But though metaphysics is certainly treated with a considerably greater degree of tolerance than it was some twenty years ago, one can hardly claim that it is much practised, not at least under the name of "metaphysics". Well, here is an example of explicit metaphysical thinking by a philosopher who is evidently giving us the fruits of prolonged and sustained personal reflection. The result of his reflection can reasonably be described as a world-vision. And world-visions are, it is true, generally frowned on by those who prefer either to insinuate their own, without explicitly stating it, or simply to presuppose its validity. But it is natural for the reflective mind to attempt to form a coherent interpretation of the world; and world-visions are often present even when they are not acknowledged as such. It is desirable that they should be made explicit, and that presuppositions should be revealed. Hence I cannot see any cogent objection to the author's enterprise on the grounds that it results in a world-vision. Whether one agrees or not with his interpretation of "the world" is a matter for rational decision, a decision which should be taken only after one has examined his line of argument.

Preface

by Professor Jean Ladrière

Is a Christian philosophy possible? According to all appearances, this question calls for a negative answer. Indeed, philosophy is an effort by which human minds relying upon their own resources—that is to say, upon reason—try to grasp, as radically as possible, the meaning of reality, such as it is given to us in experience. One might say that philosophy is a discourse which tends to identify itself with experience; it is an effort which aims at expressing in an appropriate conceptual apparatus the totality of what is given to us in reality as lived by us, not only in its explicit aspects but also (and mostly) in its implicit aspects, which are not immediately perceptible. On the other hand, Christianity is a religious experience based upon a revelation—that is, upon a word spoken by God to man. On one side the discourse of reason (merely human), on the other the word in which God gives himself. Between the two, a radical discontinuity. Never will a philosophical discourse, however developed, successfully reconstitute God's word and so absorb it in itself. On the other hand, if human reason, making use of the resources of philosophical thinking, endeavours to understand, so far as it can, the content of God's word, it must necessarily begin by accepting this word; thus it relies no longer upon itself but upon the light which this word contains and it makes itself its instrument—such an undertaking is no longer philosophical. Therefore philosophy seems unable to meet Christianity: if it tries to reduce it to itself—that is, to interpret it according to its own categories—it destroys it; if it makes itself the instrument of an explication of Christianity—if it accepts from the start whatever Christianity contains—it is no longer philosophy, it becomes theology.

However, there is a possibility of conceiving the relation between philosophy and Christian faith as something else than an inclusion of the one in the other. Revelation, as implied in its concept, is a manifestation to man of God's world; therefore, by nature, it is such as can be effectively received by man; conversely, human reality includes in itself that which enables it to open itself to revelation. Revelation is not entirely extrinsic to human reality. No doubt with regard to human discourse, it presents itself as something absolutely new, as a break, an event in the strongest meaning of the word. But it is an event which concerns man in what he really is; it could not be an event if it did not insert itself in a real history in which is initially included the possibility of its arising. If revelation is not something vain, it must open to man a new field of experience, possibilities of self-realization which man could not give to himself through the mere resources of his own discourse. But if it is something real, it must already have its place in the context of human experience, it must correspond to a secret expectation which the human being feels in himself without being able to grasp its full meaning, it must answer a call which, moved by its deepest desire, the human soul addresses, with the whole of itself, though not always acknowledging it explicitly, to that Infinite of which it has only a presentiment, a need, and yet whose reality it longs to possess.

If all this is true, it must be possible to bring to light, through a sufficiently lucid analysis, this immanent possibility, this expectation and demand, this existential desire. It is not a question here of having any explicit recourse to revelation, but simply of taking human experience as it is, of analysing its content with the help of reason alone, of accepting it as it presents itself once it is thus scrutinized by reason. But if, in fact, there is in the human being an openness to revelation, if there are potentialities which enable him to hear God's word to the extent that it is addressed to him, then a truly and exclusively philosophical study of experience must be able to bring to light whatever, in the human being, is, as it were, constitutionally attuned to revelation as lived by Christianity. No doubt, this bringing to light will never constitute any kind of rational demonstration of revelation, the establishing of a necessary link between the structure of the human being and the fact of revelation; the latter remains an event, it cannot be deduced from what is included in the essence of man—the only domain to which philosophical reason has access. In any case, the discontinuity indicated above between philosophical discourse and God's word remains radical. Perhaps, however, philosophical discourse is capable of disposing itself in some way for a meeting with God's word—as we find in the beautiful formula of the medieval thinkers, *intellectus quaerens fidem*—of presenting human existence as the expectation of a realization which can be effected in it only by this word, of making itself, therefore, an expectation of this word. Waiting for God's word is not yet listening to it or accepting it; the man who waits still remains entirely on this side of faith, he still remains within the sphere of jurisdiction of rational effort; however, his expectation is already secretly attracted towards the term, inaccessible to it, which, by its very structure, it indicates, though in a merely potential manner. Such a conception of philosophical effort rightly deserves the title of Christian philosophy. Philosophy it is, undoubtedly; at no time is there any reliance on resources other than the data of experience and the mechanism of rational analysis. As such, this philosophy is not specifically Christian. But, on the other hand, by showing in human reality an opening to a possible revelation, by bringing to light an agreement, a sort of secret "collusion" between the being of man and Christian revelation, it is already marked in itself, in the direction which its effort follows implicitly, by the event of revelation as the realization of that of which it is only the presentiment. No doubt, it cannot by itself give this interpretation to its undertaking, since it must necessarily stop on this side of the event of revelation, whereas such an interpretation would already bring this event into play. Therefore it is from the outside of such a philosophy that its Christian meaning can appear. With regard to its explicit meaning—the only meaning which it can be aware of—it is philosophy through and through, purely and simply. It is only with regard to its implicit meaning, which it has not by itself the possibility of bringing to light, that it can be characterized as a Christian philosophy. Therefore, if there is no contradiction between the terms "philosophy" and "Christian", if a Christian philosophy is not only logically not contradictory but effectively possible, it can be so, it seems, only in the form of a paradoxical undertaking which rises, in its own movement, above the level of meaning which it can possibly attribute to its own effort, which goes beyond itself without ceasing to be itself, which constitutes its discourse only to prepare, in this very discourse, the surpassing of all discourse.

Such, if we are not mistaken, is the conception of philosophy which underlies the monumental work of Father Winckelmans. But, if that is so, it is only by examining how effectively he has succeeded in carrying out his original intention that we shall grasp the full significance of his undertaking. A truly philosophical effort must be inspired by the intuition of a radical rational truth, of an entirely faithful and entirely intelligible interpretation of experience. The unfolding of such an intuition must necessarily be effected with the help of a rigorous method of analysis. On the other hand, a philosophy the implicit intention of which is to show the presence, at the very heart of human existence, of a movement which points to something which is beyond it, cannot be a purely conceptual effort, a mere logical construction. It must itself follow, not only in its intention, but also in its way of proceeding, this movement which it tries to explicate; it must be, as it were, an action of the human mind upon itself through the medium of an intellectual *démarche*. By progressively bringing experience back to its foundation, by letting the human reality gradually discover what it is in itself, what is really at stake in its various initiatives, it must make it see itself as a certain need and a certain claim, and orientate it actively, in the direction which this need and this claim indicate; it must not only reveal the truth of existence, but lead existence towards its truth. In such a philosophy, the effort by which experience endeavours to express itself, to express whatever it contains implicitly in itself, by which experience tries to go back to the very conditions of its unfolding, must be at the same time the effort by which it tries deliberately and explicitly to make its own the exercise of these conditions, by which it tries to become really responsible for itself, by identifying its action, its explicit being, with its immanent dynamism, with its implicit being. Father Winckelmans' undertaking fulfils precisely—in a very concrete manner—these two conditions: it is characterized at the same time by an exemplary methodological rigour and by a conception of philosophy which makes of thinking an action and of speculative research a progress of the soul towards its own kingdom. It makes use of a phenomenological method and assumes the form of an ethical philosophy. Thereby it is the meeting-point of two great philosophical lines, which are at the heart of contemporary thought but which, both, are a continuation of famous systems: on the one hand the phenomenological line, marked by the figure of Husserl, in which, however, the echo of Hegel can be heard (whose phenomenology, although very different from that of Husserl, expresses nevertheless the idea of a radical explication of the phenomenon), on the other hand the ethical line, marked by the figure of Blondel, in which the echo of Spinoza can be heard (whose metaphysic, although very different from that of Blondel, expresses nevertheless the idea of a philosophy-conversion, which must raise us to a fully authentic mode of existence).

First, what about the method? A true philosophy must provide itself with an instrument fully appropriate to its ambition, which is the elaboration of a true discourse; it must devise a method which enables it to master its subject-matter according to a well-defined order in full consonance with the indications of experience, and to exercise at every moment a precise control of the steps it takes, the concepts it utilizes, the concatenations it forms. Therefore it must be animated by a desire for rigour as great as that which characterizes science in its own order and which gives it its efficacy and its authority. Husserl was perfectly right when he proposed the ideal of philosophy as a rigorous science. But philosophy is not science. Whereas each science is concerned only with a well-defined sector of experience, which moreover it gives itself beforehand as an unquestioned presupposition, philosophy endeavours to grasp the totality of experience, in its global aspect as well as in its particular articulations, and aims at reaching the *right* beyond the *fact*—that is, to bring to light the foundation of experience, the source of its legitimacy, that which makes of it precisely what it is. Its object is experience in its integrality and it questions it in an integral manner. In other words, whereas particular sciences study the content of the different regions of experience, philosophy takes as its task the elucidation of experience as such, the comprehension of what constitutes experience in itself, of that by which there is experience. But how is such an understanding possible? There is no question of simply making observations, of simply recording facts such as we see them, for such a way of proceeding would not enable us to bring to light what makes experience possible, the dynamic principle which gives it life from inside. If we stay in the realm of facts—considering them in their factualness—we shall never grasp either the totality (which is by no means a collection of facts but the unity to which all facts belong and out of which they can arise) or the foundation (which is immanent in facts, no doubt, but is not identical with the mere external manifestation in which a fact consists). There is no question either of contemplating any justification of facts from principles laid down beforehand, any *a priori* deduction of all data. For we cannot have recourse to principles of deduction unless we provide some kind of justification for these principles. If we seek to found them upon principles which are even more fundamental, the result is an endless regression. If we maintain that these principles are given in an appropriate evidence, we must show how they are given. But it is clear that they cannot be given to us in the way in which the facts of immediate experience are given; therefore, if they are given, this can only be in a mediate manner. There is already need of a reflection, and consequently of an interpretation of immediate experience, to discover the way in which such principles manifest themselves. Indeed, if it appears that, at such or such a moment of our philosophical enquiry, we can have recourse to basic principles, we must still show how, from what is immediately given, we can discover these principles, how the very structure of what is given points to their existence. If there are principles—that is, intelligible elements in whose light concrete reality such as it presents itself can be made transparent and be justified—they must pertain to the internal texture of reality. We can make use of them only to the extent that we have first succeeded in discovering them through a detailed analysis of this texture. But this analysis must start from reality such as it is given to us at the level of facts. Are we not thus caught up in a situation from which there is no way out? If we remain at the level of facts, we shall have no means of understanding them really in accordance with the radicalism which characterizes the philosophical undertaking, and if, to give a foundation to facts, we want to make use of terms which are not immediately given, we are left with no alternative but to justify these terms on the basis of facts. Indeed, all hope of a justificative comprehension would be vain if facts presented themselves to us as nothing but mere facts, as perfectly free spheres without any connection with each other and without internal structure.

But, in truth, this is not the way in which experience presents itself, in which reality is given to us. We must look more attentively at the manner in which the meeting of facts, the gift of the given, takes place, in which the realm of phenomena presents itself. As indicated by its etymology, the word "phenomenon" means the appearing of reality, its self-revelation within experience; it means reality itself as appearing, as leaving its isolation to come and meet consciousness, to offer itself to its grasp. In the phenomenon, reality, while remaining itself, without abandoning itself, comes our way; it comes towards us from itself, it manifests itself in a manner conformable to its own resources, without relying on anything but the internal dynamism which resides in it and which gives it precisely the power of unfolding itself in the field of manifestation. Therefore, the phenomenon is not at all the presentation of a closed, opaque and impenetrable surface, a mere crude datum which does not go beyond itself and comes into being inexplicably, in an irremediable isolation, out of something which cannot be determined. The phenomenon is the unfolding of reality from an origin which is immanent in it, which belongs to its own structure, which determines its most essential possibilities. Hence, by grasping the phenomenon as phenomenon, we penetrate into the very manifestation of reality, into that unfolding which it is and in which it gives itself; we witness the coming of reality towards us; we somehow accompany it in this revelation in which it manifests itself. From this moment, we have only to follow the indications of which the phenomenon itself is the bearer to be able to travel this road in the opposite direction—that is, to go back from the manifestation towards that which makes it possible, from the external surface where reality shows itself towards the origin of its self-unfolding, that is, towards its principles. Therefore, it is possible to go beyond facts, because facts are phenomena, not pure undecomposable data, but a process of manifestation. It is possible to go back towards the principles because the phenomenon itself, as a movement from an origin towards a self-manifestation, as the unfolding of a principle, gives us the leading thread which enables us to rediscover this principle, to grasp again the origin behind the self-manifestation and in it. But once we have gone beyond the immediate self-manifestation, we must carry on our course. Once we have undertaken the regressive movement which must lead us towards the heart of experience, towards the centre from which everything unfolds, we realize that we are penetrating into a vast region of reality the structure of which is extremely complex. We are then in the field of principles, but we reach them not as *a priori* elements—as if they were purely logical elements, premises assignable to possible deductions—but as concrete elements, which belong to the very texture of reality, which have in themselves the density of things such as they are given to us, the density of whatever offers itself unquestionably to our apprehension. We have then to determine the topography of this domain, to make out the leading threads which enable us to carry our analysis further, to penetrate even further into the realm of foundations until we succeed in bringing out the most fundamental condition of our experience, the very centre from which it is organized, the principle of unity which makes of it a totality, the hidden mainspring which makes it unfold itself before our eyes, constitute itself in us, in all the complexity of its multiple articulations. The field of principles, the realm of foundation, presents itself as a diverging network organized in the form of an arborescent structure. We start from the periphery—that is, from the most exterior, the most diversified branches—and, from embranchment to embranchment, we go back little by little towards the centre of the network, the root of the tree, the hidden activity which incessantly projects around it this complicated ramification and makes its terminations emerge into our immediate experience.

Thus it is the very structure of the phenomenon which opens a way to interpretation; we have only to acknowledge the phenomenon as phenomenon, to surrender ourselves to it, in order to be carried, by the solicitations of the phenomenon itself, into a fundamental network the description of which must provide speculative discourse with both the schema of its own organization and the detail of its content. Philosophy, as a discursive justification of experience, will be the bringing to light of this internal structure which gives experience its unity and coherence, establishes its rightfulness, guarantees and legitimizes its intelligibility. The method of philosophy will be to follow the indications of the phenomenon, and this method will be rigorous because the internal organization of the phenomenon is a real immanent logic which ensures the systematic and necessary concatenation of all its constitutive terms. The explication of the phenomenon is the explication of this logic; therefore it is governed through and through by the imperatives of liaison which constitute the very content of this logic. A philosophy which follows such a method deserves to be called a phenomenology, a science of the phenomenon. This is the methodological perspective which Father Winckelmans has adopted.

Now, what about the ethical aspect?

A vigorous and really coherent philosophical effort must be entirely understandable from the methodological decisions on which it is based. Fr Winckelmans' choice of a resolutely phenomenological method is the starting-point from which his thought unfolds the totality of its movement. It is from his methodological positions that we can understand the central essential *démarche* of this thought, what makes of it precisely an ethical thought. A resolute phenomenology, determined to persevere to the end of its undertaking, must include a double movement: as indicated above, a regressive movement by which, following the solicitations of the phenomenon, it goes back step by step towards the central principle of experience, and a prospective movement by which, from this central point, it tries to reconstitute the whole of its operations, to understand how it exercises its foundational function, how, from itself, it brings out the totality of experience, in the multiplicity of its aspects and the unity of its fundamental movement. After having travelled from the manifestation to the principles and having reached the principle of all principles, we must follow the opposite road, come back from this principle and from the kingdom of principles towards the manifestation, reproduce the foundational action of the principle, understand how the principle is principle, what is finally the movement of expression by which the phenomenon exists both in its manifestation and in the logic of its internal structure. Only then shall we really understand experience as such, understand how there is such a thing as experience. Only then shall we begin to identify ourselves with the immanent life of experience, with the incessant movement of its self-production. This is, indeed, the way in which Fr Winckelmans proceeds. At the end of a very searching analysis of the phenomenon, he shows us that there is, at the very heart of experience, a central activity, an essential operation which is the foundation of the whole realm of manifestation and is called life-act. Then, in a prospective *démarche* rigorously organized, he endeavours to show how this prime act unfolds itself and how we can reconstitute, from its operations, the whole diversity of experience in all its structural layers and in all its sectorial articulations. But this reconstitution of experience from this central act is nothing but the analysis of the structure of this very act: the articulation of experience is its own articulation. Thus it is by a study of its internal constitution that we shall finally be able to account for experience itself. Therefore, by coming back from the life-act towards experience, in its concrete manifestation, we do not abandon this act, and pass on to a term which is exterior to it; once we have discovered the life-act, we progress in it, from the beginning till the end. It is by entering into its operation that we can understand from this act the complete organization of experience.

As the central operation of experience in which experience unfolds itself and offers itself to us as it is in its manifestation, the life-act is the real principle of unity of experience, that which makes of it not a plurality of juxtaposed contents but a real totality, a unified wave, an undivided expanse. It is at the same time the unity of meaning and the source of meaning of this totality. Experience is pregnant with meaning, it is, as it were, immersed in an atmosphere of meaning. At the level of the phenomenon, meaning expresses and diversifies itself for us in a multiplicity of particular meanings which, though different, are related to one another in numberless ways. But there is a principle by which the various contents of experience have a meaning, by which the world is given to us as a system of meanings, by which experience as such is inhabited by meaning, by which there is a universal life of meaning. This principle must be such as can produce meaning, as can secrete it in the very exercise of its function as principle; in other words, this principle must be an operative term, therefore an act. As this act is source, incessant movement of genesis, production of meaning, it really deserves the name of life-act.

This life-act is the meeting-point of two movements of constitution: in relation to one of these movements, it is produced, in relation to the other, it is source. In other words, it is at the same time constituted and constituting; it is constituted as a power of constitution, it is constituting to the extent that it is itself constituted. Therefore, if it is act of constitution, it cannot be so in an absolute manner, but only from an "already-there" which it must necessarily take up in its constituting activity. As act, it is operation, active position rooted in itself, unfolding from itself, source. In living itself as such, it unfolds around it and before it a totality which embraces and unites a unified system of contents—that is, a world. In so far as it thus posits a world in its exercise, it can be called act-world. But it posits its world not in a direct manner, but through the medium of its incarnation: it is through the mediation of its body that it refers itself to the world. But this body itself is not a mere given for the life-act, it is object of constitution, it is in the course of the universal operation of constitution which the life-act takes up into itself. It is while constituting its body, while positing itself as source of incarnation, that it becomes act constitutive of its world; it is to the very extent that it projects itself into an incarnate form that it enables itself to unfold around it this meaningful totality which we call world.

But this life-act, while constituting, is also constituted, and this in a twofold manner: on the one hand it is inserted into a world which is anterior to it and which conditions its constituting operation itself; on the other hand it is inhabited by potentialities which it has not given to itself but in which it finds itself given to itself. Its world-positing operation is not an absolute position; rather, it is a super-position in the sense that it is from an already constituted world of which it is, as it were, the heir that it can unfold the world which is its own. No doubt, this pre-constituted world is not exterior to it—otherwise it could not influence it in its very operation—it is, as it were, inserted into its own being, it conditions it from inside, so that it is only by making use of the resources which it contains and by following the indications which it offers that it can unfold itself and, by this very fact, give existence to the world of which it is the centre. It is none the less true that this pre-given world is independent of it—in itself the life-act transcends all given, but it is only from a given, not from an absolute beginning, that it can exercise its own initiative. Therefore, although it is source, it is dependent; it is even *as source* that it is dependent, in the sense that it is in its constituting activity that it is conditioned by a reality which is anterior to it. Naturally this pre-given world refers to other constituting acts; thus we discover behind us all the historical density of human life, the concatenation in time of the life-acts which have brought forth this cultural world in which we live and exercise our activity. But beyond this historico-cultural world, there is the pre-human world of nature. Here we must have recourse to other non-human constituting acts, to "cosmic persons", according to a very original and attractive theory put forward by the author. At the origin of all world, at the origin of each one of those worlds which together form what we simply call the world, there are acts-worlds and all these acts, each in its own manner, are conditioned; no one is an absolute beginning. This dependence which affects them in their exercise is the sign of a transcendental dependence, which affects them in their very being, which is the foundation of their very possibility. The analysis of this transcendental dependence enables us to bring to light their most fundamental structure, which is that of their created-being, that by which they are given to themselves in an absolute manner.

Moreover, and more deeply, every life-act is conditioned by its own content, by that which defines it as act: there is question here no longer of a dependence upon an already constituted reality, but of a dependence upon that which belongs to it essentially, in the form of potentialities which are inserted into it and form what might be called its essence. This constituting operation of the life-act is nothing but its realization of these potentialities, the projection of them in the field of exteriority which is formed by the pre-given world. But, just as the already constituted world refers to an antecedent constitution and, therefore, to other acts, so also these internal possibilities of the life-act refer to a constituting activity which operates inside this act and makes it precisely what it is: a life-act determined in such and such a way. There is, in the life-act, a setting in motion of its very actuality, an actuation which makes of it source, constituting activity. This principle is a creative dynamism, a will, an intention which gives it an internal tension, by which the potentialities of the life-act ordain themselves towards their realization. But the adequate fulfilment of such an expectation cannot be anything but the goal for which the life-act is created as it is—that is, its end. The intention which is at work in it is the volition in it, and the anticipation of its end; it is the force which drives it towards the realization of its end.

Precisely here, the phenomenological reflection becomes ethical reflection—not in virtue of a new intellectual decision, of an intervention which comes somehow from outside, but in virtue of its internal methodological dynamism, following the requirements of its progress. The life-act, we have just seen, is set in motion by an internal actuation which is the volition in it of its own end. But, at the same time, the life-act has in itself the possibility of making its own this movement, of identifying with itself the operation by which it is constituted. This fundamental possibility makes of the life-act a personal act. The personal-act is nothing but the integration, in an operation which is both reflective and volitive, of what the life-act contains in itself. The destination of the life-act, one may say, is to realize itself in the personal-act so that it does not really perfect itself unless it raises itself to the level of personal existence. The personal-act is really reflection—that is, it is really a returning of the constituting operation upon itself, an active identification of this operation with itself, it is the process by which the life-act takes itself up consciously; but it is also—at the same time, in the same movement—a real voluntary act—that is to say, it is really a positional activity, a radical initiative, it is self-conquest, dynamism of self-affirmation, a seizing up in its own operation of the constituting dynamism which animates the life-act and makes it what it is. Reflection is here really active self-grasp, integral self-conquest, and the positional activity is really reflection, self-grasp. The union, in one and the same operation, of this reflective aspect and of the voluntary aspect constitutes precisely the ethical moment of this thought and brings us to the real core of its meaning.

While taking up in its own operation the intention inherent in the life-act, the personal-act, *ipso facto*, ratifies this intention, makes it its own. Thus it adheres fully to the creative intentionality which, in positing the life-act, gives it both the power of unfolding itself as such and of positing its world, and the power of going beyond itself, of taking itself up in the personal-act in which it must find its realization. Hence in the integrating operation effected by the personal-act, we must discover again whatever constitutes the life-act, whatever belongs to it: the creative operation which posits it, its own unfolding, the world which it itself posits, the pre-given world which it takes up in its own initiatives, the potentialities which it bears in itself and on the basis of which it can operate, the tension towards its end which animates it and constitutes the mainspring of its action. Thus the personal-act takes up and integrates the life-act in its totality, in all its extension—that is, in all its dimensions, in the fullness of its experience—it is this experience coming into full light, reaching its total efficacy. In it, experience finds both its truth and its meaning, its foundation and the goal of its unfolding. Therefore the personal-act is truly, more than the life-act of which it is itself the truth, the heart of experience; in it, everything finds itself, realizes itself. Hence, it is not astonishing that we should find, in the personal-act, the synthesis of whatever phenomenological analysis has enabled us to discover.

The human being becomes a person only in the act by which the explicit will, the "willed will" as Blondel would have said, coincides with the implicit will which animates and constitutes it, with what Blondel called the "willing will", which makes of the human being a dynamism tending towards an absolute end, which makes him appear in his own eyes as a limitless need and a limitless claim. This coincidence is essentially acceptance, ratification by the being-as-will of the being-as-essence; but, since the being-as-essence refers to the creative will which posits it, the proper act of the person, which comes from the person and at the same time constitutes it, is the adhesion of the finite will to the infinite will; it is a submission of the human being to the solicitation by which the absolute, having posited him outside himself, calls him back to himself. Therefore the personal-act is fundamentally obedience.

Man, however, does not live necessarily and spontaneously in obedience. His being is given to him, but, at the same time, depends on him. He cannot fail to be what he is, but he can refuse himself; it is up to him to be for himself what he is in himself; the realization of what he is depends on this acceptance. The reason for this is that his being is given to him not as fully realized being, but as being to be perfected, as a tension towards an end—that is to say, as a destiny. It is precisely the realization of this destiny which depends upon him. Only through the medium of his own will can it be realized. But, since this will is really his, it is really up to him to decide what is to become of him. The meaning of his existence is really in suspense for itself and in itself. Therefore, in the human being, there is a twofold possibility as to the manner in which he will realize his destiny: that of inauthentic existence and that of authentic existence. Inauthentic existence is that which does not really integrate itself, which refuses to take integrally upon itself the dynamism which animates it. Authentic existence is that which shows itself capable of so doing, which follows the road of obedience. But this road is also that of truth, in the double sense of fullness of meaning and of the end in which existence realizes itself.

This is precisely the content of the *Pater*, the Christian prayer *par excellence*: "Thy will be done on earth as it is in heaven." Therefore, at the horizon of this thought, it is the Christian experience which we discover. But it is merely announced, at the conclusion of an effort which remains through and through an effort of reason—of reason based upon itself and aiming at itself, aiming at a radical rational comprehension. This effort leads us to a point where we discover what is the reality of human existence, what is really at stake in it, what, in it, must be decided. It shows us how the structure of experience is in itself of an ethical nature, contains in itself the indication of an essential need, of a call, and assumes by itself the form of a vocation. But have we by ourselves the possibility of answering the call which is our very being? Can we, through our own strength, go to the end of our vocation, travel effectively the road whose direction and even whose end we have discovered through a lucid intellectual effort? In itself, philosophical discourse is already a call, it is already of an ethical nature; but, as discourse, it is only the indication of ethical existence, it is not the realization of it.

Must we not, to realize in fact what the discourse gives us in the form of a presentiment, abandon the discourse and turn towards a word which is at the same time authentic life? Must we not, to become really this personal-act the conditions of which are analysed by speculative thought, leave speculative thought and turn towards a person who is in himself way, truth and life? These questions no longer belong to philosophy, they already take us to the threshold of religious experience.

Fr Winckelmans' intention was to do the work of a philosopher. He has given us, at the end of an elaboration which is bold, vigorous, complex, but wonderfully unified, which contains an infinite number of shades and an extreme variety of contents, an exegesis of human existence the radical character of which fulfils the demands of the most severe logic and of an uncompromising will for comprehension and justification. But the view he offers us is not locked up in itself in the manner of a closed system; on the contrary, in proportion as it develops, it opens us for a continually wider, a more and more infinite, horizon. At the moment it reaches its final and decisive point, at its conclusion, it leaves us, as it were, in suspense before a threshold which it is no longer the task of philosophical thinking to cross. The greatness of his undertaking is to have led us up to the point where philosophy, without ceasing to be faithful to itself, in the very name of this fidelity, in the name of its most intimate demands, of its deepest will, prepares itself for its own abdication, not in bitterness for its own inadequacy, but in the joy of a presentiment. Its imperishable merit is to make us experience the virtue of this presentiment and to establish its truth.

Contents

Part Two

EXPLORING THE HUMAN WORLD

Part One

DISCOVERING THE PERSONAL FIELD

CHAPTER I

The World

When I look at the world in a rather superficial manner, I see it as a vast container in which innumerable objects co-exist. No doubt, I realize that all these objects act upon each other, but nevertheless I consider them as essentially exterior to one another; I exclude the very possibility of their penetrating each other. Thus my view of the world is that of a totality made up of many different units subsisting together without merging. Each of these units appears to me as something definite, something which makes sense by itself, which is complete in itself. Those houses which I see through the window standing in a row along the street are in their massiveness, in the clarity of their features, entities which raise no problems, which need nothing in order to be themselves. Each of them is a whole which exists where it is by excluding anything else than itself. No. 32 is for ever that mass of plastered bricks pierced with six holes occupying that portion of space. It allows No. 34 and No. 36 to be what they are in their proper places, but it requires nothing from them and gives them nothing: it exhausts itself by being No. 32, by standing there *partes extra partes*, by offering itself to my sight and affirming itself as itself and no more than itself. Thus each object is characterized by its compactness, its self-sufficiency, its definitiveness, its exclusiveness—in a word, it is "in itself". This is what appears to me from the natural standpoint.

But there is another way of looking at the world.

I am sitting at my table. Before me: a few sheets of white paper, four or five books, an ink-bottle, a clock, a crucifix. Around me: the other pieces of furniture, the white walls, the door, the window. Beyond: the other rooms of the house, the great city, the whole world.

My eyes are fixed on the clock which stands there on my table. It is an object[1]—that is, a spatial configuration which reveals a certain unity. This unity is not simply the massiveness of my alarm-clock, its geometrical peculiarities, but it is something which is present in this very massiveness and makes it exist as alarm-clock: like the unity which binds together the letters of a word and the words of a sentence, the unity of my alarm-clock is a unity of meaning. Indeed, as soon as I fix my eyes on my alarm-clock, it "tells" me something. *Its existence as object is existence as meaning*, as "telling-something".

Now this unity-meaning may be considered from two different angles: (1) It is a unity *which expresses itself* in spatial modalities; (2) it is a unity *which is conditioned* by the spatial modalities in which it reveals itself.

Considered from the first angle, my alarm-clock is a meaning which takes possession of a portion of space and fills it in order to manifest itself in it, it is a *movement of expression*. This meaning and the spatial modalities in which it expresses itself are inseparably one. Indeed, the particular unity which constitutes my alarm-clock has no existence apart from the particular spatial configuration in which it appears; in order to be itself, it must occupy this precise portion of space and fill it in this particular manner. Thus my alarm-clock is *essentially* a particular meaning-existing-and-manifesting-itself-in-appropriate-expressive-modalities.

Looking at my alarm-clock from the second angle, I can describe it as a unity which results from the putting together of various elements, from the shaping of these elements into an appropriate significative ensemble. From this angle, I see my alarm-clock no longer as a meaning which unfolds itself in a portion of space, but as a meaning which is *generated* in an organized diversity of spatial modalities—just as the meaning of a word springs from the arrangement of its various letters.

These two aspects are essentially complementary: my alarm-clock is a meaning which expresses itself (first aspect) and, in this very process, is conditioned, determined, brought forth (second aspect) by the spatial modalities in which it appears. (Throughout this book, we shall use the expression "aspect a" to refer to the first aspect and the expression "aspect b" to refer to the second.) This presence of a particular meaning in an appropriate spatial texture constitutes the

[1] The term "object" is taken here and in the following pages to mean a thing, not as opposed to subject.

singularity of my alarm-clock—that is, its existence as an original object distinct from the other objects that surround it.

Now I notice this fact: on the one hand my alarm-clock taken as a whole has a definite meaning, on the other hand its different parts have different meanings. Let us examine how the parts are related to the whole.

(*a*) I focus my vision on a detail of my alarm-clock: the figure 6 at the lower part of the dial. Assuredly, this figure means something of its own. Its meaning is not identical with the meaning of the figure 3, or with that of the glass which protects the dial, of the small hand of the clock, of the different components of its inner mechanism. Should I say in consequence that the global meaning of my alarm-clock is nothing more than a conglomerate of these different meanings? If so, each particular meaning is confined within the detail in which it expresses itself, and the unity of my alarm-clock is very hard to explain. This is not the right solution. We must proceed in another way.

I want to grasp the concrete meaning of this figure 6. I must broaden my vision, and include the other figures, the hands of the clock, the whole dial; I must look at the whole clock in order to understand the meaning of this figure 6: the whole clock gives it the precise meaning it has in the place which it occupies.

I fix my eyes on another detail: the copper frame in which the protecting glass is enclosed. I make the same discovery: this accessory does not make sense apart from the glass which it keeps in place, from the dial which the glass protects, from the whole clock—in other words, its meaning is derived from the unity-meaning which constitutes the whole clock. Thus my alarm-clock is a structure each element of which has its value not by itself, but by its communication with the other elements, its insertion in the whole. *Each element of my alarm-clock is an expression of the unity-meaning*; it is a local detail in which the complete meaning is reflected. To affirm this is simply to acknowledge that each part of the clock exists as a modality of that movement of expression which constitutes the whole clock (aspect a).

This fact remains true even if the part is accidentally detached from the whole. I remove the winder of my alarm-clock and put it on the table. What is that little metal ring lost there among my papers and my books? To understand its meaning I must see it as something which belongs to my alarm-clock. Thus even now the unity-meaning of the clock expresses itself in the winder and, thus, constitutes it as something meaningful.

(*b*) I said above that the different elements of my alarm-clock have different meanings. Now I acknowledge that all these elements mean what the whole clock means—nothing more and nothing less. Is there no contradiction between these two assertions?

To answer this objection I have only to observe the way in which the unity-meaning of my alarm-clock expresses itself in its spatial modalities. Assuredly, the clock is one, but its unity is diversified, modulated, so to speak, in that expressive field formed by its spatial make-up. The meaning of the figure 6 and the meaning of the winder are not two different meanings—as in common parlance I would say that my alarm-clock and my dictionary are two different things; however, the unity-meaning of the clock as expressed in the figure 6 is not identical with this same unity-meaning as expressed in the winder. *Each element* of my alarm-clock has its individuality because it *expresses the whole clock according to its particular modalities.*

In this simple fact, the complementary character of the "aspect a" and "aspect b" reveals itself in a very concrete manner. To the extent that each particular meaning—e.g., the meaning of figure 6, of the protecting glass, of the winder—is derived from the meaning of the whole clock, participates in this meaning, and expresses it, there is unity—aspect a. On the other hand, there is diversity in so far as the unity-meaning expresses itself in each element *according to the particular modalities of this element.* To this extent, the unity-meaning is a qualified unity; to this extent, *each detail* of the clock *contributes according to its particular modalities towards forming the meaning of the whole clock* (aspect b).

This contribution of each part to the whole—or this dependence of the whole on the parts—is an obvious phenomenon. At the place which it occupies at the lower part of the dial, the figure 6 plays a role which concerns the whole clock. If it disappears, the unity-meaning is affected. My alarm-clock-without-the-figure-6 is not the same thing as my-alarm-clock-with-the-figure-6. The small crack visible at the upper left angle of the protecting glass is not a mere local detail without significance for the whole. It may not be of great importance, yet it somewhat alters the value of the clock. Some elements have an essential role to play. If the hands of the clock or a part of its inner mechanism should drop off, the whole clock is mutilated; it becomes a useless instrument, a disintegrated unity which stands there on my table lifeless and stupid.

Thus the unity-meaning of my alarm-clock is continually fashioned (aspect b) by all the spatial modalities in which it expresses itself (aspect a). It constitutes each element as a meaningful detail (aspect a); at the same time, it is so intrinsically conditioned by the modalities of each element that the suppression or the alteration of an element affects it in a decisive manner (aspect b) and, thus, affects the meaning of all the other elements. Remove the hands of the clock, you change the meaning of the whole clock and of all its elements: the winder becomes the winder-of-a-clock-without-hands—something different from the winder-of-a-clock-with-hands.

(*c*) Whenever I look at my alarm-clock, I fix my eyes instinctively on its hands. These are indeed the centre of the clock—that is, the elements in which its unity-meaning reveals itself in the most expressive manner. All the other elements have their importance too, but in a subordinate manner: they refer to the hands as to the centre which gives them their meaning as parts of the whole clock. Thus each detail of the clock expresses the meaning of the hands—in other words, the unity-meaning of the clock springs from its hands and, from this centre, spreads throughout the different parts of the clock. *To the extent that my alarm-clock is a meaning which unfolds itself* (aspect a), *it is a centrifugal movement.*

On the other hand, *in so far as this unity-meaning is conditioned by the modalities of all the elements of the clock* (aspect b), *it is the resultant of a centripetal phenomenon.* Indeed, the hands of the clock—that is, the element in which its unity-meaning expresses itself primarily—have no usefulness, no value apart from the other elements, apart from the whole clock. In other words, they play their central role in dependence on all the other elements, by virtue of the converging action of these elements.

I have taken my alarm-clock as an example. A similar structure can be shown in any object. My table, like my alarm-clock, is a unity-meaning which unfolds itself in an appropriate spatial configuration (aspect a), and, in this movement, is conditioned by all the spatial modalities in which it expresses itself (aspect b). My table is also made of different elements which have different meanings: the legs of the table are meant to support the top, the top to hold my books, my papers, to enable me to write. However, no element of the table makes sense by itself: a single leg is no better than no leg, and four legs together do not make a table. Thus each element, if it is to be an element of my table, must be related to the whole table; each part is a place in which the whole table expresses itself in a particular manner.

I have shown how each part of my alarm-clock refers to the hands as to the centre in which the meaning of the whole appears fully. There are many things in which such a central point cannot be strictly determined. I could possibly say that all the parts of my table are subordinated to that place on the top on which I put my papers and where I write. But what is the natural centre of my dictionary, of this white sheet of paper, of those coconut trees which I see there among the houses? Such a centre cannot be determined in every object. However, it remains true that any object is *a unity which unfolds itself in a portion of space* even though no centre can be determined from which this movement of expression originates (in which case, the "aspect a" cannot be strictly described as a centrifugal movement). The meaning of an object is always concretely identical with those inter-relations by which the various elements of this object are made into a single whole. Each page of my dictionary is connected with the whole dictionary, each section of this sheet of paper with the whole sheet, each palm of that tree with the whole tree. Because of such connections, each particular element, in its place, contributes towards forming the global meaning of the object to which it belongs (aspect b—in those objects which have no special centre of reference this aspect cannot be strictly described as a centripetal movement). This is the reason why a local mishap—a page of my dictionary torn away, a blot on this white sheet of paper, a palm of the tree broken by the wind—is never confined to the place where it occurs—it always modifies the global value of the thing which suffers it.

Let us sum up our main observations:

(i) Each object is a unity-meaning which expresses itself in a texture of spatial modalities (aspect a), and, in doing so, is conditioned by these modalities (aspect b).

(ii) The meaning of each part of an object is derived from the unity-meaning (aspect a).

(iii) Each part expresses the unity-meaning according to its particular modalities and, thus, contributes towards forming the unity-meaning (aspect b).

(iv) Some objects have a centre of expression—in which case, the "aspect a" may be described as a centrifugal movement and the "aspect b" as a centripetal phenomenon.

So far we have considered isolated objects. We must now examine in what relationship objects stand to each other.

I let my glance wander over the things that are scattered before me. My first impression is that these objects are lying on my table next to one another without penetrating each other, that each of them is a sharply delimited entity, clearly distinct from all the others. However, a closer observation reveals to me a quite different reality.

I take my dictionary and my alarm-clock and place them on the chair which stands next to my table. I notice first that in that place these two things do not mean what they meant when they were on the table. The alarm-clock-on-the-chair and the dictionary-on-the-chair are not identical with the alarm-clock-on-the-table and the dictionary-on-the-table. Moreover, something in the table itself is altered since I removed these two objects from it. My table-without-my-alarm-clock-and-my-dictionary is not the same thing as my table-with-my-alarm-clock-and-my-dictionary. Similarly, the chair-standing-next-to-my-table-with-my-alarm-clock-and-my-dictionary-on-it is different from the chair as it was before I put these objects on it. Such observations can be multiplied *ad infinitum*. In front of me, there is a picture of the Annunciation hanging on the wall. I remove it and place it on my bed. This operation considerably affects the wall and the picture itself; neither of them means now what it meant before. The coconut trees which I see through the window are essentially those coconut-trees-among-those-houses. They would have a quite different meaning if they were coconut-trees-on-the-Maidan.

All these facts show that there is no such thing as an isolated object. Each object has its concrete meaning not simply by itself, but also in relation to the objects around it; in other words, *its surroundings express themselves in it and give it its concrete meaning.* Thus the different objects are not simply next to one another, but do in fact penetrate each other; they are not merely distinct from one another, they condition one another. When the alarm-clock is there on the chair next to the dictionary, the chair and the dictionary are in a true sense present in it since the unity-meaning which constitutes it *contains* the chair and the dictionary.

More widely, I must say that each object is an expression of the *system* in which it is included. By this I do not mean simply that each object, as I have just shown, reflects the other objects next to which it stands, but that the concrete meaning of an object is greatly dependent on the concrete situation which it occupies among the other objects which surround it and the concrete relations which all these objects have to one another. If, without removing anything from my table, I alter the position of all the objects that are lying on it, I observe that the meaning of the table and of all these objects is affected by this change. My alarm-clock is still alarm-clock-on-the-table, yet, where it stands now next to my crucifix and my fountain-pen, it does not mean exactly what it meant when it was alarm-clock-next-to-my-ink-bottle-and-my-dictionary; similarly, the table-with-all-the-objects-disposed-on-it-in-this-particular-manner is different from what it was when all these objects were lying on it in a different order. In the same way, I can easily imagine that to change the meaning of those coconut trees, it is not necessary to transplant them to the Maidan. It would be enough to change their positions in relation to the houses. This new situation would make them appear in a different way; at the same time, the houses would acquire a new significance.

In a practical way we feel this interpenetration of objects, the dependence of each object on the system in which it is included, when we try to arrange in the best possible manner a collection of things—e.g., the furniture of a drawing-room, the different articles in a show-room. There is a way of relating them to one another which makes them look awkward; there is another way of disposing them which sets off each one of them.

What is the implication of all these phenomena? A consideration of "collective" units such as my room, the house of which my room is a part, the city all around, the whole world, will help us to answer this question.

From where I sit, I look at all the things which surround me: the shelf with a few books, my prie-dieu and my table, my bed close to the window, the lamp hanging from the ceiling, the electric fan turning, all these objects enclosed within the four walls of my room. This ensemble is not a loose conglomerate of various elements but a unified reality. There is a sort of dialogue going on among all these objects, a dialogue in which they express their common inclusion in the totality which I call my room. Each object expresses this totality in a particular manner. Thus I see my room not as a mere collection of things put together in a certain order, but as a unity-meaning which reveals itself in various ways (aspect a). This unity-meaning—

like the unity-meaning of my alarm-clock—is inseparable from the spatial modalities in which it appears. It constitutes these four walls with the pictures hanging on them, my table, my chair, my bed and these other pieces of furniture, my books, the breeze coming from the fan, the light and the air pouring in through the open window. It does not exist apart from this texture of expressive elements.

The unity-meaning resides in these elements and makes them what they are. Indeed, whatever I see here around me receives from it its concrete meaning, its existence as object of my room. Each thing, in its own place, "tells" the whole room. This is so true, that if I remove a piece of furniture from my room and take it to some other place, its meaning is immediately altered. My chair-on-the-veranda is not the same thing as my chair-in-my-room. Wherever I put it, its surroundings assimilate it and express themselves in it.

But if the unity-meaning of my room constitutes all the objects contained in it, it is also conditioned by all these objects (aspect b). My room-with-my-chair and my room-without-my-chair are not the same reality. If my chair breaks, the entire room is affected by it: my room-with-a-broken-chair has not the same meaning as my room-with-a-whole-chair. If I hang a new picture on the wall, I add something to the whole room. If I remove my books from the shelf and put them on the table, not only the meaning of the shelf and of the table but the meaning of the whole room is altered. Thus each object present in my room contributes by its very presence and situation, and according to its particular modalities, towards forming the unity-meaning of my room.

The conclusion of these considerations is that the structure of a "collective" unit is identical with that of a particular object. In both cases, the totality is prior to the elements which it contains and constitutes, but inseparable from these elements. It never exists as a pure idea, but always as a concrete unity expressed in spatial modalities and conditioned by these modalities.

Where do these observations lead us? To answer this, we must carry our investigation to its farthest limits. My room is still a restricted totality; it does not make sense apart from the house of which it is a part. The house is itself included in the city, the city in the country, etc. . . . Finally, we come to the consideration of the whole universe as the totality of all totalities. This is the picture which imposes itself upon us:

The universe as a whole is a unity-meaning which manifests itself in the innumerable expressive modalities which constitute space (aspect a). This unity-meaning is inseparable from the spatial diversity in which it appears. Each portion of space—whether it be a totality like Calcutta, the house in which I live, my room; or a particular object like my dictionary, my crucifix, my alarm-clock; or even a part of an object like a page of my dictionary, the winder of my alarm-clock—expresses the unity-meaning of the universe according to its particular modalities, according to its situation, according to the peculiarities of its environment. Thus the meaning of each spatial unit is derived from the unity-meaning constitutive of the whole; each object *is* the whole expressing itself in a particular manner. This means that each limited reality has a double aspect: as a *particular* reality, it occupies a definite place, it is circumscribed (aspect b); as a *meaningful* reality, it is co-extensive with the whole universe (aspect a). These two aspects are *essentially complementary*, but they are not of equal value. The "aspect a" comes first because it is the totality which gives existence, meaning, to the particular elements—these elements are nothing apart from the whole in which they are included.

However, the totality does not exist apart from its expressive modalities—it exists in them and is conditioned by them; it is fashioned by the partial totalities which it constitutes (aspect b). Thus each portion of space, however small, while conditioning the meaning of the object to which it belongs, contributes towards determining the unity-meaning of the whole universe, of which this object is essentially a part.

This integral perspective explains why objects interpenetrate without ever merging into one another. They interpenetrate to the extent that they constitute one another, to the extent that each of them reflects all the others; they remain distinct in so far as each of them expresses its surroundings, expresses the whole in a particular, localized, and thus radically incommunicable, manner.

All the facts we have observed enable us now to reach some final conclusion regarding the structure of the universe.

The universe is first of all a unity-meaning. However, this unity is essentially spatialized—that is, expressed in a great diversity of situations and relations. Let us suppose that, in our analysis of phenomena, we reach what we may call the ultimate components of the universe, very minute spatial modalities inside which no relation whatsoever can be established. We must affirm that these entities are *by themselves* absolutely meaningless, unnameable, and nonexistent; *by themselves* they are nonentities. Let us explain this.

We have seen that each portion of space expresses the unity-meaning of the universe *according to its particular modalities* and according to its situation and, *thus*, reveals itself as something meaningful. The implication of this fact is that a significant unit has always a certain internal diversity—otherwise, it cannot *express*—that is, manifest—the unity-meaning of the whole, and, therefore, cannot *mean* anything, cannot be an *individuality*. Thus we understand that the ultimate components of the universe, because they are posited as absolutely simple, have *by themselves* no expressive value, no meaning, no reality whatsoever. Thus, *in themselves*, they cannot be defined, localized, isolated, differentiated—they are nothing and they are nowhere. This suggests that the names which are given to them, in so far as they mean something positive, already express relations—that is, properties of a system. They do not point to anything absolutely inherent in these ultimate components, but they qualify them as aspects of a significative ensemble by which and in which they exist. The conclusion of this consideration is that the smallest possible meaningful unit—that is, the smallest portion of space in which the whole universe can express itself—is already a system—that is, a structure which has in itself a certain diversity of relations and aspects.

These reflections throw some light on the deeper nature of what we call "spatial modalities". The descriptions contained in this chapter are based on observation. I see around me many objects. Each of them has a certain configuration and volume, is a certain manner of filling, of being a portion of space. I use the expression "spatial modalities" to designate this concrete spatiality such as it appears to me. Thus this expression refers to a phenomenon of which I have experience. Now I am forced to admit that this same expression should designate first of all a structure of which I have no direct perception, but which I infer from what I observe. This infra-perceptual spatiality is the foundation of phenomenal spatiality. Their relation may be expressed thus: the variations which take place in a certain field on the phenomenal scale are the translation of variations which constitute this same field on the microscopic scale.

This view gives us a deeper understanding of the way in which each portion of space expresses the universe. Each spatial unit, as we know, expresses the whole *according to its particular modalities*.

This should mean first of all that the expressive value of a spatial reality is determined by its intimate structure. We need a certain knowledge of this structure if we wish to handle the universe and create new significative ensembles. The better we know it, the better also we grasp the structure of the whole.

This intimate structure determines also the way in which things appear—since there is an essential relation between phenomenal and infraperceptual spatiality. As a rule, we must say that objects which are structurally different are also different in appearance. An iron pipe does not look like a lead pipe, even if they are both painted green. The brown colour of a leather suitcase is different from the brown colour of a fibre suitcase. Each spatial unit has a special way, determined by its inner structure, of being blue, red, golden, silvery, black, of appearing soft or resistant, strong or fragile. In one word, each object has a particular manner, which depends on its intimate structure, of "telling" the universe.

In conclusion, let us indicate how the observations contained in this chapter reconcile two trends of thought which are apparently irreducible.

The problem of unity and multiplicity is, no doubt, at the centre of every question we raise about the universe. In every phenomenon—whether it be on the perceptual, on the infraperceptual, or on the cosmic scale—there is unity and diversity. How are we to explain the simultaneity of these two aspects?

In the sixth century B.C., Parmenides initiated a philosophical tradition whose tendency was to over-emphasize unity at the expense of multiplicity. He maintained that the only abiding reality is the One—that is, undifferentiated Being, transcending all differences and limitations, all-pervasive, indivisible, and self-identical throughout. Faced with this Absolute, the changing world is no more than confused and deceptive appearance. Plato did not adopt the doctrine of Parmenides—its exaggerations were too obvious. However, to the extent that he considered the world of sense-experience as a quasi-nonbeing compared with the eternal and perfect World of Ideas, he leaned towards the Eleatic school. This tendency to explain away multiplicity by reducing to the minimum the reality of the changing material world is characteristic of the Augustinian tradition. After Descartes, Spinoza and Malebranche gave it new vigour—the former by reproducing in a new form the monism of Parmenides, the latter by emptying the created world of all dynamism and of all life. Not long ago Husserl tried to direct philosophical thinking along new lines, but he remained strongly attached to the Platonic tradition in so far as he concentrated his attention on the sphere of pure essences, and banished from his philosophy all consideration of the existing world.

Another philosophical tradition lays great emphasis on multiplicity to the detriment of unity. In the fifth century B.C., Democritus described the world as an immense whirl of atoms combining in various ways. Thus he considered multiplicity as the essence of things, and unity as adventitious and ephemeral. Aristotle was by no means an atomist. Nevertheless, endowed as he was with a scientific mind widely open to the world of sense-experience, he was struck by the reality of change and multiplicity. To explain these, he developed his admirable theory of form-in-matter, and described the world as a hierarchy of beings rising from Mere Matter to Pure Form. This was, no doubt, a remarkable attempt at synthetizing unity and multiplicity, permanence and change. Not only is the world a unified diversity, but each thing, in so far as it is form-in-matter, is at the same time one and multiple, permanent and changing. But here we are faced by an insoluble problem. Aristotle admits that there is in the world a plurality of forms, that each thing is a form-in-matter and, thus, a substance. Where is the limit of this division? If we carry it too far—and where can we draw the line?—we come to a new form of atomism hardly more understandable than the atomism of Democritus. The whole difficulty arises from the fact that the system of Aristotle is a *reconstruction* of unity from multiplicity. This constructive mentality has, to a great extent, pervaded the whole philosophical tradition to which Aristotle gave birth. No representative of this tradition was an atomist. The unity of the universe was admitted by all. Yet, the universe remained a synthetic totality in which many distinct substances co-existed without interpenetrating. The somewhat extrinsic notion of *ordo universi* was used to explain the relations between the different beings, to harmonize them, and obtain a unified view of the whole.

During the last few decades, Western philosophy has become increasingly conscious of the structural character of the world. Existential phenomenology, under the inspiration of Heidegger, considers the world as a totality to which every particular reality is essentially related. For Heidegger, each object is first of all a tool. But a tool is never alone. It refers to other tools. All these tools form a system from which each of them receives its being. No tool can be understood apart from the complex of which it is a part. This complex refers to broader systems and, finally, to a global structure which is not the sum total of all tools, but an organic totality presupposed to the existence of each particular object.

The notion of totality plays an important role also in the phenomenology of Merleau-Ponty. The world is the total presence which is implied in each particular phenomenon. Each object refers to the world, is a concretion of the world. The world is the background against which all particular things stand out.

As we notice, these phenomenological views, while they are concerned with the existing world—the world of experience—acknowledge that the totality is always presupposed to any particular phenomenon; and thus they tend to posit unity as the foundation and the condition of all diversity.

Our aim in this chapter was not to propose a new way of reconciling unity and diversity. No theoretical reflection on this theme can lead to really satisfactory conclusions. Unity, no less than diversity, is *a fact* that we can observe. Analysing our experience, we have indicated how unity and diversity are reconciled *de facto*. We have affirmed the priority of unity because it imposed itself upon us as a fact. But we have shown that unity is never pure, never absolute; it is *essentially* diversified—spatialized—unity. Thus diversity has revealed itself as constituted by and expressive of unity. Concretely, this was what we saw: all particular objects, all particular spatial units are, in the places which they occupy, particular expressions of the unity-meaning of the whole.

This position indicates, we believe, the concrete framework within which the views of existential phenomenology regarding the structural character of the world must be replaced and understood. At the same time, it prolongs and corrects the Aristotelian solution. Let us show this briefly:

(1) There is affinity between the notion of form-in-matter and that of unity-meaning-in-spatial-modalities. Both indicate that the world is at once unity and multiplicity. Moreover, as Aristotle conceives a particular object as a particular form-in-matter, so we acknowledge that a particular object is a particular unity-meaning-in-spatial-modalities.

(2) However, we notice that the Aristotelian notion of form-in-matter, however much it aims at expressing concrete reality, is too

rigid to account for the interpenetration of the different objects, their intrinsic dependence on the whole. This notion forces us to posit sharp distinctions where we should acknowledge intercommunication, and, thus, to reconstruct the unity of the whole with a plurality of elements. By contrast, the expression "unity-meaning-in-spatial-modalities", because it clings to facts, has the flexibility of reality itself. The integral unity-meaning is the unity-meaning of the whole. Each particular meaning is derived from this integral unity-meaning and has no existence apart from it. Thus the totality has not to be rebuilt; it is a first given, and each object reveals it in its own particular manner.

No doubt, this perspective raises a number of problems. But we hope that answers will be found not through the elaboration of "theories", but—in keeping with our method—by looking closely at reality and observing the way in which these problems *are* solved *de facto.*

CHAPTER II

The Act

For the average man, the world is built on a geometrical pattern. It is a spectacle offered to our sight, a vast expanse in which innumerable objects co-exist. From this spectacle, we can abstract any element and study it for itself in an "objective" manner in the same way as we study the properties of a triangle. This common-sense view has given birth to the notion of science as a strictly analytical discipline: to study something scientifically is to analyse its components in a more and more detailed manner; in other words, it is to explain the whole from the parts. At the philosophical level, the geometrical mentality leads first to the notion of the duality subject-object, then to that of the universe as a plurality of objects sharply distinct from one another. Thus, in every sphere, the common conception is that of a world in which exteriority prevails and unity is obtained by putting together and harmonizing scattered elements.

The observations we have made in the previous chapter have revealed a quite different reality. Objects are not there in front of me purely distinct from one another. They shape each other, communicate with one another; they are essentially parts of an integral field which they express, from which they receive existence and meaning.

There is, we believe, a close relation between these views and the picture of the universe which contemporary science gives us. Let us mention only one aspect. Scientists tell us that the stuff of the universe is both continuous and corpuscular. These two aspects are essentially complementary. This means that every particle of matter is in one aspect of itself co-extensive with the whole system in which it is included. Scientific analysis must take this fact into account when it studies local phenomena. When it neglects this aspect (as classical science did), it indulges in what L. de Broglie calls "static idealization". On the other hand, the notion of a pure state of movement, of a wave without corpuscles, is the product of a "dynamic idealization". These views reveal that science has become conscious of the structural character of the universe, of the inseparability of particularity from totality. In the sphere of philosophy, as we have indicated, a similar consciousness animates the researches of the phenomenological school. No doubt, phenomenology presents itself as a descriptive analysis of experiences, but it is an analysis which progresses essentially within a vision of the totality and sees each particular phenomenon in relation to the whole. Our own phenomenological study has shown us that there is a dialectical relation between the intuition of the whole and the analysis of particular aspects. The efforts we made to discover the meaning of these aspects would make our perception of the totality more vivid; this clearer intuition of the whole, in its turn, would deepen our understanding of particular phenomena. The reason for this reciprocal effect is obvious: each particular phenomenon is essentially expression of the totality; the totality does not exist apart from the various structures in which it expresses itself.

Now this particular fact strikes me: in so far as I have a body, I am part of the world like all these objects which I see here around me. This body of mine is a unity-meaning expressing itself in spatial modalities. As such, it is essentially related to its surroundings—it pervades them and is pervaded by them; it forms with all the other objects a system from which it cannot be separated.

What is the unity-meaning of this system—that is, the unity-meaning of the world of which my body is essentially a part?

This is the question which we shall begin to answer in this chapter. As in the previous chapter, we shall proceed in a progressive manner, starting from particular experiences, gradually widening the circle of our investigation until we obtain an overall view.

1. My Life-Experience Constitutes the Unity-meaning of the Universe

Some two years ago, I entered this room for the first time. Never before had I seen that table of pine wood which stood there against the wall close to the window. There was, however, nothing unfamiliar in it. Indeed, from a child, I had seen a great many tables. People used them to write on and to take their meals. I myself had been trained to do the same. Thus that wooden structure which everybody called a table became to me synonymous with a certain number of attitudes and actions, it became a particular modality of my daily existence. This is why this table on which I am now writing was already familiar to me when I first came into this room—it was already pregnant with my own life. Since that time, I have been working every day in my room. The table is still in the place where I found it on the day I came, but it has become "my table". The hours I have spent working at it are, so to speak, present in it. This whole living experience constitutes its actual meaning, the particular value it has for me.

My eyes are fixed on my table lamp. Its meaning is a whole history. From my childhood, I have been accustomed to switch on the electric light when it became dark. This action was prompted by the desire to carry on my activity. In the midst of my leisure, my reading, my study, I would turn on the electric switch when the darkness made it difficult to see what I was doing. Thus the lamp, as it hung from the ceiling, or as it stood on my table, became for me the concretion of a certain need, of a certain desire, the accompaniment of my evening activities. This experiential complex is present in this lamp which I see before me. Moreover, this lamp gathers in itself all the evenings I spent in this room reading or writing in its light. My life-experience makes it what it is for me.

It is again my life-experience which gives to those coconut trees their meaning-for-me. They remind me of the hours I spent as a child looking at some illustrated magazines, fascinated by pictures of tropical landscapes. They evoke also the atmosphere of a Bengali village where I passed a summer.

Even the moon which I see there shining among the clouds is full of my personal history. My whole past—my studies, my readings, my experiences—determine the way in which I look at it and the manner in which it shines for me.

These observations may be extended to "collective" units.

When I first set foot in this room, it had a familiar look for me because it was already situated within the field of my experience. Now it is pregnant with the hours I have spent in it. As the place where I pray, work, and sleep, it is instinct with my daily life.

When I arrived in Calcutta some thirteen years ago, my mind and my eyes were still filled with the things I had experienced and seen in Europe. Everything appeared to me both strange and familiar. It was familiar because the new world into which I penetrated and the world in which I had grown were both parts of the great human world. Those men I met were similar to those with whom I had been living before; they had the same needs and the same desires. By seeing them moving, working, talking, I often knew what they were after; I communicated with the inner movement of their lives. Not only the people, but the whole city was familiar to me. I knew those taxis and those trams, those streets and those parks; I knew those houses and all that was going on in them. Yet, Calcutta was strange to me. I looked at it with the eyes of a newcomer; not with the eyes of those boys playing in the street on their way home from school, of those rickshaw-men striking their little bells on the shafts of their vehicles, of all those people who had grown up in the city and were earning in it their daily pittance. Calcutta was the very substance of their daily life; it was the place of their first joy and their first sorrow, of their successes and failures, of their toil, their love and their hope. To me, Calcutta was a new field. It had been for long the pole of my aspirations and desires, but, till then, no part of my life had been rooted in it. I imparted to it a meaning made up of experiences, contacts, and studies which were linked with a very different sphere of life. Since that time, I have spent several years in Calcutta. I have known the hard sun of April and May, the monsoon with its alternations of cooling showers and steamy heat, the glorious winter months. I have walked in the streets among the crowds—the rich and the poor—breathing in the atmosphere of the city. I have penetrated into many houses and been stirred by the example of many humble families, I have studied the language and worked daily in contact with people who exercised their influence upon me. This whole sum of experience constitutes the meaning which Calcutta has for me today. It is somehow present in each detail of the city: on the threshold of each house, in each little shop, in each sound which rises from the street and penetrates into my room.

But my experience of Calcutta is still, as such, a particular experience. No doubt, it is richer than my experience of my table, of my alarm-clock, of those coconut trees, but it is nevertheless the experience of a restricted reality. Wider than any particular experience, there is what I call my experience in general, a living whole which is continually growing, made up of the education that I have received, of my daily contacts with the world, of my readings, studies, and undertakings, of all the influences which have acted upon me, in one word, of all my past life. *This totality—my life-experience—constitutes the meaning which the world has for me.*

Thus we have given a first answer to the question raised: what is the unity-meaning of the universe?

In the first chapter, we saw that the unity-meaning of the whole expresses itself in each object according to its particular modalities, that each particular meaning is derived from the integral unity-meaning, that the integral unity-meaning does not exist apart from the structures in which it unfolds itself. The observations we have just made enable us to express these views in the following terms:

(a) My integral life-experience expresses itself in each object, in each spatial unit—in my table, my dictionary, my room, in those houses, in my whole environment—according to its particular modalities and, thus, gives it its meaning-for-me, makes it what it is for me.

(b) Therefore the meaning of each object is derived from my life-experience. It *is* my integral life-experience expressing itself in a particular manner.

(c) Thus my life-experience is essentially a spatialized totality. It exists *in* the objects which I see around me, *in* my environment; it is inseparable from the spatial structures which it animates and in which it reveals itself.

This life-experience, it must be noted, is not present in the objects of the world as a number of memories. No doubt, the perception of an object sometimes reminds me of some definite events of the past, but this occurrence is rather exceptional. I possess my whole past as a "lived" totality which forms the riches, the very substance of my present. This living experience—my own life—is present in the world and animates it, it is expressed in all the things which surround me and makes them what they are to me.

2. My Present Concern Constitutes the Unity-Meaning of the Universe

I am working at my table. My eyes follow the movement of my pencil on the paper. This pencil which I hold in my hand receives from my thinking, from my act of writing, the particular meaning which it has for me at this very moment. This meaning is different from the meaning which it had when it was simply lying on the table before I sat down to work. Not only my pencil, but my papers, my chair, my table, my books, my room, my environment, the air I breathe and the light of the sun . . . are taken up in my act of thinking and writing. All these realities form a system the meaning of which is my present activity. Some objects collaborate in this activity in a direct and definite manner; all the others in a more general and undetermined fashion, as modalities of my environment, of the universe, of that total presence in which my act unfolds. Some of the objects which form my horizon may at any moment come out of that generality in which they are wrapped and reveal in a more precise manner their inclusion within the world of my present occupation. Now and then I stop writing and look at the objects which surround me: the books on the shelf, the window, the trees and the houses, the clouds in the sky. Shaking off their anonymity, these things lend me their assistance, they stimulate my thinking and co-operate with my work.

I get up from my chair and walk towards the door. Immediately, the meaning of my environment and of the world is altered. The objects around me no longer reflect my act of thinking; they become signs expressing my new intention, landmarks which direct the movement by which I proceed towards the door.

Thus, at every moment, the things which surround me are integrated in my activity, *their concrete meaning is a function of my actual concern.*

This concern is not simply the intention which I form and the actions by which I carry out this intention, but the totality of my present vital attitude; it comprises my affections, desires, feelings, dispositions. When I feel joyful, the street in which I walk, the people I meet, the shops along the pavement and the cows lying on it, the heat of the sun all reflect my happiness. If I am angry or disheartened, the whole world becomes the world of my anger or of my discouragement: everything in it is harsh and irritating, or hostile and depressive. If I feel sick, my whole environment is affected by my illness: it becomes languid and morbid.

In Tolstoy's novel *Anna Karenina*, there is a passage which well illustrates how much a man's affectivity colours his vision of the world. Levin, the central character of the novel, is on the eve of his marriage. Full of happiness, he feels himself in loving communion with other people. Here he is at a meeting of the council of which his brother Serge Ivanovitch is a member:

"The secretary was reading the minutes, evidently not understanding what they were all about; but Levin could see by his face and from the way he stumbled and hesitated over the reading that he was a kind, sensitive man. When he finished, the speeches began. They were discussing the disposal of certain sums and the laying of certain drains. Serge Ivanovitch made an eloquent speech, completely crushing two other members of the council. Another member, after making a few notes, began replying to him, at first timidly, next very sarcastically. Sviajsky, who happened to be there, got up next and made a grand high-flown speech. Levin listened to them, feeling that the money to be spent, the sewage pipes and the rest, were of no serious importance and that all these dear excellent people were not really quarrelling, but were enjoying themselves immensely. What surprised Levin so much was that he seemed to be able to see through them. And they were all such dear good men and appeared to like him so much. Even strangers came up and talked to him."[1]

Let us quote also a passage from Pasternak's *Doctor Zhivago*:

"The travellers clung to the sides of the cart as it jolted over the ruts. Their hearts were at peace. Their dream was coming true, they were almost at the end of their journey. The last hours of the still, clear day lingered generously with a lavish splendour.

"Their way led sometimes through woods and sometimes across open fields. Driving through the forest, they were thrown into a heap every time the cart-wheel hit a root, and they sat hunching their shoulders, frowning and clinging together. But in the open fields, where space itself seemed to salute them out of the fullness of its heart, they sat up, relaxed and held up their heads.

"It was hilly country. The hills, as always, had their own expression. They rose huge and dark in the distance, like proud shadows, keeping a silent watch over the travellers. But a comfortingly rosy light followed them across the fields, soothing them and giving them hope.

"Everything pleased and astonished them, above all the unceasing chatter of their cranky old driver, in whose archaic idioms, traces of Tartar influence and local oddities of languages mixed with those of his own invention."[2]

[1] L. Tolstoy, *Anna Karenina*, tr. Rochelle S. Townsend; Everyman's Library, no. 612; vol. 1, pp. 392–3.

[2] Boris Pasternak, *Doctor Zhivago*, tr. Max Hayward and Manya Harari, p. 264.

These descriptions show us that our actual concern—that is, both our present occupation and the disposition in which we carry it out—our living present—gives to our surroundings and to the whole world the meaning which they have for us.

Like our life-experience, this living present is a spatialized reality:

(a) My present concern expresses itself in my body, in the objects which surround me according to their particular modalities and, thus, gives them their meaning-for-me.

(b) Therefore the meaning of each object depends on my present concern.

(c) My present concern does not exist apart from the situation which it animates and in which it expresses itself. It exists *in* my body, *in* my surroundings.

In fact, my life-experience and my present concern are one. Indeed, my present activity takes up my past and keeps it alive. My experience lives in what I do, in what I feel, in what I am concerned with now; it guides my decisions and the way in which I carry them out; it pervades my environment in as much as it thus lives in me. In other words, *my actual-concern-pregnant-with-my-life-experience is the reality which gives to the objects of the world their meaning-for-me.*

3. My Life-Act

All my activities are more or less transitory. An hour ago I had my breakfast, at the moment I am working in my room, after some time I shall go out for a walk. Each one of my occupations flows into another occupation; some of them will be taken up again, but none of them covers my whole life.

However, there is a continuity in my existence. Each one of my activities relates to a certain "I live" from which it receives its impulse and its meaning.

Can we determine the nature of this "I live"?

(a) My life appears to me as a movement forward. It cannot, however, be described as a mere succession of instants, each sinking into nothingness as it is replaced by the next. Each stage of my progress is the result of a whole history, each moment of my existence lives on the totality of the past—my personal past and, in it, the past of my country, the past of the continent of which this country is a part, the past of the universe. Each stage of my progress also bears in itself a whole future; the time to come is contained in it in an undetermined and embryonic manner.

The subsistence of my past in each one of my occupations, together with the potential presence in it of my future, shapes my individuality and conditions its growth by enabling my experience to develop. Let us explain this.

During the first years of my life, I had little personal experience. No doubt, from its very start, my existence was already charged with and conditioned by a whole history which I may term my pre-personal past, but this initial accretion did not constitute what I usually call my experience. At this early stage of my childhood, my familiarity with the world hardly extended beyond the circle of my daily occupations. I was concerned chiefly with the present and could not take far-reaching decisions. Gradually, by the simple fact of living in the world, undergoing its multiple influences and showing some personal initiative, I acquired a certain sense of my life as a whole. Thanks to this enrichment, I began to view my future as a totality which was somehow at my disposal—a totality that I possessed in germ and that I myself would have to determine. Thus I took decisions not only for the present but also for the time to come. Little by little, my experience attained a degree of maturity which enabled me to decide my whole life. I formed a general intention which was to inspire all my activities and become my life-intention.

This life-project may be characterized in two ways:

(1) It is the act which gives its meaning to each moment of my life. My present concern is essentially integrated in it and receives from it its meaning and its inspiration.

(2) It does not exist apart from my particular occupations. It is wider than any of them, but it lives in them and realizes itself through them. Thus my present concern is the actuality of my life-project.

Let us explain these assertions by an example. I want to go to Burdwan: I pack my suitcase, call a taxi, let myself be carried through the city, get down at Howrah Station, accept the help of a coolie, buy a ticket, proceed towards the platform. . . . All these actions are the progressive realization of my intention:

(1) My desire to go to Burdwan gives to each action its meaning.

(2) My intention exists to the extent that it realizes itself through these particular actions. It perishes if, instead of packing my suitcase and calling a taxi, I remain sitting in my room. Going to the station,

buying a ticket, getting into the train are the actuality of my decision to go to Burdwan.

But a decision of this kind is still a particular event of my life. It is essentially related to the general intention which gives their meaning to all my particular projects.

All the preceding considerations have brought out three main elements which are found together at each moment of my life:

(1) *The persistence of the past*—which constitutes what I have called *my life-experience.*

(2) *A potential presence of the future*—which enables me, in the light of my experience, to form *a life-project.*

(3) *A particular behaviour* (my present concern).

The concrete unity of these three elements may be expressed in this way: *My present is an act-project*—essentially orientated towards the future—*expressing itself in a particular behaviour and*, in so doing, *actualizing the whole past.*

(b) Thus I have discovered at the very heart of my life a continuous and unifying act. It is a general intention which all my occupations more or less express. Would it not be the very "I live" to which all my activities refer, from which they receive their impulse and their meaning?

To a certain extent, it is. Yet, this general intention cannot be simply identified with the fundamental act of my life. Indeed, this act-project has taken shape in me gradually, it has affirmed itself clearly at a definite moment of my life. But it is obvious that whatever happened to me *before this* historical *moment* must be considered as an event *of my life* as well as any occurrence *that followed it.* This means that the "I live" to which all these circumstances referred—to which all my present actions refer and all my future undertakings will refer—is, in its deeper reality, an act more fundamental than my act-project.

The existence of this prime act is also apparent from two other factors. First, my act-project is a fragile reality. At any moment, I can disown it; my particular behaviour can betray it instead of expressing it. Now, whatever action I posit contrary to it is part and parcel *of my life* as well as any particular behaviour inspired by it and expressing it. Therefore my life-act and my act-project are not simply identical. The other factor has already been alluded to. I have shown above that my present concern is both what I do now and the affective disposition, the existential atmosphere, in which this action is posited. Now on the one hand my present doing expresses directly, intrinsically, my act-project—it is my life project realizing itself; on the other hand my affective disposition, however much it is integrated in my present occupation, and thus in my act-project, is not a mere expression of this act. It reveals the existence in me of a vital layer which my act-project must take up in order to realize itself. The act constitutive of this original life field is the prime act to which all the circumstances of my life refer.

This act came into existence at the very instant of my conception—its appearance at that moment was identically the beginning of *my life*. Thus, with that act, I possessed my own individuality—an individuality which in it would remain unaltered and which, under its impulse, would continually expand and realize itself. Let us explain this.

I have described my life as a process of accretion: each moment of my life merges into the next, and thus a continual growth takes place. This process must be understood *precisely as the progress of my life-act*. This act was present from the moment of my conception as a dynamic reality orientated towards the future. But, at that moment, it had not yet realized itself; as a temporal act, it had to unfold gradually. This unfolding took place during my growth (and still continues today). My life-act was continually driving forward; at every moment of its progress, it took up and totalized in itself all the situations which it traversed. *This whole process* shaped my individuality, guaranteeing its permanence, enabling it to develop, and gradually to reveal its hidden potentialities. When this maturing was sufficiently advanced—when my experience had become wide enough—my life-act actuated itself into a life-intention through which it was thenceforth to realize itself in a conscious and deliberate manner. This fact explains how my act-project is in a real sense the "I live" to which all my present activities refer. It is this "I live", in so far as it is one with the prime act of my life, in so far as my life-act expresses itself in all my activities through it. In other words, *the "I live" to which all my actions refer is my life-act realizing itself through my act-project.*

This description shows that my life-act and my act-project are not two different acts which co-exist in me—the latter being somehow superimposed upon the former. My act-project proceeds from my life-act; it *is* my life-act actuating itself as personal act.

Nevertheless, my life-act remains independent of my act-project to the extent that it forms a life-field—the field of my affectivity, of my "natural" life—to which my act-project must give a definite orientation, in which it must realize itself. We shall indicate later on how this sort of dualism must be understood.

In conclusion, we should complete the schema drawn up at the end of (a). I have mentioned there "three elements" which are found together at every moment of my life. They must be understood in this way:

(1) The persistence of the past (my life-experience) is my life-act—including my act-project—considered in so far as, at every moment of its progress, it takes up, realizes in itself the whole past.

(2) The potential presence of the future is this same act considered in so far as, in taking up the past, it continually tends—through my act-project—towards a more perfect realization of itself.

(3) My present concern is the conscious self-realizing of my act expressed at a particular moment in a particular behaviour.

This perspective shows clearly that the "three elements" are not three different realities, but three aspects under which my life-act can be considered. Each one of these aspects exists in and by my act, and is, in it, concretely identical with the other two. This act is the "I live" to which all my actions and feelings refer, in which subsists whatever pertains to me.

4. My Life-Act-Realizing-Itself-Through-My-Act-Project Constitutes the Unity-meaning of the Universe

In the first and second sections of this chapter, I have shown that my whole past, living in my present concern, gives to the world its meaning-for-me. Now I have discovered that this living present is constituted by my life-act-realizing-itself-through-my-act-project. Thus, fundamentally, it is my personal life which gives to the world its meaning-for-me.

Indeed, "my world" is first of all the concretion of my act-project. The general orientation of my life makes of the universe as a whole and of every particular circumstance what they are concretely for me. It determines the basic meaning which all the situations I pass through, all the objects I use, have for me. My way of looking at the world, of judging persons and events, of reacting to external influences—in one word, my way of "living" the world—is fundamentally an expression of this general orientation.

This act-project must be understood first of all as the pursuit of a certain aim. I undertake this particular work, I act in this particular manner because I have given this concrete direction to my life, because such is the end towards which I tend. Correlatively, this situation in which I find myself, these objects which I perceive around me and utilize, these circumstances which influence me, have this meaning because such is the goal I have in view. I make them exist as prefigurations of the end which I wish to reach and which I wish them to reach with me and in me.

Community of aim, of aspiration, is the basic element which brings men together. It gives to their existences an identity of meaning and makes them live "in the same world". Fundamentally, there is a greater affinity between a doctor and a shopkeeper who both pursue a materialistic aim than between this same shopkeeper and another shopkeeper who gives to his life a supratemporal goal. The vision of the world of these two shopkeepers, their understanding of history, are basically different; so also is their way of living the various situations in which they find themselves, their manner of looking at their customers, at the articles they sell and the money they earn.

All my particular projects are different expressions of my act-project considered as the orientation of my whole life towards something final. Each one of these particular projects constitutes a particular world within the broad world of my life-intention. First, there is the world of my occupation, understood in its most general meaning. In all I do, I remain what my profession makes of me; and the world around me is the field in which this profession expresses itself. The street in which I walk, the crowd which surrounds me, the illuminated advertisements, the little lamps and sticks of incense which I see burning in front of sacred images in some of the little shops are lived by me as modalities of my general status in life. I can readily imagine that for this businessman squatting in front of his cash register among his wares, the night illuminations, the passing crowd, the noise of the street, the whole world have a quite different meaning. Different also is the world of this gentleman who looks like a University professor, of those rickshawmen who ring and shout their way among the crowd.

The world of my life occupation is a stable reality—it is, so to speak, the body of which the world of my life-intention is the soul. But, within it, different worlds succeed each other. At this moment, my world is constituted by my act of thinking and writing; after a while, it will express my intention of visiting my friend Robin and the actions by which I carry out this intention; then it will be the world of my evening prayer. . . . Each world flows into another world.

All these different worlds do not succeed one another within the world of my life-project and of my profession like the different scenes of a drama on a stage. As my act-project lives in my different activities and realizes itself through them, so also the world to which my act-project gives existence—in which it subsists—takes shape essentially in and through the particular worlds which these activities constitute; it forms the fundamental unity of all these worlds.

There is another aspect. I have indicated above that my life-act remains independent of my act-project in so far as it forms an original life-field which my intention must continually take up and personalize—provisionally, I have called this field the field of my affectivity, of my "natural" life. It contains whatever in my life is not derived from my personal decisions. I have mentioned in section 2 my feelings, affections, dispositions—the list could be extended. All these elements may be considered as different expressions of a fundamental existential complex which I may call my temperamental inclination. The meaning which the world has for me depends greatly on this basic factor and on its various manifestations.

A man who is by nature shy and timorous lives in the world as a concretion of these temperamental modalities. Whatever he has to face—persons or events—is *from the first* wrapped in a special existential atmosphere: the world which his act-project directs towards a certain aim is the world which his timidity *already* pervades through and through (his original life-field). This is doubtless an existential situation very different from that of a man who is by temperament overbearing. These two persons live *from the start* in two different universes. If they happen to travel together, they will never be really in the same train, among the same people, they will not cross the same bridge, or leave the train at the same station. The world which A takes up in his act of travelling is a field which his timorous temperament has *already* strewn with dangers and problems, whereas the world of B is *from the first* an oversimplified phenomenon.

Not only our temperamental inclination in general, but, as we have already seen, our particular dispositions create a certain atmosphere which our act-project must take into account and integrate. When we undertake some kind of work in a state of irritation, the world which our personal act must take up has from the first a certain existential value corresponding to our disposition. The environment in which we exercise our activity, the people with whom we deal, the instruments which we handle always form a field which our life-act already pervades and shapes in some way or other.

The relation between our temperamental inclination and our particular affective states is similar to that between our act-project and our particular occupations. Our temperament exists and manifests itself *in* our various feelings, affections, tendencies, just as our act-project realizes itself in and through our successive activities. (This is why the anger or the joy of a timid person is not simply anger or joy in general, but a particular type of anger or joy constituted by, expressive of, his fundamental disposition. The anger or the joy of an arrogant man would be a quite different phenomenon.) Correlatively, the universe expressing our temperamental inclination is always individuated in a particular world constituted by our particular affective state.

Normally, there is no split between our personal decisions and our affective dispositions, between our personal life intention and our temperamental inclination. Our temperament is presupposed in our decisions, as our life-act is presupposed in our act-project; but our affective dispositions are integrated in our personal activity *to the extent that our life-act realizes itself through our act-project.* Correlatively, there is no split between the world existing as our life-field and the world constituted by our act-project. The latter presupposes the former, but the former is taken up in the latter: it exists essentially *in* the movement of our personal life.

* * *

The phenomenological analyses contained in the first chapter have revealed the structural character of the universe. The world is a system each element of which receives its meaning from the totality in which it is included; it is a unity-meaning which expresses itself in a great diversity of spatial structures according to the modalities of these structures. At the beginning of this chapter, I noted that my body is a part of this system: it cannot be abstracted from the world, separated from the other objects. I have asked this question: what is the unity-meaning of this whole system of which my body is an element? My subsequent inquiries have shown me that my own life ("I live") constitutes the meaning of the universe: the world of which I have experience is essentially the field of my existence; in other words, my existence *is* the existence of the world-for-me. Thus, to understand the world I must first understand myself. Analysing my experience, I have discovered that I am fundamentally a life-act given to itself, forming an original life-field—a field which was there before I was conscious of it, before I could take it up in a personal manner. This experience can be expressed as follows: all my personal undertakings are preceded by the fact that I am there, that the world is *already* lived by me in a certain manner—this "already-being-lived-by-me-in-a-certain-manner" constitutes the original meaning of the world-for-me. Now, on this basis, I build my personal life. My life-act actuates itself into an act-project and realizes itself through it. This act-project expresses itself in my body, in my surroundings, in the whole world, and continually reshapes them. My original life-field is thus personalized. This is the movement which constitutes "my world", in which every object that I perceive receives its existence and its meaning-for-me.

CHAPTER III

The World Before "Knowledge"

In relation to the world, man is primarily a knowing subject, and the world, with regard to man, an object of knowledge. This is a fundamental postulate which modern European philosophy has accepted with surprising ingenuousness. Was it due to the powerful influence of Descartes, the "Father of modern philosophy"? Not exclusively. The intellectualistic attitude, of which this postulate is the mainstay, is in fact as old as philosophy itself. Plato and Aristotle, the two great builders of Western thought, were the originators of two philosophical currents characterized essentially by two different cognitive attitudes, two different ways of relating man, the owner of knowledge, to the objective world. During the Middle Ages, intellectualism was paramount, in spite of the predominantly theological or religious preoccupations which Christianity infused into the minds of medieval thinkers. Consider, for instance, the importance given to the doctrine of Illumination and to intellectual contemplation in the Augustinian tradition largely under the influence of Neoplatonism; consider, too, the dialectical relation which St Thomas Aquinas, in the wake of Aristotle, posited between man understood as *principium intellectivum* and the world described as a sum of *intelligibilia*.

This prevalence of intellectualism in the Western philosophical tradition—not to speak of other traditions—is due not simply to the prestige of a few outstanding thinkers, but primarily to the more discreet but more effective influence of common-sense philosophy. The common man believes naturally that he himself with his body is one thing, and that the houses, the trees, the people he sees around him are other things; he believes that all these things are just as he perceives them: white, green, brown shapes distinct from one another; he believes that the ideas he has of them correspond to realities present in them. Accepting these common-sense notions without discussion, intellectualism defines the world as an objective sphere of being containing sensible qualities and intelligible determinations, and man as a subject endowed with sensations and intellections. On these assumptions, the main task of philosophy is to show how the two levels of knowledge—and the principles in which they are grounded, matter and spirit—how the objective world and the knowing subject stand in relation to each other.

However, this influence of common-sense philosophy on the minds of professional thinkers does not alter the fact that modern intellectualism has been formulated largely under the inspiration of Descartes. The problems raised by Cartesianism have for a long time directed the reflection of European philosophers in one particular direction, and to a certain extent have hampered its freedom. The main difficulty of the Cartesian system was its dualistic character. How should we conceive the union of the soul defined as thinking substance and the body considered as pure extension, of thought and objective reality? This problem has given birth to a double current of thought: the rationalistic current prolonging and refashioning Cartesianism, and the empirical current reacting against Descartes' theory of innate ideas, yet remaining tributary to the Cartesian system.

At the same time, Descartes stimulated philosophical thinking not simply by raising thorny problems which he left unsolved, but even more by forcing philosophers to readopt a truly reflective attitude. The importance which he gave to the *cogito* as the starting-point of philosophy was the real positive element from which modern intellectualism took its main inspiration and derived much of its vigour. This influence is still powerfully felt in the works of Husserl and the contemporary phenomenologists.

* * *

Intellectualism is based on the conviction—at least implicit—that the relation between man and the world is essentially a relation of knowledge. This means that, in the intellectualistic perspective, the dyad subject-object is the first datum, the experimental ground from which philosophy must begin its inquiry. We shall now indicate the main directions in which reflection can proceed in order to explain what kind of relation unites the two terms. As we shall see, explaining this will often mean positing some sort of transexperimental unity at the root of the phenomenal duality—a sign that dualism as such does not satisfy our reason. In the following considerations, my aim is not to define or criticize the positions adopted by this or that particular philosopher but to expose briefly what I have felt strongly in the course of my philosophical investigation: the intellectualistic problem is not susceptible of any satisfactory "intellectualistic" solution because it is an artificial problem.

The subject and the object are two distinct antithetic realities. Neither, however, exists apart from the other. Consciousness or knowledge is the bond which unites them.

Is this unifying factor an extrinsic element, or is it a relation which pertains to the very essence of the subject and the object?

The answer would appear to be obvious:

(1) We have a certain consciousness of reality. We are subjects in so far as this knowledge belongs to us—that is, in so far as we are conscious. Thus the fact of our being subjects is identical with the fact of our being conscious; the very notion of subject implies knowledge —*consciousness is constitutive of the subject as such.*

(2) The object is essentially something which is known. Take away from it this reference to knowledge and nothing remains but an indefinable entity, a vague phenomenon of which nobody has ever been able to say whether it has any ontological consistency. This objectiveness of the world (i.e., the fact of its being an object) is its very inherence in consciousness. Thus *knowledge is constitutive of the object as such.*

(3) As a mere relation without substratum knowledge has no intelligibility: it implies both a subject—that is, somebody who knows—and an object—that is, something which is known. It follows that no subject can stand without an object, and no object without a subject: whoever is conscious must be conscious-of-something, and whatever is known must be known-by-somebody. In short: posit the relation of knowledge and you posit its terms; posit one term and you posit the relation and the other term. We conclude, therefore, that in spite of their opposition, the subject and the object have no independent reality: *they are constituted by the bond of knowledge which unites them.* Both have knowledge as their essence, though each one of them partakes of it from its particular standpoint. This funda-

mental difference in the way of sharing the same essence is the foundation of the opposition between the subject and the object. It explains how it is that, in spite of their intrinsic connection, they always appear as two distinct or even antithetic realities.

Throughout this book, I shall call *intellectualistic* every philosophical doctrine which acknowledges the duality object-subject as the first datum of consciousness and thus, explicitly or implicitly, accepts knowledge as such as the essence of reality.

Now the question arises: to which term of the relation must we give priority? Either the subject posits the object and knowledge is thus primarily the act of the subject—this is the line of idealism—or the object imposes itself. In this case, knowledge is essentially an apparition, and the subject is produced in the very process by which the world springs to consciousness. This is the line of realism.

1. Idealistic Monism

Let us examine the first alternative. We give priority to the subject because the act of knowledge proceeds from him. In this case, the object is no more than a creation of the subject. We must develop this point.

(a) In the objects of the world, there appear many different qualities and aspects which express the variety of their relations with our senses and our mind. These aspects have no meaning apart from these relations. I see a white house with a red roof. These colours are qualities which belong to that house in so far as it is an object for my sight. They mean something to my eyes that contemplate the house, but they have no relation whatsoever to my hearing. I listen to an orchestra executing a symphony. My eyes follow the gestures of the conductor and the musicians, but, beyond them, my attention is captivated by the theme which develops itself so amply, so harmoniously. This melody is not an object for my eyes; it is a structure of sounds which interests my hearing alone. Similarly, the hotness of my window sill exposed to the noon sun is a quality which only my touch experiences. I feel it in my hands; I do not perceive it as something offered to my sight, I do not receive it as an object for my hearing. Thus each objective quality has a certain relation with one of our senses. We do not imagine any sensible property free from such distinct connection with our sensorial apparatus. In order to apprehend a quality of a new kind, we should first be endowed with a new sense.

This experience reveals more than a mere order of established relations. If a quality is meant only to be seen, it has a constitutive relation to our visual faculty: the very notion of sight is implied in its definition. But sight, defined as a perceiving power, is essentially an act and—by hypothesis—the subject has priority in relation to the object. We conclude: whatever is visible is constituted by our visual power. This conclusion—*mutatis mutandis*—applies to all the other sensible qualities in relation to the other senses. Thus the things of the world, to the extent that they are objects for our sensorial faculties, are simply produced by the activity of these faculties.

(b) But the object is not a mere conglomerate of sensible qualities. There is in it a unity which is prior to the diversity of these qualities, a unity which is constitutive of them. The country in which I am travelling is not first of all a road covered with dust, a certain extent of brownish and greenish slopes, the murmur of a torrent in the valley, the heat of the sun, and the smell of a few pine trees. The country is an untamed majesty, a certain severeness which enfolds me and enters me. No doubt, this general quality is immanent in all those aspects that by an effort of analysis I can sort out and enumerate, but it is much more than their sum. It constitutes them and, at the same time, transcends them.

This higher unity is not produced by our senses. Our sensorial faculties are manifold and highly specialized; they produce objective qualities specifically distinct from one another; they cannot be the principle of a unity which transcends the diversity of these qualities, a unity which they do not formally precontain. Yet, this unity pertains to the world to the extent that it is an object of consciousness. Thus it is constituted by our mind, a faculty more universal and more unifying than our senses.

This constitutive action, it must be noted, gives birth not only to the external world but also to our senses. Our mind, indeed, produces the unity which pervades and constitutes the sensible qualities. But these qualities are essentially the acts of our senses. Thus the complex of world-sense is object in relation to the subjective operations of our mind.

Thus we have sketched the first *démarche* of idealism. We call it *phenomenal idealism*. It is essentially a reduction of the objective world to our sensations and to the ideas of our mind. Some philosophic systems do not go beyond this stage. They no doubt transcend the excessive diversity of the sensible impressions, but they nevertheless imagine reality as a perpetual flux: the flux of our ever changing mental conceptions.

(c) We have to go further. There is in the objective world a unity far more perfect than that incipient harmony created in it by the ideas of our mind. Before perceiving those green pine trees and hearing the rustling of the wind in their branches, before apprehending the sober grandeur of this landscape, I was conscious of their reality. The countryside is included in Being, that total presence which pervades all the objects of the world and constitutes their fundamental unity. All colours are real, all sounds are real, all sensible impressions and mental conceptions are real, but Reality is one and, therefore, transcends the diversity of these qualities and transient projections. Reality is the unique fact of their being—that is, the fact that I am conscious. Immanent in my senses and in my mind, but higher than all of them, there is in me that universal faculty the very act of which is the totality of the Real. We discover here in the very fact of our subjectivity the Absolute Principle of all things, a unity prior to all differences, a Pure Consciousness free from all limitations.

The reduction of the real to the ideas of our mind was only a preliminary stage of our analysis—it is now transcended; it gives place to *transcendental idealism*, that integral thought-process by which we posit an initial situation: our very Self realizing in its act the absolute and fundamental identity of Being.

Here we should note a further point. Some idealistic systems describe themselves as merely epistemological. According to them, we cannot pronounce on the metaphysical value of the transcendental Ego. It is a first principle which essentially pertains to the realm of knowledge; it conveys the absolute independence and spontaneity of the subject qua knowing subject, but it cannot be made the ontological source of reality.

It is evident that such a split between the ontological order and the epistemological order is quite untenable. From the outset we have made it clear that, as soon as we accept the distinction subject-object as the first datum of consciousness, we adopt the intellectualistic perspective—that is, we acknowledge consciousness or knowledge as the essence of reality. A split between knowledge and reality leads to the absurd conception of a reality which is never what it appears to be, and of a knowledge which is ignorant of what it claims to know.

However, we must make a concession to the epistemologists. Our subjectivity, as has been explained, is an act which contains and constitutes the totality of Being. Thus there is, *ontologically*, no *démarche* by which we rise from a given multiplicity to the unity that generates it. Unity is first and absolute; it is the unity of our own Self. Thus the regressive thought-process that we have followed (that is, phenomenal and transcendental idealism) was a mere propaedeutic devoid of metaphysical consistency. We were logically compelled to go through it from the moment we gave priority to the subject in relation to the object, but now that our analysis has come to a definitive conclusion it loses all significance. There is no phenomenal world distinct from us; there is only the act by which we assert ourselves and by which we assert Being as identical with ourselves. *Monism* alone is true.

2. Realistic Monism

Idealism is dualistic at the bottom and strictly monistic at the top: it takes its start from the experience of the opposition subject-object and ends in reabsorbing all diversity into the absolute unity of the transcendental Self. Idealism deprives the object of all independent reality and asserts the total liberty and spontaneity of the subject. This position follows from the moment we give priority to the subject in relation to the object and, thus, define knowledge as the proper act of the subject.

Let us come back to the initial experience. Another aspect strikes us: in every perception or intellection, the objective reality is exterior to us, independent of the knowledge we have of it. We do not arbitrarily create it, we discover it as it appears to us. Thus the essence of knowledge is not the act which proceeds from us and posits the object, but the process by which the object reveals itself—reality is prior to us.

What does this mean?

Knowledge, as we have said, implies both a subject who knows and an object which is known. This is an indissoluble structure. Now if, in this structure, the object is the primal element and if knowledge is the apparition of this object, it follows that the subject is produced in the very process by which the object reveals itself.

Let us examine the implications of this view. In describing idealism, we have risen from the diversity of the sensible qualities to the unity of Being. We have shown at each level of our experience the dependence of the objective elements on the subjective activity. In our present analysis, we shall raise ourselves from the start to the level of Being and determine, from our new viewpoint, the ontological status of the Self in relation to Reality: then we shall examine the lower aspects of our experience and describe their connection with the Absolute.

(a) **Transcendental Realism.** Of all our concepts, the idea of Being is obviously the most universal. It applies to all objects of knowledge (Being includes all particular beings), it refers to the real considered in its totality and in its transcendental unity. Now, according to the realistic postulate, all contents of knowledge have an objective value—that is, they are mere expressions of an external reality which exists independently of us. It follows that the universe taken in its entirety as an Absolute is the fundamental reality on which all particular beings depend.

What is our proper relation to this Absolute?

As is obvious, we apprehend the universe first of all as an object of knowledge—that is, as a reality whose essence lies entirely in the fact that it is known. Thus we are produced as subjects in the very process by which the Absolute posits itself. In other words, we are subjective modes of the Absolute, entirely related to that objective and transcendental Being which is the only substantial Reality.

(b) **Phenomenal Realism.** Our phenomenal knowledge is made up of intellections and sensations. According to idealism, these cognitive operations are real creations: they give birth to the phenomenal world.

The realistic view is just the opposite: Intellections and sensations depend on their objects. Thus the outside world is ontologically prior to the operations by which we know it. This world comprises two distinct realms: a spiritual realm made up of objective ideas,[1] and a material realm which consists in sensible forms and qualities. These different spheres of reality generate respectively our mind and our senses in the very process by which they become for us objects of knowledge.

(c) **Relation between the two.** Matter and spirit[2] appear to us equally

1 We use the expression "objective ideas" in order to stress the intellectualistic character of reality as conceived by realism.

2 We use the copula "is" whenever we predicate an attribute of matter and spirit. We say: matter is extensive, spirit is all-pervading. This copula has two different meanings: (1) It signifies the identity between the subject and the predicate; (2) it expresses the reality of the subject. We are concerned here with the second sense.

real. How can we account for this sort of identity between two objects of essentially different nature?

We know the answer of idealism: the being of all things is their fundamental identity with the act constitutive of our subjectivity. But, in our present position, the subject has no proper activity. There is only one solution: both matter and spirit are related to the Absolute Object, both of them participate in the one and substantial Being. We have already described this relation when we wrote that the universe considered as a totality is the fundamental Reality on which all particular beings depend.

In short: the being of matter and the being of spirit lie entirely in their participation in the Absolute Being. We acknowledge this relation in all the judgments we form about them. The essential dissimilarity between matter and spirit, let us add, is due to their respective modes of being—that is, to the respective manners in which they partake of being.

Such are the main features of realistic monism. It is a philosophical doctrine which acknowledges the Absolute Object as the unique Substance from which the Self, the world of ideas, forms, and qualities, and, through its instrumentality, the phenomenal subject, are derived. In this perspective, the subject is a mere witnessing presence without initiative and autonomy. His subsistence depends entirely on the permanence of his object. As a transcendental subject, he is possessed of immutability because his object is the Absolute itself. But this indestructibility can in no way be assimilated to the eternal sufficiency of a self-creative principle. It is the permanency which the unique and eternal Substance communicates to a mode entirely and necessarily derived from it.

On the phenomenal plane, the situation is different. The objective ideas and the sensible qualities are of a fleeting character. They come to life and die away, succeed one another without establishing themselves. Thus the mind and the senses (i.e., the phenomenal subject) are in a state of incessant fluctuation. The unsteadiness of the objects on which they depend lays them open to a continual menace of disintegration.

Note: Some theories whose inspiration is integrally realistic do not include any consideration of the Absolute. They aim at a "scientific" explanation of the different activities of consciousness. In these theories, the human body is treated as a part of the world. Sensations and intellections are phenomena which take place in the organism under the influence of stimuli coming from the environment. Sometimes these phenomena are described as mere chemical processes, sometimes as contiguous or successive biological events taking place according to fixed laws. Each type of consciousness is connected with a definite region of the nervous substance. A survey of the brain reveals in it visual, auditory, olfactory, tactual centres, imaginative and retentive centres, centres of intellectual and rational knowledge. But the analysis seeks to proceed still further. As each type of knowledge contains a great variety of aspects, each region is divided into subregions, so that each element of consciousness is finally reduced to a strictly localized phenomenon. In this respect, memory is explained by the presence of tiny traces left in some specific region by previous experiences, traces which associate themselves with every new phenomenon occurring in any other region of the brain. Generally speaking, the synthesis of knowledge is achieved through the manifold relations existing between the various centres and subcentres. Thus human consciousness is entirely accounted for by phenomena taking place in the objective sphere. The subject is no more than the sum total of these phenomena.

3. A "Media Via"

Realistic monism and idealistic monism are two antithetical positions which at no stage of their development can be reconciled. Let us try a *media via* (which we shall call moderate idealism or moderate realism).

The reason which impels us to reject monism is that—whether it be idealistic or realistic—it does violence to our common experience. We are not conscious of being absolute subjects creating the universe in the act by which we know it; neither do we feel purely passive in the presence of a world which reveals itself to itself through us. The fact is that we are both active and passive; therefore truth resides in a synthesis of the two extreme positions, in a *media via.*

The starting-point of moderate realism is also the dyad subject-object. Thus we remain in the intellectualistic perspective: man and the world are tied to each other by a relation of knowledge. But knowledge cannot be defined either simply as the act of the subject, or as the mere self-revealing of the object. From the outset, in order to safeguard the complexity of experience, we assert that knowledge is essentially ambivalent: it is a double movement—from the subject towards the object, from the object towards the subject—it is a synthesis of subjective spontaneity and objective determination. Thus neither has the subject pure priority over the object, nor the object over the subject. Each of them has a certain priority in its own line; but this priority is always accompanied by a subordination. In other words, the subjective aspect and the objective element of knowledge are essentially complementary. This is the fundamental postulate of the moderate school.

Let us try now to determine in what particular manner the subject and the object contribute to the cognitive synthesis.

I am looking through the window. I see a few trees among the houses. In so far as this perception is a real *act* of knowledge, it is mine: I am the only author of this act. But my perception considered concretely is not the mere fact that I am conscious, it is the fact that I see those particular trees. My act of knowledge is *specified* by an object independent of it. Therefore we must distinguish in knowledge between *the act of grasping as such*, which is elicited by the subject, and the *specification* of this act, which is effected by the object.

At first sight, this is a simple and satisfactory solution. But let us look at it more closely.

I see those trees at a certain distance from me. As the subject of this act, I am first of all a certain power of seeing, I am a body endowed with a visual organ. Now, as such, I am not a complete reality. I am essentially orientated towards a visible world—that is, a world which enables me to realize myself as power of seeing. This world (as visible world) is a sphere of reality whose being resides in its capacity of being seen. Such a reality does not exist "in itself". It is essentially related to my visual faculty, it is constituted by its reference to me as power of seeing. In this consideration, we simply apply to visual perception what we have said previously of consciousness in general: the subject and the object are constituted by their mutual relation.

I posit the act of seeing those trees. The trees specify my act. To specify means to individuate. My visual faculty is by itself universal: its object is the whole visible world. To become act of seeing—i.e., to actuate itself—it must concentrate on a particular point. These trees are the point which enables it to achieve this actuation. They actuate me as power of seeing by detaching themselves from the visible totality in which they are included and becoming trees-seen-by-me—in other words, by passing from the state of visibleness to that of "seen-ness", by realizing themselves *in my act*.

This whole process does not entail any specific activity on the part of the trees. Indeed, to the extent that they are object specifying my act of seeing, their whole being consists in being-seen-by-me: they are constituted by the act which proceeds from me. Therefore act and specification are not two distinct elements of my perception; my perception is purely and simply my act-of-perceiving-those-trees, a reality in which everything is act. We are led back to idealism from the moment we acknowledge the active role of the perceiving subject.

However, there may be a way of solving this difficulty. It is a fact that those trees exist even when I do not look at them. This implies that their being is distinct from my act of perceiving them. Did we not assert a moment ago that my act of looking at them made them pass from the state of visibleness to that of "seen-ness"? Thus, before existing as those trees-seen-by-me, they already existed as visible trees, therefore as real trees.

But this argument does not bring us closer to a solution. As we have shown above, the world, to the extent that it is visible, has a constitutive relation to my visual faculty; therefore it has no independent existence. Of this world as a whole, I cannot even say that it specifies my act of seeing, since it cannot be the object of any definite perception—it simply *is* the unfolding of my power of seeing. Thus, far from escaping idealism, we seem more and more compelled to accept it as the right solution.

Nevertheless, the fact is that those trees oppose a resistance to my look which tries to pierce them through and through, they transcend my power of seeing. This indicates that the trees as existing realities are more than the trees which I perceive, that the real world is more than the visible world.

But is not this "being more" the mere fact that the world, in addition to being a visible world, is also an intelligible world—a fact which my eyes are unable to grasp? Let us see whether idealism can be avoided at the level of intellectual awareness.

At this level, my act is the act of asserting the reality of those trees; the object which specifies this act is not simply the trees as they stand there among the houses, but the trees-seen-by-me: my intellection is based upon my sensation. Now my sensation is by itself particular, adherent to its object: it is direct perception of those green shapes. This purely sensible material offers itself to my intellectual apprehension—it is universalized: I see those trees (i.e., I understand those green shapes to be trees); it becomes object of a judgment: I acknowledge those trees as real trees.

According to our position, these attributes of universality, reality, which pertain to the trees as object of my intellectual knowledge, are not simply derived from my mind. They are present in the trees as they stand there at a hundred yards' distance from me, they are present also in the trees such as I perceive them (even though they do not reveal themselves to my sensation). Thus the trees are constituted as intelligible trees before I actually grasp them with my intellect. *As intelligible trees*, they specify the act by which my intellect apprehends them.

What exactly does this mean?

The intelligibility of those trees is precisely the fact of their being trees (their "treehood"), their reality as trees. Now intelligibility means capacity of being apprehended by my intellect—and that capacity, by itself, is not an activity but a passivity, a dependence. Thus those trees—as real trees—are constituted by their relation to me as power of understanding. When I actually grasp them, I actuate this relation, I constitute them as trees-existing-concretely-for-me—a reality in which everything is act. Thus once more the notion of specification—in so far as it implies an activity on the part of the object—vanishes for ever into thin air.

However, can we not maintain that the world, even though as reality-for-me it is entirely derived from my intellectual activity, exists as reality-in-itself independently of me?

This position is hardly tenable. If the reality of the world is absolutely beyond its objectiveness, my knowledge is pure deception. Indeed, in all my judgments, I claim to know things as they are; I am convinced that this claim is well founded. Even if there is a world-in-itself apart from the world-for-me, it is only the latter which interests me—the world which I make to exist in the act by which I know it.

The conclusion of all these considerations is that moderate realism destroys itself when it really tries to define itself. From the moment we acknowledge the active role of the knowing subject—a role which can hardly be denied—we are caught in the snares of idealism and driven to the extreme position that we are trying to avoid. However, our common experience rebels against this necessity. *We know for certain that idealistic monism cannot be true*. In our attempt at finding the flaw of the argumentation which leads us to it, we cling to the *media via* because it is the position which accounts most satisfactorily for the facts of experience.

Thus we have exposed the main difficulties which moderate realism has to face. Besides these, let us indicate two other problems—connected with those just mentioned—to which various solutions are given.

(a) Where does perception take place? If my perception of those trees occurs in my body, it is difficult to understand how it can be perception *of those trees* situated at a definite distance from me. If it takes place in those trees, it can hardly be *my* perception of them.

According to some philosophers, we do not perceive the objects themselves, but images of them that are present in our visual faculty. These images play the role of objective signs—that is, of impressions produced in us by the objects, and representing them.

This theory, besides endangering the objective character of knowledge, reduces the subject of sensation to a merely passive form. But pure passivity means pure dependence. Thus from representationism we are led inevitably to extreme realism, which makes of the objective sphere the source of consciousness.

Another view is that we perceive the objects themselves through impressions which do not represent them, but enable us to apprehend them in an active manner, to inform them with our sensorial activity.

This position may be difficult to understand, but it tries at least to safeguard the active role of the perceiving subject and the objective character of sensation. However, its very insistence on the activity of the subject necessarily inclines it towards idealism.

(b) The other problem we must mention is that of the relation between sensation and intellection. If the intellect has to receive its object from the senses, it depends on them, it allows itself to be penetrated by them. But it is hardly tenable that a physical faculty should act in this way upon a spiritual faculty.

To meet this difficulty, some philosophers maintain that all ideas are innate in the mind, and that therefore there is no action of the senses upon the intellect.

This view is a transposition of the theory of images to the intellectual level. It supposes that the mind contains from birth impressions produced in it by objective reality, and faithfully representing reality. Ultimately, this position leads to realistic monism, which makes of the subject a mode of the Absolute and considers all ideas present in the mind as particular reflections of the Absolute.

Other philosophers explain that the intellect abstracts actively from the sensible representations the matter of its knowledge and elaborates it into an object proportionate to itself.

We have here an adaptation on a higher plane of the other theory of sensation mentioned above. It paves the way to extreme idealism to the extent that it stresses the active role of the intellect, its priority over the objective reality.

Note: Some of the positions that I have sketched in this section are closely related to certain views expressed pretty consistently by St Thomas. The texts containing these views are from time to time counterbalanced in St Thomas's writings by other texts in which he tries, as it were, to free himself from intellectualism (some of these texts will be mentioned in my "Note on Thomist Psychology" at the end of Chapter IV). It is my conviction that Thomism is a doctrinal complex which takes its fundamental inspiration from an experience in reality much deeper and much more genuine than the basic experience of intellectualism. If St Thomas expressed himself in the language of intellectualism, this was due, I think, to the influences which acted upon him, rather than to requirements of his system. St Thomas, like any other thinker, had to pay his inevitable tribute to the conditions imposed upon him by the historical development of philosophical thought.

Bearing this in mind, let me indicate briefly the main intellectualistic elements of the Thomist synthesis. I do so because these elements have done much to stimulate my own philosophical thinking. The views expressed in this book are to some extent my answer to the questions which the "intellectualism" of St Thomas has raised in my mind.

(1) According to St Thomas, the world and man are two realities exterior to each other. However, they are mutually related by the bond of knowledge: the external things are essentially "sensibilia"—things which can be grasped by the senses—or "intelligibilia"— that is, realities which are to be apprehended by the intellect.

(2) But these realities considered in themselves are only "intelligibilia in potentia" (potentially intelligible),[3] they must be perfected, that is, become "intelligibilia in actu" (actually intelligible)—

[3] "Intelligibile in actu non est aliquid existens in rerum natura." (*Summa Theologica* I, LXXIX, 3, 3um.)

real objects possessing actual existence—by the act of the intellect,[4] in other words, *the intellect is the very actuality of the objects of the world.*[5]

(3) The act of the intellect—that is, the act of knowledge—is the human act *par excellence*, the act which reveals the very essence of man.[6]

(4) The intellect—the principle by which man has knowledge and understanding of reality—*is* the soul of man—that is, the principle which constitutes man as man.[7]

(5) To the degree to which the intellect is the soul of man, it informs his body, it communicates to the body its own *esse* and makes it exist as a human body.[8]

4. The "Pre-Predicative"

For many centuries, philosophers have tried to solve the antinomy idealism-realism without abandoning the intellectualistic perspective. In spite of the great ingenuity they have often displayed, their attempts have not been successful. The extreme views are nothing but mental constructions elaborated without regard for the facts of daily

[4] "Diversificatur potentia intellectus agentis, et intellectus possibilis: quia respectu eiusdem objecti aliud principium oportet esse potentiam activam, *quae facit objectum esse in actu*; et aliud potentiam passivam quae movetur *ab objecto in actu existente*; et sic potentia activa comparatur ad suum objectum ut ens in actu ad ens in potentia." (*Ibid.* I, LXXIX, 7, ad Resp.)

[5] "... sensus fit in actu per speciem sensatam in actu, et similiter intellectus possibilis fit actu per speciem intelligibilem actu; et hac ratione *intellectus in actu dicitur ipsum intelligibile in actu.*" (*Summa contra Gentiles* II, LXXVIII.)

"*Intellectus agens est actus ipsorum intelligibilium.*" (*De Veritate* I, 1, ad Resp.; VIII, 6, ad Resp.; *Summa Theologica* I, LXXXVII, 1, ad 2um.)

[6] "Natura uniuscuiusque speciei ex eius operatione ostenditur. Propria autem operatio hominis in quantum est homo est intelligere, per hanc enim omnia animalia transcendit ... oportet ergo quod homo secundum illud speciem sortiatur, quod est eius operationis principium: sortitur autem unumquodque speciem per propriam formam. Relinquitur ergo quod intellectivum principium sit propria hominis forma." (*Summa Theologica* I, LXXVI, 1, ad Resp.)

[7] Cf. text immediately above.

"... Hic homo intelligit quia principium intellectivum est forma ipsius: sic ergo ex ipsa operatione intellectus apparet quod intellectivum principium unitur corpori ut forma." (*Ibid.*)

[8] "Intellectus, qui est intellectualis operationis principium, est humani corporis forma ..."

"Anima ... principium quo primus intelligimus, sive dicatur intellectus, sive anima intellectiva, est forma corporis." (*Ibid.* I, LXXVI, 1, ad Resp.)

"Intelligere enim est actus qui non potest exerceri per organum corporale, sicut exercitur visio: sed in materia est, in quantum ipsa anima, cuius est haec virtus, est corporis forma." (*Ibid.* I, LXXVI, 1, ad 1um.)

experience; moderate realism keeps in touch with experience but does not succeed in establishing itself in a position of equilibrium—the synthesis it tries to achieve is a compromise rather than a genuine solution. All these positions, as we know, are based on a common assumption: man and the world are two distinct realities bound together by the relation of knowledge. Thus all philosophers accept the relation subject-object as the experimental ground in which their philosophical reflection must be rooted. This intellectualistic attitude, as has been explained at the beginning of this introduction, is a rationalization of the natural attitude.

Since the beginning of this century, philosophical research—mainly in continental Europe—has been stimulated by the conviction that there exists a field of experience deeper than the so-called experience of the distinction subject-object, a field which it is the real task of philosophy to unveil and describe.

This primordial experiential field has been identified by Husserl with pure consciousness. Husserl acknowledges the opposition between consciousness and the world as an irreducible fact, but he refuses to make of it the theme of his reflection. Philosophical reflection, he says, must eliminate all consideration of the objective world in order to concentrate itself on the pure subject. This mental conversion (phenomenological reduction) is possible because consciousness is radically distinct from reality. Moreover, as consciousness is essentially intentional, it contains in itself the pure essence of every possible experience and of every possible object. This pure consciousness is the domain which philosophy (or phenomenology) must explore in the light of pure intuition.[9]

This position, however revolutionary it may claim to be, still belongs to the most authentic intellectualistic tradition. It introduces, however, a new element into the intellectualistic debate: Husserl claims that the dyad subject-object is not purely identical with the relation consciousness-world, but is already present in consciousness independently of its relation to the world. This enables him to consider consciousness as a kind of universal archetype which can be studied for itself.

This separation between the realm of consciousness and the world

[9] Husserl defines phenomenology as "a *pure descriptive* discipline which studies the whole field of transcendental consciousness in the light of pure intuition." (*Ideas, General Introduction to Pure Phenomenology*, translated by W. R. Boyce Gibson, London, 1952.)

has been rejected by all the phenomenologists of the existentialist school. They consider the very idea of pure consciousness as an aberration and believe that the operations of consciousness make sense only in a world. Accordingly, they look upon phenomenology not as a philosophy concerned only with essences but, in the words of Merleau-Ponty, "as a philosophy which replaces essences in existence and does not believe that man and the world can be understood save on the basis of their state of fact."[10] In this context, the term "existence" does not mean simply the fact of existing, but expresses the way in which man is inserted in the world—not a relation of knowledge, but a vital "being-in" and "being-towards". This original situation—deeper than the relation subject-object—is the experiential field which existential phenomenology tries to bring to light.

The philosophical views which I develop in this book have not been inspired initially by a study of the phenomenological movement. In fact, my acquaintance with a number of works considered as basic by the historians of this movement is quite recent. The starting-point of my reflection has been the study of Scholastic philosophy. In keeping with the Thomist theory of knowledge and psychology, I first adopted a decidedly intellectualistic view of the relation between man and the world. The effort I carried on during many years to understand the universe in its totality and to replace every single experience within my general intuition led me gradually to a deeper and more integrated vision of the place which man occupies in the world and of his relation to God. This deepening of my understanding of reality has been in fact the progressive discovery of that existential stratum which underlies the world of our daily experience and gives it its true meaning: in particular, it has been the discovery of our living unity with the world—an existential situation deeper than the duality subject-object—of our membership in a community of persons co-extensive with the whole created reality.[11]

10 *La phénoménologie de la perception* (Paris: Gallimard, 1945), Avant-propos.

11 Throughout this reflective process, I have never broken with the Thomist tradition. All those who are truly familiar with the philosophy of St Thomas will acknowledge that the present work remains Thomist in its inspiration and, very often, in its formulation. I am more and more convinced that Thomism, before being an intellectualistic doctrine, is a philosophy of existence. Quite often, when reading some texts of the *Summa*, I felt that St Thomas's intuition went deeper than the conceptual apparatus in which he tried to express it. This made me understand that true fidelity to the doctrine of the great Doctor has necessarily to be more than verbal fidelity: it has to be first of all a true understanding of what

I am not first of all a subject facing a world of objects distinct from me; I am the act-of-a-certain-world in tension towards its realization. As act, I am not primarily a certain "I know", but a certain "I live" existing for a certain aim. All the objects of the world (and first of all my body) are essentially modalities of this existential movement (which is myself)—they express it and condition it, they subsist in it and by it. Therefore the meaning of things is not primarily of an intellectual or cognitive character, but of an existential character—it is life-meaning.

This is the perspective in which henceforth all problems of knowledge must be studied. It is too early to examine the different aspects of the question. I shall merely touch upon one or two points.

(a) **Consciousness pertains to the Life-Act and therefore cannot be studied for itself.** As it appears now, the fundamental error of intellectualism is to conceive the relation between man and the world as fundamentally a relation of knowledge; consequently, to consider knowledge or consciousness as a domain which can be studied in itself. This error prevents intellectualism not only from rightly understanding man and the world, but even from explaining coherently the meaning and structure of human knowledge. If we consider knowledge or consciousness as such as an act, and if we define man essentially as the subject of this act, we posit *a priori* a sharp distinction between man and the world, between the "for-itself" and the "in-itself" (the fact of admitting the intentional character of knowledge, far from attenuating this distinction only emphasizes it). Once this duality has been artifically created, the whole problem is how to resolve it. The only practical way is to make knowledge a synthetic activity, and, finally, a purely creative activity. (From Kant to Fichte there is only one step.) But, as it appears now, the act constitutive of man is not an "act of knowledge"; it is a life-act which from the first occupies a certain field, constitutes a certain world, exists as a continually self-transcending act. Now, in this

---

St Thomas means to say—that is, coincidence with his intuition—and then fidelity to his intention.

I do not claim to have achieved such identity of view. The point of view of my study has never been that of an interpreter of St Thomas's philosophy. I have constantly tried to understand reality as it is, to discover its structures, to coincide with its movement, and to express what I saw and felt as adequately as I could. But this laborious effort has been carried on within the philosophical tradition to which I had been introduced. To the very degree to which it has succeeded, it has, I hope, made me coincide with the intention constitutive of this tradition.

movement, this act is essentially conscious. Conscious of what? Of itself, of course, and of everything as included in, constituted by, this movement which is itself. *Consciousness is, thus, the property which the human life-act has of being self-transparent.* This fact, to be sure, will have to be further elucidated; but, from now on, we must admit that there is no such thing as a pure act of knowledge or consciousness. The human act is always life-act, consciousness is a property of this act, and cannot therefore be understood apart from it. Every form of consciousness is first of all a certain manner of living. This fact shows that to make of man a pure subject of knowledge is to falsify *a priori* what we are trying to explain: it falsifies knowledge, it falsifies man, and it falsifies the world—it excludes from the start any experiential contact with reality. This lack of contact with living reality leads to the notion of philosophy as an abstract science whose task is to deduce the *a priori* conditions which render possible our awareness of the objective world and the existence of the world as object—human psychology is almost entirely reduced to a theory of knowledge. In this perspective, the idea of a descriptive philosophy developing within experience and showing how man and the world exist *de facto*—instead of explaining how it should be *de iure*—is declared non-metaphysical, dismissed as phenomenism or empiricism. This reminds me of the fox and the grapes. I have shown that the intellectualistic position is based on a misunderstanding of facts. The negative attitude which many intellectualistic philosophers adopt with regard to existential phenomenology is derived from their failure to grasp a perspective into which their postulates prevent them from entering.

(b) **The Concrete "Universals".** According to Aristotle, there is no *intellectual* knowledge of individual objects. From the sensorial images which are singular, concrete, the intellect abstracts the "forms" of the objects and expresses them in universal concepts. Thus intellectual knowledge is essentially knowledge of quiddities, not of individualities; the meaning of a thing is a universal which is by itself impersonal, free from all "subjective" elements.

Our study has brought to light the following facts:

(1) The meaning of a thing depends on the spatial modalities of this thing, of its situation among the other things which surround it, on the system in which it is included. The meaning of a thing

is a particular expression of the unity-meaning of the whole universe.

(2) The unity-meaning of the universe is constituted by my life-act-taking-up-my-life-experience-and-realizing-itself-through-my-act-project; thus it is life-meaning.

(3) Each particular object is a particular expression of this act: it is constituted by my act, it expresses my act according to its particular modalities and situation. Thus my personal life constitutes the concrete meaning which an object has for me. In other words, the meaning of a thing *is* my act living in a particular manner its presence in the modalities of this thing.

Therefore:

(1) There is no such thing as "*abstractio conceptus a phantasmate*", because man is not primarily an intellect facing a world and communicating with this world through a body which is essentially a sensorium. I know the objects which surround me because my act lives in them, animates them, makes them exist for me. (The different aspects of this "informatio" will be studied in the next chapter.)

(2) My knowledge of things is concrete, singular, personal. These objects which surround me have a unique meaning for me constituted by their relation to me, their inclusion in the field of my life, of my present concern. Nobody can see, experience them as I see, experience them now. If another person wishes to live and know them exactly as I do, he should first become myself—his life and my life should become one and the same act.

(3) My knowledge of things is universal to the degree to which my integral life-act (the act constitutive of the whole universe) animates each one of them, to the degree to which each object, in its very singularity, expresses the unity-meaning of the whole.

Let me explain this last assertion in more detail.

My life-act-realizing-itself-through-my-act-project constitutes the unity-meaning of the whole world. Now this act exists essentially as a reality in tension towards something final. Thus the world-in-me is in a state of genesis, it is being built, it is ordained towards an end which will be the full realization of its constitutive act (my personal life). In other words, my world exists essentially towards an end, it is meant for an end. This "being-meant-for-an-end" forms the unity-meaning—the being—of the world-in-me, and, thus, the meaning of every particular object. This fact shows that each particular object, in spite of its singularity, is *radically* identical with all the other objects: its meaning-for-me—that is, its being-for-me—is first of all its "being-meant-for-the-end".

Now my act-project realizes itself through particular decisions and actions—that is, through particular projects. Fundamentally, the end of all these projects and the end of my act-project are one. However, in so far as they are particular projects, they have also particular aims in view. In reference to these particular aims, the different objects are defined by their particular utility; in other words, their "being-meant-for-the-end" is specified as "being-meant-for-a-particular-end". This designation constitutes the "categorial" meaning of objects: it classifies them, it makes them susceptible of being named. Owing to this specification, the meaning of each object remains to a great extent permanent whatever the environment in which it is situated, whatever my affective disposition and my actual concern. (At a further stage of our study, we shall indicate the deeper foundation of this permanence.)

It must be noted carefully that this classification of objects does not induce a perspective different from the structural perspective in which our study has introduced us. Each object, as a "universal", is the specification of the unity-meaning of the whole universe. As a particular "tool", it refers (as Heidegger has shown clearly) to other tools, it expresses the whole system in which it is included—it has no existence and no meaning apart from this system.

Let us observe also the concrete, "personal", existential nature of these universals. The general meaning which an object has for me—whether it be its general destination (its being-meant-for-the-end), or its specific destination (its being-meant-for-a-particular-end)—is made of my life-experience and of my act-project. Thus each object, as a "universal", is already a concretion of my personal life. My life fills the world, it is present in all things in the form of intentions, each of which expresses in its own manner my general orientation towards the end.

Part Two

EXPLORING THE HUMAN WORLD

CHAPTER IV

The Act Incarnate

The world has revealed itself to us as a structural totality, a unity-meaning expressing itself in a great diversity of significative elements, in the relations which all these elements have to one another. Further inquiry has shown us that this unity-meaning is constituted by my life-act-realizing-itself-through-my-act-project (my personal act). Thus the world exists as the field of my life ("my world"), and my personal life as the act of the world. In this chapter, I shall study in a more detailed manner the structure of my world—that is, the different aspects of my personal act. In doing so, I shall make more explicit the observations gathered in the preceding chapters.

Among all the objects, my body has certainly a central role to play in the making of my world. It is a fact that my act exists first of all in my body, and, from this centre, "occupies", constitutes, the whole universe. It is a fact that all the objects which surround me refer to my body and receive from this relation their existence as parts of my world. Thus my world is a totality which has a definite centre of reference.

In the first chapter I have observed that an object which has a natural centre, in so far as it is a meaning which unfolds itself in a diversity of spatial modalities, is a centrifugal movement (aspect a). This observation applies to this totality which I call my world (in which all objects are included): my world, in so far as it is the unfolding of my personal act, is a movement which originates in my body—that is, a centrifugal process.

On the other hand, I have seen that an object which is centred is the resultant of a centripetal process in so far as its unity-meaning is conditioned by the modalities in which it expresses itself (aspect b).

Thus I shall say that the very existence of my world entails a convergence of all worldly phenomena towards my body to the extent that the constitutive act of my world, which unfolds from my body, is conditioned by the modalities of the whole spatial field which it animates, in which it lives.

In the course of this study, I shall examine in detail the concrete implications of these two complementary aspects. To proceed methodically, I shall first observe the way in which my act is present in my body, then analyse the relationship between my body and the surrounding world.

I. MY ACT IN MY BODY

The tendency of idealism is to derive the whole of reality from the activity of the subject understood as pure consciousness, or pure interiority. In this line of thought, the body, to the extent that it is active, is conceived as a moment of the act of knowledge. On the other hand, in so far as it exists in the manner of an object, it is considered as an element of the world—that is, of that sphere of being in which consciousness extrapolates itself.

Conversely, empirical realism tends to consider the body as a purely extensive reality, existing *partes extra partes*. According to it, all phenomena of consciousness may be explained by a "scientific" study of processes which take place in the "objective" sphere.

These two conceptions have one thing in common: they do not take any notice of my body as this living reality of which I have personal experience; and this for obvious reasons. Considering man as pure consciousness, idealism is obliged either to identify the body with the act of knowledge, or to objectify it. On the other hand, anxious to explain everything "objectively", empiricism reduces the whole human psychology to a blind process, to a combination of elements. In either case, the "phenomenal" body is ignored.

The truth is that I am never a pure act of consciousness existing above space and time, but always a life-act expressing itself in spatial modalities; and that my body is never a mere synthesis of distinct elements, but always the incarnation and expression of its constitutive act—that is, the diversification of a fundamental unity. Therefore consciousness and body, as they exist *de facto*, are but two aspects of one reality which is my life-act-existing-spatially.

The act which constitutes my body and my world is my life-act-realizing-itself-through-my-act-project. As we have seen, my life-act and my act-project are not two different acts which are somehow juxtaposed: my life-act is the prime act by which I exist, and my act-project is the personal actuation of this "I live". However, a certain distinction has to be maintained between them in so far as my life-act forms an existential field which is presupposed to all my personal initiatives, which each one of my projects must take up and activate in a specific manner. In the following pages, I shall first study my body as constituted by my life-act; I shall then consider its integral reality as the expression of the total movement of my personal life.

A. My Life-Act in My Body

Preceding all my personal decisions, there is the fact that I am there—not as a pure consciousness hovering over the earth like the Spirit of the God of Genesis, but as a life which is already structured, which has a direction, or directions. I do not create myself; I "find" myself as a living individuality which is already involved in, committed to, a certain world. Here where I stand, there is flesh, there are bones, there is a nervous system, there are desires, inclinations, repulsions, there is a temperament, there is a past and a potential future, there is consciousness. All this forms an original situation which may appear to me auspicious or frustrating, but from which I cannot dissociate myself; I must take it as it is and make use of it to build my personal life. This original situation is my life-act-incarnate-in-my-body. Through several concentric approaches, I shall survey it so as to understand more and more deeply the nature of the existential humus in which my act-project is rooted.

First Approach

My body—as any other object—*is a unity-meaning which expresses itself in a diversity of spatial structures* (*aspect a*), *and is conditioned by the modalities of these structures* (*aspect b*).

My body is first of all a unity, but this unity is not simple: within my body there is a great diversity of elements—of limbs, of systems, of organs; within these limbs and organs, there is a diversity of parts, of aspects. Each of these elements has a meaning of its own: the meaning of my hands and the meaning of my feet are not simply identical; different also are the meaning of my stomach, that of my heart, of my lungs. . . . However, these particular meanings do not differ from one another as one thing differs from another. No element of my body makes sense apart from the whole body. Therefore the meaning of each element is a particular expression of the unity-meaning of the whole—it *is* this unity-meaning expressing itself in a particular manner.

This last proposition means two things: (1) The meaning of each part of my body is really *derived* from the unity-meaning of the whole (aspect a); (2) Each element expresses this unity-meaning *according to its particular modalities, according to its situation, to its relation to all the other parts of my body;* it contributes in its own way towards forming the unity-meaning of the whole (aspect b). This contribution of each part to the whole is an evident fact: my arms, my hands, my feet have irreplaceable roles to play in building this totality which I call my body. Suppress any of these limbs, and my body will no longer be *this* body, I shall no longer be what I am now.

Second Approach

My life-act constitutes the unity-meaning of my body. This act animates the various structures of my body (aspect a), and, in so doing, is conditioned by the modalities of these structures (aspect b).

My life-act is present in my body, in my world, as a dynamic principle which tries to perfect itself, to realize itself. In describing the way in which it is incarnate, I shall consider first the "aspect a", then the "aspect b".

Aspect a: My act expresses itself in the modalities of my body; its mode of existence is therefore spatial. My act animates the various elements of my organism; it gives them their existence as parts of my body. Thus my head, my hands, my feet, my stomach, my lungs . . . —in the places which they occupy—are really constituted by my life-act, the life which is in them is entirely derived from my act, they *are* my act expressing itself in various ways, their existence is my act-tending-towards-its-realization.

In unfolding itself in my different limbs and organs, my life-act, though remaining essentially one, diffracts itself in a variety of functions. Each of these functions is my act as present in a given part of my body (thus a function is the act—the meaning, the life, the very existence—of the organic modalities in which it operates). In fact, the process by which my act expresses itself in the various structures of my body and the movement by which it diffracts itself in a plurality of functions are one and the same phenomenon: the different organs of my body have no meaning, no life, apart from the functions which manifest themselves in them; on the other hand, each of these functions is essentially the act of a particular organ, it is nothing apart from the organ in which it operates.

All the functions of my body are different aspects of my life-act, different variations of its movement towards its end. As such, they are different "intentions", incipient behaviours—they are characterized by the different roles they play, by their respective finalities, within the context of my integral teleology. My whole body is occupied by these functions—being in its entireness the original field in which my act expresses itself, through which it realizes itself. Thus my body is the original behaviour of my life-act, its primordial manner of ordaining itself towards its end, of fixing the directions in which its striving after this end will be carried on.

Each organ of my body, though localized in a definite region of my body, is, in reality, co-extensive with my whole organism. Each function of my body, though it is the act of a particular organic structure, is, in reality, constituted by my integral life-act. Therefore each organ of my body is built, constituted, by all the other organs; the exercise of one function supposes that of all the other functions. This synergy is simply the fact that my life-act always operates as a single principle, even though, at a given moment, it expresses itself mainly through the exercise of a particular function. Therefore all the functions of my body are involved in each pulsation of my life-act.

This synergy indicates also that, in the human body, there is no function which is narrowly specialized—that is, ordained *exclusively* to a specific aim. The notion of the human body as a synthesis of sharply delimited organs, of faculties, each of which has its own independent activity and strictly predetermined *objectum formale*, is a product of the geometrical mentality. Each organ is meant for the whole body; in other words, the integral finality of each function is the finality of the whole person to whom it belongs. This does not mean that the human body is an undifferentiated expressive field (to be "expressive", a field must be differentiated). Each part of the body has, indeed, a particular and irreplaceable role to play within the context of the entire organism—that is, within the whole movement of the human life of which this organism is the expression. But this "utility" is not reduced to a striving in one particular direction—even though each organic structure should naturally be defined by a predominant destination which, indeed, manifests itself in it—it is essentially a particularization of the utility of the whole body. The exercise of each function, therefore, must be integrated in the activity of the whole system, it must be concretely identical with the movement of the integral life-act—in other words, each function must follow the course which the entire life-act incarnate follows. An example will illustrate what is meant here. The sexual organs are naturally defined by their relation to the generative act. This does not imply that their function is merely generative, that they operate only when this act is posited. At every moment, these organs are at work but their activity is canalized in the direction which the life-act concretely follows, it is an aspect of the actual movement of the act.

Aspect b: We have studied so far the manner in which the life-act animates, constitutes, the whole body and the different functions of the body. We must analyse now the other aspect: the act is conditioned by the modalities of the organic structures in which it expresses itself.

Considered under the "aspect a", the body appears as the very concretion, the self-unfolding of the life-act: it exists by, in, and for the act. Now, from the point of view of the "aspect b", we see that the act "finds" itself involved in, fashioned by, the organic structures which it activates. From this point of view, the act seems to express itself in a body which is *already there*: the body "moulds" the act *according to its particular modalities.*

The whole life-act is conditioned by the biological substratum in which it is incarnate, because the act, even though it diffracts itself in a variety of functions, remains essentially one. Accordingly, the life-act manifests itself as a unified complex of propensities, aspirations, aptitudes, deficiencies; it reveals a fundamental affective disposition; in short, it exists in the form of a more or less definite temperamental inclination. This temperamental inclination may be defined as the basic vital attitude which the life-act tending towards the end assumes owing to its incarnation in this particular body. This fundamental disposition manifests itself, to some extent, in every particular pulsation of the life-act incarnate.

Each function, as a particular variation of the life-act, is also conditioned by the organic modalities in which it manifests itself. In fact, if, in a certain part of the body, the act expresses itself as visual power, this is due to the particular structure of this part in relation to the whole; likewise, if, in another part, the life-act is the function of speech, this is due to the peculiar constitution of that part, to its situation in the whole body. The diffraction of the act in a plurality of functions is due, therefore, to the division of the body into a variety of organs and systems. Moreover, we observe that the perfection of a given function depends on the integrity of the organic system in which this function operates. As a matter of fact, the good "functioning" of an organ is the criterion which enables us to say that this organ is well constituted and healthy. On the other hand, functional irregularities point to "organic defects"—this means that the life-act-incarnate-in-this-or-that-part-of-the-body suffers some violence on account of peculiarities of its expressive field. These peculiarities are said to be defects precisely *because* they are the source of some malfunctioning. An application of this is that functional troubles can be artificially provoked through some manipulation of the organic substratum; conversely, a function can be restored to health through some modification of the organ in which it lives.

What we have said just now must be understood in a structural perspective. Each organ is essentially related to the other organs, to the whole body; each function is essentially a particular variation of the integral life-act. This means that each organ contributes, according to its particular modalities, to the functioning of all the other organs; more fundamentally, it means that each organ has its vital role to play in forming what we have called the temperamental inclination: each part of the body conditions the act according to its inner structure. This fact shows us once more that an organ can never be the substratum of a function operating in a single direction. Each organ has, no doubt, a predominant destination by which it is naturally defined, but this specialization is not the whole of its utility: its specific action contributes to the activity of the entire organism—that is, to the "shaping" of the life-act which is incarnate in the whole body.

We understand also that temperamental peculiarities may sometimes be ascribed to definite organic factors, and sometimes to no one factor in particular (but to the whole physiological set up). Sometimes psychological irregularities can be corrected through some definite modification of the organic substratum, sometimes through some action on the whole system. Conversely, affective troubles can be provoked sometimes through the impairment of some definite organic ensemble, sometimes through some constitutional alteration.

In the human body, there is no purely local happening, and there is no purely organic process. Whatever takes place in a particular organ affects the whole body and has a certain "psychological" significance. When a given part of the organism is in a bad condition, the whole system suffers (we never say: my throat, or my stomach, or my heart is sick, but: I am sick), the whole personal structure is altered.

The fact that the life-act is thus conditioned by the modalities of the organic structures in which it is incarnate accounts also for a great part of our needs. Steps must be taken to keep the body in working order—that is, to enable the act to express itself in it in an adequate manner, to tend in a truly human way towards its ultimate realization. In this perspective, we can say that there is no such thing as a purely physical need. Hunger is not simply a bodily phenomenon; it is an existential situation; it conditions the whole life of a man; it has a significance in relation to his final destiny. Each want influences the way in which the life-act incarnate realizes itself.

Complementariness of the two aspects: Each function of the body is at the same time:

(1) A particular concretion of the life-act-in-tension-towards-the-end (aspect a: the division of the body into a number of organs and systems is due to the fact that the life-act diffracts itself into a variety of functions—the visual system has this particular structure *because* the act lives in it as sight; similarly, the organs of speech are constituted in that way *because* the act expresses itself in them as power of speaking).

(2) A structure which conditions, incarnates the act according to its particular modalities (aspect b: the diffraction of the act into several functions is due to the way in which the body is structured—the act lives in a given part of the body as sight *because of* the specific structure of this part, in another part as power of speaking *because of* the particular constitution of this other part).

Thus: the life-act *constitutes the body* as its expressive field (aspect a)—at the same time, *it "finds" itself involved in, conditioned by*, the structures of the organism *as though they were "already there"*, as though the life-act itself were fashioned, brought to existence in them.

The process of self-expression through language may help us to understand this paradoxical fact. I have a certain idea in mind and express it in a sentence: "man is an act-incarnate". The different words of this sentence, the letters which form these words, the relations which all these elements have to one another, are really constituted by my intention; they have no meaning, no being, apart from it: my intention creates its expression. Yet, all these letters, these words—with their particular meanings—were "already there", they were at my disposal, ready to be used. My act of self-expression is, therefore, the taking up and the re-creating of a pre-existent expressive field. Similarly, my life-act, in constituting my body and the various functions of my body, takes up and re-creates vital structures which are, in a way, offered to it "ready made".

To determine the significance of this phenomenon calls for further investigation.

THIRD APPROACH

My body, as the concretion of my life-act, is a centrifugal movement; as a structure by which my act is conditioned, it is a centripetal process.

Among the different parts of my body, my head—more particularly, my brain inside my head—has a dominant role to play. Indeed, it is the place where my life-act affirms itself as a real human act (endowed with self-consciousness); thus it is the centre in reference to which my body exists as a real human body.

Centrifugal movement (*aspect a*): I have shown how my life-act, in expressing itself in the modalities of my body, diversifies itself in a variety of functions. Although I have just described the mutual interpenetration of these functions, I have not yet assigned any order to them. The brain, we have said, is the most important region in my body, and we should now consider the role it plays in my organism considered as a movement of expression.

My body, as we have seen, is the original behaviour of my life-act, its primordial manner of tending towards its end, of fixing the directions in which its self-actuating movement will be carried on. My head is the part of my body in which this movement really begins: my act comes into being first of all in the modalities of my brain. My brain is, therefore, the first concretion of my life-act-in-tension-towards-its-end; it is my act expressing itself in a still undivided manner and ordaining itself towards its unfolding into various functions, towards its actuation through specific behaviours which are the exercise of these functions. Thus my brain is my whole organism at its initial stage, my life-act activating my brain is my whole behaviour—the whole movement of my life—at its source. The different functions of my body are what they are in virtue of their relation to my brain; each of them begins in my brain and prolongs this central function according to its particular modalities.

Centripetal movement (*aspect b*): In the very movement by which it constitutes my brain as its primordial centre of expression, my life-act is conditioned by the modalities of this centre. My brain, therefore, for all that it expresses my life-act, "shapes" it according to its inner structure. In this sense, the functional ensemble which I call my brain precedes the act which is incarnate in it and, therefore, precedes the movement by which my act constitutes my body. But my brain has no existence apart from my other organs and functions: isolated from them, it is nothing but a lump of bleeding and decaying matter. My brain is fed, it is vitalized, by my entire organism: each part of my body, connected with all the others, has, according to its modalities and situation, a special role to play in shaping my central organs. Thus, prior to the movement by which my life-act incarnates itself in my brain and, from this core, constitutes my body, there is the fact that the functions of my organism converge towards a centre (my brain) where they build themselves into a single functional nucleus. In other words, the centrifugal self-expressive expansion of my life-act is built on a "pre-existent" centripetal phenomenon. This perspective throws some light on the way in which my act is conditioned by the structures in which it expresses itself. I have observed above (2nd Approach, Aspect b) that *my whole act* is regulated by the biological substratum in which it is incarnate because, even though it diversifies itself into several functions, it remains essentially one. My act, therefore, exists in the form of a temperamental inclination which manifests itself in all its different variations (it assumes a fundamental behaviour because of its incarnation in this particular body). Now, I have discovered that my life-act existing as a unitary principle is first of all my act expressing itself in my brain (more particularly, in the central modalities of my cerebral system). Thus my temperamental inclination is due primarily to the inner structure of this centre. However, as my brain is built on my entire organism, I can say that each part of my body, each organic process, has its own particular role to play in determining my fundamental vital attitude. This conditioning activity is a regulated activity in the sense that the more closely a biological fact is connected with the central functions of my body, the more decisive also is the role it plays in influencing my life-act, and thus in determining my temperamental inclination.

Not only is my whole life-act conditioned by my biological system, but each function of my body, as a particular variation of my act, is shaped by the organic modalities in which it manifests itself. Now, I have observed that each function of my body, in so far as it is constituted by my act, *begins in my brain* and prolongs this functional centre according to its particular modalities. On the other hand, I have noticed that each function, to the extent that it conditions my act, *culminates in the modalities of my brain.* Thus each function of my organism, as a centrifugal process, is conditioned by the same function existing as a centripetal phenomenon.

Clearly, this fact must be understood in a structural perspective. Each process which takes place in my body—whether it be considered as a centrifugal or as a centripetal phenomenon—is essentially integrated in the whole. Consequently, my whole-body-existing-centripetally conditions each function-existing-centrifugally; conversely, each function-existing-centripetally conditions my whole-body-existing-centrifugally.

Complementariness of the two aspects: My body, in so far as it is constituted within the centrifugal movement of my life-act, is, so to speak, the first draft of my personal behaviour. As such, my body is really my act beginning to express and realize itself. Now, as I have shown, this movement is based on another phenomenon (the centripetal aspect) which is not properly *constituted* by my life-act (since it conditions or "shapes" my act). Considered "in itself", this centripetal process may be called a pre-personal phenomenon (pre-personal with regard to me). Thus I must say that my individual life develops essentially within a pre-existent field—that is, within vital structures which are relatively independent of me.

Yet, in reality, my body-existing-centripetally has no existence apart from my act. Without my life-act, there cannot be any convergence of my organic functions towards my brain, there cannot be any biological process existing as the substratum of my personal life. Therefore, in the order of reality, my life-act is the existence of both my body-existing-centripetally and of my body-existing-centrifugally. Not in the same manner, however: my act gives existence to the latter by expressing itself in it, to the former by exerting a pull which creates in it a polarization. These two aspects will become clearer as we proceed. My act, as we shall explain, comes to life in an existential field which is already prepared; it takes it up (pull, polarization, centripetal process), and re-creates it (self-expression, centrifugal movement). Thus my body-existing-centripetally and my body-existing-centrifugally are not two different realities: the latter *is* the former taken up by my life-act and re-created by it in its field of expression (in the same way as each one of the sentences I write is the re-creation, within my act of thinking, of a certain pre-existent linguistic material).

Fourth Approach

In my previous considerations, I have spoken of affectivity and aspirations. These are without doubt notions which imply *consciousness*. I shall now study more carefully my life-act incarnate in my body in so far as it is thus self-transparent. The purpose of this study is not to analyse the structure of knowledge, but simply to indicate a few facts within the limits of my present investigation. As I proceed in my work and widen the sphere of my phenomenological analysis, I shall complete the description of these phenomena and indicate their meaning in reference to the totality in which they are implied. In so doing, it will be borne in mind that consciousness and its different modalities pertain to life: each state of consciousness is, first of all, a certain manner of living; it refers to a particular variation of the life-act incarnate.

i. *The Life-Act Existing in the Body in the Form of Thoughts*

Earlier (Third Approach), I have shown that my brain, as the first expression of my life-act and the summit of the centripetal activity, is the most important part of my body: it is the centre in reference to which my body exists as a real human body. I must conclude, therefore, that my life-act-existing-consciously is first of all my life-act-incarnate-in-the-modalities-of-my-brain. Now, this central conscious state is always specified in some way or another. It exists in the form of thoughts, ideas, or "mental images" loaded with a certain affectivity (which may attain various degrees of intensity).[1] These thoughts—which may be the continuation at a non-reflective level of a previous reflection, or of a past reading, the resurgence of a past experience, the crystallization of a certain preoccupation, feeling,

[1] I am not speaking here of my act of thinking, but of those thoughts and imaginations which come to me "by themselves" and succeed one another without my fixing them deliberately.

desire, etc.—considered from the point of view of my present study, may be described as *self-transparent expressive variations of my life-act-incarnate-in-the-modalities-of-my-brain.* As such:

(1) They are *constituted* by my life-act, in so far as they *are* my life-act-expressing-itself-in-a-particular-manner-in-the-modalities-of-my-brain-while-tending-towards-its-end.

(2) They *condition* my act, in so far as they proceed from my biological life—being particular condensations of my centripetal activity at its summit.

In short, these thoughts are particular ways in which my life-act is given to itself in the modalities of my brain (aspect b), while positing itself in the same modalities (aspect a). We recognize here the two functions of my life-act: (1) its function with regard to the centripetal aspect: the taking up of a "pre-existent" reality; (2) its "positive" function: the re-creating in itself of this living "given".

These observations show us that our thoughts are in a true sense spatial: not in the sense that they have size and shape, but in the sense that they are variations of our life-act within the modalities of our brain—variations which are really constitutive of these modalities. In other words, our thoughts are spatial because they are different ways in which our life-act is consciously present to itself, and expresses itself in the spatial modalities of our central organ (self-expression means self-spatialization).

But if our thoughts are somehow localized in our brain, this does not mean that they are purely local phenomena. First, they exist within the movement by which our life-act constitutes our body as its expressive field while orientating itself towards its ultimate realization (centrifugal movement). Considered within this movement, our brain, as we know, is our whole behaviour at its origin. In this context, our thoughts are concretions of our life which naturally tend to unfold themselves in our whole body (following specific directions according to their particular nature), to realize themselves through concrete behaviours; in other words, they are pointers, crystallized intentions, which, "left to themselves", would become what they aim to be. Secondly, as particular condensations of our centripetal activity, our thoughts and imaginations, as we have said above, proceed from our entire biological activity. The "pre-personal" life of our perceptive apparatus, of our whole organism, converges towards our brain and expresses itself in it in a synthetic manner in the form of suggestions, of vital motions, of proposed behaviours, which are taken up by our act.[2]

The vital character of our thoughts indicates clearly that there is no such thing as a *purely* cognitive mental state. The pure knowing subject of Kantian and Post-Kantian idealism is nothing more than a fiction. Our thoughts have from the first a functional and dynamic character because they belong to us as living incarnate beings striving towards our ultimate realization: they are essentially modalities of this movement which is our life.

ii. *The Life-Act Existing in the Body in the Form of "Percepts"*

Each one of my functions, as a centrifugal movement, begins in my brain and prolongs this central function in a particular direction; conversely, all my functions, as centripetal processes, culminate in my central organ.

I have just shown how my life-act expresses itself in the modalities of my brain in the form of thoughts and imaginations. Now, I observe that, in those organic systems which form my sensory apparatus, my act is present in the form of percepts. These percepts are traditionally said to be of five different types: the nature of each percept depends on the modalities of the perceptive system in which it is present. Like my thoughts, these percepts must be considered both as expressive variations of the centrifugal movement of my act and as modalities which condition this movement. From the point of view of the aspect a, they are—like the very organs of which they are modifications—my act evolving partial self-expressions in the movement by which it actuates itself—they are various concretions of this movement; from the point of view of the aspect b, they are modifications of my

[2] As our study proceeds, we shall continue to appreciate more clearly the full content of what we call "centripetal biological activity", "the pre-personal life of our senses and of our whole organism". We shall see that the reality which these expressions designate is far richer and more intensely human than the phenomena habitually referred to by expressions such as "organic determinisms", "biological life", etc. The point of view of our study is not that of any natural science; it is integral in the sense that it embraces the totality of our experience; it indicates the perspective in which the different scientific views of the universe and of man must be integrated in order to become really intelligible. Any "explanation" of the whole human universe from a point of view narrower than that of our *integral experience* is bound to be a distortion, a levelling down, an impoverishment of reality. Scientists—particularly those whose field of study is man—must acknowledge the limitation of their research, and realize that only a vision of the whole, both extensive and intensive (the two always go together), gives their full meaning to the phenomena which they study.

perceptive apparatus presenting themselves as various possibilities and calling in particular elementary ways for the act by which they could realize themselves. These expressive motions may develop into thoughts and so exercise their suggestive influence in a more integrated and thus more luminous manner. They may also be taken up by my life-act in their primitive state and be immediately translated into actual behaviours. This happens, for example, when I react to stimuli in a direct instinctive manner, or out of habit convert stimuli into definite attitudes and actions.

We see from all this that there is no percept which is a *mere* visual percept, or a *mere* auditive percept—that is, a modification of a subject who is essentially a sensorium. Each percept has a vital connotation because it exists essentially within a living whole; it is carried and constituted by the life of the entire organism. Some percepts have from the first a certain value which betrays their link with a particular function of the life-act incarnate. They are the life of this function crystallizing itself in particular suggestive modifications of the sensory apparatus.

iii. *The Life-Act Existing in the Body as Affectivity*

We referred earlier to the fact that our thoughts are loaded with affectivity, that some of them present themselves as concretions of our feelings, desires, etc. Let us now examine the various manifestations of this affective life, considering them as different aspects of our life-act-incarnate-in-our-body. The expression "affective life" is used here to designate our emotions, reactions, feelings, interests, desires, passions, etc.

I have already shown that my life-act exists in my body in the form of a temperamental inclination. With my body, I have an individuality made up of a certain fundamental affective disposition, of tendencies, aptitudes, deficiencies. This complex which forms an incipient behaviour is my life-act assuming a certain vital attitude as it incarnates itself in my body. We recognize here the two aspects:

Aspect a: My act makes my body exist as the incarnation of its fundamental tendency (centrifugal movement);

Aspect b: My body shapes my life-act incarnate according to its particular modalities (centripetal aspect).

This prime disposition is not originally a conscious state; yet, as it expresses itself in some way or other in all the particular behaviours in which and through which it actuates itself, it gradually becomes self-transparent: *as I live*, I become conscious of my fundamental way of facing life, of my possibilities and of my limitations—that is of my individuality.

This individuality manifests itself in a special way in my emotions, reactions, desires—that is, in the various aspects of my affective life. These different motions are not simply, like my thoughts and percepts, conscious self-expressions of my life-act in the modalities of my brain and of my perceptive apparatus; they are my act consciously accentuating the movement by which it constitutes the various functions of my body. Some affective states are, as it were, motions of the whole life-act incarnate; others are pulsations of the act living in the form of a particular function.

The existential structure of these affections is identical with that of the whole life-act incarnate: they are centrifugal movements (aspect a) conditioned by the organic situations in which they develop (aspect b); or better: they are biological situations taken up by my act and lived by it as different vibrations or tensions within its existential movement.

These situations are of various types. Some of them are *constitutional*—that is, existing in some way from birth. Such are, for instance, the situations created by some peculiarity of the nervous system, by some organic malformation, by some glandular irregularity. Such situations contribute first of all towards determining the temperamental inclination of the life-act incarnate. Subsequently, they underlie a number of affective states to which this original disposition gives rise and in which it manifests itself. This can easily be understood; as it actuates itself, the act continually takes up the organic situations in which it is incarnate and lives them in the form of impulses and motions which are the very actuality of its fundamental attitude. Other situations are *adventitious*. Without trying to classify them, we can group some of them under the following headings:

Penury Situations: In order to realize itself harmoniously, the life-act must be conditioned by adequate organic structures. From this dependence of our life-act upon the biological system in which it is incarnate, arise many of our needs: need of food, of drink, of air, of rest, of comfort, etc. A lack of these provokes organic alterations which are lived by the act in certain typical ways: feeling of hunger or thirst, desire of relaxation, despondency, irritation, etc.

Disturbance Situations: Various organic modifications are induced by diseases, by the absorption of various kinds of substances, etc. These situations are also taken up and "experientialized" by the act in the form of motions, "psychological states", tensions, etc.

Mutilation Situations: The loss or removal of a limb, of any element of the body, organic lesions, are also biological situations which "move" the act in some way or other.

(It must be emphasized again that there is no such thing as a purely organic or a purely psychic event. Every disturbance or mutilation of the organic stuff is lived by the act in some characteristic manner, and every motion of the act incarnates itself in a more or less definite "physical" way. Moreover, the way in which the act is affected depends greatly on the region of the organism which is impaired and the manner in which the organism is disturbed. This should not surprise us. We know that the whole life-act is present in every part of the body, but not everywhere in the same way; we know that the life-act expresses itself first of all—originally and integrally—in the modalities of our cerebral organ (especially in a particular area of our brain) and that the more closely an organic element is connected with this core of our personality, the more vitally it conditions the act. This explains why disturbances and injuries close to the centre or in the centre itself affect the life-act much more essentially than the impairment of less central organs. From this circumstance arises the distinction which is commonly made between mental and physical diseases. But, as can now be seen, this distinction is only a matter of emphasis. There is no sick person who is not to a certain extent psychologically affected by his ailment, and there is no mental patient who is not physically affected in some way or other.)

These various organic situations may be considered as *crisis situations*. They develop special types of affectivity which could be exemplified *ad infinitum*. It must be noted, however, that there is no stereotyped reaction for each kind of situation. Each situation exists in a totality which is the whole organism, the whole life-act incarnate; each person "experientializes" his organic tribulations according to his particular temperamental constitution and individuality. This is why we said earlier that a person's fundamental affective disposition manifests itself in a special way in the various aspects of his affective life. On the other hand, we must also say that crisis situations—especially when protracted—influence a person's affective disposition and alter it. The reason for such a modification is that the life-act is always conditioned by the situations in which it is incarnate. This temperamental alteration will manifest itself in the whole behaviour of the person who undergoes it—that is, to some extent, in all his subsequent affective motions.

From the observations we have just made, it should not be concluded that only crisis situations are loaded with affectivity. In fact, *every organic disposition*—whether it be a *crisis* or an *equilibrium* situation—is lived by the act in some particular manner and is, therefore, the substratum of a certain affective state. This is clear to us once we understand that affectivity is identical with the very movement of life, that it is *the existential vibration of the act within the life-field which it occupies*. In crisis situations, this vibration becomes irregular, anxious; sometimes tense, violent, desperate; sometimes, on the contrary, weak and sluggish. In equilibrium situations, conversely, it tends to be regular and peaceful: there is contentment, optimism, psychological harmony. This smooth flowing of the act-in-equilibrium is as much a type of affectivity as the more jerky movement of the act-in-crisis.

The most important biological situations with regard to our affective life are, no doubt, those which exist in the form of thoughts and percepts. These are, as has been explained, self-transparent expressive variations of our life-act in the modalities of our brain and of our sensory apparatus (about which much more will have to be said). About our thoughts, we have said that they exist essentially within the movement by which our life-act unfolds itself in our body; that they are, thus, concretions of our life which tend to develop into behaviours. Similarly, we have indicated that our percepts are situations influencing our act and provoking vital reactions. Now, these tensions and reactions are nothing but affective motions consequent on our sensations and representations. The difference between the way in which these thoughts and percepts "move" our life-act and the way in which the constitutional and adventitious situations described above develop into vital motions may be described as follows:

(1) Some biological facts are taken up by our act and lived by it in the form of thoughts and percepts and, concomitantly, in the form of vital attitudes prolonging these thoughts and percepts and manifesting in some particular manner our temperamental inclination.

(2) The organic situations which do not exist in the form of per-

cepts or thoughts[3] are translated into affects by the simple fact that they are modalities of the life-field which the act takes up and in which it unfolds itself. (Thus we understand the way in which there arise in us those many feelings and desires which cannot be referred to any perception or cogitation.)

iv. *Complementariness of our Thoughts, Percepts and Affects*

Through this first approach to incarnate consciousness, we have come to realize that our various conscious states are different modalities of our life-act which cannot be separated from one another. In so far as the relation of our thoughts and percepts to our affective states is concerned, we have chiefly emphasized the fact that the former are expressive variations of our life-act in the modalities of our brain and perceptive apparatus which naturally develop into feelings and desires. Thus we have indicated affective motions which exist in us as the prolongations of our sensations and cogitations. On the other hand, we have also observed the presence in us of affects which are not derived from the latter and arise, so to speak, spontaneously. Moreover, we have mentioned that our thoughts may at times be concretions of our affective life. Let us now, even though it will involve considerable repetition, look at the unifying perspective within which these different observations must be integrated and understood.

The fundamental situation from which everything starts is the life-act existing in the form of a certain temperamental inclination produced by its incarnation in a particular organism. This fundamental situation may be considered from two different angles:

(1) The life-act *constitutes* the body as its field of expression—from this point of view, the body exists by and in the act; it is the act diffracting and expressing itself in various ways as it orientates itself towards its final realization (aspect a, centrifugal movement).

(2) The life-act *is conditioned* by the organic structures in which it unfolds itself—from this point of view, the body exists for the act;

3 We suppose the constitutional and adventitious situations mentioned above to be of this type. This is not always the case. It is evident that these situations are often "accompanied" by sensations, imaginations, thoughts; in other words, that they often are concomitantly, modifications of our perceptive or cogitative apparatus: in which case, these modifications contribute naturally to the shaping of our affective motions.

it determines the act according to its inner structure (aspect b, centripetal process).

This complex, which is prior to the awakening of consciousness, may be synthetized thus: the life-act comes to existence in pre-existent vital structures, takes them up, and re-creates them into its field of expression. Now, as the life-act actuates itself, it "vibrates" in various ways within the vital structures in which it is incarnate: these existential vibrations of the life-act incarnate constitute different affective motions in which its temperamental inclination manifests itself. This fact shows that affectivity is the very pulsation of the life-act: to live is to be affected in a certain manner, to experience oneself as living is to experience oneself as feeling, desiring—that is, as being *already* preoccupied in some way or other.

What is, within this frame, the place of our percepts and thoughts? They are expressive variations of the life-act within the modalities of our brain and perceptive organs. As centripetal phenomena (aspect b), they are possible behaviours suggesting themselves to us in a more or less integrated or articulate manner. They present themselves as potentialities already linked with the entire organism of which they are parts, often closely related to some power latent in the biological system. As parts of the centrifugal movement (aspect a), they are the same phenomena taken up by our life-act with the whole organism of which they are expressive elements, "experientialized" in the form of "indicators" reflecting our vital movements.

Therefore:

(1) Our sensations and mental conceptions *take place essentially within a certain affective atmosphere.* Therefore it is not enough to say that *some* percepts and thoughts are preceded and influenced by affective dispositions; we must assert that *no* perception or cogitation *can* occur except within an affective current. This is clear to us once we realize that the act constitutive of our percepts and thoughts is our life-act—that is, an act which exists in the form of a temperamental inclination and keeps existing by developing within itself affective motions in which its fundamental vital attitude manifests itself.

(2) Our sensations and mental conceptions *are essentially expressions of our affectivity* (aspect a). As modifications of our sensorial and central organs, they are expressive variations of our life-act and of its various movements—as the words of a sentence are expressions of its unity-meaning, of the various shades of this meaning. This

accounts for a great number of psychological phenomena. First, at the "mental" level; the motions of our organism, our desires, feelings, concerns, express themselves in the modalities of our brain and thus develop into ideas, images, and dreams—which may acquire a fantastic character if these vital motions, as the result of some maladjustment or disturbance of their organic substratum, become unruly. At the sensory level, our affective motions impregnate our percepts and "colour" them; sometimes they even create them (hallucinations, "imaginary" sensations, etc.). Thus our mental conceptions and sensations have their concrete meaning within the whole symphony, or tragedy, of our biologico-affective existence; they are reflections of all those tensions and impulses which characterize our condition as life-acts incarnate.

(3) Our sensations and mental conceptions *condition our affectivity*, and give rise to affective motions (aspect b). Not only do our life-act and its various movements constitute the perceptive and cogitative variations of our sensorial and central organs as their very expressions, but they themselves are determined by these expressive modifications, as they are determined by our whole biological structure and by our different organic situations. From this point of view, our percepts and thoughts (together with the whole biological system in which they occur) precede in existence the movement by which our life-act expresses itself in them—though they do not really exist apart from our act (this paradox, we hope, will become more intelligible as we proceed). This dependence of our affects upon our sensations, imaginations, and mental conceptions is also a matter of daily experience. Our perceptions arouse in us feelings and desires which are at times vehement and tyrannical; they provoke emotional reactions which often manifest themselves in our face, in our gestures, in our whole demeanour. Our thoughts and imaginations also modify our affective states: they rejoice or sadden us, bring us peace, irritation, or anxiety, stir up our instincts and provoke us to action.

All these facts show that no aspect of our incarnate consciousness can be studied in isolation. Our life-act-incarnate-in-our-body is a dynamic structure each element of which has its existence only in relation to the other elements, to the totality in which it is included. Each element is constituted by all the other elements, by the whole system; each element influences all the other elements and contributes to the determination of the whole. This dependence of each aspect on the entire structure and of the entire structure on each particular element shows how misguided is any attempt at studying the different modalities of consciousness "in themselves" with the idea of arriving at a definition of "pure sensation", "pure desire", "pure feeling", etc. The notion of human psychology as a composite of such entities is as meaningless as the notion of body as a composite of organs which can be understood independently of the whole in which they are integrated. Both notions are typical products of the geometrical mentality which has for so long thwarted scientific and philosophical research.

In so far as the relation between our percepts, thoughts, and affects—different aspects of our incarnate consciousness—is concerned, it has become clear that the whole problem cannot be solved simply by declaring that our affects follow our percepts and concepts. At the root of such an exclusive statement is the intellectualistic notion of life as a derivative of knowledge. We have seen that many of our affective motions are indeed prolongations of our sensations and mental conceptions, but we have realized also that the latter are nonentities if they are separated from the vital current within which they occur, and of which they are expressions.

No doubt, it will be objected that the views developed in this chapter reduce knowledge to a mere "subjective state". The answer is that they do nothing of the kind, because the problem of the nature and value of knowledge has not yet been raised (though we have already found indications which point to the perspective in which the solution will be found). So far we have examined our percepts and thoughts as facts taking place in our body considered as the first incarnation of our life-act, and we have determined the nature of these facts *within the limits of our investigation.* It is only at the end of our inquiry that these observations will reveal their full meaning. "In themselves" they have little sense; they must be understood within the whole perspective of which they are expressive elements.

Conclusion of the Four Approaches

Through four concentric approaches, I have tried to analyse the situation formed by my life-act-incarnate-in-my-body, and so understand its nature as the existential ground in which my act-project is rooted. Whatever I have described so far is "already there" before I take any personal initiative: it is myself as given to itself, as "thrown into the world", the stuff of which I am made, the original soil on which I have to build my personal life, my individuality. This dynamic situation seems, from many points of view, very unstable and fragile, torn by inner conflicts and crises, threatened by many dangers, continually in a state of need and dependence. Nevertheless, it is a system which reveals in itself a planned harmony: it has a centre to which its different elements refer, in which its various processes culminate, and from which the movement which constitutes it takes its origin. I must now examine what this system becomes when it is integrated—as it must be—in the vital project of my personal act.

B. My Body as the Incarnation of My Integral Personal Act

Some time ago, when I came back to my room after breakfast, I had the intention of resuming this study. In order to carry out my project, I sat down at my table, took from the drawer four or five sheets of paper, revised and corrected the few lines that I had put down yesterday, and then laboriously set about writing. Throughout this process, the various movements of my body, its various positions, attitudes, were entirely moulded by my preoccupation. I wanted to carry on my work: this very will quickened my limbs and my senses. The same occupation is going on now, and the very intention which made me start my work still keeps me sitting at my table: my body is bent forwards, slightly reclining on my left elbow, my eyes follow the movement of my pen on the paper—this is my intention in act.

This description reveals my body as a reality very different from the body which I have analysed in the preceding pages. It is no longer a system which is merely given to itself; it is now the expression of my personal project, a reality which I constitute as the concretion of my act-intention and of the particular projects through which my integral act realizes itself. Let us study carefully this new reality.

To realize itself in a truly human manner, the act must be conditioned by adequate biological structures. That is why each man must go through a process of growth—that is, of physical, affective, perceptual, mental development—before his personality attains real emancipation. As the central organ perfects itself, the life-act expresses itself in it in the form of more and more elaborate concepts (that is, thoughts, imaginations, reminiscences). Through the mediation of these concepts, thanks to the development of its entire biologico-affective set up, the act asserts itself in a more and more conscious manner. In so doing, it realizes its transcendence with regard to the organic structures in which it is incarnate; it begins little by little to "hold them at a distance". Thus emancipated, the act expresses itself in the central modalities of the brain in a more perfectly integrated and integrating manner—that is, in the form of "reflects", "projects". Subsequently, it prolongs these reflects and projects into personal behaviours and, in this movement, re-creates the whole body into a new reality. We shall now analyse this new structure from various angles.

1. My Personal Act as Constituting My Body (Aspect A)

The process that we have just described summarily is the real personal actuation of my life-act. We have explained in the previous chapter that our life-act realizes itself through our act-project. We begin to see how this self-realization takes place. Let us show first in a more detailed manner that this personal actualization of our life-act entails a real re-creation of our organic structures (centrifugal movement, aspect a).

In the first part of this chapter, I have indicated that my life-act comes to existence in vital structures which, from a certain point of view, are "already there", and recasts them into its field of expression. My body thus recast is my body existing as the self-unfolding of my life-act—what we have called a biologico-affective system. This system is, fundamentally, my life-act diffracting itself in various functions within organic structures; subsequently, it is this primary movement accentuated in the form of vital tensions and impulses. Now, in the central modalities of my brain, my life-act, taking up my entire organism, realizes itself as act-project—it becomes self-possessed, self-determined. In this new mode of existence, my act breaks its close adherence to the organic structures in which it is incarnate—as we have said, it realizes its transcendent character. From this moment, I am no longer simply given to myself in the form of a vital process unfolding itself in a succession of affective states, but I become, in a true sense, the author of my life: I form personal intentions, I take personal decisions, I give myself an aim, and I tend towards it in a deliberate manner through personal behaviours: I become responsible for what I do. Consequently, my body is no longer a mere biologico-affective system, but the dynamic expression of my act-project. Everything is recast: the whole life which circulates in my limbs and animates them becomes my act-project-actuating-itself; the modalities of my different organs become the expressive field of this intention-in-act; my features and my whole bodily attitude become its vivid manifestations; my brain, my senses, and my limbs become channels or conductors. In this movement, my thoughts, sensations, feelings, and desires are not eliminated, but are taken up, canalized, ordinated, sublimated; they become modalities of my progress towards my personal end. This orientation tends to become more and more pervasive, permeating and underlying even those moments of relaxation when my personal act, so to speak, entrusts itself to the "mechanisms" of the biologico-affective system in which it is incarnate. Thus my body, as the living expression of my personal project, is in a true sense a new creation. In so far as it is now constituted by a vital impetus which transcends its "native" dynamism and the movement through which this dynamism expresses itself, it is really personalized and spiritualized.

2. My Personal Act as Conditioned by My Body-Already-Constituted

But my life-act-realizing-itself-through-my-act-project—in spite of its transcendent character—remains deeply conditioned by the structures in which it is incarnate (centripetal movement, aspect b). First, as we have said, the harmonious development of these structures is required for the emancipation of the act. This is so true that the presence of organic malformations—either in the form of localized traumata, or in the form of generalized deficiencies—may at times prevent the act from realizing itself in a truly transcendent manner. In such cases, the whole personal structure either remains infantile, or develops in a narrow, twisted, abnormal way: human life remains a largely impersonal process which appears poignantly monstrous.

In this connection, it must be noted carefully that abnormal cases cannot be understood from the point of view of intellectualistic psychology. A "mental" patient is not first of all a person whose life is irregular *because* he has defective percepts, concepts and ideas. On the other hand, it must not be said either that abnormality is *solely* the result of affective troubles. In fact, there is, proper to each person affected by mental irregularities, a certain existential structure characterized primarily by a lack of transcendence—that is a certain "imprisonment" of the act within its biologico-affective make-up. From this excessive adherence—due, as we know, to some organic or constitutional maladjustment—there results a certain eccentric way of living. This eccentricity manifests, no doubt, certain typical characteristics, but it never affects the exercise of only one "faculty" —it is always a structural phenomenon. This remains true even if the mental trouble is due to a localized injury of the cerebral apparatus. In this respect, we must also guard ourselves from what may be called an intellectualistic or "geometricist" conception of cerebral localizations. We must admit that the different areas of the nervous substance have particular relations to different aspects of the psychological make-up, but, in doing so, we must avoid two misunderstandings:

(1) No area in the nervous substance has any exclusive reference to the "cognitive side" of our activity because the act which is incarnate in it is never and nowhere a pure "I know", but always a life-act.

(2) No area in the nervous substance refers to a psychological modality which can be isolated from the whole personal structure. Indeed, each area is essentially related to all the other areas, *to the whole system*; as such, each area is essentially a particular centre where *the whole life-act* is expressed and incarnate.

It must, accordingly, be acknowledged that each area of the nervous substance conditions the act according to its particular modalities. This means that the act expressing itself in this particular centre is not identical with the same act expressing itself in some other centre —in other words, that each particular centre contributes in a unique manner towards building the whole psychological make-up. This contribution consists in the fact that each area of the nervous substance is responsible for a certain dimension of the personal structure. Therefore the impairment of a certain area will be the origin of disturbances and tensions which affect the whole psychological make-up, even though they manifest themselves mainly through some definite infirmities or irregularities.

All these observations show how deeply the emancipation of our act is conditioned by our organic structures. As a rule, we must say that each personal act (that is, each life-act-realizing-itself-in-a-personal-manner) is characterized by a unique manner of transcending its biological make-up *which is still determined by that make-up*. This means that our most personal decisions are still temperamental: they are expressions of aptitudes, inclinations, aspirations which we "find" in ourselves; they are also marked by our constitutional deficiencies. Some people are born artists, others have an aptitude for scientific studies, others are men of action, etc.—each one's life-project will naturally be the personalization of his native predispositions. A man who embraces a profession for which he is not made is in danger of remaining a misfit throughout life—a situation which is surely not conducive to spiritual freedom. The dependence of our personal act on our physico-psychological structures is a phenomenon which we experience every day. Often we feel unable to carry out decisions which we have taken because they are above our capacities, because our act is too deeply buried in our biological apparatus. It seems as though our life were still to a great extent a drama enacted for us in the form of motions and tensions which absorb our personal will. At times of sickness and exhaustion, our personal life tends to dissolve into morbid affectivity. We are forced to give up, or to modify projects which we have formed; we feel too weak to carry on our work, to think, or to face our daily responsibilities. Conversely, when we are in good health, in a state of physical fitness, our act transcends more easily its biologico-affective structures and takes them up more thoroughly; we feel more alert, we are in a better position to carry out our projects and take new decisions.

Besides these general facts, we can also observe the way in which all our particular projects are tied to our physical apparatus. To be truly effective, my present will of pursuing this study must express itself in a certain attitude of my body, in the movement by which my hand grasps my pen and makes it move across the paper. The connection between my intention and these bodily modalities is so close that a change in the latter would entail the cessation of the former: I cannot *effectively* will to carry on my work and, at the same time, lie down on my bed or go out for a walk. Similarly, if I wish to recollect myself and pray, I must adopt a suitable attitude. If, instead of disposing myself in the proper way, I move about and look around me, there will be no true recollection, there cannot even be any serious will to pray. A lame person can no more intend to go for a long journey on foot than a dumb man can plan to make a speech. These are impossibilities, because the very formation of such intentions requires a certain organic substratum which, in these cases, is missing. All these observations point to the same fundamental fact: our personal act is, in its very existence and at all the moments of its actuation, conditioned by the vital structures in which it is incarnate.

It can realize itself only by taking up these structures and allowing itself to be fashioned by them.

3. Complementariness of the Two Aspects

The two series of facts that we have just described separately are always found together—they are essentially complementary aspects of a single process: my personal-act-incarnating-itself-in-my-body. From the point of view of its genesis and development, this process presents itself as follows:

(1) My life-act comes to existence in vital structures which are already there, is conditioned by these structures, takes them up, and recasts them in its field of expression. This original situation is already myself, but it is myself as given to itself—prior to all my personal decisions and projects.

(2) My life-act actuates itself in the modalities of my brain into an act-project. As such—that is, as personal act—it goes on taking up the same vital structures, recasting them in a new expressive ensemble. From this moment, my life becomes really personal; I am no longer simply given to myself, but I shape myself in a deliberate, self-determined manner: the modalities of my brain become my personal act expressing itself in a synthetic, all-integrating manner; my whole body becomes my personal act shaping itself into a concrete behaviour in the movement by which it tends towards its ultimate realization. However, this movement is never purely creative. At every stage of its actuation, my personal act is conditioned by the very structures which it constitutes as its expressive field; in other words, it unfolds within a pre-existent vital ensemble which determines its manner of realizing itself, which offers it a certain resistance and forces it, so to speak, to adapt itself. At this moment, my personal act actuates itself through my act of thinking and writing. As such, it shapes itself first of all into a certain cerebral situation. But this primordial self-expression is, in fact, the recasting of a vital centre which is "already there" as the apex of a converging process. I make my brain exist as the first concretion of my act of thinking, yet my brain is already constituted as the summit of a pre-personal activity, it models my act according to its inner structure. My act of thinking and writing, however, does not remain confined within the modalities of my cerebral organ—it unfolds itself. This unfolding of my act is my body bent forward, my look

fixed on my paper, my left hand holding this sheet, and my right hand filling it with strange signs; the unfolding of my act is the whole life which animates this dynamic system. Thus my personal act makes my whole body exist as the very realization of itself. Nevertheless, this is not a *creatio ex nihilo*. In the very moment by which it thus unfolds itself, my act is conditioned by the organic structures which it constitutes. Therefore my body precedes my act and delineates *a priori* the way in which it must actuate itself. In other words, my present occupation is the reorienting and the reshaping of pre-existent vital structures which are already inclined in some more or less definite directions.

Now, it must be noted that the actuation of our life-act into an act-project and, consequently, the personalization of our body, is not an operation which brings about a rigidly permanent situation. There are moments of creative tension when we direct all our vital energies towards our aim. At these moments, our act becomes more intensely personal, takes up more thoroughly the biological structures in which it is incarnate (though it remains always conditioned by them), pervades and drives them on in a more powerful and compelling manner. At other times, a certain relaxation takes place: the act allows itself to adopt a looser mode of existing, it lets itself live. This relaxation may be of various types:

(1) It may be deliberately intended, or consented to, either as a recuperating process, or as an answer to a temptation. In the first case, it may have its place within a life-project which remains operative throughout. If so, the act-in-relaxation remains self-possessed and capable at any moment of resuming its former tension. In the second case, it may create a downward movement, which is at variance with the movement of the act-project. If so, there will be an inner conflict which may lead to the weakening of the life-project—that is, to a depersonalization. In both cases, the relaxing initiative comes from the personal act, even though it is conditioned by certain biologico-affective circumstances.

(2) The relaxation may be forced upon the personal act as a result of some physico-psychological disposition. This is a consequence of the fact that the emancipation of the act is greatly dependent on the development—and, thus, to the fluctuations—of the organic structures in which it is incarnate. At times of sickness and fatigue, the biological system ceases to give the personal act the assistance

which it normally expects from it, and the body becomes lazy and heavy. At such moments, the act is, as it were, glued to the disturbed modalities of the organism and does not succeed in realizing itself with its usual dynamism.

However, in this connection, an important fact should be noted. Organic disturbances do not *automatically* lead to a sort of depersonalization. Experience shows that men who live in a state of physical fitness are not always those who tend in the most purposeful manner towards their aim, and realize the most creative types of personalization. In fact, "unfavourable" biological situations often act as stimulants; personal eminence is often linked with organic penury, and with biologico-affective tensions. Beethoven did not write his ninth symphony in spite of his deafness. He did so because he had been able to take up his infirmity and transform it into a hymn of joy. Theresa of Lisieux discovered her "Little Way" and became a saint because she had converted her constitutional deficiency into an act of love and unwavering confidence.[4] Thus sickness, infirmity, fatigue may be the occasion of an astounding spiritualization. It seems as though a disabled organism may be the very channel through which the human act may rise above mediocrity and manifest its dynamism in a really creative manner. We meet here the real transcendence of the personal act with regard to the structures which condition it. In its movement forward, our personal act has the power to overcome biological circumstances which should apparently ruin it; and it can thus tend more effectively towards its end. This spiritualizing process, let us note carefully, never implies a refusal or negation of our incarnation. To overcome our biologico-affective tensions never means to ignore or deny them, but to sublimate them—that is, to integrate them within our personal project. Indeed, it is the very stuff in which we find ourselves embodied that we spiritualize along the line of our directive intention; it is with the

[4] Merleau-Ponty argues on similar lines in *La structure du comportement*:

"A visual defect in an artist can receive, through his meditation, a universal meaning, and become for him the occasion of perceiving a 'profile' of human existence.

"The deficiencies of our bodies can always play that revealing role, provided that, instead of being suffered as pure facts which dominate us, they become, through the consciousness we gain of them, a means of enlarging our knowledge . . . El Greco's alleged trouble with his eyes was overcome by him and so deeply integrated into his manner of thinking and living that it finally appears as a necessary expression of his being rather than as a peculiarity imposed upon him from outside" (p. 219).

substance of our biological processes that we build our personal existence. These limbs which support us, this flesh which our life-act animates, are the very realities that we reshape into conductors of our will, into a network in which we express our desires and our love. In its very essence, in all its initiatives and manifestations, our personality remains an act incarnate. A fundamental acceptance of this incarnation is the very condition of our authentic spiritualization.

4. My Personal-Act-Incarnate-in-My-Body as Consciousness

In some previous considerations, we have tried to characterize the different aspects of incarnate consciousness. We must now study what these various phenomena become once they are integrated within the movement of my personal act; more broadly, we must analyse, step by step, the different conscious modalities of my personal-act-incarnate-in-my-body.

i. *The Reflectiveness of My Personal-Act-Incarnate-In-My-Body*

From its expressive centre, my life-act actuated into an act-project unfolds itself in my whole body and personalizes it. This personalizing activity is rooted in reflection, or thinking; or rather, it is essentially reflective. Let us try to understand the nature of reflection as an aspect of my personal-act-incarnate-in-my-body.

My concepts (thoughts, mental images, memories), such as I have already described, are variations of my life-act in the modalities of my brain which "by themselves" do not express any transcendence of my act with regard to the biological structures in which it is incarnate. They pertain to me as given to myself, as living in the world without being the author of my life; they succeed one another without my producing them in a really personal manner. My reflects, on the contrary, are *my personal act* expressing itself in the modalities of my brain; they proceed from me as possessing myself, as leading my life in a really transcendent, self-determined manner. This is the main clue which will guide us in this inquiry.

My life-act exists essentially as an act-in-tension-towards-an-end—each of its modalities is a modality of its movement towards its final realization. Now, as has been explained, it realizes itself through my act-project—as such, it transcends the organic structures in which it is incarnate. This transcending takes place primarily in the modalities of my brain—that is, in the centre towards which all the biological phenomena which constitute my organism converge, and from which the movement of my life takes its origin. It may be characterized as the process by which the act—which is myself—consciously takes possession of itself and, thus, actuates itself into a transcendentally conscious, self-determined vital endeavour—that is, into an act-project.

We should be careful to note the modalities of this movement. I have already pointed that my life-act attained emancipation through the development of the biological structures in which it was incarnate. This process of growth entailed, together with the enrichment of my vital centre, the formation of more and more elaborate concepts—in other words, as I grew, my life-act (as a result of the development of my whole biologico-affective system) expressed itself in the modalities of my brain in a more and more lucidly conscious manner. In this way, I finally reached self-determination. Throughout this ascent, *the rise towards emancipation was identical with the rise of consciousness*—that is, my act took possession of itself by achieving a more and more self-transparent mode of living. It its present state, my act transcending the biological structures which condition it—my act tending towards its end in a self-determined manner—is identically my act transcendentally or reflectively conscious of itself. Thus reflective consciousness is an essential property of the life-act which has realized its transcendence; it is the personal act luminously present to itself in the movement by which it tends towards its ultimate realization—in other words, the reflectivity of the act is identical with its freedom.

This notion of transcendental consciousness formed through an analysis of concrete experience has, it will be noted, little in common with Husserl's pure consciousness. We are not in the presence of a pure *cogito*—that is, of an act which is by essence pure disincarnate awareness. *The act remains the life-act-in-tension-towards-its-end:* in so far as this act is simply self-given, biologico-affective, it is, so to say, phenomenally self-conscious (thus phenomenal consciousness is a property of the act as involved in, adherent to, the structures of the organism); but to the extent that it actuates itself into a real personal act tending purposively towards its end, it is transcendentally self-conscious. In other words, transcendental consciousness pertains to a certain "I-*live*-towards-an-end" which has actuated itself into an "I-*live*-towards-*my*-end". This act, even though it transcends the biological structures which condition it, remains an act incarnate—

that is, the act of a particular body, depending on this body and expressing itself in it.

Now, as we know, the emancipation of the act and, therefore, its accession to reflectivity are only the beginning of our true personal existence. The act emancipated is as yet far from being the act fully realized. The real progress of the act follows the line of a more and more perfect personalization, and therefore entails a continual rise in consciousness. In the same way as the ascent of the life-act towards true personal existence is a gradual illumination, so also the tension of the personal act towards its end is accompanied by a progress in self-understanding. But the whole process is henceforth largely self-possessed and self-controlled: the act endeavours in a personal manner to understand itself better and better and so realize its self-hood in a more and more integrated manner—that is, *attain a more and more perfect manner of living*. Thus we see that the personalization of the act is identically an intellectualization—not in the sense that the act becomes a pure "I think", but in the sense that it now deliberately aims at a more and more penetrating self-understanding in order to perfect itself as personal life-act. Here we begin to see the meaning of reflection, of all intellectual pursuit in our personal life. Within the limits of our present investigation, this intellectual activity must be described as follows: as it constitutes the modalities of my brain, my personal act expresses itself in them in an increasingly luminous manner in order to reach a more intense and more perfect manner of living. Thus my reflects, transcendental concepts, and projects are expressive modifications of my personal-act-striving-towards-its-end.

The structure of these states of consciousness is identical with that of the personal act incarnate: (1) As just described, they are moments of the centrifugal movement of my personal act (aspect a): they are my act developing an expressive central field in which it mirrors itself in many ways (reflects) and directs itself towards specific aims (projects). (2) But, in doing so, my act is not purely self-creative; in other words, I do not produce this expressive field in a perfectly spontaneous manner. In the very process by which my personal act concretes itself in it in the form of reflects and projects, it discovers itself as a reality which is already constituted and oriented towards an end (aspect b), a reality which it has to delve into and bring to clear consciousness at the price of intensive efforts. This "self-givenness" of my personal act is particularly apparent in the fact that my thinking is never a pure starting-point but always the taking up and the revitalizing of ideas and experiences which are already formed: I think myself by continually infusing new life into "myself-already-thought".

There is a corollary to these considerations. This central expressive field of my personal act may be described as language. Indeed, my thinking is identically a speech process: it is my personal act telling and foretelling itself to itself in embryonic linguistic forms (which my articulate speech articulates and makes explicit). From the point of view of aspect a, this telling is my act casting itself in a self-revealing, self-anticipating linguistic mould at the outset of its self-actuating movement. But this language—which is myself-expressed-to-myself—is not a mere evolution of my act. Prior to my shaping it, it already exists in the form of a constituted speech, of a definite tongue: I tell and foretell myself by continually revitalizing "myself-already-told".

These observations reveal the original nature of language: in its primitive form, speech is identical with thinking—it is the *personal-act-expressing-itself-to-itself*. Therefore thought and speech can never be separated: my personal-act-constituting-the-modalities-of-my-brain, my personal-act-expressing-itself-in-the-form-of-reflects-and-projects, and my personal-act-telling-itself-to-itself are one and the same reality; likewise, the fact that in constituting my brain my act is conditioned by the modalities of this expressive centre, the fact that in thinking itself it must continually take up "itself-already-thought", the fact that in casting itself into a linguistic mould it finds itself "already told" (that is, makes use of a language already constituted) are one and the same fact. This identity between thought (self-understanding) and speech is a reality of which we have continual experience. The efforts we make to express our self-knowledge in articulate language—spoken or written—render this consciousness more vivid and more luminous: words reveal ourselves to ourselves because, originally, they are our personal act-expressing-itself-to-itself; originally, they are the very articulation of our experience. We understand from this that our thinking faculty and our speech faculty are fundamentally identical. They are first of all circumscribed within our brain; subsequently, as our personal act unfolds itself in our body, they actuate themselves through those organs which we term organs of self-expression. As I express myself orally—making use of my vocal cords, of my tongue, of my lips—or in writing—through the movement of my hand which makes my pencil cover the white sheet of paper—I do not simply give "external" formulation to thoughts and statements which are already well formed in my head, but I actuate my thinking, I bring to clarity a world which was only confusedly self-conscious. In other words, through the activity of my organs of expression (through the words I utter and the sentences I write), my whole self-understanding perfects itself—my personal act, as it "speaks itself out", becomes more deeply and more widely acquainted with itself, more knowingly committed to the pursuing of a definite aim.[5]

ii. *My Personal-Act-Incarnate-in-My-Body as Act-Volition*

Self-understanding — self-intellectualization, self-verbalization — does not exist for its own sake. My reflects and transcendental concepts are expressive modalities of my personal act—that is, of a life-act which exists for an end and directs itself towards it in a self-determined manner. This end is not my accession to the realm of Pure Thought, but the attainment of a more perfect—more intensely human, more deeply personal—manner of living. Thus my thinking takes place essentially within an existential movement which is my progressive realization as a living person: I aim at a more and more adequate self-understanding because, through it, I gain a continually firmer possession of myself and of the world and thus achieve a continually better mode of existence. Let us now reconsider once more from the beginning the movement of my personal life, in order to bring to light other aspects of my transcendental consciousness—that is, other conscious modalities of my personal-act-incarnate-in-

[5] All these considerations emphasize the inherence of speech and thinking in our living experience: they *are* our personal life-act taking luminous possession of itself, orienting itself in a conscious manner towards its end. This means that, to remain meaningful, speech and thinking must be continually vivified by intuition: it is experience which gives their fundamental value to our concepts, to the words we utter and the sentences we write—in other words, the "pre-predicative" constitutes the "predicative".

Now, we notice that, as it becomes more and more elaborate, speech gradually constitutes itself into an independent superstructure. Concomitantly, the connection between thinking and intuition grows looser and looser, reflection tends to take constituted notions, words, speech forms, as its object, and to imprison itself within these categories: the geometrical mentality is born—leading to verbalism, conceptualism, essentialism, formalism, atomism, etc. To avoid such blind alleys, it is necessary constantly to vitalize speech and thought through a renewed contact with living experience.

my-body. What I propose now is to examine explicitly—within the limits of my present study—my "voluntary activity".[6]

At a certain stage of my growth, my life-act—as a result of the development of my biologico-affective structures, of my whole organism—realized itself in the central modalities of my brain as personal act. From that moment, I ordered myself towards my end in a self-determined, transcendent manner; thus, at its summit, my act-incarnate became personal appetence for the end, deliberate motion towards the end—my personal will affirmed itself and became the leading force of my life. This primordial role which my will assumed as the constitutive and creative element of my personality-in-tension-towards-its-ultimate-realization indicates that the cerebral centre in which my life-act realized itself—and continues to realize itself—as a self-determined principle is the most important part of my organism, the nucleus in reference to which my body exists as the incarnation of my personal act, as the expression of its deliberate movement towards the end.

Let us analyse the main articulations of this movement.

From the vital centre where it "voluntarizes" itself, my act unfolds in my whole body and personalizes it (aspect a). My body thus re-created into an expression of my will may be called *my transcendental body*—that is, my body animated by, manifesting, an energy which transcends its "natural" dynamism (by which it exists as a biologico-affective system). In this self-actuating movement, my act-volition (which is my whole life-act existing as will) first illumines itself within the modalities of my brain, following the process described above.[7] Thus illumined, my will "takes shape" in my body: it incarnates itself into concerete behaviours, significant actions, creative attitudes. Through these comportments, my life-act achieves various modes of self-realization.

Throughout this process, my act-volition is continually conditioned by the vital structures in which it unfolds itself (aspect b).

[6] The reflections which follow contain many repetitions of earlier considerations —see above paragraphs i, ii, iii, of this section. We think these repetitions useful in the present passage where we analyse explicitly volition as an aspect of our personal-act-incarnate. It should be noted that the following reflections do not explore a different field from that already studied in the preceding paragraphs. We are describing the same reality, but bringing out some further points with greater precision.

[7] We shall analyse in the following paragraph the relation between reflection and volition.

Above all, it is conditioned by the modalities of the cerebral nucleus which it first animates. The particular way in which this nucleus is structured determines to a large extent the peculiarities, the scope, the resistance of my will. Perturbations of this centre may at times paralyse my will or, at least, weaken and unnerve it. But this connection between my voluntary capacities and the structure of my brain is in fact a dependence of my will on my whole body. Indeed, the "volitive kernel" of my brain has no existence apart from my whole organism; prior to the self-positing initiative by which my act-volition makes it live as the first concretion of its self-realizing centrifugal movement, it is already constituted as the summit of a pre-personal activity which is my body-existing-centripetally. Therefore the constitution of my brain is related to that of my whole organism; consequently, the temperamental individuality of my will depends on my physical peculiarities. Not only the first existential pulsation of my act-volition in its primordial expressive centre, but the whole self-realizing movement of my act-volition is thus conditioned by the modalities of the organic field in which it unfolds itself. We have shown how in the very process of illuminating itself—that is, of constituting the reflective centres of my brain and my organs of self-expression, as the very substance of its self-intellectualizing endeavour—it finds itself already illumined—that is, conditioned by the very expressive entities which it constitutes. Further, as it translates itself into various comportments, my will is conditioned by the very modalities of these limbs, of this whole body which it quickens, moves, renders expressive of itself. In short, in the very process by which my act-volition gives existence to my transcendental body, it finds itself, as it were, generated by my body already existing, and conditioned by the modalities of this body—it actuates itself by continually taking up and re-creating this already existing organism.

To continue our analysis: In the first section of this chapter, I described at length my phenomenal body—that is, my body existing as the incarnation of the prime act of my life: myself given to myself, alive, yet not the author of my life.[8]

In so doing, I showed that my phenomenal (biologico-affective) existence is already a centrifugal expansion tempered by a centripetal movement: my life-act unfolds itself from the centre from which it first animates and constitutes my body as the concretion of this

[8] See the section entitled: A. My Life-Act in My Body, pp. 59 ff.

existential movement (aspect a); yet, throughout this process, it is conditioned by my organism as though the latter were already structured prior to its being animated by my act—in other words, my life-act unfolds itself within a pre-existent organic field which it takes up and revitalizes. Now it must be noticed that this phenomenal body taken in its entirety is not simply identical with the "already-existing-organism" which—as I have just indicated—my act-volition continually takes up and re-creates. Indeed, this pre-existing body taken "in itself"—as described a few lines above—is a mere *centripetal* reality; it must be identified with the pre-existent organic field which, as we are seeing, my life-act revitalizes while unfolding itself.

The relation between my transcendental body and my phenomenal body (or my biologico-affective system) must be understood as a dialectical process. Innately, I am a life-act incarnate—as such, I am given to myself, "thrown into the world", made to exist. Thus my original existence is essentially phenomenal (not exclusively, however: from the beginning, it is radically, potentially, "appetitively" transcendental—my accession to transcendental existence will be the realization and manifestation of something which is latently present from the day of my conception) and so is my consciousness at the moment of its awakening. Not only at the beginning of my life, but throughout my existence I remain self-given: I never cease to be a life-act-incarnate-in-a-body. Thus, until the end, my existence remains largely phenomenal; and similarly, my body remains to a great extent a biologico-affective system. This fact explains why it is that, however self-determined I may be, I still experience my life as "something which takes place", a process which unfolds without my causing it to do so: days follow one another; changes occur in my organism; as years pass, I become older and older. It is in this atmosphere of self-givenness that I must lead my personal existence. In the modalities of my brain, my life-act "voluntarizes" and "intellectualizes" itself; actuating itself further, it personalizes my whole body—"transcendentalizes" it. Nevertheless, the movement of my phenomenal existence goes on, my life-act remains self-given, and my body remains a biologico-affective system. My authentic self-realizing act is my act-volition consciously ordaining itself towards its end in a self-determined manner, continually animating my body and re-creating it into the purposeful expression of its inner tension, into the symbolic prefigurement of the goal towards which it tends; this self-realizing cannot, however, take place without a continual surrender of my act-volition to the conditions imposed upon it by its incarnation in biologico-affective structures. On the one hand, the spiritualizing influx of my will truly moves the totality of my organism down to its most inert elements; on the other hand, the biologism of my phenomenal existence permeates my will and underlies even its most personal decrees and its most spiritual yearnings.

This incarnation of my act-volition in a phenomenal field, the necessity in which it finds itself of accepting the conditions imposed upon it by this involvement, of regulating its course according to the rhythm of biological existence, accounts for the fact that its movement towards the end and its spiritualizing action are a slow process. My personal act cannot realize itself fully through a single self-actuating initiative. As an act-incarnate, it must illumine itself progressively, actuate itself through particular intentions, limited decisions which are various moments of its total progress, its various reactions to the biological circumstances in which it finds itself involved. These various decisions and intentions—in order to be real—must translate themselves into definite movements of my body, into vital attitudes, into "external" activities.

iii. *Relation between Volition and Reflectiveness*

Let us examine explicitly the relation between volition and reflectiveness, and so open up a first approach to the problem of freedom.

From my previous observations, I know that my thinking activity is my personal act—that is, my life-act-actuated-into-an-act-volition—taking luminous possession of itself, expressing itself to itself in the modalities of my brain. This means that my reflective activity *is* a volitive activity—free, transcendent, self-controlled. This freedom of my act illuminating itself appears in the fact that, in the process of reflecting upon itself, it emerges more and more from the current of its phenomenal existence; it breaks its adherence to the organic structures in which it is involved, dominates its biological situation, sheds its native blindness, pierces the opacity of being, grasps the totality of itself, determines the modalities of its future behaviour; it liberates, personalizes, "transcendentalizes" itself. However, as it thus frees itself and takes possession of itself through reflection, my act does not become purely self-creative. This is clear from the painful efforts it has to make to illuminate itself and keep itself illuminated: it has to inquire laboriously into itself, to bring itself to clear consciousness through an intensive and ever renewed self-penetrating exploration. Even at those moments when it totalizes itself and becomes, as it were, all light to itself, it does not posit itself in a perfectly spontaneous manner. My act always experiences itself as given to itself; it always "finds itself there", made to exist, a reality which it has to study "objectively", to discover *as it is*. Thus submission to facts and acknowledgment of things as they are are essential aspects of my self-illuminating activity: my self-understanding actuates itself in a climate of dependence. Now, it must be noted carefully that the freedom of my act reflecting upon itself and its submissive attitude are not two conflicting aspects of one and the same act. On the contrary, *it is precisely in accepting itself as fact that my act perfects itself as free act.* The more my personal act discovers and affirms the truth of itself, the more it acknowledges itself as it is, the more also it liberates itself, possesses itself, determines itself, the freer, the more dynamic, self-controlled its thinking activity becomes: my act personalizes, "transcendentalizes" itself to the extent that it submits itself.

This general conditioning of my act-reflecting-upon-itself is, in reality, the very law of life of my personal act incarnate. As we know, reflection is never intended for its own sake; it must always be envisaged within the existential movement of the life-act, its movement of self-realization. We have just considered it in its most explicit form: as deliberate thinking. In fact, reflectivity, being identical with freedom, is a property of all my activities in so far as they are true personal activities. In other words, in all its different self-actuating initiatives, my personal act is self-illuminating. From the point of view of our present study, this fact must be understood as follows: as it unfolds itself in my body in the form of definite actions, movements, behaviours, my act-volition expresses itself to itself in the modalities of my brain and, through reflection, possesses itself, directs itself. Now this self-mastery of my act achieved through self-illumination is precisely submission: as it "sees through itself"—because it does so—my act-volition incarnate actuates itself according to the requirements of its inner constitution; *through this submission to facts*, it controls itself, realizes itself as free act. In other words, my activity possesses itself and, so to speak, creates itself in so far as it accepts itself as it is, in so far as it unfolds itself *as it must be unfolded.*

My personal act realizes itself through successive self-actuating moves. Each one of these moves proceeds from a particular decision, and is constituted by a particular intention. As it tends reflectively towards its end, my act-volition finds itself carried and conditioned by the organic structures which it continually takes up and personalizes. Involved in this biological set up, it illuminates its various situations through reflection: in the expressive modalities of my brain—which it constitutes—it reveals itself to itself as it is (that is, involved in this way). Thanks to this enlightenment, my act dominates its situations, sees them in the perspective of its integral finality, directs them and itself through them, and lives them as variations of its movement towards its ultimate realization; it lives them, accordingly, as particular self-actuating syntheses animated by definite intentions which express in various ways its integral volition. In forming these intentions, my act would appear to be essentially self-determined. Yet, in each case, it wins its liberty through the conscious acceptance of the requirements of its biological conditioning. In other words, my decisions and intentions are free to the extent that they *are* acts of submission.

From all these observations it is clear that reflection and volition are not the acts of two "faculties" distinct from one another. Fundamentally, there is only one act, which is my life-act—the prime act by which I am constituted. This life-act realizes itself through my act-volition, which is not an entity superimposed upon it, but is its transcendent self-actuation within the modalities of my brain. All my personal activities are various expressions of the movement by which my act-volition incarnate tends towards its ultimate realization. This fact shows that there is in my life no transcendental act of knowledge distinct from my voluntary activity. More precisely, transcendental knowledge or consciousness, *as such*, is never an act or an activity but the luminous presence to itself of my personal act or activity—hence a modality of my transcendental existence. This personal activity assumes different forms: at this moment I am busy thinking and writing, this afternoon I shall go for a walk, then I shall read a book, clean my room, attend a meeting, etc. Some of these activities are called intellectual activities because they aim at increasing my knowledge, that is, at achieving a mode of existence characterized by a deeper self-understanding; others are considered to be non-intellectual—though they too are transcendentally self-conscious. All these activities have this in common that they are constituted by my act volition-in-tension-towards-its-end; they are different variations of the movement by which my personal act actuates itself.

In the opinion of some philosophers, to affirm that our intellectual activity is constituted by our will is to make a profession of absolute subjectivism. Their idea is that volition and intellections are the acts of two different "faculties", the one being free, self-determined, the other essentially dependent on some "external given". Will, they say, is a faculty independent of matter; it is the power which *moves* to action all the other faculties—self-determination is absence of subjection. The intellect, on the contrary, *is moved* by outward reality—its activity consists in the assimilation of something which is distinct from it, something "objective". To affirm that intellect and will are one is to destroy the "objectivity" of knowledge—that is, its relation to and dependence on something other than itself.

Such thinkers base their whole argument on an idealization of will and intellect. They analyse volition and knowledge in the abstract, outside the concrete totality from which they are inseparable. This is a typical example of linguistic illusion: a reflection on notions and words detached from the living reality which they are meant to express (and from which they receive their "objectivity"). The different modalities of our personal existence, which are different facets of the same dynamic reality, are first solidified, then examined and defined "in themselves": volition and intellection are made into two different "activities" proceeding from two different "faculties"; freedom (or independence) becomes the attribute of the will, subjection (dependence on something else) the characteristic of the intellect.

Very different is the picture obtained from an analysis of the living reality. Experience shows us that volition is the transcendent dynamism of our life-act incarnate and that intellection is the luminous self-expression of our personal act in the modalities of our brain—thus our volitive activity and our intellective activity are concretely one. Experience shows us also that our freedom is identical with the "intellectiveness" of our act-volition incarnate—that is, both with its luminous self-possession and with its luminous self-acceptance. In this perspective, the "objectivity" of knowledge (its "passivity") is not its dependence on some "outward reality" but the fact that our personal act incarnate always experiences itself as "already there".[9]

What is exactly this self-givenness of my personal act?

So far, I have shown it to be two things: (1) It is the fact that, in the process of unfolding itself, of constituting my body as the concretion of its self-actuating movement (aspect a—centrifugal), *my act-volition is continually conditioned by my body already existing* (aspect b—centripetal); (2) it is the fact that my act-volition, *as a self-determined centrifugal movement* (aspect a) *remains life-act and experiences itself as such*—that is, as an act which is not self-creative but created. Now, in the course of this study, I have shown that a certain distinction must be maintained between my life-act existing and actuating itself as a process which unfolds itself without being self-controlled, and my life-act existing and actuating itself as act-volition. To the extent that my life-act incarnate is a mere act-process, my existence is purely *phenomenal*: it is the mere continuation in me of that pre-personal existence (aspect b) by which I am continually conditioned and maintained. To the degree to which my life-act is an act-volition, my existence is *personal, transcendental*: I take up and personalize the pre-existing field in which I find myself incarnate. Now, it must be noted carefully that **my** existence *has never been purely phenomenal.* Indeed, **my** life has never been the mere continuation of something which was already there before me. Had it ever been that, no "I" would ever have come to existence. Moreover, the fact that my life-act actuates itself into an act-volition shows that it was potentially transcendental right from the beginning. Had my life ever been *purely* phenomenal (that is, purely impersonal), there would never have been any possibility of its becoming personal. Thus, right from the beginning, my existence was something more than the mere evolution of a reality which existed already before me. Now, in several passages of this study, I have practically identified self-givenness with "phenomenality", giving thereby the impression that my personal act *qua dependent* is exclusively my act realizing itself in dependence on a pre-existing reality (or that my life *qua fact* is

[9] It may be objected that our definition of the objectivity of knowledge is valid when applied to self-knowledge but that it does not hold good in the case of knowledge of reality.

We may answer the objection by pointing out that we have overcome the opposition subject-object by disclosing the unity of person and universe. The second part of this chapter will show in detail how our definitions apply to the whole of human knowledge.

essentially my life qua continuation of a pre-existing life). From this notion, it would follow that the act of submission which—as we have seen—my freedom implies is essentially submission to the conditions imposed upon me by the existential field in which I find myself incarnate—that is, submission of the personal to the impersonal. But it is absolutely impossible that this submission should be constitutive of my freedom. Indeed, we have just seen that *my personal, transcendental existence cannot be constituted by its dependence on a pre-personal existence*, it cannot be simply the evolution of a reality which was there before it. Yet, my act *qua personal, qua transcendental*, experiences itself as self-given, as constituted. *This dependence can only be a relation to a Transcendent Creative Source.* Thus I have to distinguish between my phenomenal self-givenness—that is, my incarnation in a phenomenal field—and my transcendental self-givenness—that is, my relation to a Transcendent Source of life (by which I am constituted as personal act, i.e., as free act). It follows from this that the act of submission which is constitutive of my freedom is essentially submission to the Creative Source of my personal existence. No doubt, the exercise of my freedom implies the acceptance of the biological structures in which I am incarnate and the right to use them, but this acceptance, to be really personalizing, must still be fundamentally submission to the Creator: I am created as a personal act incarnate, that is, as an act concretely involved in biologico-affective structures—my personal acceptance of this situation is essentially submission to the Act which creates me in it. If, instead of being an act of transcendental obedience, my acceptance of myself-incarnate becomes simply surrender of myself to the biologico-affective motions which condition me—mere "phenomenal submission"—my freedom, instead of perfecting itself, alienates itself. Such a submission, far from being personalizing, is essentially depersonalizing—an evident sign that the reality which *constitutes me as person* is not my incarnation but my relation to a Transcendent Creative Source.

Let us now examine in this context the essence of reflection. I have shown that the freedom of my personal act is identical with its reflectivity: my act-volition (as free act) is my life-act taking luminous possession of itself in the movement by which it actuates itself—that is, *my act-reflecting-upon-itself.* Now, as has just been pointed out, I am constituted as a free person by my relation to the Creator and I actuate this freedom by an act of transcendental obedience. In terms of reflectivity, this assertion becomes: I am constituted as a life-act reflectively conscious of its ontological dependence, possessing itself by virtue of this illuminative relation, actuating itself through the luminous realization of this subjection. This means that I am the product of an Act of illuminative creation, that the process by which my act incarnate illumines itself within the modalities of my brain is entirely derived from this light-giving Source. These considerations help us to clarify the notion of "objectivity". As we have seen, the objectivity of my knowledge is not the dependence of my act on an "external given", but the fact that my personal act experiences itself as "already there", sees itself as it is, or as it should be—a self-realization which is identical with the freedom of my act, that is, with its transcendence. Now, as I have just explained, this transcendental self-givenness of my act cannot be reduced to its incarnation, to its dependence on the biological structures which condition it; it must be understood as its ontological dependence on a Transcendent Creative Source. Thus *the objectivity of my knowledge is essentially constituted by my luminous realization of my relation to the Creator.* The act by which I experience myself as I am is acknowledgment of my condition as creature—this is the essential "passivity" of my knowing activity, not a passivity with regard to "outward reality", but the transcendental passivity of my createdness. It does not follow from this that the objectivity of my knowledge does not include the acknowledgment of my biological situation. It includes a realistic assessment of my incarnated condition, just as the freedom of my personal act implies my acceptance of this condition; but no more than my freedom is it *constituted* by my dependence on my biologico-affective structures. In the same way as the free self-possession of my act entails its acceptance of the structures in which it finds itself involved *in submission to the Transcendent who creates it as act-thus-incarnate*, so also the objectivity of its self-knowledge implies its cognition of its phenomenal field *as the very concretion of its createdness* (such a cognition takes place essentially within the Creative and Illuminative Initiative which constitutes me as personal act incarnate). In fact, as we know, these two aspects are one: the objectivity of my knowledge *is* the very luminosity of my transcendental submission—in other words, my personal free activity is constitutive of my reflective perception of reality.

iv. *Relation between Transcendental and Phenomenal Consciouness*

Our last step in this study of transcendental consciousness will be an analysis of the relation between the act-volition and phenomenal consciousness.

I have already shown that my life-act exists in the form of a certain temperamental inclination. This general affective disposition is due to the fact that, in the very process of energizing the vital structures in which it finds itself incarnate, my life-act is conditioned by the modalities of these structures. I have shown also that my act (1) expresses itself in my brain in the form of thoughts, imaginations, and in my sensorial apparatus in the form of percepts, and (2) lives in my different organic systems in the form of affective motions. These various aspects of my phenomenal consciousness are closely interrelated. Let us examine now the way in which they are integrated in the movement of my act-volition.

My Personal Act and My Temperament. The accession of my act to true personal existence has been a slow process. My act has gained its freedom as it was becoming more and more self-transparent—my consciousness has become more and more reflective as my act was liberating itself. The movement goes on: my act-volition is my life-act tending consciously, reflectively, towards its end. In its daily endeavours, my act makes of my body the expression of its inner tension, it personalizes the organic structures in which it is incarnate. However, my personal act remains deeply conditioned by these structures. Therefore, though it is essentially self-determined, it has still a temperamental bent, it is characterized by a fundamental affective disposition. This individuality manifests itself in all my initiatives and decisions, in all the self-actuating moves of my act-volition; it pervades my whole personal life. This temperamental factor, it must be noted, is not simply imposed upon me; it is integrated in the self-realizing movement of my act-volition, and is thus personalized: my personal-act-striving-for-the-end, as it reflects upon itself, becomes more and more conscious of its innate disposition and aspirations, and translates them deliberately into projects, into vital attitudes. As we can see, this personalizing integration of my temperamental inclination and affective dispositions implies a real acceptance of them. In this respect, what we have just been saying finds a new application (in fact, we are dealing with the same reality): my liberating acceptance of my temperament, of my emotionality (that is, of myself-incarnate), is not mere submission to the impersonal, but obedience to the Creator. Conditioned as I am, I proceed from a Creative Source which orders me towards a certain end to be reached in some specific way—thus, as a personal act incarnate (possessing this particular temperament, characterized by these particular aptitudes, aspirations) I am a certain *intention*. As my act-incarnate becomes reflectively conscious of its innate disposition and accepts it, it discovers the intention which constitutes it and identifies itself with this intention. This is the fundamental obedience which liberates and personalizes me—not a mere surrender of myself to my affectivity, but a submission to the Transcendent who creates me as I am. If, instead of being obedience to the Creator, my acceptance of my affective disposition becomes mere yielding to it, my will is, as it were, reabsorbed by the biologico-affective structures which condition it; my life tends to reduce itself to a mere temperamental process (a reduction which, of course, can never be complete, since my life-act, however deeply involved it may be in biological structures, always remains constitutionally transcendental). These considerations enable us to clarify the notion of individuality. My phenomenal individuality is my incarnation in a particular organism; it is my temperamental disposition. This individuality has no existence by itself: it is constituted by my transcendental individuality—that is, by the unique intention which constitutes me as this particular person ordained towards a specific end. In this context, we understand better how my discovery of reality takes place essentially within a free act: in the act by which I identify myself with the intention constitutive of my individuality (that is, in the act of submission by which I actuate myself as free person), I become reflectively conscious of this individuality—that is, of myself as I am. This act takes place essentially within the Creative and Illuminative Initiative from which I hold my existence.

My Personal Act and My Affectivity. Let us now analyse the relation between my personal act and my different affective motions. As we have seen, each biological situation in which I find myself incarnate presents itself from the first with a certain affective value, in the form of a vital impulse which "left to itself" would develop into an emotional behaviour. Conditioned by such a situation, my act-volition can either let itself be carried and, to a certain extent, absorbed by it, or integrate and "transcendentalize" it. If I "let myself go", a depersonalizing surrender takes place—my will alienates itself, my act tends to degrade itself into a mere affective behaviour. If, on the contrary, my act-volition takes up the situation which conditions it in a reflective, personal manner, it transforms it into an expression of its self-realizing endeavour, it converts the emotional urge with which this situation is charged into a transcendental affect. This personalizing process is most perfect when my act-volition sees its conditioning situation in relation to the Creator as a particular concretion of the intention which constitutes it as act-incarnate, accepts it as a gift, and lives it as a modality of its movement towards the end for which it is created (thus making its own the Transcendent Will which creates it as act-incarnate-in-this-particular-biologico-affective-situation).

I have just introduced the notion of "transcendental affect". It must be understood in connection with that of transcendental body. As my act-volition constitutes my organism as the expression of its self-actuating movement, it vibrates in it, and thus gives birth to new feelings. This emotivity is no longer made up of vital impulses arising, as it were, from below; it consists in affective motions, manifesting in a direct manner the tension of my personal act, which are under the control of my will. These transcendental affects are often produced through the sublimation of phenomenal affects. Incarnate in vital structures which have, so to speak, their own movement, my act feels itself vibrating in them in various ways: it experiences desires, attractions, repulsions, various affective states such as contentment, euphoria, optimism, or discouragement, depression, sadness, etc. From the centre where it "transcendentalizes" itself, my act takes up personally the biological situations which it already "experientializes" in such phenomenal ways, controls them reflectively, reshapes them into variations of its movement towards its final goal, and thus gives them a new dimension. Other transcendental affects are directly intended and voluntarily produced. This happens, for instance, when my act-volition shapes itself into a feeling of benevolence, sympathy, respect, into a definite desire or regret. All these affects, it must be noted, are never pure creations of my will. Whatever their relation to my voluntary activity, the movement by which my personal act makes them exist as the very vibrations of the existential field in which it unfolds itself is conditioned by the modalities of this field. In other words, I shape myself into the subject of a definite affective disposition by reshaping myself-already-affectively-disposed-in-some-way-or-other.

In the consideration of affectivity, we must always remember that the act, though realizing itself as act-volition in the central modalities of the brain, remains life-act incarnate. Together with or, rather, within the movement of my transcendental existence, a great variety of affective motions occur which are not directly derived from my will. I decide to go to visit a friend. As I carry out this project—that is, as I make of my whole body the concretion of my intention—I experience a diversity of feelings. Thus, even though it constitutes my organism as the expression of its personal volition, my act still feels itself vibrating in many ways in this same body. Some of these vibrations may at times become so tense that they overwhelm my will. Sometimes my act-volition may, as it were, lose itself in an affective motion which it has itself produced. This happens, for instance, when I let myself be carried away by a sentiment of pity which I have reflectively created within myself; or when, after rousing myself to indignation, I let this feeling develop into an irrational anger. In such cases, my personal act, instead of controlling the existential vibration to which it has given rise, tends to reduce itself to this vibration: a real decentralization of my personality takes place—the transcendental affect is degraded into a phenomenal emotion.

In this context, we must observe once more how affective motions can influence the act-volition. This influence is due, as we know, to the fact that my act, even though it transcends the biologico-affective structures in which it is incarnate, remains conditioned by these structures—in other words, it is due to the fact that my personal act never ceases to be temperamental (its freedom is always imperfect, threatened). Involved in a certain biological situation, my act lives this situation according to its particular modalities—that is, it moves "itself-already-moved". This moving may be of various types:

(1) My act-volition may surrender itself to the phenomenal urge characteristic of this situation—in this case, my freedom alienates itself.

(2) My act may take up personally this biological situation—that is, integrate it within its voluntary movement—and, *at the same time*, be deeply determined by it—in this case, my freedom is real though very imperfect: my act-volition is all at once transcendentally moving and phenomenally moved.

(3) My act may accept this situation as the phenomenal expression of its createdness and, by an act of transcendental submission,

coincide with the intention which constitutes it as act-incarnate-in-this-situation (in other words, I may make of this situation what it must be: a variation of my movement towards the end which I am meant to reach)—in this case, I perfect my freedom: there is a liberating harmony between my will transcendentally moving and my act transcendentally moved.

To these three ways of living a situation correspond three types of knowledge.

In the first case, as it lets itself be absorbed by its biologico-affective make-up, the act no longer dominates the situation in which it is incarnate; consequently, its reflectiveness (which implies transcendence) decreases, its consciousness is imprisoned within narrow limits.

In the second case, there is already a certain breadth of vision, a reflective self-discovery. However, the act interprets itself in a defective, prejudicial manner due to its imperfectly personal mode of existence.

In the third case, the act, because it transcends its situation by linking itself with its Creative Source, sees itself in the light which emanates from this Source. Thus its reflectiveness and self-understanding are freed from those prejudices which have their origin in a narrow way of living: the act realizes itself luminously. These reflections show us that the personal act incarnate reveals itself to itself according to the way in which it lives; they will lead us to the conclusion that, to be grasped, truth must first be lived (because it *is* life).

My Personal Act and My Imaginative, Perceptive Consciousness. In our study of phenomenal consciousness, we have described the way in which the life-act illuminates itself in the modalities of the brain and in the sensory apparatus. Let us see now how these expressive variations of our life-act incarnate are integrated in the movement of our transcendental existence.

As I carry out my activity, translating reflectively my projects into concrete behaviours, my life-act goes on illuminating itself phenomenally in various ways (in the same way as it goes on vibrating emotively). Conditioned by these expressive phenomena, my act-volition may either take them up reflectively and, thus, convert them into modalities of its self-actuating endeavour, or let its movement be slowed down by them (let itself be absorbed by the biologico-affective motions of which these thoughts and percepts are the concretions). The integration of these elements in the movement of my act-volition may be effected in various ways. Sometimes, these expressive modifications of my life-act remain practically unheeded and the vital urges which they represent are simply fused with the transcendental impetus of my personal act. At other times, these thoughts and percepts are taken up in the reflective current of my act-volition and so become part of its self-illuminating activity. When this movement takes place, my whole biological system is harmoniously integrated in my transcendental activity.

From time to time, stimulated by some thought or perception, I decide *reflectively* to adopt a new course of action. When this happens, the thought or percept in question is not the *cause* which acts on my will and makes me change my behaviour. As a phenomenal reality, this concept is an expressive modification of my life-act—it is my life-act-revealing-itself-as-involved-in-a-particular-situation. Were this phenomenon to "cause" my decision—that is, to carry my will with it—there would be surrender of myself to a biologico-affective motion, alienation of my freedom. In fact, what happens is this: my personal act, as it discovers itself—through the medium of this thought or percept—phenomenally modified in some particular manner, takes up reflectively this situation and accepts *itself-involved-in-it*—that is, submits to the Act which creates it as act-incarnate-in-this-particular-situation. Thus the decision which is taken, even if it implies a change of activity, is not a surrender of myself to the impersonal, but submission to the Creator.

From this it is clear that the relation between the various "levels" of knowledge cannot be explained in a mere intellectualistic perspective. As the subject of percepts, concepts, and reflects, I am not a mere *cogito* but first of all a living person. Therefore the integration of my percepts in my reflective activity cannot be understood as the subsumption of particular data under universal principles. This does not imply that the whole intellectualistic analysis of knowledge is totally meaningless. It has, no doubt, a certain schematic value, but because of its excessively conceptual or abstract character, it cannot be put forward as a faithful description of knowledge as it takes place *de facto*. The valid elements of the intellectualistic schema appear when it is referred to the living reality as our experience discovers it, and vitalized by this contact. Let us show by an example how this vitalization can be effected.

Intellectual knowledge, we are told, is essentially universal, whereas perceptive knowledge is particular. I have pointed out that the life-act incarnate realizes itself as a personal reality in the central modalities of the brain. As personal act, the life-act transcends the limits of its biological situation, and so apprehends the totality of itself in reference to its final goal and in relation to its Creative Source. We see here the concrete universality of the self-knowledge achieved by the act which has freed itself from its phenomenal entanglement—in other words, the universality of reflection, of intellectual knowledge. Let us look now at sensation. Our percepts are expressive variations of our act in the modalities of our sensory apparatus. Now, our life-act existing within our perceptive organs does not—*as such*—transcend the biologico-affective situations in which it is involved—its mode of existence in these organs is narrow and adhesive; consequently, its self-knowledge is superficial and very limited. Thus we discover in a concrete manner in what consists the particularity of perceptive knowledge. Now how does the subsumption of the particular under the universal take place? We have explained this above: the personal act, as it discovers itself—through the medium of sensation—phenomenally involved in a particular biological make-up, "transcendentalizes" this make-up—that is, accepts "itself-created-in-it" and, through this submission, actuates itself as free act. In this process, the limits of the phenomenal situation open up: the restricted self-transparency of the "act-in-bondage" broadens out into the luminous self-discovery of the "act-at-liberty".

This explanation of the relation between sensation and reflection, it must be noted, is somewhat artificial in so far as it implies *first* an analysis of reflection, *secondly* an analysis of sensation ("in itself"), and *thirdly* a description of the link between the two. More realistically, perception must be considered within the movement of the act-volition. As it actuates itself through a definite behaviour, my personal act, just as it vibrates affectively within the vital structures which it animates, expresses itself in the form of sensations within the modalities of my perceptive apparatus. Thus, in its self-actuating movement, my act-volition evolves not only transcendental affects, but also transcendental percepts—that is, percepts which directly express the transcendental dynamism of my personal act. Such percepts cannot be reduced to the narrow self-expressive variations of the act-in-bondage (of which we have just spoken). As they exist essentially within the reflective self-actuating movement of my act-volition, they must be seen as particular concretions of this movement, as reflections of my transcendental project. What we said about transcendental affects is similarly applicable to these transcendental percepts. If my act, instead of living a particular perception as a moment of its self-actuating movement, allows itself to be seduced by it, it is, to a certain extent, absorbed by the biologico-affective situation which this perception represents. When this happens, the act loses something of its freedom; consequently, the perception no longer reflects in the same way its transcendental movement (since this movement has slowed down); it becomes the concretion of the narrower mode of existence which the act has adopted—the transcendental percept is degraded into a phenomenal sensation.

Interpenetration of the Different Aspects of Consciousness. In this section devoted to the study of the integration of phenomenal consciousness in the movement of transcendental existence, I have analysed first the taking up of affectivity by the act-volition, then the "transcendentalization" of phenomenal knowledge. I must now make a few concluding remarks about the interrelation of the different aspects within the current of transcendental existence.

The reality constitutive of the whole personal structure is the life-act-tending-through-the-act-volition-towards-its-final-realization. Owing to its incarnation in biologico-affective structures, this act is characterized by a temperamental inclination, a fundamental affective disposition. All the different forms of consciousness that we have studied in this chapter must be understood as interrelated aspects of this act-incarnate-in-tension-towards-its-end. The diversity of these aspects arises from the fact that the act, while unfolding itself in the different organic structures, expresses itself in many ways, diffracts itself in various self-actuating motions, vibrates in many different ways. Each of these modes has no existence apart from all the others, apart from the whole personal structure; each of these modes also influences all the others, conditions the whole structure. Thus perception conditions reflection, volition, affectivity, and depends on them; affectivity permeates reflection, volition, perception, and is, in various ways, subject to them; volition constitutes reflection, perception, affectivity, and is determined by each of them; reflection leads volition, liberates perception, influences affectivity, and is, at the same time, tributary in a particular way to each of these elements. Let us note, however, that the act-volition-reflectively-conscious-of-itself is the leading principle of the whole personal structure. This means that it does not depend on affectivity and perception in the same way as they depend on it. The dependence of reflective volition on the lower strata of the personal structure is *phenomenal.* This fact implies that the personal act, *as a freely self-actuating principle*, however much it is conditioned by the whole existential field which it moves, is not *constituted by*, *derived from*, any process taking place in this field. On the other hand, the dependence of affectivity and perception on volition and reflection is *transcendental.* Therefore perception and affectivity, in so far as they are integrated in the movement of personal existence, are *constituted* by the act-volition-actuating-itself-reflectively.

What about these percepts and affects which occur without any apparent connection with my act-volition? Are they purely phenomenal?

Let us note first that nothing happens in my life which is totally independent of my act-project; as I progress reflectively towards my end, I carry along whatever takes place in my field of existence. But this is not yet the full answer. Even if some of my percepts or affects were totally independent of my act-volition, they would not be purely phenomenal. Indeed, even so, they would be mine, they would be *constituted by my life-act*—by an act which does not come to existence as an evolution of that pre-personal existential field which it takes up and by which it is conditioned, but as a product of a Transcendent Creative Initiative. Were some phenomena to occur *as mere evolvements* of the pre-existent field, they would in no way pertain to me; with regard to me they would be purely phenomenal, purely "not I". Therefore there is nothing *in me* which is mere phenomenon. This means that the adjective "phenomenal" applied to any aspect of my personal structure has an essentially relative meaning. To call a reality transcendental is fundamentally to express its relationship to, its dependence upon, the Creative Source. Thus I call my personal existence transcendental because its principle—my act-volition—is myself-qua-immediately-related-to-the-Transcendent, it is my personality considered in the fullness of its created being, my Ego qua least-evolving from the pre-existent non-ego, my act possessing the plenitude of its freedom, reflectiveness, self-determination. With regard to my personal existence, I call my biologico-affective existence phenomenal, because I myself as the subject of this existence am more deeply involved within organic structures, more closely adherent to the pre-personal existential field, more intensely conditioned and determined by the modalities of this field, less vitally related to the Creative Source and, therefore, possessing less being, less freedom, less reflectiveness, less self-determination. However, this existence "in itself" is also transcendental to the extent that it is constituted by my life-act—that is, by an act which takes its origin from the Transcendent. Even the pre-existent non-ego which, with regard to me, is purely phenomenal is—as will be seen later—fundamentally transcendental because it also has its being from Above.

Note on the Method

Now that we have covered a good deal of ground, we may pause for a while and try to characterize our method of investigation.

It may be objected that this should have been made clear before we began this study. This occurred to me on several occasions, but every time I rejected the idea. The method followed in this work has not been determined beforehand, it has taken shape in the very effort I made to get at the heart of things and it is still taking shape as my investigation progresses. Moreover, the way in which my philosophizing develops cannot be separated from the reality which it illuminates; this thinking activity cannot be separated from the effort I make to express it in a "methodical" manner. In other words, the method followed in this study is the very act by which reality illuminates and expresses itself in me. It was not possible, therefore, for me to clarify it beforehand: I had to be "in it" in order to realize the way in which my study would develop. The reader must make his own the experience which this book tries to articulate and the thinking activity of which it is the expression, if he is to understand the way in which the whole work proceeds.

The study in which I am engaged is the progressive self-revealing of my act-incarnate. This means that my method is entirely *reflective* (in fact, all human knowledge, because it is always a certain manner in which the act reflects itself, is in some way reflective). However, it is not perfectly uniform: my reflection assumes various forms which correspond to the various ways in which my act incarnate reveals itself to itself.

I have begun this chapter with a study of my act incarnate in my body as *life-act*. This study must be characterized not simply as the self-revealing of my act incarnate existing as life-act, but already as a particular self-revealing of *my integral personal act*. This becomes clear when we understand that my life-act, as distinguished from my personal act, cannot take luminous possession of itself. The light which, in the course of my study, I have thrown on my incarnate existence was already the light of my transcendental being. This means that the sphere of my "natural" existence has revealed itself not as it would be "in itself" ("in itself", it could not be self-transparent, it could not exist as I described it, since my act of describing it, while illuminating it, "transcendentalized" it), but as a dimension of my integral personal structure. This aspect of my personal structure is, in the main, the sphere constituted by my act *as phenomenally self-given* (in the main, i.e., not exclusively: my personal act incarnate, in so far as it *is*, can never be a mere "third person" phenomenon): my personal act has described itself *as it felt itself living*. In this operation, its main effort has not been to coincide luminously with its transcendental self-actuating movement, but to let its light spread within the lower strata of its incarnate existence. While doing so, it had not, of course, to lose itself in these strata, but, holding them, so to speak, at a distance, retaining its transcendental character, it had to make them become explicitly what they generally are implicitly and obscurely. The method implied in this operation may be called *phenomenological*. It is a reflective process through which a world of interconnected facts is brought to light, analysed without being yet integrated explicitly in the total perspective from which it receives its full meaning; it is a method through which is revealed what is immediately given in a particular sphere of our experience.

In the second part of the section just completed, I have analysed my body as the incarnation of my integral personal act. In this study, a new mental operation has taken place. My personal act, reflecting upon itself, has tried to be all light to itself, to express itself, to express the whole movement of its own life, in a clear and detailed manner. The difference between this reflective operation and the phenomenological thought process just analysed is evident. There is no longer any question of my personal act's standing aside from its field of study, no question of illuminating particular structures of its incarnate existence while remaining, so to speak, above these structures. My personal act's effort is now one of luminous and articulate self-identification. In this respect, let us note the following:

(1) The method followed in this analysis remains a descriptive

method. My personal act gives expression to the experience it has of its transcendental *esse* and of its "transcendentalizing" operations. My study, therefore, remains throughout *in the realm of facts*. It does not aim at elaborating explanatory theories, it is concerned with what is: my personal act tries to grasp the totality of itself-living—in doing so, it discovers as facts (by living and realizing them luminously) the concrete and universal conditions of its unfolding.

This descriptive reflection reaches the very heart of things. In the effort it makes to penetrate to the innermost of itself, my personal act incarnate apprehends its self-givenness—in other words, it experiences its createdness, its transcendence with regard to any worldly, bodily reality, its dependence on a supramundane Creative Source. This realization illuminates the whole of my personal structure; henceforth, I see it in the light which proceeds from my central discovery. My descriptions of myself-incarnate are thus raised to the level of metaphysical aperçus: everything is related to the fundamental fact.

In this context, we understand that, as our study progresses, the distinction between the two reflective methods indicated above tends to disappear. Every phenomenon is immediately and instinctively integrated in the whole perspective; it is apprehended *within* the central fact, as a particular manifestation of this fact. Thus the reflective effort, even though it is carried out at various levels and, therefore, assumes a variety of forms, tends to become more and more homogeneous.

(2) In the effort it makes to grasp the totality of itself, my personal act never reaches perfect luminous self-identification. This is due not to any accidental factor but to my very condition as an act-incarnate-tending-towards-an-end. Indeed:

(a) As an act incarnate, my personal act is a continually self-expressing, self-spatializing reality: it never coincides perfectly with itself, it never exists as Pure Act. The implication of this is that my act always apprehends itself in a certain expressive context. It is literally true to say that it always looks into itself from a certain distance.

(b) As a reality tending towards an end (a pro-ject), my personal act is a self-transcending principle whose existence (ek-sistenz) is in the very movement by which it goes beyond itself-already-realized.

This means that my act continually escapes itself, it is perpetually ahead of itself-apprehended; it never grasps in a definitive manner the totality of itself because it never exists in a perfectly actual manner.

Concretely, these two aspects of my personal act incarnate are one and the same reality.

Concluding remarks. Some readers, I fear, will find me tediously repetitive, but I would ask them to bear in mind what follows.

This whole study is the unfolding of a single intuition. It brings to light a fundamental perspective and analyses it from various angles, at different levels. Each restatement of the central fact is designed to introduce new developments, and must always be understood in relation to the whole context in which it is made. When this connection is established, the restatement of what is fundamental is seen to be not a mere repetition, but the bringing out of a new aspect, or dimension, of reality. Repetitions are not made for their own sake, but continually to restate the central perspective to which the various elements which analysis brings out must be related if they are to be understood. Apart from the fundamental structural whole, everything is not only unintelligible but simply non-existent.

In using so many cumbersome hyphened expressions, am I not taking too great liberties with language?

It may be so, but it must be remembered that language is meant to be an expression of reality. As I have just said, at the heart of all my analyses there is the vision of reality as a structural whole the elements and aspects of which have no independent existence, no independent intelligibility. Hyphened expressions designate in various ways, or from various angles, the fundamental dynamic personal system which includes, in some way, the whole of reality or the different aspects of our experience. Sanskrit could, no doubt, elaborate harmonious compounds to express such a structural fact, but, in English, only the use of hyphens can, it seems to me, give a perception of this reality.

II. MY WORLD

In the first chapter of this study, I have shown that the universe is a unity-meaning which expresses itself in a great variety of significant elements, and in the relations which all these objects have to one another. The second step has been an inquiry into the nature of this unity-meaning. This inquiry has revealed that my experience, my activity, my affectivity, my projects, constitute the world in which I live. The conclusion of this investigation was: my life-act-realizing-itself-through-my-act-project is the act constitutive of "my world". The present chapter is an analysis of the structure of my world. It had to include first a study of *my act-in-my-body* because my body is the centre of my world—that is, the first unfolding of my life-act. I have shown in this study that my activity, my affectivity, my projects, are different modalities of my personal-act-animating-my-body. This observation enables me to conclude that the various aspects discernible within the unity-meaning of my world have their origin in the different variations of my act-incarnate-in-my-organism. I shall now examine carefully the constitution of my world—that is, analyse in detail the role of my organism as the centre, the *fons et origo* of my world, describe my world as the continuation of that movement of expression of which my body is the beginning. The method of this investigation will be parallel to that followed in the first part of this chapter: I shall study my world as the total incarnation (a) of my life-act, (b) of my integral personal act.

A. My World as the Unfolding of My Life-Act

By nature, I am a life-act incarnate. This life-act is "located" primarily in my brain which it constitutes as its first expressive centre. From this centre, my act unfolds itself and, in this process, diffracts itself in a variety of life functions, of vital motions. This unfolding of my life-act constitutes my body as a biologico-affective system, a living organism. However, my body is not simply *produced* by this centrifugal movement of my life-act. Indeed, as it unfolds in my organism, my life-act is conditioned by the structures of this vital field as though it were already in existence before being constituted by my act. This complex situation may be expressed thus: my life-act comes to existence in pre-existing vital structures and, while being intimately conditioned by these structures, takes them up and makes them live as the very concretion of its self-actuating movement (makes them exist as *my body*). All this has been explained in the first part of this chapter.

Now, my body is essentially the centre of my world (as my brain is the centre of my body): it has no meaning—it is nothing—apart from the environment in which it is situated. This fact shows that the limits within which my investigation has hitherto confined itself are to a large extent arbitrary. Considered in its totality, the original situation which underlies all my personal initiatives is constituted by my life-act animating my body, my surroundings, and the whole world (aspect a)—being conditioned, moreover, in this process, by the world, my environment, and my body existing centripetally (aspect b). In other words, my original life structure is my act coming to existence in a certain nucleus which offers itself as the convergence of pre-existent cosmico-biological phenomena and, while being conditioned by these phenomena, taking them up, energizing them, making them live as its total expressive field. I shall now study this integral life structure, placing myself within it at different levels of integration.

First Approach

My act gives existence to *my world* as it gives existence to *my body*: from the centre in which it is originally created, it constitutes my body, my environment, the whole world as its field of expression, as an immense living structure. This fact indicates that my act is not merely the act of my body but the act of the world: every object, in so far as it means something to me—*in so far as it exists for me*—is created within me—that is, within the life-act which I am, as a particular concretion of this life-act. The discovery of this all-embracing breadth of my life-act forces me to break the narrow frame within which I enclose my daily thinking. I realize that, as a human person, I am not merely confined within a small portion of space, but in reality co-extensive with the whole world (even though I am centred in my body); or rather, I realize that the world *is* this very person which I am—that is, this life-act unfolding from a centre, actuating itself in various ways, constituting space as its total expressive field. I have not, therefore, to imagine the existence of a material universe *outside me*; the universe, to the extent that it exists for me, *is* this structure constituted by my life-act incarnate. In this perspective, I must consider the movement of my life as the very progress of the universe-in-me.

This all-inclusiveness of my life-act does not suppress all differentiations; it excludes only the geometrical perspective according to which I am constituted with my body as one thing essentially distinct from an "external world" made of many other different things—in other words, it excludes the notion of the universe as a collection of beings which are placed side by side without interpenetrating. In my study of my life-act-incarnate-in-my-body, I have pointed out that my body, even though it is not a mere spatial entity existing *partes extra partes*, has a real internal diversity. Each part of my body occupies a certain place, has a particular structure which distinguishes it from any other part—it is, therefore, a particular expression of my life-act. However, no element of my organism has any existence or meaning apart from the other elements, or apart from the whole bodily structure: each part is constituted by its relation to all the other parts, in particular by its relation to my brain, which is the foremost expressive centre of my life-act. This perspective shows how illusory is an analytical study of the organism which isolates each element from the whole in which it is included. Considered apart from their connection with the entire bodily structure, and in particular from their essential relationship to my brain, my eyes, my heart, my hands are meaningless fictions, they are nonentities. These reflections must now be carried further. My world is constituted by my life-act unfolding itself and, in this process, expressing itself in many different ways; therefore it is a field characterized by an internal multiformity. Each element of this field has a particular situation, a unique texture, which differentiates it from any other element—it is, therefore, a peculiar concretion of my life-act. However, my life field is not a collection of elements which are simply juxtaposed: each object which I see around me is constituted by its inclusion in the whole system of which it is a part (i.e., by its relationship to all the other objects which surround it), fundamentally by its relation to my body, which is the centre of this system. This fact shows that the notion of an isolated object-in-itself is perfectly meaningless. Each object exists within a structure which is primarily a living whole. It does not offer itself first of all as something which must be known, but as a certain variation of the existential field constituted by my life-act-in-tension-towards-its-end.

Let us now examine in more detail the manner in which my world is constituted.

Aspect a: My life-act is essentially a reality moving towards a final goal; my body is the initial concretion of this vital project. Now, as has just been pointed out, my life-act is the act of the world. This means that its striving after an end is identically the movement by which the universe-in-me proceeds towards its ultimate realization. My body, as the crystallization of my existential movement, is the form which the universe-in-me first assumes while building itself, while tending towards its end; it is the seed of my world. My environment and, beyond it, the whole world are the evolution of this vital nucleus, the actualization of its potentialities. It is clear, therefore, that my body is inseparable from its ambiance. The centrifugal movement of my act which constitutes it goes beyond its limits. It constitutes and animates all the objects which form my environment (my table, my lamp—and the light which radiates from it—my books, my whole room, the house of which my room is a part—and all the noises with which it resounds—the street—with all its traffic—and the houses along the street, the coconut trees which stand there among the houses and the evening breeze which shakes them gently, the kites which fly around the trees, the clear winter sky and the crescent moon which appears in it, the freshness of the air, the light of the setting sun . . .); beyond my environment, it constitutes the whole earth, the solar system, the entire universe with all its galaxies—thus my act gives existence to the totality of my world. This movement is simultaneously one and diverse. I have pointed out that my life-act, as it unfolds in my body, though it remains undivided, casts itself into various functional systems, into many vital motions. Each of these existential vibrations of my act tends to create a certain world within my total life field. When a particular motion reaches a certain degree of intensity, it may become all-absorbing, posit itself as the totality of my life, swell itself for a moment into the unique act of my world. My world, therefore, is a fluctuating reality made of intercommunicating currents carried within a main stream. In the same way as each form assumed by my life-act-incarnate-in-my-body contributes towards giving to my whole existential movement its general tonality, so also each of these currents plays a certain role in the building of my world, and is responsible for a certain dimension of the existential climate which characterizes my whole life field.

In all these considerations, it must be noted, I am not dealing with a self-controlled activity, but with the "natural" evolution of my life-act. This total situation is myself as I am created: I am given to myself as a life-act-already-existing-in-the-form-of-a-world-which-it-constitutes-from-an-expressive-centre; I "find" myself in the process of shaping my environment, of giving existence and meaning to the universe.

Aspect b: As it unfolds itself from my brain in my body, from my body in my surroundings, my life-act is conditioned by the whole cosmico-biological system which it constitutes: it is conditioned by the modalities of my brain, by the structures of my body, by the peculiarities of my surroundings and, through these surroundings, by the whole world. Thus the world is not simply a reality which my act fashions as the expression of itself, but also a structural ensemble which it finds already there, by which it is phenomenally generated, vitally promoted. I have shown that my brain as the centre of my organism draws its expressive vigour from my whole body—in other words, that my life-act-expressing-itself-synthetically-in-the-modalities-of-my-brain is conditioned by my body already existing centripetally. I understand now that the process by which all the biological phenomena which take place in my organism converge towards my brain is the continuation of a movement which originates in the world and reaches me through the environment in which I happen to be. This process can be described in many ways. Let us consider a few of the ways in which it can be seen.

(1) The world exists before my act shapes it as the expression of itself. Pervading it through and through, there are cosmic "forces" which constitute it as an earth-centred reality, which fashion the earth—with its atmosphere, its climate, its fluctuating characteristics—and make it converge towards my body, which shape my body—with all its organic functions—and centralizes it in my brain. Thus my act-expressing-itself-synthetically-in-my-brain-at-the-outset-of-its-self-actuating-movement is conditioned by the whole universe existing centripetally. This must be understood in a very concrete way. My human life is tied to some conditions. These conditions are realized in my body existing actually on earth as the convergence of a cosmic synergy. Therefore, in my present state of life, I exist *essentially* as an earthly being—not a being who just happens to live on earth, but a being fashioned by the earth and, through the earth, by the whole cosmos. Moreover, the way in which I live at the present moment is closely related to the conditions in which I find myself now—that is, to the precise structural ensemble in which my life-act is presently incarnate. This setting is the universe, the earth fashioning my environment, my body, my brain in the precise way in which they fashion them now. I would not be living *just as I live now* if, at this moment, it was day instead of night, if it was summer instead of winter, if the night was stormy instead of calm, if I was on the seashore instead of in Calcutta, on the Maidan instead of in my room, if Calcutta was a soundless place instead of a noisy city. . . .

(2) (A corollary of 1) My body draws from its ambiance the very substance of which it is made and much of its vitality; the life-act

which animates my brain, my limbs, my surroundings receives from the whole world its "phenomenal" energy. Each of my functions, as a centripetal process which conditions my life-act, is not something improvised in my body; it is the term of a movement which is none other than the world, my surroundings shaping themselves in a specific manner in order to bring forth in my organism a particular biological phenomenon.

(3) The way in which "external" influences act upon me must be understood in a structural perspective. The universe-converging-towards-my-body-and-my-brain is essentially the universe-for-me: my life-act is its unity-meaning. Each element of this system contributes from the place which it occupies to the constitution of the whole—that is, to the shaping of all the other elements in reference to my body and my brain. Thus I am conditioned by each "external" occurrence to the extent that it is an element of the total structure in which my act is incarnate.

Each influence, it must be noted, is from the start a biological reality, since it pertains to a system whose unity-meaning is my life-act—therefore whatever conditions me "from outside" is not simply the physical cause of biological effects, but originally a life-process—not a life-process in general, but an element of a structure which pertains essentially to my individual life. This is the perspective in which I must understand how the modalities of my environment mark my organism and thus have a real influence on my personal life.

Complementariness of the two aspects: The centrifugal movement of my life-act and the centripetal activity by which it is conditioned are always two complementary aspects of the same reality. My life-act animates my body, my environment, my world; yet, in this process, it is internally fashioned, continually subtended by the world, my environment, my body already existing. This winter night in which my room, the house, the city, are immersed exist for me to the extent that I live it—that is, in so far as my act unfolding itself from my brain in my body, and in my environment, constitutes it as its life-field, as the actual concretion of its movement towards its end. Nevertheless, this winter night exists before I constitute it, and conditions the expansive movement of my life-act according to its modalities. Therefore my existential initiative is not a purely creative move, it is not an absolute beginning; it is the taking up and the re-casting of a pre-existent universe—that is, of cosmico-biological structures which are already there and have from the start a definite existential significance. These structures condition the movement of my life-act by their convergence towards its expressive centre.

Now, an important fact—which has already been referred to—must be stressed again. However real the pre-existence of the vital structures by which my act is conditioned, I cannot affirm that the world-converging-towards-my-brain has its concrete existence independently of me. In fact, it exists essentially for me—that is, in dependence of my life-act. However, it is not related to my act in the same way as the world-existing-centrifugally. My act gives existence to the latter by constituting it as the concretion of its self-actuating movement—that is, in a direct, intimate, quasi-creative manner—whereas it gives existence to the former by attraction: it polarizes, centralizes in its expressive nucleus, a world which is already there—*in this sense*, it constitutes the world-existing-centripetally, even though it is conditioned by this world, even though this world exists before being polarized.

These observations lead me to the following conclusions:

(1) The world-converging-towards-my-expressive-centre does not *as such* precede in existence the centrifugal movement of my life-act since it is constituted as this converging world by the polarizing virtue of my act (that is, of an act which exists essentially as a reality unfolding itself from a centre).

Therefore:

(a) My act does not in any way *proceed* from the world, from any pre-existent vital structures.

(b) Absolutely speaking, what is prior to and constitutive of any reality existing qua related to me in any way is my life-act-positing-itself-in-the-form-of-a-world-which-it-constitutes-from-an-expressive-centre (aspect a)—or rather, it is the Transcendent Initiative which creates me as act-of-the-universe and the whole universe as the expressive-field-of-my-act.

(2) However, the world-converging-towards-my-expressive-centre is made of pre-existing stuff. Prior to the coming into existence of my life-act, there are already vital structures, a universe extant. Thus I am essentially a being who has been born one day; nay more, I am a being who continually comes to life in an already existing universe. As my life-act is brought to existence, it constitutes the world as the concretion of itself (aspect a) and, at the same time, polarizes the already existing universe and lets itself be conditioned by it (aspect

b). Thus we see in what sense the world-converging-towards-my-expressive-centre precedes in existence the centrifugal movement of my act: it pre-exists *to the degree to which it is made of pre-existent cosmico-biological material* (but it follows in existence the movement of my act—that is, exists in dependence on my life-act-unfolding-itself—*in so far as it is made to converge towards its expressive nucleus*).

Second Approach

Let us examine now my life-act-in-my-world from the "psychological" point of view. In my study of my life-act-in-my-body, I have pointed out that my act exists as a temperamental inclination because of its incarnation in this particular organism, that it expresses itself in the form of percepts in the modalities of my sensory apparatus and in the form of thoughts, imaginations, concepts, in my central organ, that it vibrates affectively in the different structures of my organic system. I must now analyse these same realities within the wider perspective of my present study. I shall first examine these various phenomena separately, and then indicate their essential complementariness.

i. *My Act-World as a Temperamental Inclination*

My act has a fundamental affective individuality—in other words, it is from the start characterized by a basic existential attitude, an original manner of "facing life", of ordering itself towards its final goal. This temperamental inclination is constitutive of, and manifests itself in some particular manner in, each motion of my life-act-incarnate-in-my-body; however, it is not a phenomenon confined within the limits of my organism: it shapes my whole world because my life-act—of which it is the basic determination—is essentially act-of-the-world. Thus my environment, my world, are from the start concretions of my temperamental disposition. The situation in which I find myself, the obstacles which I meet on my way, the persons with whom I deal, all the things which I see around me, the whole world, have for me from the start an existential meaning which is made up of this fundamental manner of living. This shows that the world-in-me is originally a deeply individualized reality: its concrete essence is constituted by my individual life—by the desires, the apprehensions, the vital dispositions which characterize my life-act incarnate.

Phenomenally, this temperamental inclination of my act is due to the constitution of the cosmico-biological structures in which my life-act expresses itself—in other words, it is due to the way in which my act is fundamentally conditioned by these structures-existing-centripetally. To the extent that these structures precede in existence the movement by which my act animates them—that is, to the degree to which they are made of pre-existent cosmico-biological material—the temperamental inclination of my life-act is the product of an activity independent of its centrifugal self-positing movement. In so far as its fundamental affective disposition is thus fashioned by the world, my body and my brain that already exist, my life is the mere continuation in me of the movement constitutive of this pre-existent world. We must, however, note that to the degree to which these cosmico-biological structures exist qua structures-converging-towards-my-expressive-centre—that is, to the extent that they are polarized and thus exist as structures of my life—they are dependent on me, they exist in dependence on the centrifugal movement of my life-act and, therefore, in dependence on my temperamental inclination. Thus the whole truth is not merely the fact that my life-act exists in the form of a basic affective disposition *owing to its being conditioned* by the cosmico-biological structures in which it expresses itself, but first of all the fact that these structures *are constituted* as structures-conditioning-my-act-in-this-particular-manner *in dependence on the fundamental disposition of my act*. This explains why the circumstances in which I find myself (a danger which I have to face, a person I meet, the ringing of the phone . . .), the peculiarities of my environment and of my body (the coolness of this winter night, the noises of the street, a mosquito bite . . .) are situations which condition and influence me not simply according to their particular modalities but primarily according to my individuality—that is, according to my fundamental existential attitude. In this perspective, I shall maintain that my life-act-unfolding-itself-from-its-expressive-centre is the *a priori* which gives its meaning-for-me—its conditioning value—to whatever is related to me, I shall maintain that the fact of my being individuated ("temperamentalized") by the modalities of my life field is not primarily the fact of my being vitally conditioned by cosmico-biological structures which exist independently of me, but the fact that, in the very process of fashioning my life field, of animating it in my own typical manner, I am *transcendentally* given to myself as act-living-in-this-field-in-the-form-of-a-temperamental-inclination. Thus the fundamental existential attitude of my life-act is not merely due to the way in which it is conditioned by the modalities of the already existing vital field which it takes up (my "phenomenal" individuality); it is first of all constituted by the Transcendent Initiative which creates me as this particular life-act having this particular basic disposition, creates the universe-in-me as this particular world expressing my innate disposition, creates all particular circumstances as concretions of my fundamental attitude, creates me as act living these particular circumstances in this original manner (my "transcendental" individuality).

ii. *Perception*

The intellectualistic tradition considers the subject of sensation essentially as a spectator facing a world which offers itself to be perceived. On this assumption, the task of the philosopher is to account for the existence of sense data which represent faithfully the external reality—in other words, to explain the coincidence between sensation and its object. We have mentioned that one of the most thorny problems encountered in this study is that of determining exactly where perception takes place: if we maintain that it occurs in the object, we must still show how it really pertains to the subject; on the other hand, if we hold that it takes place in the perceptive faculty, we must clarify the way in which it can be perception of the object itself. Another difficulty is that of determining with any precision the subjective and objective elements of the perceptual synthesis.

All these problems are based on erroneous presuppositions. As we know, there is no such thing as a "subject of perception" facing a world of "objects" which exist side by side; there are no objects which exist in the world as complete entities and must be perceived "in themselves"; there is no such phenomenon as a synthesis of subjective activity and objective specification. The reality is my life-act existing from the first in the form of a world which it occupies and animates from an expressive centre. No part of this field has any meaning "in itself"—that is, independently of the whole system. All the elements of this universe receive from their relation to my body their existence as parts of the totality. My life-act-in-tension-towards-its-end is the movement of this totality towards its completion. This is the perspective in which perception must be studied.

In the first part of this chapter, I have shown that my life-act expresses itself in the modalities of my sensory apparatus in the form of percepts. Now these percepts are phenomena which are essentially relative to some elements of my environment. At this moment I have perception of those houses which stand there along the street. This perception entails, no doubt, a modification of my visual organ, but this modification refers essentially to those houses which I see through the window. Let us study this system.

Aspect a: From its expressive centre, my life-act constitutes my body as the concretion of its self-actuating movement, as the embryo of my world; from my body, it expresses itself in my environment, in the whole world, and constitutes them as the unfolding of my organic potentialities. Now, in this movement, my act illuminates itself, becomes self-transparent. My present perception is a moment of this vital process: the structure formed by my eyes fixed on those houses which stand there along the street at a certain distance from my body *is* my act-world (i.e., my life-act existing qua act-of-the-world) expressing itself to itself in a certain manner, illuminating in a particular way its existential movement. How does this illumination take place?

Let us always remember the original situation from which the whole process begins: my life-act-constituting-everything-as-concretion-of-itself. Therefore, from the start, my body, those houses along the street, the concrete distance which separates those houses from my body are my life-act-existing-in-a-certain-manner: they are modalities of the total centrifugal movement of my act. Now, in the very process by which my act constitutes my environment, my world, as its life field, it makes itself present to itself in a particular manner—that is, it expresses itself to itself visually. In its origin and development, this phenomenon may be described thus:

(1) My act shapes itself in my body into a capacity of apprehending its life-field in a certain manner (i.e., of apprehending a certain aspect of itself-incarnate); concomitantly, it gives to my world in relation to this faculty the possibility of being apprehended (in a certain manner)—thus, while unfolding itself in my body and in my world, my act becomes capable of illuminating itself in the mode of visual perception.

(2) In the movement by which it constitutes my world, my life-act actuates this perceptive capacity: as it shapes the various elements of its existential field and lives in them in various ways—as it thus realizes itself—my act perfects its visual faculty, it actuates the link

which unites my world with my visual organ; my act incarnate becomes present to itself in a specific manner, it becomes visually self-transparent.

This particular illumination of my act-world always takes place within certain limits which manifest the finiteness of my incarnate existence. My act is centred in my body; though it animates the whole world, it lives first of all within the portion of my life field which constitutes my immediate surroundings. In this restricted area, it expresses itself to itself in the mode of visual perception. This is what takes place now as my eyes are fixed on those houses. In the situation formed by those houses-standing-along-the-street-at-a-certain-distance-from-my-body-situated-in-my-room, my life-act incarnate develops that very humble type of self-awareness which I call my perception of those houses. In agreement with my different observations, I shall characterize this perception in the following negative and positive ways:

(1) *As such*, my perception of those houses is neither an act, nor a motion of my act. The reality constitutive of my present situation—that is, of my eyes-fixed-on-those-houses-standing-along-the-street, of the concrete distance which separates those houses from my body—is my life-act-incarnating-itself. Thus my situation exists first of all as a particular embodiment of my life-act, as a particular concretion of the movement by which my act constitutes the whole world and leads it towards its end. My perception of those houses is *the presence of my act to itself within this situation* which it thus constitutes as a particularization of the totality of itself-incarnate. In this context, we understand that perception is always expression of life: I perceive my environment according to the way I live it. I have alluded to this phenomenon in my study of my act-existing-in-the-form-of-a-temperamental-inclination. This fact will become even more manifest when we analyse the complementariness of our various psychological phenomena.

(2) My perception is not a synthesis of various elements. It develops entirely within the movement of my act. Its constitutive unity is the unity of my life-act itself and the diversity which it reveals is the very diversity of self-expressive forms which my act evolves as it spatializes itself.

(3) My perception is my act-world illuminating in a particular manner its movement towards its end; therefore it does not refer to

an "object" which exists outside me and must be apprehended "in itself". My present situation, as a part of my total life-field, is a structure each element of which has no existence, no meaning, apart from its relation to my body (and also apart from all the other elements). Thus:

(a) Realizing that those houses—as parts of my life field, as concretion of my life-act incarnate—receive their existence from their relation to my body, I shall admit that my present perception—in order to be perception of those houses *such as they are in fact*—must be vision of those houses-qua-related-to-my-body; I shall admit that those houses-perceived-as-they-are-in-fact are those houses-related-to-my-percept.

(b) I shall not wonder how my percept represents those houses "objectively", but realizing that my body, as it exists concretely, is the beginning of the movement by which my act constitutes my present situation, my world, I shall understand that my percept is the inception of the process by which my act, while constituting my present situation (i.e., those houses-standing-along-the-street-at-a-certain-distance-from-my-body-situated-in-my-room), while living it as a particular concretion of its total existential movement, makes itself present to itself in it in a particular manner—in other words, that my percept—as such—is those houses-beginning-to-exist-as-luminous-expressions-of-my-life-act-incarnate.

(c) In conclusion, I shall not wonder whether my perception takes place in my body or in those houses, but realizing that my perception is my life-act-incarnate-expressing-itself-to-itself-in-a-particular-manner, that my act constitutes the whole of my life field, I shall acknowledge that my perception of those houses is in my body, in my visual faculty to the degree to which my body is my environment, my world, beginning to exist as the expressive field of my act incarnate, that it is in those houses to the extent that they are the unfolding of this potentiality, the portion of my life field which actually reveals my act to itself.

Let us understand clearly the implications of these observations. As we know, the existence of my life-act is essentially centrifugal. From its expressive centre, my act constitutes my body as the initial concretion of its self-realizing movement; from my body, it unfolds in my environment, in my world, and constitutes them as the realization of my organic possibilities—that is, as the continuation of the movement by which my body is framed. My perception of my environment is not an activity distinct from this existential movement of my act, but it is this movement illuminating itself. It takes place originally in my body because my body is the embryo and the centre of my world; it is concerned with my environment because the movement of my life is essentially centrifugal. Moreover, let us note this: while revealing my act to itself, my perception makes me aware of my organic potentialities, of the vital urges latent in my body because its objects—that is, the media through which it makes my act incarnate present to itself—already exist as the extension of my corporality, as the evolving of the different aspects of my life-act-existing-corporally. These facts show that the objects which I perceive do not present themselves as mere conglomerates of static qualities, but first of all as suggestions, allurements, proposed behaviours, ways of action (tools, in Heidegger's terminology). More than this: since the objects which I perceive and my apprehension of them are constituted by my life-act-actuating-itself-in-a-particular-direction, any perception implies as its substratum an already existing behaviour. This is the perspective in which we must understand these observations of Merleau-Ponty: "Before being an objective spectacle, quality is revealed by a type of behaviour which is directed towards it in its essence, and this is why my body has no sooner adopted the attitude of blue than I am vouchsafed a quasi-presence of blue. We must therefore stop wondering how and why red signifies effort or violence, green restfulness and peace; we must rediscover how to live these colours as our body does, that is, as peace or violence in concrete form. When we say red increases the compass of our reactions, we are not to be understood as having in mind two distinct facts, a sensation of red and motor reactions—we must be understood as meaning that red, by its texture as followed and adhered to by our gaze, is already the amplification of our motor being."[10] Also: "Whether it is a question of perceiving words or more generally objects, there is a certain bodily attitude, a specific kind of dynamic tension which is necessary to give structure to the image; man as a dynamic and living totality has to 'pattern' himself in order to trace out a figure in his visual field as part of the psycho-somatic organism."[11]

[10] M. Merleau-Ponty, *Phenomenology of Perception*, translated by Colin Smith, p. 211, London, Routledge, 1962.
[11] *Op. cit.*, p. 236.

To these considerations let us add a few concluding remarks:

(1) It is while constituting my whole world—as act-world, that is to say—that, in each situation, my life-act reveals itself to itself through the medium of particular objects. Each particular object, therefore, while making my act present to itself, in some way expresses the totality. This universal expressiveness of each situation manifests itself in the fact that each object which I perceive is inseparable from the other objects which surround it and from the whole setting in which it is situated. It manifests itself also in the fact that particular objects are media through which my act incarnate becomes aware of its potentialities. Let us explain this: each fundamental impulse of my life-act exists first of all as a certain dimension, a particular function of my body; subsequently, it takes the form of a world which comes to existence as the unfolding of this organic potentiality: particular objects illuminate this physical urge to the extent that they are expressions of the world which it constitutes.

(2) The process by which my life-act constitutes my world is identically the movement by which it tends towards its ultimate realization, and by which the world-in-me tends towards its completion. This movement is essentially centrifugal: it originates in my body and expels me from it, it transforms me into a field in which my central potentialities must continually actuate themselves. This process does not take place *in space*, but is constitutive of space. Thus the world does not open itself before me first as a spectacle which I contemplate serenely without being committed, but as a task which I have already undertaken and has to be pursued. The world offers itself to my perception as a call or an attraction; it stretches around me as a field of action, a hollowness which I must fill, a depth formed by my existential ecstasy and demanding of me a continual self-transcendence.

(3) In the intellectualistic perspective, the perception of a particular object implies the formation of a particular perceptual synthesis. This synthesis will remain in existence as long as this perception endures. As soon as a new object presents itself, there will be a new "act of perceiving" and, consequently, a new synthesis. Thus, in the same way as it reduces the world to a collection of objects distinct from one another, so intellectualism makes of the life of our senses a succession of particular perceptive states each of which is self-sufficient. This shows us that to a view of the world inspired by

geometricism there corresponds necessarily a geometrical conception of human psychology; in either sector, unity is artificially rebuilt from an original multiplicity.

Our experience does not in any way support this atomistic view. The authentic perspective is this: in the same way as it constitutes the world as a unified field containing a variety of forms, so my act constitutes my perceptive life as a continuous process in which various moments can be distinguished. These various elements do not form a succession of independent temporal atoms any more than the different objects situated in my perceptive field form a collection of co-existing entities. In my study of temporality, I shall try to show how the various perceptive moments are related to each other. However, it is important to realize here and now that the life-act incarnate reveals itself first as a unity, *whatever be the aspect under which it is studied.*

Aspect b: So far I have analysed my perception of the world as an aspect of the centrifugal movement of my act. Now, as we know, each structure in which my act unfolds itself is conditioned by the same structure existing as a centripetal process. Thus my body is not only the form which my life-act assumes at the outset of its self-realizing movement, but also the convergence of that cosmico-biological activity which already forms the world before I constitute it as my life-field. From this point of view, each phenomenon taking place in my body is the term of a movement which originates in the world. Considering my perception in this perspective, I shall no longer say that it occurs in my environment in dependence on my body; I shall say that it occurs in my body in dependence on my environment; I shall no longer describe it as the process by which I become aware of my organic potentialities through the medium of objects, but as the process by which objects become in me aware of themselves through the medium of my body. This "process b" is an aspect of the vital movement by which the structures in which I am incarnate condition my act, in the same way as "process a" is an aspect of the movement by which my life-act constitutes my world. Let us explain this.

Perception is not only a phenomenon which occurs within the self-actuating movement of my life-act, but also a fact which somehow precedes this movement and *guides* the way in which this movement takes place concretely—in other words, my life-act does not only posit itself-illuminated while constituting my world, but constitutes my world *in accordance with* the way in which the world finds itself already illuminated in me. This means that the world-conditioning-the-centrifugal-movement-of-my-life-act is to a great extent the world-already-luminously-present-to-itself-in-me. What exactly is this world-expressing-itself-to-itself-in-me? The process by which my environment converges towards my body and my brain shapes my sensory apparatus (as it shapes all my other organs). Now this particular phenomenon is precisely the world-conditioning-*luminously*-the-centrifugal-movement-of-my-life-act (i.e., the world conditioning my act *qua world-luminously-present-to-itself-in-me*). Indeed, while shaping my eyes, the world reveals itself to itself in me as a visual field containing many forms and colours; while shaping my ears, it casts itself into sounds (the ticking of my alarm clock, the chirping of birds, the barking of a dog); while shaping my whole body, it takes the form of tactile modalities (the hardness of the table, the dryness of the air). These percepts which are *the world-luminously-present-to-itself-in-me-under-different-aspects* are elements which contribute dynamically towards making my life-act what it is concretely—that is, towards conditioning its centrifugal movement. As such, they are not primarily objective qualities presented to my senses from outside, but modes of living, concrete behaviours proposed to me through my sensory apparatus (which they shape in order to realize themselves in me) from a certain place in space, taken up by my act and converted by it into luminous modalities of its self-actuating movement. These views have been adumbrated by Merleau-Ponty in the following terms: "The subject of sensation is neither a thinker who takes note of a quality, nor an inert setting which is affected or changed by it, it is a power which is born into, and simultaneously with, a certain existential environment, or is synchronized with it. The relations of sentient to sensible are comparable with those of the sleeper to his slumber: sleep comes when a certain voluntary attitude suddenly receives from outside the confirmation for which it was waiting. *I* am breathing deeply and slowly in order to summon sleep, and suddenly it is as if my mouth were connected to some great lung outside myself which alternately calls forth and forces back my breath. A certain rhythm of respiration, which a moment ago I voluntarily maintained, now becomes my very being, and sleep, until now aimed at as a significance, suddenly becomes a situation. In the same way I give ear, or look, in the expectation of a sensation, and suddenly the sensible takes possession

11—W.O.P.

of my ear or my gaze, and I surrender a part of my body, even my whole body, to this particular manner of vibrating and filling space known as blue or red. Just as the sacrament not only symbolizes, in sensible species, an operation of Grace, but is also the real presence of God, which it causes to occupy a fragment of space and communicates to those who eat of the consecrated bread, provided that they are inwardly prepared, in the same way the sensible has not only a motor and vital significance, but is nothing other than a certain way of being in the world suggested to us from some point in space, and seized and acted upon by our body, provided that it is capable of doing so, so that sensation is literally a form of communion."[12]

These facts explain the driving force of our sensations. Each perceptive contact between our body and the world conditions the movement of our existence dynamically. Each perception has its own determining influence—an influence which may at times overwhelm our personality.

Complementariness of the two aspects: My eyes are fixed on those houses which stand there along the street. This perception takes place simultaneously: (1) in the centrifugal movement by which my life-act constitutes my world, (2) in the process by which the world converges towards my body and my brain. Considered from the first angle, my perception is my act-revealing-itself-to-itself-in-a-particular-manner-through-the-medium-of-those-houses; from the second angle, it is those houses (and in them the whole world)-revealing-themselves-to-themselves-in-me-through-the-medium-of-my-percept. To the extent that the world-converging-towards-my-expressive-centre is made of pre-existent cosmico-biological material, my perception as an aspect of the world-existing-centripetally precedes this same perception subsisting within the centrifugal movement of my life-act. In this perspective, I shall explain the whole process in this way:

(1) Those houses—as parts of the pre-existent-world-converging-towards-my-expressive-centre—become aware of themselves in me through the medium of my percept.

(2) My act takes up this already existing perception (as it takes up the whole field in which it comes to existence) and converts it into *my* perception (i.e., into myself-present-to-myself-through-the-medium-of-those-houses). This explanation would account for both the

[12] *Op. cit.*, pp. 245–6.

"active" and the "passive" sides of my sensation, for its dependence on an "objective" reality distinct from myself.

But does this conception of the "mechanism" of perception really make sense?

Let us analyse the facts more carefully. Considered within the movement by which the world centralizes itself in my body, my perception of those houses, as has just been stated, is those houses-revealing-themselves-to-themselves-in-me-through-the-medium-of-my-percept. Now, as is abundantly evident, this phenomenon—as it exists concretely—cannot precede my perception qua modality of the centrifugal movement of my life-act. Indeed, if anything takes place *in me*, it must exist first of all within this centrifugal movement, since this movement is my existence. If at any moment there is in my body a percept through the medium of which something reveals itself to itself in me, this percept must *first of all* be constituted by my life-act-unfolding-itself-from-its-expressive-centre (otherwise it cannot pertain to me). Now the presence in my body of a percept constituted by the existential movement of my act implies the presence of a perception taking place within this same movement. Thus to speak of my perception of those houses occurring *in any way* antecedently to the movement by which my life-act-unfolding-from-its-centre constitutes those houses as itself-illumined-in-a-particular-manner is, in the order of reality, simply meaningless. Existentially, my perception of those houses qua modality of my centrifugal movement is a necessary presupposition to the existence of this same perception as the process by which those houses illuminate themselves in me through the medium of my percept. Therefore the whole perceptive process must be understood in this way: while unfolding itself from its expressive centre and constituting my body, my environment, my world as its life field, my act shapes those houses as luminous expression of itself-incarnate-in-my-body (phase a)—no sooner has this phenomenon taken place than *my act returns to its source and, in this regressive movement, fashions my percept into the luminous expression of itself-incarnate-in-those-houses* (phase b).

Clearly, this must be understood in a broader perspective (since "phase b" as described here is but an aspect of the whole centripetal activity by which my life-act-unfolding-itself-from-its-centre is conditioned). This broader perspective may be described in these terms:

—my act comes to existence in a centre,

—from this centre, it unfolds itself and, in this movement, constitutes my body, my environment, the whole world as its life field (phase a),

—this quasi-creative movement has no sooner taken place than, from everywhere, my life-act returns to its source and, in this regressive process, conditions itself-continuing-to-unfold-from-this-source (phase b).

In this system, we observe the following:

(1) Existentially, phase a has priority—indeed, it constitutes my world, it is presupposed to phase b.

(2) Phase b is the world-*already*-constituted-by-my-life-act conditioning my life-act-*continuing*-to-constitute-the-world. To the extent that my act-already-realized (my essence) thus underlies the actual self-realizing movement of my act (my existence), the former has a certain anteriority with regard to the latter—however, it has no existence apart from it: my act-already-realized-in-the-form-of-a-world exists by and for my act-continuing-to-realize-itself.

(3) These facts show that my life-act exists as a reality which is continually ahead of itself: my existence consists in the very movement by which I continually transcend myself-already-existing (ek-sistenz).

(4) My act-in-tension-towards-its-final-realization (phase a) is not constituted by my act-already-realized but conditioned by it. Nevertheless, I must affirm that I am constituted as an act-world-continually-conditioned-by-itself-in-the-movement-by-which-it-realizes-itself—in other words, that I am continually given to myself while tending towards my end. This experience is that of my ontological dependence on the Creative Source, the experience of my createdness.

(5) To the extent that my body, my world, exist within the centrifugal movement of my life-act (phase a), I may truly say that *I am* my body, my world; to the extent that my body, my world, exist within my act-continually-returning-to-its-source (phase b), I must say that *I have* a body, a world.

A further consideration will complement what has just been said. I have pointed out that the world-converging-towards-my-expressive-centre (phase b), however dependent it is on my life-act-unfolding-itself-centrifugally, is made up of pre-existent cosmico-biological material (the nature of which will be specified at a further stage of this study). In this perspective, I remarked earlier that I was bound to be born one day—in other words, I was bound to come to life one day in an already existing world, on an already existing earth. Taking this fact into account, I can describe my coming into being in these terms: I came to existence at a given moment in an already existing nature in the form of a life-act co-extensive with the whole but animating the whole, re-creating it from a definite centre (phase a). No sooner had my act thus posited itself as act-of-the-universe than it found itself conditioned by itself-returning-to-its-source-from-every-place-it-occupied-and-animated (phase b). This regressive movement of my life-act was in fact the whole-pre-existent-nature-conditioning-my-act-continuing-to-unfold-from-its-expressive-centre. Now let us note this fact: from the moment the universe-already-existing began to condition my act-unfolding-itself-centrifugally, this nature *qua nature-conditioning-my-act* began to exist by and for my act-continuing-to-unfold-itself—thus, existentially, my act-ek-sisting has priority over my whole nature. The fact that it finds itself conditioned by this nature is in no way the fact of its being derived from, of its evolving from, of its being constituted by pre-existent cosmico-biological structures, but the fact of its being created by the Transcendent as life-act-having-a-nature.

This complementary observation must now be connected with my preceding considerations. I have shown that I am a life-act-continually-realizing-itself-from-a-centre-in-the-form-of-a-world (my existence)-and-, in-this-movement-, being-continually-conditioned-by-itself-already-realized (my essence). Now I see that my act-already-realized-conditioning-my-act-continuing-to-realize-itself includes the whole pre-existent universe and is absolutely undistinguishable from it: my nature and my essence are concretely one.

At this stage of our inquiry, let us halt for a while and look back at the ground we have covered:

(1) In my study of my life-act in my body, I made the following observations:

(a) *My life-act constitutes my body* as its expressive field (aspect a)—at the same time, *it "finds" itself involved in, conditioned by, the structures of my organism as though they were "already there"*, as though it itself were fashioned, brought to existence in them.

(b) The centrifugal movement of my act (aspect a) is underlaid by another phenomenon (the centripetal aspect) which is not properly speaking *constituted* by my life-act-unfolding-centrifugally (since it conditions or shapes this movement). Considered "in itself", this centripetal process may be called a pre-personal phenomenon. Thus *my individual life develops essentially within a pre-existent field*—that is, within vital structures which are relatively independent of me; yet, in fact, *my body-existing-centripetally has no existence apart from my act.* In the order of reality, my life-act (unfolding centrifugally) is the existence of both my body-existing-centripetally and of my body-existing-centrifugally. Not in the same way, however: my act gives existence to the latter by expressing itself in it, to the former by exercising a pull which creates in it a polarization.

(2) In the description of my body as the incarnation of my integral personal act, a new fact has been established: my act is in no way constituted by, derived from, the biological structures by which it is conditioned—*it proceeds from a Transcendent Source* and is created as life-act-unfolding-itself-from-a-centre-and-being-conditioned-by-the-structures-in-which-it-expresses-itself.

(3) In this section dealing with my "act-world", I have first summed up in a wider perspective the various elements just mentioned. I have shown first that my life-act actuates itself by continually taking up and recasting pre-existent cosmico-biological structures; then I have qualified this affirmation by remarking that these structures, in so far as they condition my life-act, are existentially dependent on it, and, therefore, that my act gives existence to both the world-existing-centrifugally (by constituting it as the expression of itself) and to the world-existing-centripetally (by centralizing in its expressive nucleus a world which is already there). In this context, I have emphasized the existential priority of my life-act with regard to any reality existing qua related to me.

Finally, the study of perception has made me realize that the world-converging-towards-my-expressive-centre, is constituted by my life-act-continually-returning-to-its-source-and-, in-this-regressive-movement-, conditioning-my-act-continuing-to-unfold-itself-from-this-source. This discovery has shown me that my act-realizing-itself (my existence) is continually underlaid by my act-already-realized (my essence), even though my act-already-realized (my essence) has no existence apart from my act-realizing-itself (my existence). Complementing this, I have pointed out that the regressive movement of my life-act (my essence) is identically the process by which the whole pre-existent universe (my nature) conditions my act-unfolding-itself-from-its-centre (my existence). This new development does not supersede all the previous statements, but shows in what light they must be understood.

In all these descriptive sketches many assertions will be found which contradict each other when taken absolutely. I affirm that my life-act comes to life in vital structures *which are already there, which are independent of me* (thesis), yet I maintain that these structures *have no existence apart from* my life-act (antithesis). I assert that my life-act *constitutes* the world-existing-centripetally (thesis), yet I declare that this world conditions my life-act as a reality which is *already constituted* (antithesis). I say that my existence *precedes* my essence (thesis), yet I acknowledge that my essence *is anterior to* my existence (antithesis). I affirm that my nature and my essence *are one* (thesis), yet I admit the pre-existence of my nature (antithesis).

These antinomies cannot be resolved by devising some sort of synthetizing theory. To be effective, my attempts at reconciling these apparently contradictory elements must be based on the conviction that they *are* reconciled *de facto*. Through an experiential contact with the living reality, with the concrete movement of my incarnate existence, I must find in what sense each of these facts is related to all the others and, thus, in what sense each of my assertions is valid.

My observations have shown me that my dependence on a Transcendent Source which creates me as act-world and re-creates the whole world in me—my createdness—is the central reality which contains and illuminates all the rest. It contains the fact of my existence as a life-act-continually-realizing-itself-centrifugally; it contains the fact of my being continually conditioned by myself, by the universe already realized. It illuminates the existential priority of my act-in-tension-towards-its-end, the existential dependence on it of my act-world-continually-returning-to-its-source (my act-continuing-to-realize-itself continually "sucks back" itself-already-realized). It illuminates the relative independence of my act-world-already-realized of, its relative anteriority with regard to the actual existential movement of my act (I "find" myself as an act-conditioned-by-itself-already-realized-in-this-specific-manner—a fact which my act cannot change *because it is created in this condition*). Finally, it illuminates the fact that my act-already-realized-conditioning-itself-continuing-to-realize-itself (my essence) is concretely identical with the world-already-existing-conditioning-my-act-unfolding-itself (my nature), even though the latter is made of pre-existent cosmico-biological material.

Let us now come back to the study of perception which was the starting-point of these new developments. Through the open window I see those houses which stand there along the street. In the process by which my life-act constitutes my world, it shapes those houses as luminous expressions of itself-incarnate-in-my-body (phase a)—while returning to its source, it fashions my percept as luminous expression of itself-incarnate-in-those-houses (phase b)—thus my act-continuing-to-constitute-those-houses-as-luminous-expression-of-itself (phase a) is continually conditioned by itself-already-illumined-in-those-houses (phase b): my perception-taking-place is continually moulded by my perception-having-already-taken-place (phase b). However, it is my perception-actually-taking-place (phase a) which is the existence of the whole perceptive system: my perception-having-already-taken-place (phase b) exists by and for my perception-continuing-to-take-place (phase a).

From these facts we understand in what consists the "passivity" of sensation. It does not reside in the dependence of my perceptive faculty on an "outward given" (a notion of intellectualistic origin), but in the fact that, in the very process of constituting those houses as myself-illumined, I find myself *already* illumined—that is, I am given to myself. Fundamentally, the passivity of my sensation is identical with my createdness.

iii. *Imagination*

As I carry on my different activities, thoughts and fancies continually cross my mind. In my study of my life-act-incarnate-in-my-body, I have indicated the nature of these phenomena as expressive variations of my life-act within the modalities of my brain. I shall now analyse their function as expressions of the totality of my act-world. As has been explained, my world is formed by my life-act unfolding itself from a centre—constituting my body with its different functions as the first expression of its self-realizing movement—constituting my environment with all its peculiarities, the universe with all its galaxies as the extension of my body (phase a)—returning to its source from all the places which it occupies and animates—and, in this regressive movement, conditioning itself-continuing-to-unfold-from-this-source (phase b). This totality is myself such as I exist from the first moment of my life, the fact in which all subsequent developments take place. We have just tried to understand the nature of sense perception as a modality of this integral movement. A few more remarks on this subject will help us to see the difference between sensation and imagination:

(1) *Within phase a*, there is *the fact* that my life-act unfolding from its centre constitutes my body and, as an extension of my body, those houses standing there along the street. My present perception, as a modality of phase a, is *this particular fact* becoming luminous *in a particular manner*: it is my act-incarnate-in-my-body making itself present to itself in those houses in the mode of visual perception.

(2) *Within phase b*, there is *the fact* that my life-act-already-existing-in-the-form-of-those-houses returns to its source and, in this process, conditions my life-act-continuing-to-unfold-from-this-source (continuing-to-constitute-my-body-and-those-houses). My present perception, as a modality of phase b, is *this particular fact* becoming luminous in a *particular manner*: it is my act-already-existing-luminously-in-the-form-of-those-houses conditioning my act-continuing-to-constitute-those-houses-as-particular-luminous-expression-of-itself.

These observations aim at emphasizing or, at least, at indicating the following points:

(1) Perception is essentially *factual*: it starts from a fact and develops within this fact. It is this fact illuminating itself.

(2) Perception is essentially particular:

(a) In so far as it takes place within a particular fact.

(b) In so far as it is this particular fact illuminating itself in a particular manner (that is, in the mode of visual, auditive, tactual . . . perception). By this we mean that perception, *as such*, is not a process which begins in the expressive core of the act-world—that is, in the centre which the life-act animates in a still undifferentiated manner, where it expresses itself comprehensively. Though the life-act in which perception takes place unfolds from this core, though it is essential that perception should take place in a life-act which unfolds from this expressive centre, yet, *as perception*, it begins in the perceptive apparatus—that is, in a place which is already at a certain distance from the nucleus, where the life-act—while unfolding itself—has already differentiated itself, specialized itself, impoverished itself. This fact explains the rather narrow, adhesive character of perception, its lack of plasticity.

Quite different is the "state of consciousness" formed by my life-act expressing itself to itself in the form of thoughts. To picture it, we must fully grasp the existential status of my life-act-incarnate-in-my-brain. This status can be characterized in this way:

(1) My life-act-incarnate-in-my-brain is my act-world possessing the whole of itself as a potentiality at the outset of its self-actuating movement; as such, it is my whole body and my whole world in an embryonic state. Though the concrete motions of my life-act-animating-my-brain may already refer to some particular aspects of my incarnate existence, yet, *de jure*, my act qua present in this central field is not yet specialized in a particular line (though already "temperamentalized", individuated), not yet narrowed down to one of its functions.

(2) However, my life-act-incarnate-in-my-brain is never in a state of pure indetermination, of pure inception. Indeed, as my brain is the centre towards which the universe-already-existing converges, the source towards which my act-already-unfolded returns, my life-act-incarnate-in-this-centre is *de jure* conditioned by the totality of itself-already-realized, by the totality of the world-already-constituted. This means that its movement is itself-already-determined-continuing-to-determine-itself, or the world-already-constituted-continuing-to-constitute-itself. *De facto*, the way in which this conditioning takes place depends upon particular factors such as the concrete circumstances in which I find myself, my particular biologico-affective comportment, my particular occupation, etc.

From these facts, it appears that the expressive field formed by the central modalities of my brain has a great plasticity. In them, my life-act can express itself to itself in many different ways—this means that it achieves in them a mode of consciousness which is of another order than that of perceptive consciousness. We can describe this mode of consciousness in the following way.

(1) To the extent that my life-act-incarnate-in-my-brain is in potency with regard to my body and to the whole world, my thoughts and imaginations are my act-world revealing itself to itself in the form of possibilities, eventualities, probabilities, wants; they are my life-act making itself present to itself in an atmosphere of non-actuality, of indeterminate expectancy.

(2) To the extent that my life-act-incarnating-itself-in-my-brain is my life-act-already-determined-continuing-to-unfold-itself, or the world-already-constituted-continuing-to-evolve, my thoughts and imaginations are my life-act-living-on-itself revealing itself to itself

in the form of non-reflective mental conceptions, of reminiscences, reveries; they are the continuation at a non-positional level of past reflections, the crystallization of past experiences, of psychological states.

(3) The two aspects of imaginative consciousness just mentioned must not be conceived as two distinct sectors. In fact, they are inseparable from each other: it is my act-world-already-realized which, in my brain, lives as potentiality, as universe-to-be. Therefore my prospective imaginations are charged with my experience, and my act-already-realized reveals itself to itself in an atmosphere of non-actuality, non-factualness.

(4) The factual character of my perceptions prevents them from being real creations of my psychological states. Within the perceptive situations my life-act is already cast into somewhat rigid and determined structures. This is why these situations, however much they let themselves be permeated by the various motions of my life-act, however much they reflect these motions, cannot be called products of these psychological variations. On the contrary, owing to the non-factual character of imaginative consciousness, to the plasticity of the cerebral expressive field, my mental conceptions appear often as real creations of my psychological states, of the various motions of my life-act-incarnate. These facts show that we can speak in a true sense of the realism, or "objectivity", of perceptive consciousness and of the non-realism, or "subjectivity", of imaginative consciousness.

iv. *Affectivity*

Our affectivity plays a very important role in the formation of the existential atmosphere which permeates our world. We have already seen how erroneous it is to consider our affective motions as mere products of our perceptions and cognitions. It is no less a mistake to conceive them as phenomena taking place within the restricted limits of our body. The geometrizing propensity of intellectualism is at the root of these two misconceptions. In fact, our affects are widely diffusive and deeply pervasive realities; to a very large extent, our world is made up of our desires and feelings.

Aspect a: In studying my life-act-incarnate-in-my-body, I have pointed out that my affects are my life-act accentuating consciously and in various ways the fundamental movement by which it shapes my body with its various functions. Some affective states, I remarked, are, as it were, motions of my whole life-act incarnate; others appear rather as pulsations of the act-living-in-the-form-of-a-particular-function. Now, as we know, my act-constituting-my-body is essentially my act-beginning-to-constitute-my-world. This implies that each of my affects, as a variation of my life-act, is an expansive phenomenon: it diffuses from my body, spreads in my environment, pervades my whole world. This is a fact which I have already mentioned and must once more emphasize.

It is a matter of experience that, at every moment, the concrete way in which my surroundings exist for me depends very much on my mood, on my particular affective disposition. My room-for-me-joyful is not the same reality as my room-for-me-depressed. Suppose at the moment of going out for a walk I am in a state of irritation: my anger is the atmosphere in which the street which I cross, the sun which beats down on my head, the moistness of the air, the hooting of a car are "existentified" for me. The moon in the sky does not shine for me in the same way when I am worried and when I am at peace. The train in which I travel does not vibrate in the same way when I feel tired and when I am alert. My neighbour-with-whom-I-talk-with-sympathy is not for me the same individual as my neighbour-whom-I-look-at-with-annoyance. The water which flows from the tap has for me a particular vital meaning when I feel thirsty. All these phenomena point to the same reality; my affective dispositions—even though they originate in my body—permeate from the start my whole life field; every peculiarity of my environment, every incident, reveals itself within my world as a concretion of my particular existential comportment. This fact shows once more that my existence *is* the existence of the world-for-me. In other words, there is nothing which takes place outside me. I exist qua world and the world exists qua myself. Every motion of my life-act is a wave which, though emitted from the centre of my world, pervades the entire system and modifies existentially all the peculiarities of this system.

Some of the examples just given show that at times my affective disposition may aim in a special manner at a definite portion of my life field—in other words, that it may shape, or intensify itself, in the relation which unites my body to a particular element of my world. My thirst, no doubt, confers to the water which flows from that tap a very particular significance, a significance which it does not confer to that banyan under which children are playing; similarly, my feeling of sympathy is directed at this gentleman who is sitting next to me, not at those trunks piled up in the corridor between the seats. However, even in such cases, the affective wave which binds my body to a definite portion of my life field is not simply confined within the limits of this situation; though it develops mainly in this particular structure, it shapes my whole world: however significantly my thirst may concrete itself in the particular system formed by my body-related-to-that-tap, it constitutes the existential mood by which my whole environment is permeated; however much my sympathy may be directed at this gentleman with whom I talk, it forms the atmosphere in which the entire compartment, my whole world, exists for me at the moment.

Aspect b: While pervading my environment, my affective motions never reduce it to a uniform whole. As I am crossing the street in a state of irritation, the heat of the sun, the moistness of the air, the hooting of a car do not become simply the undifferentiated field of my anger. Each of these elements keeps its individuality and expresses my feeling according to its particular modalities. Therefore, as it makes of my world the concretion of its present existential disposition, my life-act is conditioned by the structures of this expressive field as though they existed before the actual motion of my act. Let us analyse the broad context in which this phenomenon must be understood.

I have already explained that each affection implies as its substratum a certain biological situation, that it is a certain disposition of the body taken up by the act and lived by it in a particular manner. In this connection, I have pointed out that some situations are constitutional and others adventitious. The facts that we must understand are these: (1) All organic situations, as elements which condition the centrifugal movement of the life-act, are the terms of movements which originate in the world; (2) all the peculiarities of the world condition the affective motions of the life-act in so far as they are centripetal phenomena—that is, in so far as, converging towards the centre, they develop into organic situations.

The most fundamental situations are those which we call constitutional because they exist in some way from birth. These situations contribute first of all towards determining the temperamental inclination of the life-act incarnate. Their genesis must be understood in this way: there is *a certain basic manner in which the world converges* towards the expressive centre of the life-act—the peculiarities of the ambiance (considered in so far as they condition the centrifugal movement of the act in a particular fundamental manner), the constitutional organic situations (which evolve from the ambiance) come to existence *as concretions of this original movement;* they are the centripetal cosmico-biological system considered under its most fundamental aspect. All subsequent centripetal phenomena must be understood as variations, or evolutions, of this substratum—they are "experientialized" by the life-act according to its native disposition, according to its fundamental manner of being incarnate.

Let us analyse the structure of these adventitious phenomena, making use of some of the examples given above:

(1) The irritation which I feel when going out for a walk is a certain existential vibration of my life-act in its expressive field. First it is a motion of my act-incarnate-in-my-body. The substratum of this phenomenon is a certain variation, a disturbance of my biological system. Now this trouble is not an event taking place in my organism existing in itself, it is a fact occurring in my body-existing-in-dependence-on-my-environment: it is a way in which the world realizes itself in me, it is a way in which my ambiance at this moment conditions my act. This situation may be due to some particular circumstance, for example, the reading of an unpleasant letter. In this case, this letter-offering-itself-to-my-eyes has been the channel through which the world has shaped itself into this particular biological disturbance which persists in me even now. As I am crossing the street, the elements which make up my immediate surroundings reflect my feeling. In this respect, I remarked above that each of these factors contributes towards shaping my present psychological state *according to its particular modalities*—that is, as though it existed antecedently to the actual motion of my act. The point to be grasped is this: the heat of the sun, the moistness of the air, the hooting of a car condition my feeling *to the extent that they are one with the biological disturbance in which this feeling originates,* to the extent that they modify this central situation. This fact can be articulated in this way: my feeling-conditioned-by-these-factors is my feeling-originating-in-my-expressive-centre—therefore these factors-conditioning-my-feelings are these factors-converging-towards-my-expressive-centre (-and-realizing-themselves-in-it-in-the-form-of-my-present-biological-situation).

(2) The thirst I feel as I am looking at the water which flows from that tap is also a vibration of my life-act developing within a particular

biological situation. Like the "irritating" disposition just analysed, this situation is a modality of my body-existing-in-dependence-on-its-environment. Now, if my thirst confers a particular vital meaning to that tap—a meaning which it does not confer to the other objects which surround me—it is because the water which flows from it has from the start a very special relation to me-thirsty, it is because my thirst-*originating-in-my-body* is from the start conditioned in a particular manner by that tap; but, if my thirst-*originating-in-my-body* is modified in a special way by a definite element of my life field, this element must be in some way present in my body, *it must be one which the organic situation which underlies my thirst*—therefore that tap-conditioning-my-thirst is that tap-passing-into-my-body-and-existing-in-it-in-the-form-of-my-present-biological-situation.

In short: (a) my present biological situation (which my life-act "experientializes" in the form of thirst) exists as the convergence of the world; (b) each part of my life field, to the extent that it conditions my thirst, exists as a significant modality of the world-converging-towards-my-body-and-hypostatizing-itself-in-it-in-the-form-of-my-present-biological-situation.

The role which sensation plays in all these processes should be noted. It is a fact that the heat of the sun, the moistness of the air, the hooting of a car reflect my irritation and modify it through the perception I have of them; it is a fact also that the tap expresses my thirst and conditions it through the vision I have of it. I shall analyse these facts when dealing with the complementariness of the different modalities of my life-act incarnate.

Complementariness of the two aspects: I have shown that my affects are centrifugal motions of my life-act which express themselves in a concrete manner in my body and in my world (aspect a); I have shown also that, antecedently to the actual motion of my act, there is the fact that the world converging towards my body shapes itself in it into a particular biological situation and, through this modification of my organism, determines my present affective disposition (aspect b). Now, it must be noted that this aspect b, however much it precedes the actual centrifugal movement of my act, exists by and for (that is, in dependence on) this movement which is my existence. Moreover, it must be noted that my life-act-conditioned-by-my-present-organic-situation-and-through-it-by-the-world is not my life-act-conditioned-by-something-extrinsic, but my life-act-incarnate-conditioned-by-itself. Indeed, the conditioning virtue of the world-existing-centripetally comes entirely from my life-act: if the moistness of the air conditions my act in *this* particular manner, it is not because this peculiarity of my environment determines me "from outside" according to its particular modalities, it is because my life-act animates it, constitutes it as a definite concretion of its present disposition and, *at the same time*, finds itself given to itself qua act-living-in-it-in-*this*-concrete-manner—in other words, it is because my act is created. This remark applies *mutatis mutandis* to the road which I am crossing, the heat of the sun, the hooting of a car—in short, to all the peculiarities of my environment: the fact that they condition my affective disposition is the fact that, in the very process of making them exist as concretions of its existential motion, my life-act finds itself given to itself, conditioned by itself-incarnate-in-them. This is the perspective in which I must understand also how the unpleasant letter provoked me to anger: my life-act constituted that situation formed by my body-in-my-room, my hand holding the letter, my eyes fixed on it, and, in the very process of animating it, found itself vibrating in it in that specific manner. The tap conditions my thirst similarly. The water which flows from it does not fascinate me "from outside". My life-act-incarnate-in-my-body makes it exist as a concretion of its present affect and, at the very same moment, finds itself solicited by itself-incarnate-in-it.

All these facts must be understood within the broad movement of my existence as disclosed to me by my previous reflections. My act continually comes to existence in a pre-existing universe and recasts it into its own life field—it unfolds from a definite centre and, in this movement, constitutes my body as the concretion of its potentiality and my world as the extension of my body, the actuation of its potentialities (phase a). No sooner has my life-act thus posited itself than it returns to its source from all the places which it occupies and animates and, in this regressive movement, conditions itself-continuing-to-unfold-from-this-source (phase b). As I am crossing the street, my life-act makes of the peculiarities of my environment concretions of its present affect (phase a)—my act returns from everywhere to its source and, in this process, conditions itself-continuing-to-constitute-the-world-as-expression-of-itself (phase b). Thus, as I am crossing the street in a state of irritation, I am continually conditioned by myself-existing-already-irritated-in-my-environment, or by my irritation-already-incarnate-in-the-peculiarities-of-my-surroundings, or by the various-aspects-of-my-environment-already-existing-as-concretions-of-my-anger (these three expressions are synonymous).

In this dynamic system, we notice the following:

(1) Phase b (my concrete essence) has no existence apart from phase a (my concrete existence). In other words: my life-act-continuing-to-constitute-the-world-as-the-concretion-of-itself (or my act-continually-ahead-of-itself) is the existence of my act-already-existing-in-the-form-of-a-world (or of the world-already-existing-as-the-concretion-of-my-act).

(2) However, phase b has a certain priority with regard to phase a:

(a) in so far as it is made of pre-existing cosmico-biological material;
(b) in so far as it is my act-*having*-realized-itself conditioning my act-continuing-to-realize-itself.

Let us conclude this study of affectivity with a few complementary remarks:

(1) There is no possibility of classifying rigidly the different situations in which the life-act can find itself incarnate in order to establish what type of situation is *always* "experientialized" by the act as "irritating" situation, what other type is "experientialized" as "pleasing" situation, etc. As we know, each situation is lived by the act according to its temperamental disposition—that is, according to its fundamental manner of being incarnate. This fact must be understood in this way: from the centre where it comes to existence, the life-act constitutes the body as the concretion of its fundamental disposition and the whole world as the actuation of this basic potentiality—from all the places which it animates, the act returns to its source and, in this process, conditions itself-continuing-to-constitute-the-world. Thus, as it shapes the world as the concretion of its basic existential project *the act finds itself continually conditioned by its fundamental-disposition-already-existing-in-the-form-of-a-world,* or by the world-already-existing-as-the-concretion-of-its-individuality—in other words, the act finds itself continually "temperamentalized". This dynamic system is the basic movement of the act, its individual *esse* of which every subsequent affect is an evolution, a variation, an expression. The root of this individualization is not primarily the unique "composition" of the cosmico-biological structures in which the act is incarnate, but the fact that

the life-act exists as the product of a Unique Creative Intention. This perspective allows us to grasp the fundamental reason why each situation in which the act finds itself incarnate is lived by it in a deeply individual and incommunicable manner.

There are two other factors which prevent us from classifying the different situations into rigid types:

(a) the fact that the life-act is never fully determined by itself-already-realized, but always ahead of itself—that is, continually transcending the situation in which it is incarnate,

(b) the fact that the way in which the act lives a situation depends very much on the mood in which it already finds itself when this situation is brought about.

I shall analyse these two factors when studying the temporality of the act.

(2) There is no possibility of reducing each affective motion, as it takes place concretely, to an abstract pattern, to an archetype to which it must necessarily conform. Indeed, as each affect is an expression of the temperamental disposition of the life-act, it has always a deeply individual character—it can never be abstracted from the current of a particular existence. Moreover, each affect occurs in an already existing particular affective context, expresses this context, and is conditioned by it. This fact also will be studied in the chapter dealing with the temporality of the act. Finally, it must be noticed that feelings, as they exist concretely, are usually "mixed". This does not mean that they are blendings of various "simple" affects. Indeed, each affective state is a structural whole which has a fundamental unity, even though it manifests a certain complexity. Each aspect of this structure receives from all the others its concrete mode of being: it is concretely one with all the others. An affective state which can be described as a state of irritation, fright, and antipathy is not a mixture of these three feelings but an original unity the various aspects of which have neither existence nor substance apart from each other. Living reality is not made up of abstract essences blended together, it is prior to any concept we use in order to express it, and irreducible to any single notion. This is why we have to struggle with language when we want to "get back to things".

(3) I have pointed out that, in the intellectualistic perspective, as each perception is a particular synthesis, our "perceptive life" must be conceived as a succession of particular perceptions. Now intel-

lectualism considers feeling as a psychological state essentially derived from sense perception or cognition. This means that our "affective life" follows the pattern of our "perceptive life": it is a succession of affective states each of which is the product of a particular perception.

This conception is hardly reconcilable with facts. I shall shortly analyse how perception and affectivity are related *de facto*. It will be enough for the present to realize that our affective life is essentially a continuous, though varying, process. As the act unfolds itself, the cosmico-biological structures in which it incarnates itself are in a state of continual fluctuation. As the expressive field of the act passes from one state to another, the act experiences a change in its manner of living—that is, in its affective disposition. Such modifications of the expressive field may be brought about either *mainly* by an initiative of the life-act, or *mainly* "from outside". The first process will be analysed in this chapter at a further stage of our investigation. About the second process, a few words of explanation can already be given. As we know, the life-act comes to existence *in an already existing universe* and continually re-creates this universe into its own life field, into the concretion of its own self-realizing movement (phase a)—as it does so, it is continually conditioned by the world existing as the concretion of itself—that is, by itself-existing-in-the-form-of-a-world (phase b). Now this universe which the act constantly takes up is subject to continual changes; therefore we must say that the life-act comes to existence *in a fluctuating universe* and continually recasts this universe into its expressive field (phase a)—as it does so, it is continually conditioned by the fluctuating world existing as the concretion of itself—that is, by itself-existing-qua-fluctuating-reality (phase b). These facts explain how the life-act, even though it is conditioned by variations of its expressive field which may be due originally to some agency other than itself, is, in reality, never conditioned by anything else than itself-incarnate. These facts show also why all the changes which take place in the environment are experienced from the start by the act as modalities of its own existence, are lived by it as concretions of its temperamental inclination. These changes, it is clear, to the extent that they are "experientialized" by the act in the form of various affective states, do not condition the act-unfolding-itself as isolated phenomena which take place somewhere in the environment; they do so in so far as, passing into the organism, they develop into modifications of the expressive centre of the life-act—that is, in so far as they are identified with the regressive movement of the act incarnate (phase b).

v. *Complementariness of Perception, Imagination, Affectivity*

In the various analyses that I have just made, much has already been said about the complementariness of perception, imagination, and affectivity, a point I shall now examine more in detail. The fact to be stressed is not merely that these states are related to one another, but that they have no existence and no meaning whatsoever apart from each other.

(1) I have shown how my temperamental individuality expresses itself in my different affective dispositions, in my way of looking at the world, and of living the various situations in which I find myself. There is no need to dwell further on this point. Let us remember that the reason for this immanence of my basic existential attitude in all the different aspects of my incarnate consciousness is the fact that all these aspects are constituted by, exist within, my life-act-temperamentalized.

(2) In the study of perception, I have alluded to the diversity of senses, showing that the various types of percepts are different modes in which the world reveals itself to itself in my body. It must be noted now that the different perceptive structures are not insulated phenomena which do not communicate with one another. The world does not offer itself to my perception as a variety of forms and colours accompanied by a certain amount of sounds, but as a unity which is entire in each aspect under which it reveals itself. Noises rise from the street and fill my room. *In them,* I perceive all the traffic, the whole street with its agitation. A screech pierces the air. *This, as I hear it,* is a jet speeding through the sky. Palm leaves are swinging. *I see* the wind rustling in them. *I see* the intense heat of an iron bar reddened in the fire. "One sees the hardness and brittleness of glass, and when, with a tinkling sound, it breaks, this sound is conveyed by the visible glass. One sees the springiness of steel, the ductility of red-hot steel, the hardness of a plane blade, the softness of shavings. The form of objects is not their geometrical shape: it stands in a certain relation to their specific nature, and appeals to all our other senses as well as sight. The form of a fold in linen or cotton shows us the resilience or dryness of the fibre, the coldness or warmth

of the material. Furthermore, the movement of visible objects is not the mere transference from place to place of coloured patches which, in the visual field, correspond to those objects. In the jerk of the twig from which a bird has just flown, we read its flexibility or elasticity, and it is thus that a branch of an apple-tree or a birch are immediately distinguishable. One sees the weight of a block of cast iron which sinks in the sand, the fluidity of water and the viscosity of syrup. In the same way, I hear the hardness and unevenness of cobbles in the rattle of a carriage, and we speak appropriately of a 'soft', 'dull' or 'sharp' sound. Though one may doubt whether the sense of hearing brings us genuine 'things', it is at least certain that it presents us, beyond the sounds in space, with something which 'murmurs', and in this way communicates with the other senses. Finally, if, with my eyes closed, I bend a steel bar and a lime branch, I perceive in my hands the most essential texture of the metal and the wood. If, then, taken as incomparable qualities, the 'data of the different senses' belong to so many separate worlds, each one in its particular essence being a manner of modulating the thing, they all communicate through their significant core."[13] These experiences make us realize that no particular aspect under which an object is perceived ever presents itself as "just itself", it is always an expression of the whole object; even if this aspect is related to one of our senses in a particular manner, all our senses are involved in its perception to the degree to which the object which expresses itself under this aspect has a meaning for them.

(3) However different imaginative consciousness and perceptive consciousness may be, there is a close relation between them. My thoughts and imaginations, as has been pointed out, are self-expressive variations of my act-world in the modalities of my brain. Now, to the extent that my expressive centre exists as the convergence of the world—that is, as the termination of the regressive movement of my life-act (phase b)—my thoughts are derived from my sensations. Let us explain this assertion.

As we know, the regressive movement of my life-act is 'my-life-act-already-realized-in-the-form-of-a-world'-conditioning-'my-act-continuing-to-realize-itself'. Now my life-act-realized-in-the-form-of-a-world is the world-existing-as-the-actuation-of-my-central-potentiality—that is, the world-existing-as-the-extension-of-my-body, or the world-constituted-by-the-unfolding-of-my-act-from-

[13] Merleau-Ponty, *op. cit.*, pp. 229–30.

its-expressive-centre-through-the-functions-of-my-body. Perception is this reality illuminating itself in various ways: it is my life-act-revealed-to-itself-in-various-ways-in-the-world-which-it-constitutes, or 'the-world-constituted-by-the-unfolding-of-my-life-act'-revealing-my-act-to-itself-in-various-ways. In consequence, the regressive movement of my act (i.e., 'my-life-act-already-realized'-conditioning-'my-act-continuing-to-realize-itself'), *to the extent that it is a luminous process*, is *primarily* 'the-world-existing-as-my-life-act-revealed-to-itself-in-various-ways'-conditioning-'my-life-act-continuing-to-constitute-the-world-as-the-luminous-expression-of-itself'. This perspective shows that my thoughts—*in so far as they are luminous variations of my expressive-centre-existing-as-the-termination-of-the-regressive-movement-of-my-life-act*—are my sensations developed into a more integrated type of consciousness.

This derivation of imaginative consciousness from perceptive consciousness is not always an actual process in the sense that my life-act-illuminating-itself-in-the-form-of-thoughts is always the integration at a higher level of my life-act-illuminating-itself-*in-my-present-environment*-in-the-mode-of-perceptive-consciousness, but it is always real in the sense that my thoughts—even if they are reminiscences, crystallization, of psychological states—are always my *act-world*-illuminating-itself-in-some-way-in-the-modalities-of-my-brain.

The looseness of the relation between my thoughts and my actual perceptions is due to the difference between the existential status of my life-act-incarnate-in-my-brain and that of my life-act-incarnate-in-my-body-related-to-my-environment. As I have pointed out, my life-act-incarnate-in-the-various-structures-of-my-organism-and-in-my-world is my act-already-realized-in-a-concrete-manner—from this fact arises the factual, adhesive character of my perceptive consciousness. On the other hand, my life-act-incarnate-in-my-brain is my life-act-existing-in-a-state-of-relatively-undetermined-potentiality—hence, the non-factual, non-positional character of my imaginative consciousness. Now, if my thoughts were necessarily derived from my actual perceptions, my imagination would be a strictly determined and factual type of consciousness. This would indicate that my life-act-incarnate-in-my-brain is, like my life-act-incarnate-in-my-body-related-to-my-world, narrowly adherent to the modalities of my present situation. But this is not the case: the relative indetermination of imaginative consciousness points to the transcendence of my life-act-incarnate-in-my-brain with regard to the concrete situation in which I actually find myself.

Nevertheless, the fact remains that my imaginative consciousness is derived from my perceptive consciousness—in other words, that my thoughts are always '*my-life-act-existing-in-the-form-of-a-world*'-illuminating-itself-in-some-way-in-the-modalities-of-my-brain-while-conditioning-'my-life-act-continuing-to-constitute-the-world-as-the-concretion-of-itself'. This shows us that my life-act-incarnate-in-my-brain is never in a state of pure undetermined potentiality, but that it is to some extent determined by itself-already-realized. In the chapter dealing with the temporality of my life-act, I shall show further how this dependence of my imaginative consciousness on my perceptive consciousness must be understood.

Now, if my thoughts *are derived* from my sensations, it must also be acknowledged that the way in which my life-act illuminates itself in the modalities of my brain *influences* the way in which it illuminates itself in my sensorial-apparatus-related-to-my-environment. However undetermined my life-act-incarnate-in-my-brain may be *de jure*, the fact that it illuminates itself at a given moment in the form of a particular thought or imagination indicates that *de facto* it already determines itself in a particular direction. Now my life-act-animating-my-expressive-centre is essentially my life-act-beginning-to-constitute-my-body-and-my-world. Therefore the incipient motion of my life-act, of which my particular thought is the expression, tends to actuate itself in my body and in my environment. This movement naturally modifies, influences, my perception of the world, since my perceptive consciousness is my life-act-illuminating-itself-while-constituting-my-world. Sometimes the motion of my life-act-incarnate-in-my-brain, of which my thoughts are the expression, is at variance with the actual movement of my life-act-animating-my-body-and-my-environment. Following the natural dynamism of the life-act, this motion, however, tends to actuate itself in my organism and in my world. When this phenomenon takes place, an atmosphere of dream and unreality pervades my life-field: my life-act, though constituting the structures of my body-related-to-my-world and living in them in the form of a particular behaviour, is, by some part of itself, disengaged from these structures—by this part of itself, however, it does not constitute a world of facts, since it tends to create life structures which do not fit in with those which my act constitutes *de facto*. As a result of this complex situation, my perceptive consciousness loses much of its realism and factualness, my perception of my surroundings becomes vague and absent.[14]

From all these observations, it should be clear that the interpenetration of my imaginative and perceptive consciousness must not be conceived as an exchange of "species" between two "cognitive faculties", but as a vital process. My thoughts depend on my sensations to the extent that my life-act-illuminating-itself-in-my-brain is conditioned by itself-already-illuminated-in-the-mode-of-perceptive-consciousness—that is, by itself-already-existing-luminously-in-the-form-of-a-world, or by the world-already-constituted-as-the-luminous-concretion-of-itself. On the other hand, my imaginative consciousness expresses itself in my perceptive consciousness to the degree to which the various motions of my life-act-incarnate-in-my-brain unfold themselves in the structures of my body-related-to-my-environment.

(4) In all the preceding analyses, I have already said much about the interrelation between my life-act-revealing-itself-to-itself (i.e., my imaginative and perceptive consciousness) and my affectivity. It is important to understand that the whole problem is not solved either by affirming that all affects follow an "act of knowledge", or by declaring that perception and imagination are products of our affectivity. Only a careful analysis of the concrete structure of our life can make us grasp the nature of affectivity and its relation to our thoughts and sensations.

The basic fact from which this analysis must start is the fact of my existence as a life-act incarnate. I am given to myself as a life-act co-extensive with the world, but animating the world from a definite centre.

Phase a: At the very outset of its self-actuating movement, my life-act frames itself into my brain and—as an actuation of itself-incarnate-in-this-expressive-nucleus (i.e., of my cerebral potentiality)—into my body. Expanding further, my life-act constitutes (a) my

[14] "As he walked he began to sing.

'Alas, my love, you do me wrong,
To cast me off discourteously,
And I have loved you so long,
Delighting in your company.'

"It was a yearning and mysterious tune. He used to sing it with Molly under the Plain, and for a moment he felt the wind in his face and felt the turf under his feet and saw Shrewford Ring before his eyes, and stopped singing.

"He began again. He was in Coromandel."

John Masters, *Coromandel!*, p. 118.

environment with all its diversity as the actuation of itself-incarnate-in-my-body, (b) my whole world as the widening of my environment, as my total life field. These facts show us that my body as the *fons et origo* of my world, and my world as the unfolding of my organic potentiality, are my life-act-realizing-and-expressing-itself. Each detail of my environment is a modality of this fundamental movement; in relation to my body, it exists as a particular crystallization of my act-constituting-its-life-field.

Phase b: Concomitantly, from every point of itself-unfolded, my life-act returns to its source. In so far as they are constituted by this regressive movement, my brain in relation to my body, my body in relation to my environment, to my whole world, exist as 'my-life-act-already-realized-in-a-concrete-manner'-conditioning-'my-life-act-continuing-to-realize-and-express-itself'. Each detail of my life field, as a modality of this conditioning process, is 'my-life-act-already-crystallized-in-a-particular-manner'-determining-'my-act-continuing-to-constitute-its-life-field'.

Taking now into account the concrete unity of these two aspects, I affirm the following:

(a) My brain is my life-act continually conditioned by itself-already-disposed-in-a-certain-manner while disposing itself to its further unfolding in my body and in my world.

(b) Each detail of my environment in relation to my body is my life-act modulating itself in a particular manner within itself-already-modulated.

These considerations—which do not introduce anything new—aim at stressing the fact that *each part of my existential field is fundamentally constituted by my act-living-in-a-particular-manner*. To come to the point, this means that there is a fundamental priority of affectivity with regard to sensation and imagination: every perception and mental conception is my act-illuminating-itself-*while-living-in-a-particular manner*; thus every perception and mental conception takes place essentially within an affective current. This affective current, in its deepest reality, must not be conceived as a stream of feelings but as the original movement of my act, my individual *esse*, the existential wave which constitutes the totality of my world, which gives to every detail of my life field its being for me. I call this current "affective" because, in it, I possess my fundamental way of being "affected", of being "modulated", of vibrating; and secondly, because all my subsequent affective motions are modifications, expressions, of this original life stream. The particular tonicity of this whole system depends initially on the existential structure of my life-act-incarnate-in-my-body.

How do my subsequent affective motions occur? Not necessarily through the medium of any sensation or imagination. Without there being any "act of knowledge", I may experience thirst, hunger, fatigue, anguish, depression, irritation, consolation, peace, contentment, etc. All these feelings are existential modifications of my life-act developing within particular situations; they are ways in which my act lives the cosmico-biological setting by which it is conditioned. Each of these affective motions, as soon as it takes place, pervades my whole life field and thus constitutes the atmosphere in which my environment and whatever is contained in it are made to exist for me.

Of course, whatever perception "accompanies" such affects will always reflect them. To take an example that illustrates this phenomenon: For some unknown reason, I feel myself in a state of euphoria. As I enter my room after a walk, the different objects which offer themselves to my sight somehow express this happiness; I see them as various concretions of this inner contentment; I see my whole room as a portion of space which this feeling permeates, inhabits, enlivens. How must I understand this fact? First, let us remember the nature of perception: it is my life-act illuminating in a particular manner the movement by which it realizes itself. At this moment, this movement is first of all the process by which my act, unfolding from its centre, constitutes (a) my body, (b) my room and all the objects it contains, (c) my whole world as its life field. This process is, as it exists now, the original life-stream of which I spoke above, the existential wave of which each object-in-relation-to-my-body is a particular modulation. My perception of my room and of all the things it contains is first of all this fundamental affective current illuminating itself in a particular manner. But there is something more: at this particular moment, the basic disposition of my life-act is actuated into this particular mood which I call my present state of euphoria. Following the natural movement of my act, this mood takes hold of my environment, pervades my whole world. This is why my perception of my room, and all the objects which offer themselves to my sight, reflect my contentment.

Not only my perceptions, but also my thoughts and imaginations express my feelings. The way in which this is done and the difference between the way in which my mental conceptions crystallize my emotions and that in which my sensations reflect them are clear enough from what has already been explained.

Thus I have shown the basic priority of affectivity with regard to perception and imagination. Following upon that, I must acknowledge now that many of my affective states are indeed the result of some perception or thought. It is a fact that some of my thoughts rejoice me, others sadden me, others excite in me some desire, some other kind of emotion; it is a fact also that, by seeing or hearing something, I often feel myself moved in one way or another. How must I conceive this derivation of affects from mental conceptions and perceptions?

First, it must be emphasized that these sensations and imaginations always take place within a basic affective context which can already be accentuated in some particular manner—they belong to a living individual, not to a pure knowing subject. In other words, my sensations and imaginations are my life-act illuminating in some way its existential movement as it takes place concretely. Now it happens that my life-act, while making itself present to itself in the mode of perceptive or imaginative consciousness in the process by which it unfolds itself, "experientializes" in a new way itself-illuminated-in-this-particular-manner—thus a perception, or a passing thought, gives rise in me to some definite affect. As I enter my room, my eyes fall on a letter which has been put on my table during my absence. This perception immediately provokes in me a certain pleasure and curiosity. What has happened? As I am coming into my room, my act, unfolding from its expressive centre, constitutes my body in motion, my room and all the objects it contains, my eyes falling on the letter lying on the table—it shapes this whole setting as itself-living-in-a-particular-manner-and-revealing-itself-to-itself-in-a-particular-manner. As it finds itself in this situation, my act, conditioned by itself-thus-existing, begins to vibrate in a new way—in other words, my perception of the letter lying on the table arouses in me pleasure and curiosity. Now, as I take the letter from where it lies, a certain thought occurs to me which immediately (without the mediation of any reflection) tends to transform these feelings into a certain sentiment of apprehension. I still look at the letter with curiosity; the contentment I experienced when my eyes fell on it is still there; yet a new emotion tries to substitute itself for these affects and to change them into a different psychological complex. Let us note carefully that this new development is a process which takes place entirely within my life-act incarnate. The disturbing thought which gives rise to my sentiment of apprehension is my life-act-revealing-itself-to-itself-in-a-particular-manner-in-the-modalities-of-my-brain. The fact that my act can express itself in this way while evolving in itself those affects which I call pleasure and curiosity indicates that these two motions (which in fact are two aspects of a single emotive state) are not the whole of my life-act incarnate. There are in myself-incarnate existential strata which do not manifest themselves *explicitly* in all my affective states, yet are capable of coming to the surface, even though the actual motions of my life-act seem to exclude them.[15] The study of the temporality of my life-act incarnate will throw further light on this point. The fact to be noted is that, as soon as it illuminates itself in this new way, my life-act experiences in itself a new existential vibration: my sentiment of apprehension. Following the natural movement of the act, this motion immediately tends to actuate itself in my whole life field, and thus to transform the existential atmosphere of my world—it tends to make me see in a new way the letter which I hold in my hand.

All these observations show that the process by which perception or imagination influences activity cannot be conceived as a causal action exercised by a "cognitive faculty" upon an "affective faculty". There is not first of all an "act of perception", or an "act of imagination", specified by an "external object", and then an "act of sensitive appetite" motivated by the former; there is no such thing as the transmission to the "appetitive faculty", by the senses or the imagination, of a "concept of the object"; there is the fact that my life-act, which is from the first co-extensive with its environment, with the whole world, finding itself incarnate in various situations and illuminating itself in these situations in the mode of perceptive or imaginative consciousness, "experientializes" in various ways itself-thus-incarnate-and-thus-illumined. Thus the whole process takes place within my life-act incarnate, not in the form of an action of one faculty upon another, of a succession of distinct acts, but in the form of a continuous movement which has, no doubt, various aspects,

[15] To understand this let us remember that *all* my affective states are in some way expressions of the basic existential movement of my life-act. This means that the pleasure and curiosity I experienced when seeing the letter were not pleasure and curiosity in general, but deeply individualized feelings which in their concreteness already expressed—however implicitly—the whole of my affective potentiality.

various moments—which are called perception, imagination, affective motion—but which remains entire in each one of its expressions: no abstract theorizing, but only an experiential contact with living reality, can make us discover how the various psychological facets of our incarnate existence are *de facto* related to one another.

B. My World as the Expressive Field of My Integral Personal Act

In the preceding section, I have analysed my act-world in so far as it is a process which unfolds itself without being self-determined, self-controlled—my "phenomenal" individuality (this expression being taken, as has been explained, in a relative sense). Going one step further, I must now study my personal world—that is, the whole reality constituted by my life-act-realizing-itself-through-my-act-project.

As we know, my life-act-incarnate-in-my-brain is in a state of indetermination, potentiality. Now, as it illuminates itself "imaginatively", it takes possession of itself, determines itself—in short, transcends itself into an act-volition, into an act-project. Thus personalized, my act reshapes my body, my whole world into the concretion of its transcendental dynamism, of its reflective movement towards its ultimate realization. I shall now examine in detail my integral personal act first as an act reflecting upon itself; secondly as a voluntary movement incarnating itself in my environment, in my whole world; thirdly as both things indivisibly combined and one; finally, I shall describe the taking up of my phenomenal act-world in the movement of my transcendental existence.[16]

1. The Reflectiveness of My Personal Act-World

In the modalities of my brain, my life-act is present in a synthetic, though largely non-actuated, unrealized manner. Whatever determination it reveals comes mainly from the fact that it is conditioned by itself-already-actuated (phase b) and, through itself-already-actuated, by the world-already-existing—thus its determination may be on the whole characterized as phenomenal. But even this determination is not truly realized in my life-act-incarnate-in-my-brain; indeed, my act-already-actuated-in-the-form-of-a-world lives on in my brain in an atmosphere of non-actuality, non-factualness—it

[16] Cf. plan followed in "B. My Body as the Incarnation of My Integral Personal Act," iv, pp. 79ff.

reveals itself to itself in the mode of imaginative non-positional consciousness.

However, as it illuminates itself in this way, my life-act apprehends itself as an act-in-tension-towards-an-end, and thereby becomes self-possessed—it transcends itself into an act-volition. This accession of my life-act to true personal existence is identically the process by which it begins to actuate itself in a free, self-controlled manner—that is, the process by which, shaking off its basic indetermination, it converts itself into a luminously self-determined act-project, into a personal appetence for its end. Thus actuated, my act expresses itself to itself in a new way in the central modalities of my brain—it reveals itself to itself in the mode of reflective consciousness.

Difference between Reflective and Imaginative Consciousness

Let us note well the difference between reflection and imagination. It derives from the difference between the existential status of my act-world-incarnate-in-my-brain-as-mere-life-act and that of my act-world-incarnate-in-my-brain-as-act-volition. As I have just said, my life-act-incarnate-in-my-brain is in a state of relatively undetermined potentiality and, therefore, my imaginative consciousness is non-factual, non-positional. By contrast, my act-volition is my life-act-determining-itself, my life-act-actuating-its-potentiality-in-a-self-controlled-manner. Therefore my reflective consciousness will be characterized by actualness, it will be a "realistic", positional, factual type of consciousness.

Difference between Reflective and Perceptive Consciousness

However, its "realism" will not be of the same type as the factualness of my perceptive consciousness (as it has been described previously). Again, the difference between the two is due to the difference between the existential status of my life-act incarnate in the various structures of my body-related-to-its-environment and that of my act-present-in-my-brain-as-act-volition. My life-act-incarnate-in-my-body-related-to-my-world is my life-act diversifying, specifying, itself in various ways. As we know, this movement is not self-controlled. To a very great extent, my life-act-incarnate-in-specific-ways-in-the-structure-of-my-organism-related-to-my-environment is my life-act determined by itself-already-realized-in-various-ways and, through it, by the world-already-constituted; therefore its determination is mainly phenomenal. To this fact are due the lack of freedom of my life - act - existing - in - the - structures - of - my - body - related-to-my-surroundings, and also the narrow, particular, adhesively factual character of my perceptive knowledge. My act-volition, conversely, is free: it transcends the cosmico-biological structures in which it incarnates itself (i.e., itself-already-realized and the world-already-constituted); it transcends the indetermination of my life-act-incarnate-in-the-modalities-of-my-brain; it is my act determining itself as it proceeds from its Creative Source. Therefore the determination of my act-volition is transcendental. Consequently, the factualness of my reflective consciousness is universal, it overflows the limits of the situation in which my act is incarnate.

These preliminary statements need, of course, the clarification which, I hope, the following considerations will provide.

My Personal-Act-Illuminating-Itself is Identically:

(a) **The World-Illuminating Itself-in-Me,**

(b) **My Situation-Illuminating-Itself-in-Me**

I am created as a life-act continually ahead of itself, in tension towards an end. This moving forward, which is my very existence, is identically the movement of the universe-in-me towards its completion. This is the fundamental fact in which and by which subsists whatever pertains to me in any way. Now, as it constitutes my brain as its first expressive centre and illuminates itself in this centre, my life-act takes possession of itself. Apprehending—at least vaguely—its end, it ordains itself towards it in a self-determined, self-controlled manner, it affirms itself as personal act-project. Thus the universe-in-me is truly personalized, its progress towards its completion becomes a self-governed endeavour. Now, this existential moving forward of my personal act-world is essentially reflective. In the central modalities of my brain my personal-act-in-tension-towards-its-end illuminates itself continually in order to possess itself in a more and more penetrating and comprehensive manner. This process of self-penetration must be understood as a modality of the existential movement of my act-incarnating-itself. From the centre in which it realizes itself as life project, my act expresses itself continually in my body, in my environment, in my whole world, and constitutes them as concretions of its transcendental movement (phase a)—from all the places which it thus occupies and animates, my personal act returns to its source and, in this regressive movement, conditions itself-continuing-to-unfold-from-this-source (phase b). This conditioning of my personal-act-incarnate shows that *my personal-act-illuminating-itself-in-the-modalities-of-its-expressive-centre-at-the-outset-of-its-self-realizing-movement is always my act-illuminating-itself-within-'itself-already-realized-in-the-form-of-a-world'*, or '*my-act-already-realized-in-the-form-of-a-world'-illuminating-itself-within-'itself-continuing-to-unfold-itself'*.

Now, it must be noted that my personal act is always incarnate in a particular situation. At this moment, my act constitutes my body situated in my room, my room situated in this house, this house situated in a definite place in Calcutta, Calcutta immersed in the chilly atmosphere of this winter morning; at the same time, my act finds itself involved within itself-already-existing-in-the-form-of-this-winter-morning,-of-Calcutta,-of-this-house,-of-my-room,-of-my-body. This means that my personal act-illuminating-itself-within-the-modalities-of-my-brain is, at this moment, my act-illuminating-itself-within-'itself-already-existing-in-the-form-of-this-particular-situation', or 'my-act-existing-in-the-form-of-this-particular-situation' illuminating-itself-within-'itself-continuing-to-constitute-this-situation-as-the-concretion-of-its-self-realizing-movement'. In other words, this means that, at every moment, the reflectiveness of my personal act—that is, its luminous presence to itself in the modalities of my brain—*is* my transcendental consciousness of my situation, and that *my awareness of this situation* (of every particular object) *is always identical with the luminous self-expression of my personal act in its centre.*

Therefore there is no Gap between the "Intellect" and the "Objective World"

These facts show once more that the problem of the relationship between the "external reality" and the "intellect" is a false problem. Intellectualistic problematic, based as it is upon erroneous presuppositions, directs philosophical investigation on a wrong track, leads to artificial solutions, and to the building of theories which do not have any close connection with experience. The mistaken presuppositions at the root of this problematic are:

(1) The notion of the world as an objective sphere of being which offers itself first of all as a *cognoscibile*, a reality which subsists "in itself" and must be known as it is.

(2) The notion of man as a subject distinct from the world, but able to know it "objectively"—that is, as it is "in itself".

(3) Consequently, the idea that the relation between the world and man is first of all a relation of knowledge.

(4) The notion of the intellect as an independent "faculty" whose operations can be studied apart from the consideration of the whole personal activity—and, what is more, the notion of intellect as the principle which constitutes the very essence of man.

(5) The notion of knowledge as a synthesis whose components can be analysed and sharply distinguished from one another.

(6) The idea that a valid "theory of knowledge" can be built independently of a "theory of voluntary activity", of a "theory of affectivity", etc.

In reality, the world is not a *cognoscibile* "ontologically" distinct from me, but my life field, the total unfolding and incarnation of my personal life-act; I am not a spectator facing the world, a disincarnate "I know" separate from reality, but I am the world living a personal existence, tending in a conscious and deliberate manner towards its end. Consequently, any investigation I may carry out in order to find a means of bridging the gulf between me and reality cannot be anything but a wild goose chase: I exist qua personal act; this act exists as a transcendental "I live" unfolding itself from a definite centre and, in this process, constituting my body, my environment, my world as itself-actuated—thus I exist qua world, and the world exists qua I.[17]

This being so, let us note carefully this point: I shall not wonder how my personal-act-reflecting-itself-in-my-brain can give itself an "objective representation" of my environment, of my world, but I shall acknowledge that the world revealing itself to me in my expressive centre is not the world-existing-in-itself-outside-me but my world—that is, the world-existing-qua-related-to-my-expressive-centre. This must be understood in a very concrete sense: those houses of which I am reflectively conscious are not those houses as they stand there *in themselves*, but those houses as they exist in myself—that is, those houses qua concretions of my personal

[17] In studying my life-act incarnate, I have shown that my life act is continually conditioned by itself-already-realized-in-the-form-of-a-world and, through itself-thus-realized, *by the world-already-constituted.* This means that, in spite of what I affirm here, there exists a world which is "not I"—a world to which I am related, upon which I depend. But, as will appear later, my relation to this transcendent world is by no means the relation of a subject to an object (i.e., a relation of pure knowledge), but a relation of person to person.

life-act, those houses qua essentially related to my body and to my brain.

It will be objected, no doubt, that this view does away with the "objectivity" of knowledge. The answer is that if the term "objectivity" refers to the power which the intellect is said to have of knowing things which stand *in themselves outside me*, this notion of objectivity—let it be stated clearly—is done away with, and rightly so. Let me add one word: if the term "intellect" refers to a faculty capable of knowing "objectively" things-in-themselves, this notion of intellect is also rejected. But if the term "objectivity" refers to the power of the intellect of knowing things *as they are in fact*—that is, things-for-us-and-in-us, things-qua-related-to-our-expressive-centres—this notion is valid. In this case, the term "intellect" means the power which our personal act-world has of reflecting upon itself and of apprehending itself as it is.

This is the perspective in which all problems of knowledge must be studied and all intellectual pursuit must be understood. In this perspective, it appears—and will do so more and more clearly—that no "epistemology" can be built apart from a description of the whole personal structure and of the whole movement of personal existence.

I shall now examine the various aspects of my *transcendental* consciousness.

The Monism of My Transcendental Consciousness

The very existence of my life-act is in the movement by which it continually projects itself, by which it continually transcends and re-creates the situation in which it is incarnate (i.e., itself-already-realized), by which it continually leads itself (and the universe) towards its final realization. As concretions of this existential tension, my world and all the particular objects contained in it exist as realities which must be continually perfected, as realities which my act must bring to completion in the process by which it realizes itself.

The actuation of my life-act into an act-volition is identically the personalization of this movement: my personal act is my life-act transcending consciously, self-determinedly itself-already-realized; it is my life-act re-creating consciously, self-determinedly, the situation in which it is incarnate; it is my life-act leading itself (and the whole world) consciously, self-determinedly, towards its final realization.

As it actuates itself in this personal way, my act, reflecting upon itself-incarnate, apprehends each situation which it traverses as a moment of this existential tension, and thus as a reality constituted by a movement which goes beyond it, as a reality which has no definitive meaning in itself, whose meaning lies in its end. *My transcendental consciousness of my situation* (of each particular object) *is* precisely *my consciousness of this situation as a modality of the integral movement of my personal life.*

Let us go one step further: my transcendental consciousness of things is my consciousness of their *radical* identity. Let me explain. Things are not "in themselves"; they are not constituted by independent self-contained ontological principles (which make of them co-existing substances), but by my personal-act-existing-towards-an-end. This means that my act-in-tension-towards-its-end is the very *being* of the world and of all the objects contained in it—in other words, this means that things exist *fundamentally* qua my act-tending-towards-its-final-realization. My transcendental consciousness of things is my consciousness of this radical and dynamic oneness of all things in me.

This fact manifests itself in what I have called the positional character of my reflective consciousness. I have pointed out that, unlike my imaginative consciousness, which is non-factual, my reflective consciousness is "realistic". As it overcomes its basic indetermination and actuates itself into a personal project, my life-act incarnate constitutes everything as concretions of its self-determined existential tension. This operation is the process by which I give to my world its concrete being, its actuality, by which my personal-act-in-tension-towards-its-end posits itself *determinedly* as the *esse* of all things, and posits all things as itself-being-actuated. This operation manifests itself in the assertive character of my reflective consciousness: my continual affirmation of the reality, the existence, of things—which is at the very heart of my transcendental activity—is nothing other than my personal act expressing its awareness of its own existence as act-world.

The Pluralism of My Transcendental Conciousness: It is Consciousness of Myself-Already-Realized-in-the-Form-of-a-Pluralized-World

It is clear that, however "monistic" it may be, my transcendental knowledge of things is never consciousness of the world as undifferentiated being. The fact remains that my life-act, in spite of its radical unity, never exists as pure act, but always as an act which unfolds itself from a centre and, in this process, diversifies itself in many ways (expressing itself in my body, in my environment, in my world). My act-volition, as we know, is not a reality superimposed upon my life-act, but the personal actuation of this act. As it realizes itself, my personal act does not simply create its expressive field *ex nihilo*, but it actuates itself in itself-already-actuated; it re-creates into the concretion of itself the existential field formed by my life-act-already-realized. In doing so, my personal act expresses its tension towards its final realization in particular motions which are ordained towards particular ends; it incarnates its basic existential project in particular decisions and projects (my life-act never exists as pure act any more than does my personal act). As concretions of these particular moves, the various objects which form my surroundings exist as particular tools, as crystallized intentions expressing in many ways the general destination of the universe-in-me—thus my world never exists as pure being, but always as pluralized being. This specification manifests itself in my reflective consciousness in the fact that my affirmation of the existence of things is never the positing of being in general, but of being existing in particular beings—this affirmation of plurality is my personal act expressing its awareness of itself-existing-in-the-form-of-a-diversified-expressive-field.

These facts must be understood within the whole system formed by my personal act incarnate:

Phase a: My personal act, unfolding itself from its expressive centre, diversifies itself into particular motions, decisions, projects (which express in various ways its fundamental tension towards its end), and, in this process, constitutes my body, my environment, my world, as the concretion of itself-thus-diversified.

Phase b: In this movement, my personal act is *from the start* conditioned by the world, my environment, my body, existing as itself-already-diversified-in-the-form-of-particular-objects (which are crystallized intentions, suggestions, proposed behaviours, particular concretions of the meaning, the destination of the whole).

With this in view, we can understand that the reflectiveness of my personal act—that is, my personal-act-illuminating-itself-in-the-modalities-of-my-brain-at-the-outset-of-its-self-realizing-movement—*is* my transcendental consciousness of a world made of many objects which have different meanings. In other words, as it posits itself in its expressive centre, my personal act apprehends itself as already realized in the form of a pluralized world—thus its movement of self-realization, its self-expression in particular decisions, projects, behaviours, will be the conscious taking up, the re-personalization of intentions which are already there and offer themselves to be fulfilled.

Let me illustrate this by an example. I am back in my room after my evening walk. My personal act, unfolding itself from its centre, constitutes (a) my body facing my table, (b) my chair, my table, all the objects lying on my table: my papers, my dictionary, my other books, my fountain pen, my pencil, etc. . . . , (c) beyond my room, beyond the whole house, the entire world. I decide to resume my work. This decision is a deliberate motion of my personal act which takes place first of all in my expressive centre: it is my life-act-determining-itself-while-illuminating-itself-in-the-modalities-of-my-brain. Subsequently, it expresses itself in my body, in my environment, in my whole world. Now let us notice this: as a deliberate motion of my act-reflectively-conscious-of-itself, my decision is not a pure initiative of my personal act. Indeed, from the start, it is present, in the form of convergent particular intentions, in my chair which I already grasp with my hand, in my books, my pencil, my papers half filled with writing, in my whole room. All these objects become reflectively conscious of themselves and "move" me as my personal-act-illuminating-itself-in-my-expressive-centre actuates itself deliberately into my decision of resuming my work. Thus my decision is the reflective taking up and the re-personalization of various intentions which are myself-already-decided.

The Pluralism of My Transcendental Consciousness: It is Consciousness of the World-Already-Existing-in-the-Form-of-Many-Particular-Objects-Intentions

To these considerations, we must now add another important observation. Through itself-already-realized, my personal act is conditioned by the world-already-existing. Now this world is not a nameless, undifferentiated whole. It is a totality which moves in a certain direction, which is diversified in many particular objects, each of which expresses in a more or less definite manner the destination of the whole. I know this fact because I am aware that there is in things a wealth of meaning—and so an abundance of life, a plenitude of being—which remains always transcendent to me; because I am aware that the being of the world, of all things which I perceive, even though it proceeds from my personal life-act, is in some way older than me; because I am aware that I give meaning to all the objects which surround me largely by making mine a meaning which was in them before me (in other words, that I live largely by receiving life from the living world in which I am continually being born). This already existing world, as we know, does not "move" my personal-act-unfolding-itself "from outside", but always through my personal act-already-realized-in-the-form-of-a-world (my personal-act-continually-conditioned-by-'itself-already-realized' *is* my personal-act-conditioned-by-the-world-already-existing). In this perspective, we understand that, as it actuates itself in the form of particular decisions and actions, my personal act, while taking up and re-personalizing itself-already-existing-in-the-form-of-a-pluralized-world (made of particular crystallized intentions), assimilates (i.e., converts into itself, actuates, brings to fulfilment) the pluralized world already existing (i.e., the world already existing in the form of a general-intention-diversified-in-many-particular-intentions). This fact must be understood in a very concrete sense. At this moment, my personal-act-actuating-itself-through-my-act-of-thinking-and-writing gives their particular meaning to the pencil which I hold in my hand, the paper on which I make this pencil run, the table on which my papers are laid, the light which comes from the window and fills my room, etc.; my act makes of all these objects concretions of its present mode of tending towards its end; yet all these objects are not pure creations of my present voluntary activity, neither is this activity a pure initiative of my personal act: as it actuates itself into my act of thinking and writing and expresses itself in my surroundings, my personal act:

(a) takes up and re-personalizes itself-already-realized-in-the-form-of-a-pluralized-world;
(b) in taking up itself-thus-realized, identifies with itself the world-already-existing-in-the-form-of-many-particular-objects-intentions (in my present act of thinking and writing, I convert into myself and fulfil in a determined way the intentions which already constituted my pencil, my paper, my table, my whole room, before I decided to use them in this particular way, before I was born to them).

The process by which I thus integrate into my personal world the already existing world, by which I convert into my personal act the intentions constitutive of the objects of this world, is *essentially* reflective. This does not mean that my relation to these objects is first a relation of knowledge and then a relation of vital assimilation. The presence in me of the world-already-existing (and of all the objects it contains) is identical with my incarnate existence: I live by continually revitalizing myself-already-realized-in-the-form-of-a-world and, through myself-thus-realized, the world-already-existing. Thus all the objects of the world are present in me first of all as modalities of my existence, of my cosmico-biological system: I live them, I live what they signify, I am carried by them, before I have any explicit knowledge of them. Now, as my life-act actuates itself into an act-volition, it becomes reflective. *My act-volition-illuminating-itself-in-the-modalities-of-my-brain-while-unfolding-itself is identically the objects-of-the-world-revealing-to-me-their-meanings-while-being-taken-up-in-my-personal-activity*. Because they are part of my daily life, the objects of the world disclose to me what they signify (i.e., their "being-towards") in the process by which my life-act-incarnate becomes transcendentally self-conscious, within my life-act-incarnate-reflecting-upon-itself. Thus I begin to use reflectively and freely—that is, to know and to master—what I was living in an obscure and dependent way.

These facts show us how vain are all attempts at separating consciousness from the world. The notion of pure disincarnate awareness is perfectly meaningless in the order of reality. I am not and I shall never be an undifferentiated consciousness: first because my consciousness is nothing by itself, nothing apart from the life-act of which it is an attribute, secondly because my personal life-act is essentially act-world. Thus my personal-act-conscious-of-itself *is* the world-conscious-of-itself-in-me; my personal-act-in-tension-towards-its-final-realization *is* the world-in-progress-towards-its-completion. As this study progresses, we shall try to visualize in some way what this end will be. However, we can already see that it will not be the realization of a state of pure indifferentiated acosmic awareness, since such a state would be pure nothingness; we can see, too, that it will not be a separation of our "self" from the world, since in us the world itself tends towards its consummation, since our personal act (which is our "self") is the act-of-the-universe.

Further Description of My Transcendental Knowledge of the World:
(1) As Affirmation of the Existence of Things
(2) As Knowledge of "Quiddities"

Let us try now to characterize adequately the way in which the pluralized world reveals itself within my personal-act-reflecting-upon-itself—that is, the conditions in which my personal act continually determines itself.

In my personal act, the world exists as a totality diversified in many objects which are intentions-expressed-in-textures-of-spatial-modalities. This situation—which is nothing else than my personal-act-incarnate—may be typified in the following manner:

—It is a situation which implies a certain degree of *determinacy*, first because it exists concretely by, in and qua my personal-act-unfolding-itself (i.e., by, in, and qua my life-act-actuating-itself-in-a-*self-determined*-manner); secondly because it exists qua my personal-act-conditioned-by-itself-already-existing-in-the-form-of-a-world (i.e., qua my personal-act-conditioned-by-itself-already-existing-in-the-form-of-*determined*-objects-intentions). In fact, these two data are one reality: my personal act unfolding itself (my existence) is the existence of my personal-act-already-realized (my essence).

—However, this situation is still characterized by *indeterminacy* to the degree to which my personal act is tending towards a final realization which it has not yet attained, and to the extent that the intentions constitutive of the objects in which my act finds itself already realized are still unfulfilled—that is, to the extent that the world-existing-qua-myself-already-realized is still in a state of incompletion, or to the extent that my personal-act-already-realized-in-the-form-of-a-pluralized world is still in a state of non-realization. These two data are also one reality: it is because my personal act-already-realized-in-the-form-of-a-world is still imperfectly realized that my act is continually tending towards a more perfect realization of itself.

It is in reference to this complex situation that I must understand the way in which the world reveals itself to me. All the objects which surround me, *in so far as they have a meaning for me*, that is, *in so far as they exist for me in a determined manner*, are constituted by my act-realizing-itself-self-determinedly.

(1) This meaning—this determination—is first of all their being—

that is, their being constituted as the concretion, the expression, of my personal-act-tending-towards-its-end, their "being-towards-my-end". The operation by which I give them this fundamental determination, their concrete *esse*, considered in so far as it is self-transparent, is my affirmation of their existence, of their reality.

This shows that my positing the existence of things, which is the very core of my reflectiveness, takes place essentially in an act of freedom: it pertains essentially to my act-realizing-itself-in-a-self-determined-manner. Therefore my freedom—that is, my existence as a personal act—is constitutive of the very existence of all the objects of my world—that is, of their fundamental determination.

We must, however, realize that the operation by which I give to the objects of my world their *esse* is not a pure creative act:

(a) As we know, my personal-act-realizing-itself, however much it constitutes my world, is always conditioned by itself-already-realized-in-the-form-of-a-world and, through itself-thus-realized, by the world-already-existing. This means that things, however much they receive their *esse* from my personal-act-unfolding-itself, already exist in some way antecedently to my constituting them. This means that, in the very process of constituting the world as the concretion of itself, my personal act is in some way dependent on the world-already-existing, that it *is* in some way the world-already-existing-continuing-to-posit-itself.

This sort of emergence of my personal act from the world-already-existing expresses itself in the fact that in the very act of constituting things as concretions of myself (of giving them their being-for-me), I acknowledge their pre-existence with regard to the actual self-positing movement of my personal act (i.e., I acknowledge the anteriority of my act-existing-in-the-form-of-the-world with regard to my act-actually-constituting-the-world). Therefore my affirmation of the existence of things is not only my conscious assertion of their being-in-me (i.e., of their being constituted by the actual self-positing movement of my personal act) but also the acknowledgment of their being-without-me (i.e., of their being in some way independent of my present existential movement, or of my existing in some way qua world antecedently to my actually constituting the world as the expression of myself).

(b) However, it cannot be maintained that my personal-act-constituting-my-world simply evolves from the world-already-there;

it cannot be maintained that, in affirming the existence of things, I am simply made to exist qua the world-affirming-itself. The fact remains that my personal-act-unfolding-itself (my existence) is never the mere continuation of something pre-existing, but always a reality which transcends itself-already-realized and the world-already-existing (my personal existence *is* freedom); moreover, the fact remains that my act-already-realized (and, in it, the world-already-existing), far from giving existence to my personal-act-positing-itself, are constituted by it—in other words, my personal-act-unfolding-itself (my existence) is the *esse* of anything existing qua related to it in any way, and, in the existential order, it has absolute priority with regard to itself-already-realized. This priority of my personal-act-realizing-itself expresses itself in the fact that my acknowledgment of things as already existing takes place essentially within my actual positing of them as expressions of my existential movement: I cannot assert anything about the world unless I first make it exist in me and for me.

Nevertheless, in giving existence to my world and in asserting the existence of things, I am continually dependent on the world as though it existed without me, as though my personal act really emanated from the world, as though my affirmation of things evolved from a certain consciousness which things have of themselves before being apprehended by me. This is in its most acute form the apparent antinomy which I have met at every step of my investigation. Its solution, as we know, is simply the fact of my createdness. I am created as a personal act unfolding from a centre, constituting the world as the concretion of its existential movement and, in this process, being continually conditioned by itself-incarnate, or by itself-created—therefore my personal act finds itself dependent on the very world which it constitutes because, in constituting it, it is transcendentally given to itself (not because it emanates from the world-already-existing). But this is not yet the full picture. The fact is that, through itself-incarnate (through itself-created), my personal act *is* conditioned by the world-already-existing. Thus I shall say that I come continually to life from Above in an already existing world in the form of a personal act unfolding from a particular centre, reshaping the pre-existent world into the concretion of itself and, in so doing, being conditioned by itself-incarnate (i.e., by itself-created and, through itself-created, by the world-re-created). But even this view is not wholly satisfactory. Indeed, the notion of a pre-existent world is essentially relative to me; it means nothing with regard to the Transcendent Initiative to which I owe my existence. Absolutely speaking, there is nothing which precedes in existence the Act which creates me; in other words, the Transcendent does not create me with the help of an already existing cosmico-biological stuff. The full picture we have to accept is as follows: there is One Transcendent Creative Act which, at this moment, gives existence to the whole universe and to myself. Proceeding from this Source, I exist qua the whole-universe-centred-in-a-definite-place (individuated in a particular manner). Proceeding from the same Source, the "not-I-universe" exists qua centred in other places (individuated in other ways). My world is made to exist as a personal act unfolding from a centre, constituting the whole and, at the same time, being conditioned by itself-incarnate (i.e., by itself-created and, through itself-created, by the not-I-world-co-created). Thus we see that my dependence on the not-I-world is ultimately also a dependence on the Transcendent Creative Source—in other words, the not-I-world is not a purely phenomenal field but a basically transcendental reality.

The experience of my createdness pervades my transcendental activity and constitutes its deepest characteristic. However truly my personal act determines itself and constitutes my world, I am never conscious of being a self-producing, all-creative, transcendent Principle: at every moment, in everything I do, I experience myself as "already-there", given to myself, made to exist. This experience expresses itself in my affirmation of the existence of things. More fundamental than my admission of their being-without-me, there is in it an acknowledgment of my-already-being-in-them: in every affirmation, I am implicitly conscious of my existence as fact in the object I affirm—in other words, I am conscious that, in the very act of giving being to things, I am created and the things are created in me (I am conscious that my personal act-world exists as a participation in a Transcendent Creative Act). In the same way as my createdness constitutes the deepest reality of my transcendental, self-determined, world-constituting activity, this acknowledgment is the basic element of my affirmation of the existence of things, the element from which the other aspects (i.e., my positing of the world as the concretion of my existential movement, my admission of the pre-existence of things) receive their meaning and intelligibility.

The fact that my personal life-act exists as act-world-tending-towards-its-final-realization not by its own self-creative initiative but by the initiative of the Creator, shows that the *esse* of things, before coming from me, proceeds from the Transcendent Creative Source, that it is first of all the dependence of things on the Creator. This Creative Action must not be conceived as though it constituted things "in themselves" where they are—that is, as though it constituted them as substances independent of one another. The Transcendent Initiative creates things as they are—that is, in me, as concretions of my fundamental "being-towards" (and in others, as concretions of their fundamental "being-towards"). This fundamental "being-towards"—my substantial *esse*—is my personal life-act considered in so far as it is created as act-world-in-tension-towards-an-end—that is, considered in so far as it is constituted by an intention deeper than all my particular intentions, desires, motions. The substantial *esse* of things (i.e., their existence-in-relation-to-the-Creator) is in their being concretions of this fundamental intention constitutive of my transcendental individuality (as well as in their being concretions of the fundamental intentions constitutive of other transcendental individualities).

In this context the following points must be noted:

(a′) As I am constituted as a personal act reflectively conscious of its ontological relation to a Transcendent Source, of its being ordained by the Creator towards an end, so my authentic existence consists in my conscious and deliberate tending towards the end in obedience to the Creator—that is, *in the identification of my personal will with the intention by which I am constituted.* In this obedience, by which I make myself reflectively and deliberately what the Creator intends me to be, by which I make of my personal existence the true actuation of my substantial *esse*, *I possess the fullness of my freedom and I perfect my understanding.*

(b′) The substantial *esse* of things, as has just been explained, consists in their being concretions of the fundamental intention by which I am constituted. This means that when I tend consciously and deliberately towards the end which the Creator intends me to reach (identifying my will with the will of the Creator), while making of things concretions of my existential tension, I allow them to be what they are meant to be, I give to the world of my daily life its authentic *esse*. Thus we see that, in the very process of realizing myself truly, I also allow the world to come to itself; we see that the more my world grows into what it is intended to be, the more also it becomes the embodiment of freedom, the more it illuminates itself.

(c′) *Veritas est adequatio rei et intellectus.* This classical formula means both *veritas est adequatio rei ad intellectum*, and *veritas est adequatio intellectus ad rem.* On the one hand: the ontological truth of the thing—that is, its conformity with the idea of it present in the mind of the Creator; on the other hand: the truth of our judgment—that is, the conformity of our intellectual representation of the thing with the thing itself. This conformity is possible because, by the will of God, there is analogy between our created intellect and his Creative Mind. Implied in these views, there is of course the idea of man as an intellect facing a world of objects. This conception, as we know, is based on a misinterpretation of facts. However, the classical formula is fundamentally valid. I consider first its ontological interpretation. The *res* in question here must be understood not as the object "in itself", but as the object such as it exists *de facto*—that is, the object existing in me (and in others). In so far as it exists in me, this object is not a substance distinct from other substances but essentially an element of the structure formed by my act-world-ordained-towards-its-final-realization—that is, a particular concretion of the intention which constitutes me as personal-act-in-relation-to-the-Creator. The ontological truth of the thing consists in its existing as a created expression of the Transcendent Will. In this sense, we can speak of truth as *adequatio rei ad intellectum* (the term *intellectus* being understood as the Creative Intention). To turn now to the other interpretation: the *intellectus* referred to is no longer the *intellectus divinus* but my intellect—that is, the reflectiveness of my personal act. As it tends consciously and deliberately towards its end, my personal act constitutes the world as the concretion of its existential project; at the same time, it identifies itself with the intention which constitutes it as creature. When this identification takes place, the world-existing-as-the-concretion-of-my-life-project tends to be simply the world-intended-by-the-Creator. Moreover, while my freedom perfects itself, my understanding becomes more and more penetrating: in my act-actuating-itself-deliberately-in-accordance-with-the-Creative-Intention the world reveals its authentic *esse*. Thus we can say that there is *adequatio intellectus ad rem.* Let us note well that this *adequatio* is achieved in the act by which, through the conformity of my will with the Creative Will, I attain the fullness of my freedom. Therefore, in a true sense, I can say that freedom (my authentic self-realization) is the essence of truth (my unveiling of the authentic *esse* of things).

Let us conclude this analysis of my reflective position of being. When I opened this line of thought, I wrote that all objects, to the extent that they have meaning for me, that is, to the extent that they exist for me in a determined manner, are constituted by my act-realizing-itself-self-determinedly. This meaning—this determination—is fundamentally their being, their existence. This determination, it must be noted, is by no means an abstract universal—that is, what remains of things when all particularizing elements have been removed. The being of an object is this object considered in its all-embracing concreteness. In the first chapter of this study, I have shown that each particular object has no meaning, no existence, apart from all the other objects which surround it, apart from the whole universe; I have shown that the totality *is* the meaning, the existence of each particular object. Therefore the object as being is the object considered in so far as it is one with all the other objects, with the whole universe. Now the being of the world, to the extent that it is being-for-me, is constituted by my personal-act-unfolding-itself-while-tending-towards-its-end. Thus each object as being, while expressing the whole universe, is a concretion of my integral existential tension; it is not the object detached from all its particular determinations, but the object possessing, in its very particularity, a plenitude of expressiveness.

(2) My personal-act-reflectively-conscious-of-itself is always my personal-act-conscious-of-'itself-incarnate-in-a-particular-manner'; my personal-act-tending-towards-its-end is always my personal-act-actuating-itself-through-the-pursuing-of-particular-aims. I am filling my fountain pen in order to write a letter to a friend. My personal act is incarnate in my body characterized by a particular posture, in my chair and my table, in my left hand holding the ink-bottle, in my right hand dipping the pen into it and "pressing four times the ribbed bar", in my eyes focused on this little scene. This situation, with all its elements, is the concretion of my intention of writing a letter to my friend—that is, of a tending-towards-a-definite-aim which expresses in a particular manner my tending-towards-my-supreme-realization. Therefore my chair, my table, my ink-bottle, my fountain pen, in relation to my body, do not exist simply qua "being-towards-the-end" (i.e., as being) but qua "'being-towards-a-particular-end'-expressing-'being-towards-the-end'" (i.e., as particular beings). In other words, the fundamental destination of the world-in-me (their

existence) is materialized in them in the form of particular destinations (their existence as . . .).

(Let us note carefully that at every moment my tension towards my supreme realization must necessarily be exercised through the pursuing of a particular aim. If my personal act were to intend its supreme realization in a fully actual manner, it would no longer be in tension towards it; it would posit itself in a truly definitive way. But then my world would no longer be pluralized being, but pure, fully realized, intensely concentrated being. In fact, my world is a pluralized world because it exists as the concretion of my personal-act-tending-progressively-towards-its-ultimate-realization, and my existential tension exists always in the form of a motion towards a particular aim because at every moment my personal act finds itself incarnate in a pluralized world.)

Now my chair, my table, my ink-bottle, my fountain pen, although they *are* concretions of my intention of writing a letter, do not become an expressive field reflecting in a uniform way my particular concern; they preserve their distinctive characters—in other words, my intention expresses itself in each of these objects according to its particular modalities. What does this mean exactly? As has been explained, my personal act, in constituting these objects as concretions of its particular project, is conditioned by these objects-already-existing-as-*objects-intentions* (parts of myself-already-realized and, through myself-already-realized, parts of the world-already-existing). To say that my intention of writing a letter to my friend expresses itself in my chair, my table, my ink-bottle, my fountain pen, *according to their particular modalities* is to say that, while constituting them as concretions of its particular project, my personal act is conditioned by itself-already-existing-in-them-in-the-form-of-definite-intentions. In shaping itself into my act of filling my fountain pen, my personal act, while actuating itself, fulfils in a particular manner the intentions constitutive of the objects which form my surroundings. (Actuating myself and fulfilling these intentions, it must be noted, are one and the same reality: these intentions are essentially parts of myself-already-determined, though still-largely-undetermined. When I fulfil these intentions, I go on determining myself.)

In fact, it is the totality of myself-already-realized-in-the-form-of-a-world which my act of filling my fountain pen actuates in some way. Not only my chair, my table, my ink-bottle, my fountain pen, but my whole room with all the objects it contains, the house of which my room is a part, the city, the whole world, receive some new determination from my personal-act-actuating-itself-through-my-occupation. In other words, it is the whole world which my personal-act-realizing-itself-through-my-particular-activity tends to shape into the concretion of itself.

It is clear, however, that all the objects which form my world do not fuse with one another in order to reflect purely and simply my present occupation; they keep their own specific destinations—that is, the determinations which they possess as parts of my personal-act-already-realized-in-the-form-of-a-world. These particular intentions need to be fulfilled by some types of activity, some specific behaviours, which are not adequately implied in my act of filling my fountain pen. As a result, the objects constituted by these intentions oppose a certain resistance to this particular act, they do not let themselves be converted into mere concretions of it, they remain to a certain extent outside it.

These facts show clearly that the particular activity through which my personal act presently tends towards its end is only a partial actuation of myself-already-realized-in-the-form-of-a-world; they show that my personal act incarnate is charged with possibilities which it does not actually realize—in other words, that my present activity is exercised within a field of unactuated potentialities. This field—which is myself-already-realized-though-still-largely-unrealized (a situation characterized by indeterminacy within determinacy) —reveals itself as a world of objects-intentions—that is, as a world of objects which express in various ways the dynamism of the whole.[18]

Let us try to understand more deeply the nature of this world of objects-intentions.

(a) I analyse it first from an "essentialist" viewpoint.

The objects which form myself-already-realized (the world-already-constituted) may somehow be classified into various categories. All the objects which fall into one category are characterized

[18] This perspective makes us realize once more that the objects of the world are not primarily realities which offer themselves to be contemplated by a spectator who remains distinct from them, or to be analysed by a scientist from a disinterested point of view, or to be apprehended "in themselves" by a pure intellect, but that they are parts of the living totality formed by my personal act-world—that is, parts of a totality which has already reached a certain degree of elaboration but has still to build and perfect itself, to grow, through my personal endeavours, through my daily work and activities, into what it is meant to become.

by a certain similitude of spatial structure and, hence, by a unity of meaning, of destination. Let us analyse this in some detail.

At the top of the whole categorical edifice there is, of course, the totality of the universe-already-constituted. All the objects which are comprised in this category of categories have this in common, that they are textures of spatial modalities. The unity-meaning which this fundamental "external" similitude expresses is my personal-act-already-realized (my essence). From the fact of being constituted by this act, the objects of my world possess what we may call their "thing-hood"—that is, *their essential being* (their "form"). Thus each object as a thing may be defined as a certain spatial ensemble crystallizing in itself the whole universe.

But no object ever exists as a mere thing, as a being without specification. All the objects which I see in my surroundings, according to the way in which they fill the portion of space which they constitute, are called either animate or inanimate. These two categories represent two different ways in which my personal-life-act-already-realized expresses itself. Let us note that, since each object is, in its very singularity, an expression of the totality, and since the totality does not exist apart from the objects in which it expresses itself, each particular being, whether it be "animate" or "inanimate", is constituted by all the others; therefore there is interpenetration of the inanimate by the animate and of the animate by the inanimate. In fact, *there is no object which is really lifeless*, since each particular thing is by essence a concretion of my life-act.[19]

[19] This statement must be correctly understood. I am not concerned here with the "scientific" notion of life, I am not rejecting the distinction which scientists, *from the point of view of their own observations*, posit between living and non-living beings, between organic and inorganic matter. My experience is this: *every object*, to the extent that it exists for me, that it means something to me, is part and parcel of the system constituted by my life-act incarnate, is a modality, an expressive variation of my life field. From the point of view of this fundamental experience, I affirm that no object is really lifeless. This assertion does not challenge any scientific view which is truly scientific—that is, based upon data collected through direct observation of phenomena, concerned only with reality as revealed by this type of observation. What this assertion rejects is the transference of the scientific distinction between living and non-living onto the metaphysical plane. It is only from the point of view of our integral experience that we can make statements about the "within" of things (not from any other point of view, since any other point of view is necessarily a more restricted point of view). From this all-embracing viewpoint, it appears so far that the distinction between animate and inanimate objects refers to two different ways in which my *life-act* takes possession of its expressive field and *animates* it: my life-act *animates* (makes live for me) the objects of my room as well as the birds which I hear

Further, animate as well as inanimate objects may be grouped into many classes and subclasses according to their physical characteristics. All the beings which belong to one class, in so far as they have some external similitude, are constituted by a specific intention which is a determination of the meaning of the whole. All these classes are essentially related to one another so that no one of them makes any sense apart from all the others, and, thus, no one of them can be studied in isolation.

Finally, the various classes are made up of individual objects. Each of these is a concretion of the specific intention constitutive of the class to which it belongs. Its particular meaning expresses itself in its unique way of filling the portion of space which it constitutes; it is determined by the particular environment in which it is actually situated, by the particular relationship in which it stands to all the other objects which surround it.

(b) Now it must be borne in mind that this whole system which forms my personal-act-realized-in-the-form-of-a-world (my essence) exists by, in, and for my personal-act-unfolding-itself (i.e., my personal-act-continuing-to-realize-itself—my existence). Therefore the various specifications of myself-already-realized which I have just pointed out—if they have any meaning in the real order—are first of all modalities of my personal-act-realizing-itself. This is what we must consider now.

I have already shown that the *existence* of things is their being-in-me-towards-my-end; I have shown also that it is always specified in some way (it is always existence as . . .) because my tension towards my end always realizes itself through the pursuing of particular aims. Let us return to the example given above. My personal act actuates itself through my intention of writing a letter to my friend, through the particular activity through which this intention begins to realize itself. As I fill my fountain pen, I make of the objects which surround me expressions of my act, I *tend* to mould the world into the concretion of my particular design. However, my occupation remains a very humble and limited undertaking. Its finitude, as has been indicated, consists in its being an imperfect actuation of my act incarnate: my personal life-act is loaded with potentialities which my present activity does not exercise. This indetermination persisting within the

chirping on the trees outside, not, however, in the same way. What is the foundation of this difference? As my study progresses, I hope to be able to say something about it, ***from the point of view of my integral experience.***

determination of my act expresses itself in the internal diversity which characterizes the structure formed by my personal-act-actuating-itself-through-my-particular-occupation. Roughly, this diversity consists in the distinction which is maintained between this particular situation in which the present actuation of my personal act takes place (the situation formed by my left hand holding the ink-bottle, my right hand dipping the fountain pen into it . . .) and the surrounding world. This distinction must be interpreted in this way: my personal act, while it constitutes a portion of space as the immediate and explicit concretion of itself-determining-itself, makes of the whole surrounding world the expression of its still undetermined potentiality. This means that my present activity, though it is actually one, remains virtually many. My act of filling my fountain pen is not an initiative by which I actualize the whole of myself; it takes place in an atmosphere of unactuated potentiality, it is the realization of one possibility among many.

But this picture is still incomplete. In fact, as pointed out above, the determination of my present activity expresses itself in some way in my whole world (my act of filling my fountain pen is an actuation —however humble—of the totality of myself-already-realized), and my residual indetermination appears even in the particular situation which my personal act moulds into the concretion of its present self-actuating initiative. Let me explain this last assertion a little more fully. The situation in which my particular activity is exercised comprises in itself a diversity which is not eliminated by the fact of its being the concretion of my present concern. My left hand, my right hand, the objects I use, remain different things characterized by different intentions which their present existence within my decision of writing a letter to my friend does not fulfil adequately. This means that, while making them exist as concretions of my decision-realizing-itself, I find myself living in them in the form of possibilities which my particular activity does not actuate. In so far as the things I use, while being ordained within my act towards a particular end, remain such potential beings, they are characterized by a specific utility, a sort of universal serviceableness.

Let us try now to understand better the nature of this potentiality. I am working at my table; the things which surround me, the whole world, are integrated in this occupation: I make them exist as concretions of my act of thinking and writing. However, as I look at the objects lying on my table, at the pieces of furniture scattered around me, I am conscious that each of these things is not simply what my present activity makes of it: the pencil I hold in my hand, my books, my table lamp, my alarm clock, my bed, the walls of my room, are charged with intentions which my act of thinking does not fulfil—in other words, this particular occupation is only a partial actuation of my personal-act-incarnate-in-them. Now let us note this fact: each object as a potential being is not a purely undetermined, non-actual entity; each thing *as a potential being* had already for me a relatively determined meaning. This fact must be interpreted as follows: as I make of the various things which surround me concretions of my act of thinking, I also fashion each one of them, according to its modalities, with a certain part of those possibilities of mine which my present activity does not realize. Thus each object, while being made to exist within this activity, is still, as a potential being, characterized by a destination, a serviceableness, which is ampler, more "universal" than its present use.

I just said that the modalities of each thing determine the way in which I insert in it my possibilities. This means that, to objects which are structured in the same way, I give more or less the same potential being. Thus I discover how, *in the very process of constituting the world as the embodiment of my present concern, I mould it also into a totality containing many categories of objects-intentions, of tools.*

Let us note, however, that, in the process of making from different objects of similar structures one category, I do not confer on all of them exactly the same meaning. The destination which I give to an object is always to some extent determined by its particular spatial texture and by its environment; moreover, its usefulness with regard to me is measured by its relation to my body—that is, by the possibility I have of making use of it. Pencils which lie on my table have a real meaning for me as potential beings, as particular individuals belonging to the category "pencil". Pencils, however, for sale somewhere in Bowbazar Street have little significance for me, and pencils manufactured in San Francisco are practically non-existent. It is only by abstracting myself from reality, from the concrete conditions in which I live, that I can adopt the pure categorical attitude which makes all objects of one category to be equivalent units.

We must understand rightly the way in which objects, as potential beings, are already characterized by specific destinations. It is evident that my table lamp, my dictionary, my alarm clock are *meant* for different uses—and thus they have different meanings, they are different channels along which my potentialities may actuate themselves. Yet, precisely because they are potential beings, they cannot be considered as strictly specialized, narrowly determined, tools. The specific destinations which constitute them as objects of various types are no more than impoverished expressions of my fundamental life intention—that is, of my being-towards-the-end. Thus *each of my particular activities*—being a particular actuation of my integral potentiality—*is in some way a fulfilment of the intentions constitutive of all the objects of the world*—even though, "technically", it cannot be considered as an explicit realization of their specific "towards-which". This fact must be understood in connection with another fact which has already been pointed out: the fact that each motion of my life-act-incarnate-in-my-body actuates my whole body, even though it takes place mainly along some definite organic channel. My personal life-act, whether considered as the act of my body or as the act of my world, always exists in the form of a structure the elements of which are essentially interconnected, even though they are differentiated from one another. Modifications which my personal act induces in any part of itself-incarnate are always in some way modifications of all the other parts, of the whole structure.

(c) I showed earlier that my particular initiatives are never absolute beginnings: each of my particular decisions is always to a certain extent the taking up and re-personalization of myself-already-decided. Following on from this, it must be noted that the process by which I shape the objects which surround me, my whole world, into the depositaries of my still unrealized potentialities is the revitalizing by my personal life-act of itself-already-present-in-them-in-the-form-of-specific-intentions. At this moment, as I make my table, my books, the electric fan turning above my head into concretions of my act of thinking and writing, I also give them their specific meanings by incarnating my potentialities in them in various ways. Nevertheless, I must acknowledge that these objects are constituted as potential beings of different categories antecedently to the present self-positing initiative of my personal act: in the very process of fashioning them into expressions of my capacities and propensities, I am conditioned by myself-already-incarnate-in-them-in-various-typical-ways. This fact must be understood as follows:

(a′) From the centre in which it comes into existence, my personal act, while actuating itself determinedly in some particular manner and constituting the world as the concretion of this movement, allows its potentialities to crystallize themselves in various ways in its expressive field (Phase a—my existence).

(b′) From all the places which it occupies, my personal life-act returns to its source and, in this regressive movement,

(a″) conditions itself-continuing-to-actuate-itself-in-a-determined-manner,

(b″) conditions itself-continuing-to-fill-the-world-with-its-potentialities (Phase b—my essence).

Now it must be remembered that, through itself-already-realized-though-still-largely-unrealized, my personal act depends on the world-already-constituted. This world presents itself as a totality already containing innumerable objects-intentions of various categories —that is, innumerable objects having different destinations. The process by which I constitute the things which surround me into tools of various types is to a large extent the operation by which I allow their native destinations (i.e., the destinations which they already have as parts of the world-without-me) to reveal themselves in me. This fact shows that I inherit a great part of my potentialities from the already existing world in which I continually come to existence.

(d) Let us relate what we are now saying to what we know already about the structure of the various objects of the world. At the beginning of this study, I pointed out that each object is a unity-meaning which expresses itself in a particular spatial configuration (aspect a—movement of expression) and, at the same time, is conditioned by the spatial modalities in which it manifests itself (aspect b —generation). As a unity-meaning which takes possession of a portion of space in order to express itself in it, the object is constituted by my personal act unfolding itself from its centre (my existence). As such, the object is essentially related to my body, it is a particular concretion of my tension towards my end. In so far as the unity-meaning constitutive of the object is conditioned by the spatial modalities in which it expresses itself, the whole process must be explained in this way: as it fashions the object into the expression of itself, my personal act finds itself conditioned by itself-already-incarnate-in-the-object-in-a-specific-manner and, through itself-thus-incarnate, by the object-existing-as-a-meaningful-part-of-the-world-already-constituted. This perspective shows once more that the things of the world, however I may look at them, cannot be separated from me: their existence for me and my existence are one, their essence (i.e., what they are as already constituted realities, their "quiddity") is a particular crystallization of my essence (i.e., of myself-already-realized, of my individuality). From this we see, too, that the object existing as a meaningful reality is always the object existing qua related to my body: the object already constituted (i.e., the object as a particular essence) is the object-having-already-realized-itself-in-my-body,-in-my-brain, the object-being-further-realized is the object-continually-made-to-exist-as-the-concretion-of-'my personal-act-unfolding-itself-from-my-body'. In other words, the structure of the object is concretely one with the structure of my personal life-act incarnate; the object *is* my personal life-act shaping itself and being shaped in a particular manner.

(e) The problem of knowledge can be studied profitably only in the perspective opened up for us by our investigation of reality. It is no longer the problem of explaining coherently the relation between the mind and external reality. Our study has led us to the discovery of our world as a living totality constituted by our personal-act-in-tension-towards-its-end. We are trying gradually to bring out the structure of this totality. From what we have so far seen, it is clear that the intellect is not a cognitive faculty with a quasi-independent activity; it is clear also that knowledge is not the assimilation by the intellect of an external object essentially distinct from it. As has been pointed out, my intellect is the reflectiveness of my personal act—that is, the power which my personal life-act has of illuminating itself and everything within itself; knowledge is the luminous presence of my personal act incarnate to itself. In this perspective, it appears that knowledge is essentially a function of life: as my personal life-act perfects itself, it becomes more and more self-transparent, and thus possesses itself more and more comprehensively. Thus my intellectual pursuit does not aim first of all at a disinterested apprehension of the essence of things, of the structure of the "objective world"; it is an aspect of the self-realizing endeavour of my personal life-act, of its tension towards a more and more intense, more and more fulfilling, more and more self-possessed mode of existence.

In some previous sections of this chapter, I pointed out that perceptive knowledge and imagination must be understood in relation to the existential status of my life-act-incarnate-in-my-sensorial-apparatus and of my life-act-incarnate-in-my-brain. Similarly, the various aspects of intellectual knowledge must be defined in relation to the existential modalities of my personal-act-actuating-itself.

I have just shown how my personal act constitutes the objects of the world as objects-intentions by depositing its potentialities in them in various ways; I have shown also how, in doing so, my personal act is conditioned by itself-already-present-in-the-objects-in-specific-ways. My intellectual knowledge of things, in so far as it is knowledge of "quiddities", is nothing but the reflectiveness of this existential complex: in the very process of expressing myself in the world in various typical manners, I apprehend the objects which surround me as different crystallizations of my possibilities—that is, as various potential beings. In this context, we can see what is meant by the "universality" of intellectual knowledge. As has already been said, it does not consist in the fact that the intellect abstracts from the sensible image the quiddity or the concept of the thing—in other words, that it assimilates the "form" of the thing after extracting it from the matter in which it is individuated. The knowledge of a thing as a universal takes place in the movement by which my personal act constitutes it as a certain specification of its capacities and propensities. The thing as a universal is the thing as a tool charged with relatively unactuated potentialities, constituted by unfulfilled intentions, ordained towards specific aims; it is the proposal of a certain way of living, of a typical manner of actuating my being-towards-the-end.

This knowledge of an object as a universal, it must be noted, is never knowledge of it as a potential being which has exactly the same meaning as the other objects of the category to which it belongs. Indeed, the meaning which a thing has for me, as has been pointed out, is always determined by its particular spatial texture, by the environment in which it is situated, by its relationship to my body.

We should not say that these singularizing elements—the concrete existence of the thing—are not objects of my intellectual knowledge but of my sensible knowledge; not that my knowledge of the thing, to the extent that it is intellectual, is knowledge of the "form" of the thing—that is, of the thing considered in so far as it belongs to an intelligible category, in so far as it is a certain *abstract essence*. As it actuates itself through a particular activity, my personal act constitutes the various elements of its expressive field—according to their particular modalities, their situations, their relationship to its expressive centre—as concretions of this activity and, at the same time, as crystallizations of its potentialities. My intellectual knowledge—which is the reflectiveness of my transcendental activity—is apprehension of the objects which surround me as characterized, *in their concrete setting*, by specific destinations—that is, by destinations which, abstractly speaking, other objects of similar structure may have in common with them, but which owing to their situations and their particular textures, they possess *de facto* in completely original ways. Were my knowledge of the objects to be purely sensible, it would be knowledge of them as mere concretions of my present activity, it would be a narrow and adhesive type of knowledge. Such a knowledge would not take place in a life-act which transcends the particular motion through which it actuates itself. Because my personal life-act is a transcendental act, I know the objects which surround me not only as expression of my particular activity, but also as tools charged with potentialities which this activity does not actuate. This knowledge is identical with the freedom of my personal act, with the power I have to use the objects which surround me in many different ways.

But my reflective knowledge is not *primarily* knowledge of things as potential beings. As has been explained above, the fundamental character of my transcendental knowledge is its character of positing: while tending self-determinedly towards my end, I constitute reflectively my world as the concretion of this existential tension—in other words, I give to my world its existence-for-me. Thus my knowledge of particular objects, to the extent that it is knowledge of them as real objects, is knowledge of them as ordained in me towards my end—that is, as moments of the fundamental movement of my personal act incarnate. This positive reference to the end—the very existence of the objects of my world—is constitutive of things both (a′) as concretions of my particular activity and (b′) as potential beings. It is the basic element of my intellectual knowledge of the world.

(a′) As mere sensation, my knowledge of things, as has just been said, would be knowledge of them as mere concretions of my present activity—that is, as ordained towards a particular end. Because my personal act is a transcendental act, I see each object not only as an expression of my actual motion towards a particular aim but as a modality of my being-towards-the-end. When a man is driving a car, the steering wheel he holds, the road ahead of him bordered by houses and trees, the hooting of a horn, are lived by him as elements of a structure the meaning of which is his act of driving his car. This is a fact. However, this driver knows in an existential manner that all these objects are not purely and simply expressions of his present occupation, he sees in them far more than what he does just now. This is precisely what enables him to drive his car in an "intelligent" manner; this is what impels him to drive his car into a wall and sacrifice himself rather than kill a child who crosses the road inadvertently in front of him. To a hunter walking in a forest, the grasping of his gun, the seeing of leaves shaken by the wind, the hearing of twigs that snap are concretions of his particular concern: his search for game. However, fundamentally, these objects mean for him much more than his present desire of shooting some animal. Again, this is what makes him hunt in an "intelligent" manner, what prevents him from letting fly as long as he is not sure whether the moving form he perceives is a beast or a man.

(b′) If my intellectual knowledge of things was knowledge of them as mere potential beings, it would be knowledge of mere essences, of purely non-actual, unreal entities. This is of course an impossibility. We must understand that potentiality always refers to act: my potentiality is my personal act considered in relation to its full realization; it is my act in its present state of non-realization and of tension towards its end. This means that the movement by which I constitute things as crystallizations of my potentialities is in fact the act by which I make them exist as various concretions of my integral existential tension—that is, the act by which I refer them to the ultimate goal of my life beyond the particular aims towards which my present activity ordains them. From this we may see why the things which surround me should—in their very non-actualness—appear to me as fundamentally real: as *potential* beings they are non-actual, but this potentiality is their present ordination in me towards the fullness of being.

Let us now bring together these two considerations. As it appears, the fact that my personal act lives its present self-actuating move as a particular moment of its integral existential tension, the fact that—while constituting the various elements of its expressive field as luminous concretions of its particular motion, it makes them exist also as expressions of its transcendental being-towards—is identical with the fact that, while moulding the objects which surround me into the body of my present activity, I constitute them also as potential beings—that is, as various crystallizations of my unactuated potentialities. The essence of this whole process is the transcendence or the freedom of my personal act.

(f) Let us say a few words about the way in which the various natural sciences study the universe. First, it is clear that the field which they investigate and the reality which we explore in this study are one and the same world. The integral perspective which our reflection brings to light both transcends and *integrates* the fragmentary perspectives of the various sciences.

When I study the world from the point of view of a particular science, I begin—consciously or unconsciously—by "bracketing" what is most fundamental: I eliminate all explicit consideration of the concrete existence of the world—that is, of its relation to me, of its dependence on my personal activity. The object which remains, once this fixation has been effected, is the world-already-constituted. The various objects of this world are classified according to their external similarity, to their inner structure, to their type of activity. All objects belonging to a certain category are considered to have the same scientific properties, the same potentiality. These facts show that a "scientific" study of the world is basically a study of essences.

In this phenomenological study of reality, my first step has been a consideration of the way in which the objects of the world appear to me. The second step was a reflection on the way in which their meanings are constituted. This reflection led me to the discovery of my world, of my act incarnate. Scientific analysis is quite different. It starts from a certain view of the object in its totality and then studies "how it works". In this research, the scientist is prompted by the feeling that his knowledge of the object as a whole (of its properties and potentialities) is still very unsatisfactory and that, in order to perfect this knowledge, he must analyse the various elements of which the object is "composed". In other words, the scientist's idea is that the object is a certain "what" generated in a diversity of elements; he seeks to make out the nature of this "what" by analysing the various parts of the object; he tries to determine how each element contributes to the formation of this "what". As we can see, the scientific study of an object may be roughly characterized as a study of its "aspect b" (i.e., of the object as a certain essence)—no attention being paid to the fact that this "aspect b" is essentially a part of "phase b"—that is, of the personal-act-already-realized-in-the-form-of-a-world.

Now it must be noted that the various sciences, as a rule, have a practical orientation. As a technician, as an artist, as a physicist, man wants to create something. As such, he is no longer in quest of a certain "what"; the "what" is present in him in the form of an idea, an intention, a project. The whole problem for him is how to give shape to this "what", to incarnate this unity-meaning in a portion of space, as perfectly as possible. For this purpose, he makes use of all his skill and of all his experience: he realizes that the more he submits himself to the conditions imposed upon him by the world-already-there, the more valuable, the more original, his own creation will be. This creation will be the actuation in a certain direction of the potentialities of the world.

The research of the scientist, the efforts of the technician, as personal activities, must be understood within the integral perspective which our study has brought to light. The universe exists as a personal act unfolding itself from an expressive centre, tending reflectively towards its supreme realization and, in this movement, continually conditioned by itself-already-realized.

The research of the scientist, in its concrete reality, is a personal-act-actuating-itself-in-a-certain-manner. The field of his study is himself-existing-in-some-particular-way. As a person, the scientist wants to realize himself, to live his personal life in a most perfect, most intensely fulfilling manner—in other words, the universe-in-him wants to attain its completion. The scientist feels that his personal realization is linked with a continual progress in self-understanding. Therefore he studies himself-incarnate. This effort does not simply bring to light the structure of the world-already-constituted, but produces a continual actuation of the potentialities of the world. It is by transcending itself-already-realized through the research of the scientist that the world becomes in the scientist aware of itself-already-constituted. Indeed, the scientist-already-realized-in-the-form-of-a-certain-world (the essence of the scientist) has no existence apart from the scientist-continuing-to-constitute-the-world-as-the-concretion-of-himself (his existence).

The work of the technician must be understood in the same perspective. Through his efforts, the world-in-him seeks to build itself, to actuate its potentialities. To be successful in his attempts, the technician must know the world-already-constituted-in-him, he must be skilful in handling it. This is why he tries continually to increase his experience and makes use of it in his creative efforts.

In general, the research of the scientist aims at possessing more fully what is already there, the work of the technician aims at producing new forms of existence out of the old. There is a continual dialectic between these two types of activity. The latter is in a way the existence of the former: it gives to it life, dynamism, meaning; it is the former continually beyond itself. The former is in a way the essence of the latter: it is the base on which the work of the technician grounds itself, the system by which his work is continually conditioned, guided, and inspired.

A final remark. The process by which the scientist gains knowledge of the world is not primarily the process by which he forms concepts which "correspond" to the reality which he studies. It is in the act of living his object of research, of coinciding with the intentions which animate it, that he realizes luminously the "what" of this object. This means that, in order to reach the core of the reality which he studies, he must first adopt an attitude of submission. Submission to whom? To himself-incarnate, no doubt; more deeply, to the Creative Act on which he depends in the very movement by which he constitutes the world as luminous expression of himself. This submission—which is identical with his personal freedom—is the very soul of his study, the existential prerequisite to an authentic discovery of reality.

Reflection as Speech

In the section dealing with my personal act incarnate in my body, I pointed out that reflection and speech are one—in other words, that my personal-act-incarnate-reflecting-upon-itself is identically my personal-act-*telling*-itself-to-itself. I shall examine this again in the wider perspective of the present investigation.

As has been explained, my personal act, while unfolding itself, constitutes reflectively the world and the objects of the world as concretions of its particular self-actuating movement and as expressions of its still unactuated potentialities. To the extent that I make them exist as potential beings, I constitute them as "universals" characterized by specific destinations, I "categorize" them: I name them. Thus a thing as named is a thing constituted as a luminous crystallization of a certain aspect of my integral being-towards. This means that the name of the thing and the thing itself are inseparable: the name of a thing is the thing itself existing as a luminous expression of my potentialities; the name stands for whatever the thing represents and contains. On the one hand a nameless thing is almost a nonentity, on the other hand the uttering of the name gives me a quasi-presence of the thing—that is, makes me adopt a certain vital attitude, provokes a certain vibration of my act incarnate which is already the very *esse* of the thing qua modification of my existential field, qua meaningful part of my world. This shows that a name is not first of all a *verbum mentale* but, like the thing itself, a typical manner of "patterning" myself, a modality of my life. My understanding of a name is the reflectiveness of the act by which I produce in myself the vital disposition which is—at least inchoatively—the very existence of the thing which this name designates.

But the name is not a pure creation of my personal-act-unfolding-itself any more than is the thing for which it stands. As has been pointed out, my personal act, while constituting the objects of the world as luminous expressions of its potentialities, is conditioned by itself-already-existing-in-these-objects-in-the-form-of-specific-intentions,-of-incipient-behaviours—in other words, my personal act shapes the objects as crystallizations of itself by continually taking up and revitalizing (reflectively) itself-already-present-in-them-in-various-manners.

The same complex phenomenon holds good in so far as "naming objects" is concerned. I constitute them as name-realities by continually assimilating the names which they possess as modalities of my act-already-realized. In fact, the process by which objects reveal to me the intentions by which they are constituted as parts of the world-already-there, and the process by which they name themselves in me, are one and the same vital operation.

My speech function, however, is no more confined to the naming of things than the reflectiveness of my personal act is restricted to the constitution of "quiddities". I have shown that my fundamental operation is the reflective positing of the existence of things in the movement by which I tend towards my end: the being of things (i.e., their being-for-me) is their being constituted as luminous concretions of my integral existential tension. This basic operation reflects itself in my speech in the affirmation of existence which underlies each of my reflective utterances. Sometimes, it is emphasized distinctly—for instance, in judgments such as: this *is* a house, this *is* a tree. It must be noted, however, that my judgments never introduce a distinction between the being of a thing and its "quiddity". When I affirm "this is a tree", I do not mean to say "this is on the one hand a being, and on the other hand a tree", but I say "this is an object the whole existence of which is in its being a tree". This must be related to the fact that my tending towards the end never exists as pure appetence for the end, but is always expressed in particular motions and actions, in particular variations of my existential field.

Some philosophers argue from the distinction in the judgment between the act of judging (the affirmation of existence) and the "terms" of the judgment to the real distinction between the existence of things and their essence. But there is in this reasoning a fallacy based on a geometrical view of reality and a geometrical understanding of the judgment. A sound interpretation of the judgment must be made in reference to the existential framework in which the judgment is formed and apart from which it is nothing but an abstraction. Let us analyse this framework in so far as it is the vital milieu in which the judgment "this is a tree" takes shape.

The fundamental fact from which everything starts is the fact of my personal act coming to existence in a certain centre and, from this centre, constituting my world as its field of expression, as the concretion of its vital tension. Now, in a definite place in its expressive field, my personal-act-in-tension-towards-its-end crystallizes itself into a certain living form—a particular specification of its central potentialities—and, at a certain moment, becomes reflectively conscious of this operation: it apprehends this variation of its existential field as a specific concretion of its fundamental tension—thus, in the very process of constituting reflectively a certain tree as the expression of my potentialities, I form the judgment "this is a tree". This judgment is (1) the reflective positing of an existing reality—in so far as it takes place in the movement by which my integral being-towards expresses itself in a given portion of space, (2) the reflective positing of a particular object—in so far as my integral being-towards expresses itself in this portion of space in a particular, limited symbolic form. As we can see, this judgment is the verbal expression of the reflective movement by which I constitute the thing as a certain unity-meaning expressing itself in a particular spatial configuration—that is, of the act by which I give to the thing its existence-for-me.

But there is another aspect. My judgment "this is a tree" is not only the reflective positing of an object but also the acknowledgment of an object already constituted (in Scholastic terminology: it is not only an "activity" but also a "passivity"). We know why: in the very process of constituting the tree as concretion of itself, my personal act is given to itself; it is conditioned by itself-already-present-in-the-tree-in-a-particular-vital-manner; more deeply: it is created. My judgment "this is a tree", to the extent that it is the acceptance of a fact which imposes itself upon me, is the verbal expression of the consciousness I have of being generated, created, while positing myself in a particular manner. In this respect, my judgment expresses my knowledge of the object as a reality prior to my actual positing of it, a reality by which this positing is conditioned—in other words, it is acknowledgment of the object (of myself) as a certain essence.

These reflections show that the judgment points indeed to the distinction existence-essence—it does so not by distinguishing the affirmation of the *esse* of the object (aspect of activity) from the apprehension of its "quiddity" (aspect of passivity), but by being *in its entirety* the verbal expression both of my existential positing of the object as a particular concretion of myself and of the experience I have of being created while positing myself in this particular manner.

In the first section of this chapter, I have emphasized the link between speech and experience. Speech constitutes itself in my personal-act-reflecting-upon-itself. The concrete meaning, the value of the words I use, of the sentences I form, comes entirely from the unity of my thinking with the living reality. Words signify something to the degree to which they express my intuition of things.

Now it so happens that speech, which is meant to express life, tends to become a barrier between thought and reality. As it develops, speech constitutes itself into a kind of superstructure, into a world-in-itself. When this phenomenon takes place, instead of accepting the living reality as the existential basis to which we must painstakingly refer ourselves in order to vivify our speech and render it meaningful, we tend more and more to interpret reality in reference to ready-made notions. Let me try to show the main characteristics of this strange evolution.

I have described above the existential foundation of the categorical attitude, as also the limitations which it must accept in order to remain in conformity with the facts of experience. In particular, I have pointed out that the objects of the world, as potential beings, though they are characterized by specific destinations, are never strictly determined: their integral destination is the destination of my personal act—therefore their expressiveness is really universal. Now we notice that, through speech, the categorical attitude tends to harden: all things belonging to one category are reduced to equivalent units; as they are put into words, objects are defined rigidly, they are reduced to strictly determined notions; thus defined, they become co-existing, mutually exclusive entities. As a result of this evolution, the world is conceived on a geometrical pattern: a world of static essences which it is the task of philosophy to define "rigorously", to classify and arrange into a coherent whole. We know the excesses to which this fallacious systematization, this blind pretension to perfect notional clarity, may lead.

A certain hardening of the categorical attitude is needed for our daily occupations and transactions. It must be noted, however, that in daily life speech remains in touch with the living reality; words, like things, have a wide evocative value; people feel the interpenetration of the different parts of their environment, of their world, and express this feeling through symbolical language. But this sense of reality pervading our daily speech is too much for the essentialist philosophers. They consider it as empiricism or sensationism, as a contamination of knowledge by spatio-temporal vagaries. Their idea of perfect knowledge is that of a system of strictly defined, immutable "metaphysical" notions from which all imagery and symbolism are banished. This system is supposed to be the faithful expression of the intelligible substratum of the changing world—if not the substratum itself.

This radical geometricism is the extreme to which intellects which let themselves be imprisoned within verbal superstructures can be carried. Its pretension to rigour, clarity, and objectivity is based upon fallacies; the conception of metaphysical knowledge which it implies is derived from a wrong understanding of intellectual knowledge. In fact, philosophical accuracy is obtained through a continual effort of penetration into the living reality, through a constant coming back to the "things themselves". This effort enables us to express ourselves in an "existential language"—that is, in a language which does not offer itself as its own justification, but draws its value from the living experience of which it is an integral part.

2. My Act-World as Act-Volition

I shall now analyse the way in which my act-volition actuates itself and, while actuating itself, personalizes my world.

Aspect a: In the modalities of my brain, my life-act, through the consciousness it gains of itself, transcends itself into an act-volition, and thus tends towards its end in a reflective and self-determined manner. In order to actuate this vital tension, my personal act concretes itself into an act-project—in other words, I give to my life a definite direction, I decide in a practical manner the way in which it will be spent. This act-project is the reality which gives to my world its general physiognomy, its basic value; it is the concrete orientation which the universe takes while moving in me and through me towards its completion. Every event of my life, every situation in which I find myself, every person I meet, every object I perceive, reflects it in a particular manner, and is, therefore, a particular concretion of it. This is an undeniable fact. It is evident that the whole world would exist for me in a quite different manner, that every circumstance of my life would have for me a different meaning, if I were a doctor, or an engineer, or a businessman, if I were a militant Communist or a Hindu sadhu.

Now my act-project actuates itself in a progressive manner—it realizes itself through particular decisions, actions and reactions. Each of these moves is a moment which holds its existence and its meaning from my integral life intention; each of these moves is also the act of a certain world: the world of my philosophical thinking, the world reflecting my act of conversing with my friend, the world of my evening prayer. All these worlds are fluctuations of the universe-in-me on its way towards its completion.

The relation between my act-project and the various decisions and activities through which I actuate it must be correctly understood. My act-project transcends my particular actions and, at the same time, subsists in them. It transcends them by being always ahead of them, in tension towards an aim which these particular occupations do not fulfil; it subsists in them to the extent that it needs them in order to remain itself and realize itself—my life intention perishes if it is not carried out through practical attitudes and concrete initiatives.

All these facts have already been mentioned in the second chapter of this study, but they need to be complemented. I have pointed out more than once that all my particular actions express themselves in the whole universe and are, therefore, actuations of the intentions constitutive of all the objects of the world. In this connection, let us note that there are so to speak two ways in which my daily activities move and transform my surroundings. On the one hand, most of my actions produce what may be called tangible transformations of my immediate environment. At this moment, my hand grasps my pencil and, with it, fills a white page with writing. When I dust my table, my left hand moves the different objects which lie on my table and my right hand, holding a duster, cleans its surface. When I walk in the country, my feet stir the dust of the path, my body, moving along the canal, continually modifies the relationship in which it stands to the paddy fields, the coconut palms, the dinghies tied to some trees growing on the bank of the canal, the huts of the Bengali peasants. But these perceptible alterations of my surroundings which my activities bring about is not the whole influence which I exert on my environment. As it unfolds itself from its centre, as it actuates itself in various ways, my personal act, while inducing such modifications of its expressive field as I have just described, expresses itself in my whole environment and, through my environment, in my whole world. Thus nothing remains unaffected by what I do: it is the whole created reality which my activity casts into the concretion of itself, unifies in a certain perspective, moves towards its goal.

Aspect b: As it actuates itself in various ways, as it expresses itself in my environment and transforms it, my act-volition is continually conditioned by the world-already-constituted. My act of writing is not simply the creation of this particular setting formed by my body in my room, my chair and my table, my pencil and my papers; it is the reorganization, in reference to the particular aim of my present activity, of an already existing environment. This reorganization implies the continual submission of my activity to the conditions imposed upon it by the various elements of this milieu: to be able to write, I must dispose my body in the right way, keep the window open to prevent the atmosphere from getting stuffy, light my table lamp by turning the switch in the right direction, use my pencil in the proper manner, etc. All these humble realities are factors which contribute to the smooth actuation of my present will of carrying on this study. Thus, to be really effective, this will must be a continual surrender of itself: my activity must be the carrying out of intentions present in my body and in the objects which surround me. When I converse with a friend, I do not invent the words through which I communicate to him my thoughts. I make use of an already existing language, I form sentences according to commonly accepted grammatical norms. This submission of myself to the requirements of speech is the factor which enables me to get across what I have in mind, to give intelligible expression to my inner desires and feelings.

Sometimes the circumstances in which I find myself oblige me to give up or modify my plans. I am travelling by cycle from Calcutta to Raghabpur. The suburbs of the city are already behind me. Soon I am moving along the canal beyond Kaurapukur. Suddenly a few drops of rain begin to fall, heralding a heavy shower. Immediately I understand that my journey to Raghabpur has come to an end. Were I to proceed on my way along the canal, in a few minutes the mud of the path would jam the wheels of my bicycle and prevent all movement. I want to spend the evening working at my table. Now, at about 7 o'clock, because of a power failure, my room is plunged in darkness. I must give up my writing and wait patiently for the reappearance of light. These commonplace examples show how much my act-volition is dependent on the particular circumstances in which it must actuate itself, how much it is conditioned by the modalities of the existential field in which it must express itself.

Complementariness of the two aspects: Each one of my personal decisions is at once a quasi-creative initiative and an acceptance of myself-already-realized and of the world-already-existing. These are not two conflicting aspects. It is precisely through its submission to the conditions imposed upon it by the existential field in which it continually incarnates itself that my personal act wins its freedom, overcomes the obstacles which prevent it from tending effectively towards its goal, masters itself and the universe. The examples given in the previous paragraph illustrate this truth.

With regard to those events which oblige me to give up or modify particular projects, an important remark must be made. There are no circumstances in the world which can force me to cease tending towards my end. The self-determined movement by which I realize myself continues whatever the situation in which I am placed. Now each of my particular activities is essentially a moment of this integral tension. Each of my actions actuates this tension to the extent that it is acceptance of the circumstances in which I am created. This shows us that, even when I give up a particular project because of unavoidable circumstances, I still actuate my freedom, since I submit myself in a truly personal manner to the Act which creates me in these circumstances.

In this connection, it is important to emphasize once more the exact nature of true personalizing submission. It is not by yielding to all the forces which act upon me, or by giving up my efforts when faced by difficulties and obstacles, that I realize myself as a free person. When I surrender myself without due consideration to worldly influences, my life tends to become the mere continuation in me of the movement, of the fluctuations, constitutive of the world-already-existing; it tends to become a mere phenomenal process. This "phenomenalization" of my life, far from being a strengthening of my individuality, is a weakening of my personality, an alienation of my freedom. The reason for this is clear. My personal act, however much it is conditioned by the modalities of its expressive field, is not *constituted* by its dependence on itself-already-realized and on the world-already-constituted (i.e., it is not a product of evolution). Therefore its surrender to worldly suggestions and influences, its fatalistic "passivity" in the presence of adverse circumstances cannot, by itself, actuate my freedom. This surrender, on the contrary, because it tends to eliminate the transcendence of my act with regard to the expressive field in which it is incarnate (i.e., with regard to itself-already-realized, to the world-already-constituted), tends also to suppress my freedom, to extinguish my personal existence.

My personal act is constituted as a transcendental reality by its dependence on the Creative Act. Therefore the only attitude which may strengthen my personality in an authentic way and liberate me is the submission of my will to the Creator. It is by surrendering myself to the Transcendent Source of my existence that I realize myself as a free person. This shows us that, if my acceptance of the circumstances in which I find myself, my acceptance of my limitations, is to be an authentic actuation of my freedom, it must already be an act of transcendental obedience. As a liberating attitude, my acceptance of my situation must be submission to the Transcendent who creates me as a personal act incarnate in this situation—that is, it must be acceptance of my createdness.

I am created as a personal act in tension towards an end. Thus it is clear that any surrender to worldly influences that tends to slow down or bring to a halt my authentic progress towards my end cannot be an act of transcendental obedience. I may find myself faced by obstacles which I *must* overcome in order to act according to the Creator's will. In a more general way, I must say that, in order to actuate myself in compliance with the Creative Act, I may never simply "let myself go"—that is, let myself be carried along by worldly influences. Indeed, my personal existence consists in my being always ahead of myself-already-realized. I am created as the act which leads the world towards its completion, not as an act which must be simply carried along by the world-already-constituted. Therefore the movement of my existence, in order to be a personalizing process (in accordance with the Creator's will) must be a continual effort of transcendence—each moment of my life must not be a mere repetition of the past, but a genuine creation.

It is precisely in the power it has to overcome difficulties that the transcendence of the personal act with regard to all the structures in which it is incarnate is most strikingly apparent. As the personal act is able to transform organic deficiencies into spiritual attitudes, so also it can take up worldly obstacles and influences of a corrosive or depressive character and re-create them into expressions of faith, into modalities of a world made of love and hope. When such an integration takes place, the whole personal universe tends towards a more and more perfect spiritualization.

3. Relation between Reflection and Volition

The self-actuating movement of my act-volition, the main articulations of which I have just described, is essentially reflective.

First, it is evident that it is through reflection that my personal act has shaped itself into an act-project. At a certain moment of my life, my act incarnate, apprehending itself as a movement towards an end, discovering the world as its field of expression, as a reality which it had to build while realizing itself, while becoming conscious of its individual potentialities and of its fundamental inclination, took the form of a definite life intention—thus I determined in a responsible manner what my life would be.

This life project formed through reflection was my own decision. An important point should be noted in this connection. I have already explained that the fact of my existence as a personal act incarnate characterized by a unique individuality shows that I am the product of a unique Creative Intention—in other words, that I am created for a unique purpose. In this perspective, it appears that the life project I formed, in order to be a truly self-determined, deeply reflective, authentically personalizing decision, had to coincide with the unique intention by which my transcendental individuality was constituted—in other words, it had to be the personal realization of a certain mission entrusted to me—a mission which I was—it had to be an act of transcendental submission. Later, I shall show on what conditions a life project can become the luminous realization and the personal acceptance of the divine intention.

All the self-actuating initiatives of my personal act, the activities through which I carry out progressively my act-project, are characterized by reflectiveness. I do not mean to say that consciousness is an "accidental" property of these activities; I mean to say that consciousness pertains to their very existence as free actions ordained towards particular aims, as processes through which my personal act actuates its tension towards its end. The notion of an act ordaining itself towards a goal as a "blind process" is a sheer absurdity.

Reflectiveness pertains to my activities both as quasi-creative initiatives and as "obediences": each of my undertakings is both the reflective creation of a particular world and the reflective acceptance of the world-already-constituted. In accordance with my previous observations, I shall say: it is by accepting reflectively itself-already-realized, by knowing and understanding itself in an authentic manner, that my personal act is enabled to realize itself further in a truly self-determined, luminous, creative fashion. I want to go by train from Calcutta to Darjeeling. For this purpose, I consult the railway time-table. At what time will the North Bengal Express leave Sealdah Station and reach Moharajpur Ghat? How long will the steamer take to cross the Ganges? At what time will the train leave Manihari Ghat and reach Siliguri? At what time will the Himalayan toy train leave Siliguri and reach Darjeeling? These are questions to which I want an answer. Moreover, I foresee the way in which I shall spend my time during the journey, I prepare whatever I think is needed for it. This whole study of myself-incarnate-in-the-context-of-my-journey-to-Darjeeling, my reflective acceptance of the requirements of this existential field are the very elements which will enable me to be truly the master of my journey. I have to write a letter with a type-writer which I have never used. I first examine carefully the peculiarities of its keyboard and its other contrivances; I try it—and my fingers on it—by typing a few random sentences on a piece of rough paper. These preliminary examinations and exercises, this adaptation of myself to the modalities of my expressive field, enable me to type my letter with a sense of security, to assume a true personal control of myself-already-realized. Study and careful reflection are always the necessary prerequisites to creative action, to the mastery of any technique. Much experience and know-how, self-understanding and self-acceptance, is needed to actuate our potentialities in a truly creative manner, to give existence to new forms of self-expression (whether it be the writing of a poem, or the manufacture of a good razor blade, or the building of an atomic aircraft carrier . . .). In order to realize itself in a truly personal manner, my act incarnate must possess and understand itself: I must have a clear vision of my aim, I must discover the potentialities of my existential field, the intentions of which the various elements of my world are the incarnations, I must let this knowledge inspire my actions.

There is another aspect which must be kept in mind. I have stressed so far the fact that the freedom and creativeness of my personal act are based on self-understanding; they depend upon its reflective acceptance of itself-already-realized. This fact is the expression at the transcendental level of a phenomenon that we have observed since the beginning of our inquiry: the fact that my act is always conditioned by the modalities of the expressive field in which it incarnates itself. Now we must also remember that my act, however much it is conditioned by the structures in which it unfolds itself, is not a product of these structures; we must remember that the way in which the peculiarities of my act-already-realized condition my act-continuing-to-actuate-itself is itself determined by the specific form which this actuation assumes—in other words, that my essence, however much it conditions my existence, is itself constituted by my existence. This, as we know, remains true at the transcendental and reflective level which we are now exploring. My intention of going to Darjeeling is, as has been pointed out, underlaid by my understanding and acceptance of the whole setting in which it must realize itself. On the other hand—this is the point I want to stress now—the concrete initiatives I take to carry out my intention determine the way in which the knowledge I have acquired influences my going to Darjeeling; nay more, it is within these initiatives—that is, within my personal-act-continuing-to-actuate-itself—that my knowledge is kept alive. Similarly, it is according to the way in which I type my letter to my friend that my understanding of myself-incarnate-in-my-body,-in-my-fingers,-in-the-typewriter conditions my act; it is within this act that my self-understanding continues to exist. In a more general way, it must be affirmed that the way in which I build my world determines the manner in which my understanding and experience of the world-already-constituted guide me; it must be affirmed that my act-unfolding-itself is the very existence of this self-knowledge.

From this we may see that knowledge is always a function of life: it is the medium through which I realize myself as personal *life*-act, through which the universe-in-me realizes itself as a *living* totality. We may see, too, that my free initiatives, however much they are conditioned by my knowledge of myself-incarnate, do not simply result from this knowledge (since in fact they constitute it). The fact to which I am led back once more is that of my createdness: if my personal-act-actuating-itself-reflectively, however dependent it is upon its knowledge of itself-already-realized (and, through itself-already-realized, of the world-already-constituted), is not a product of this knowledge, it is because it proceeds immediately from the Transcendent Creative Act. In other words, the fact that my freedom develops in an atmosphere of luminous dependence is identical with the fact of my existence as a rational creature. Authentic self-understanding always implies the reflective consciousness of our ontological relation to the Creator. This self-understanding can develop only in a personal act which links itself to its Creative Source through obedience. Truth reveals itself to the extent that it is lived because truth *is* life.

4. Integration of the Phenomenal Act-World in the Movement of Transcendental Existence

The last part of this chapter will be an analysis of the relation between the different psychological aspects of my phenomenal act-world and my reflective existence.

i. *My Personal Act-World and My Temperament*

I pointed out earlier that my life-act incarnate is characterized by a basic existential attitude, a temperamental inclination. Transcendentally, this is due to the fact that as a creature I am constituted by a unique intention and, therefore, possess a unique individuality; phenomenally, this comes from the particular constitution of the cosmico-biological structures in which my life-act is incarnate. This temperamental inclination, as has been explained, manifests itself in my whole world—thus my body, my world, exist as the concretions of my fundamental affective disposition.

On the other hand, my body and my world are the incarnation of my act-project and of the various initiatives through which I actuate this life intention. Let us see how these two perspectives are concretely made one.

As we know, my act-volition is not a reality superimposed upon my life-act but the personal actuation of this prime act; on the other hand, my personal act remains life-act—that is, essentially given to itself—even when it actuates itself in a self-determined manner. These are the basic facts which we must keep in mind if we are to understand how my world is at once the concretion of temperamental disposition and the incarnation of my act-volition.

My act-volition is the actuation of a life-act which is characterized by a temperamental inclination; therefore, however personal it may be, it remains fundamentally temperamental. The act-project, in which my personal act expresses its tension towards the end, may be described to a large extent as the personalization of my basic affective disposition. It is a fact that my way of facing life, the concrete way in which my act-project formulates itself, the existential atmosphere which pervades it, and, therefore, my vision of the world, the meaning-for-me of all the situations in which I find myself, are to a very large extent made up of my temperamental individuality. It may happen that two persons of very different temperaments give to their lives orientations which are apparently quite similar. However, this external similarity hides, no doubt, a great divergence of aspirations, attitudes and outlooks.

The fact that my act-project may be described as the personalization of my temperamental inclination may seem to imply that freedom had very little to do with the formation of this project; it may seem to imply that my act-project was in some way determined from the very beginning of my life and came to distinct existence through a process of "natural evolution".

Had I formed my act-project simply by letting my propensities and likings express themselves "freely", the freedom of my "decision" would indeed have been reduced to a minimum; I would have alienated my personality instead of allowing it to attain emancipation and to grow in strength. However, let us note carefully the following:

(1) My temperamental disposition has never existed in me in the form of a strictly compelling urge or propensity. No doubt, from the beginning of my life, it drives me in a certain direction and, therefore, has a certain determining influence. Yet, as my life-act incarnate is a world of still unactuated potentialities, this fundamental inclination remains essentially undetermined: there is in me no "natural force" which is overpowering.

(2) The notion of a human life as a process of "natural evolution" is an absurdity. The concept of "natural evolution" implies the continual emergence of the new out of the old in a strictly determined manner. According to this view, each moment of time contains the following moment in a definite way. This means that each moment is

the mere repetition of what has already taken place, that the present is the mere continuation of the past—thus nothing ever takes place which is really new, and there is no real growth, and no real becoming.

In fact, as we know, my existence consists in my being always *ahead of myself-already-realized*; it implies the continual production of something really new out of the old. This shows that my act-project, whatever it be, can never come into existence as the mere continuation of an already existing propensity. Had I formed it simply by yielding to my likings, even then it could not be described as the mere product of determining psychological factors. In such a case, I would have to say that in fact no definite life intention has been formed, and that instead of determining myself in a personal manner (i.e., of giving to my life a personal orientation), I have allowed my life to remain a largely undetermined, a predominantly temperamental, process.

(3) To be a real "act of freedom", my act-project *had* to be the personalization of my temperamental inclination. Indeed, my fundamental affective disposition is not something "purely phenomenal"; it is in a very real way the expression of the intention by which I am constituted as creature: the fact of my existence as an individual life-act ordained by the Creator towards a specific end, to be reached in a specific manner, is the fact of my existence as this particular person, possessing this particular temperamental individuality. Now, to be authentically free, the formation of my act-project had to be an act of transcendental obedience. Therefore it had to be the reflective taking up of my "natural" propensities and aptitudes—of myself as I was—in a life intention ordering me in a personal, self-determined manner towards my end.

This taking up, it must be noted, while implying the understanding and acceptance of myself-incarnate, entailed also the understanding and acceptance of my world: this world which my particular affectivity shaped in this particular way was the existential field in which my act-project had to actuate itself, which it had to transform progressively and lead to its completion.

Not only my act-project, but each particular initiative through which this act realizes itself is intimately conditioned by my temperamental individuality. The way in which I react to the influences which I undergo, the way in which I face the various situations in which I find myself, the decisions I take and the way I carry them out depend very much on my basic affective disposition. There is in fact no possibility of distinguishing between the voluntary and the temperamental elements of my various activities. Each of my personal activities is entirely voluntary and entirely temperamental because each of them proceeds from the totality of my personal-life-act-incarnate. My whole individuality expresses itself in each of my actions.

ii. *Relation between My Transcendental Act-World and My Perception of the World*

It is through sense perception that the world illuminates itself in the modalities of my brain while conditioning my personal act; it is also through sense perception that my personal act expresses itself luminously in my surroundings, moves and transforms them consciously, "intelligently". At this moment, my eyes are fixed on my right hand holding a blue pencil, on the white sheet of paper which this pencil fills with writing. At the phenomenal level, this visual perception must be described in this way: my life-act, while unfolding itself from its centre, while constituting my table, this blue pencil, this white sheet of paper, as more or less determined expressions of its potentialities, as the concretions of the movement by which it gives existence to my world, illuminates itself in this limited setting in the mode of visual perception. This whole process is characterized by non-reflectiveness—that is, by a lack of self-determination, of freedom, of transcendence. At the phenomenal level, perception is a dim narrow and adhesive type of consciousness because, at the phenomenal level, the life-act is deeply immersed in the spatial structures which it constitutes.

But my present perception is not such a restricted phenomenon. The act which constitutes this blue pencil and this white sheet of paper is not simply my life-act. At this moment, *my personal act*—that is, the transcendental actuation of my life-act—unfolding itself from its centre, constitutes my table, this pencil, this sheet of paper as luminous crystallizations of its potentialities, of the particular activity through which at this moment it actuates its reflective tension towards its end. My present perception of my pencil and of this white sheet of paper is perception of them within this transcendental movement. This perception, no doubt, takes place in a restricted area; it is perception of a tiny part of my environment, but it is a reality quite different from the "phenomenal perception" which I have just described: I *see* my pencil, the sheet of paper, I live them visually, tactually, as modalities of a movement which goes beyond their *hic et nunc*, as concretions of my tension towards my end. Thus, in the stream of my transcendental existence, my perception of my environment acquires a new dimension; it is dilated, liberated, "transcendentalized".

In the intellectualistic perspective, the "rational element" which human perception contains is due to a sort of "contamination" of sense perception by intellection. This rational element is something superadded to "pure sensation", which is always the apprehension of a particular *hic et nunc*. We know that this view cannot be accepted because it is based on a defective understanding of human psychology and of the relation between man and the world. The fact that our perception of the world takes place in an atmosphere of freedom is not due to the infusion of some rational element by the "intellectual faculty" into the "sensible faculties", but to the fact that the personal act, while incarnating itself in our body, in our world, makes them live as concretions of its transcendental dynamism (i.e., personalizes, spiritualizes, illuminates them).

It may happen at times that the personal act, experiencing the perception of a particular object as a certain attraction, as a particularly intense vibration of itself-incarnate, allows itself to be absorbed by this situation. When this surrender takes place, the perceptive field often takes on a greater density, the objects lose a great part of their evocative power, they reflect in their own way the narrower and less flexible manner of living which the act has adopted through having in some way alienated itself: perception is tied down, it is "phenomenalized" instead of being "transcendentalized".

The way in which we perceive the world is subject to changes which are reflections of the fluctuating way in which our personal act actuates itself. Our personal act may at times concentrate itself in the pursuing of its aim; at other times—though our movement towards the end is maintained, though our act-project continues to actuate itself—it may relax its tension and adopt a looser way of living. These variations in the movement of our personal life express themselves in the way in which we look at our environment, in the way in which the world extends around us.

In my study of the relation between reflection and volition, I have pointed out that freedom is built on self-understanding and self-acceptance. Now it must be noted that my knowledge of myself-incarnate, of the world-already-constituted, is essentially perceptivo-reflective. It is through my sensory apparatus that my environment becomes in my brain, in my personal act, reflectively conscious of itself; it is through my sensory apparatus that my act-already-realized-in-the-form-of-a-world conditions luminously my act-continuing-to-realize-itself. In the light of this, I must affirm that my personal act actuates itself effectively, that it masters itself and transcends the structures in which it is incarnate, to the extent that its self-actuating initiatives conform with the knowledge it gains of itself through my perceptive organs. I walk towards Raghabpur. At a certain moment, I want to cross the canal on a bamboo bridge arching high above the water. I venture carefully upon it, putting my feet where I feel it is safest to do so. This conformation of my act of crossing the bridge with the data of my visuo-tactual perception is the very factor which makes it master of itself and enables me to arrive safely at the other bank of the canal. Examples of this kind can be multiplied *ad infinitum.* The fact to which they point is again that of my createdness: my self-actuation through conscious submission is, in its deepest reality, obedience to the Transcendent who creates me as personal act incarnate.

Let us now analyse the relation between perception and thinking.

Thinking is a personal activity—in other words, it is my personal-act-actuating-itself-in-a-certain-way-while-tending-towards-its-end. Through this activity, my personal act incarnate wants to possess itself in a more luminous, more comprehensive, way. This activity reaches its goal to the extent that I let myself and the world manifest in me their authentic being, to the extent that I let this knowledge grow into a luminous expression of the whole reality. This process, it must be noted, is in a real sense a creative activity. I do not simply produce in myself a "representation" of the existing world, I *live* the totality in a personal manner and, while living it, make it express itself luminously in the modalities of my brain. This act of living the whole reality is not simply the re-enacting in me of what has already taken place, the re-enlivening in my personal act of what is already there, already constituted; it is a transcendental activity, it takes place within my personal-act-continuing-to-constitute-the-world—that is, within my personal-act-continually-ahead-of-itself: the act by which I let the world-already-constituted illuminate itself in me *is* the act by which I give an ever new existence to my world. My act of thinking is a discovery of reality to the degree to which it is a creative activity; it is a creative activity to the degree to which it is luminous acceptance of reality as it is—fundamentally, to the degree to which it is conscious submission to the Creator, luminous fulfilment of the Creative Intention.

Perception has an important role to play in this thinking activity; in fact, perceiving is an essential aspect of the act of thinking: it is through my perceptive functions that, while thinking, I constitute my environment as luminous expression of myself (aspect a); it is also through my perceptive organs that, while I think, the world illuminates itself in the modalities of my brain (aspect b). The whole process must be understood not as a synthesis of elements but as a unity:

Phase a: While taking reflective possession of itself, my personal act constitutes my body (my perceptive functions) and, through my body (through my perceptive functions) my environment as luminous expressions of its potentialities, of itself reflecting-upon-itself. Thus the things which I see around me—my pencil, my table, those houses, those trees, etc.—*such as I see them*—are constituted as modalities of my thinking activity.

Phase b: From all the parts of my environment which it animates, my act incarnate returns to its source and, in this process, conditions luminously itself-continuing-to-realize-itself. Thus the world which illuminates itself in my personal-act-reflecting-upon-itself is the world-already-constituted-as-luminous-expression-of-myself. This conditioning illumination takes place in my perceptive organs in so far as the world manifests itself to me "visually", "auditively", "tactually"; it takes place in my expressive centre in so far as my act-already-realized-in-the-form-of-a-world reveals the totality of itself to itself-continuing-to-realize-itself. From this we can see once more that the whole process cannot be conceived according to the schema external reality-sensation-intellection. The world which reveals itself to me is from the first the world-already-living-as-concretion-of-myself, the world which my act of thinking already elaborates into its vivid expression. This world reveals itself to me in the act by which I constitute it, by which I live it. Each one of my senses manifests an aspect of it, an aspect which has no meaning, no existence, apart from the living totality to which it belongs. This whole perspective shows also that I do not think simply with my brain but also with my eyes, my hands, with all the objects which surround me, with my whole world: it is my whole world, as it exists concretely in my personal act, which thinks itself in me. This does not exclude the fact that my brain is the centre where this thinking activity takes place primarily; it means simply that my brain is nothing apart from my whole body, from my whole world; that my personal act, though centred in my brain, is really the act-of-the-universe.

Finally, let us bear in mind the basic factor which gives the whole system its ontological dimension. The continual return of my personal-life-act-incarnate to its source is its acknowledgment of its ontological dependence on a Creative Principle; the fact that my act is continually conditioned by itself-already-realized is identically the fact of my createdness; the fact that each one of my personal initiatives, in order to be really free and self-determined, must conform with the data supplied by my perceptions and by reflection, is fundamentally the fact that, in order to live an authentic human life, I must link myself consciously with the Source of my personal existence through an act of obedience: I exist as an individual person—who is at once an individual perceiving, thinking, willing, acting—by the Creative and Illuminative Initiative of the Transcendent.

iii. *Relation between My Transcendental Act-World and My Imaginations*

As I carry out my daily activities, numberless thoughts, ideas, imaginations occur to me. I shall now examine these phenomena in the context of my personal existence and study the way in which these "states of consciousness" can be integrated in the movement of my act-volition.

I have shown previously that the nature of my thoughts and imaginations must be understood in reference to the existential status of my life-act-incarnate-in-my-brain. In its expressive centre, my life-act exists in a relatively undetermined and, so to speak, uncommitted manner. Consequently, its self-consciousness is non-factual, non-positing. Now I notice that, in the very midst of my voluntary activity (i.e., of the activity by which I determine, commit, myself)—in my act of cleaning my room, of going to visit a friend, of listening to a piece of music, of writing a letter, etc.—spontaneous thoughts and fancies continue to cross my mind. This shows that I am not entirely immersed in what I do, that the action I perform is devoid of intensity, that my personal self-actuation is still weak and imperfect. In other words, though I direct myself towards my goal in a self-determined manner, my activity is still to some extent immersed in an atmosphere of unreality and dream.

These observations indicate how the phenomenon of inattention should be explained. It is possible for me to be inattentive to what I do because my act incarnate is a world of unrealized potentialities, and because my particular occupation is only a partial actuation of these potentialities. There is distraction when my act incarnate, while realizing itself in a particular manner, remains somehow abstracted from the course which it follows and, in this uncommitted region of itself, expresses itself in the form of desires, imaginations, or dreams.

This type of inattention, incidentally, must be distinguished from another kind of absent-mindedness. Sometimes, while I am performing some action, my attention is almost entirely directed towards something else. For instance, it may happen that, while taking a meal, I intentionally continue a line of thought in which I was absorbed before leaving my room. In this case, my thinking activity is the real transcendental self-actuating move of my personal act. The act of eating which accompanies it is reduced, as it were, to a "third person process", to an operation which takes place within my life-act incarnate without my being *personally* in it. Again this split in my existential structure is possible because my act incarnate is a field of potentialities which have still to be realized and can be realized in many different ways; and also because, in the various organico-environmental structures in which it is incarnate, my act tends to effect various types of self-realization.

To return, however, to our immediate subject: As we know, my transcendental activity is characterized by self-determination: as it takes luminous possession of itself in its expressive centre, my act transcends its indetermination and directs itself towards its end in a conscious and purposeful manner. Thus actuated, my act expresses itself to itself in the mode of positing, reflective consciousness—a factual, realistic type of awareness. Now I notice that, even as it illuminates itself in this transcendental manner, my act goes on expressing itself in the form of thoughts, ideas, or imaginations.

Experiencing in itself these phenomena, the personal act may adopt various attitudes:

(1) It may "transcendentalize" these adventitious thoughts and ideas—that is, actuate them, transform them into luminous expressions of its self-determined movement towards its end. We under-

stand the possibility of this personalization of phenomenal states of consciousness, because we know that the act-volition is the life-act-actuating-itself-in-a-personal-manner. This transformation of phenomenal concepts into transcendental reflects is subject to certain laws. Thoughts, ideas, imaginations, may be the expression in the modalities of the brain of numberless inclinations and motions of the life-act incarnate which are ordained towards various particular ends. Now the self-determined movement of the act, if it is to be really transcendental, to be authentically personal, must be a reflective self-orientation towards the end. This movement, it must be noted, implies a polarization of the whole personal structure, of all the potentialities of the life-act incarnate. This means that, in order to be transcendentalized, many thoughts and ideas have to undergo a transformation which practically converts them into radically new expressive realities. As a rule, we must say that the personalization of phenomenal concepts always implies a creative initiative of the personal act. Indeed, it is in the movement by which the act goes beyond itself-already-realized that this personalization takes place.

With regard to personal thinking, the stream of imaginative consciousness, though it may be a source of distraction, acts on the whole both as a stimulant and as a support. Just as the personal act is fed and energized by the whole system in which it is incarnate, so the thinking activity is fed by the lower strata of consciousness. The act-illuminating-itself-reflectively is both conditioned and supported by itself-already-thought and by itself-illuminating-itself-imaginatively.

The dependence of the thinking activity on imaginative consciousness is an aspect of its "self-givenness"—fundamentally, of its createdness. This means that the authentic personalization of phenomenal states of consciousness can be achieved only in the act-relating-itself-to-its-Creative-and-Illuminative-Source-in-a-reflective-manner. It is only in the act-living-luminously-for-its-end that a harmonious integration of the different vital structures can be realized and, therefore, that the various aspects of phenomenal consciousness can be authentically transcendentalized.

(2) Experiencing in itself thoughts, ideas, imaginations, the personal act may at times allow these phenomena to unfold themselves freely. In this case, a certain depersonalization takes place. The tension of the act towards its end relaxes, its self-determination weakens, its reflectiveness and luminosity decrease; a dreamlike atmosphere

tends to invade the whole existential field, the world of the act tends to become a world of shadows, an expanse in which unreal forms are moving in indistinct surroundings.

Thoughts and imaginations, it must be noted, are often the concretions of tensions occurring in definite regions of the life-act incarnate. These tensions, of course, tend to actuate themselves in specific ways. It is clear that, when the personal act gives free scope to these thoughts and imaginations, it tends also to reduce itself to these phenomenal processes; consequently, the personal structure tends to disintegrate.

(3) It often happens that the personal act, though it actuates itself in a self-determined way, does not integrate harmoniously the totality of its cosmico-biological structures, does not personalize intensively its existential field. (This lack of authentic personalization may assume many different forms.) When this phenomenon takes place, the reflectiveness of the act, though real, remains defective: consciousness posits as real a largely unreal mental world; ideas and imaginations which may express many tendencies within the life-act incarnate, which may be due to many different factors, are in a half-reflective but thoroughly assertive manner proposed as valid standards, as leading principles. Thus ideologies are formed: theories which are partly based on a complex of prejudices, of temperamental factors, of elements derived from a particular culture, a particular education, a particular religious background, etc., without being vivified by an authentic personalization of the existential field from which they emerge. At the root of these movements is a lack of transcendence—that is, a certain inability on the part of the act to go beyond itself-already-realized and to master itself-incarnate.

iv. *Relation between My Transcendental Act-World and My Affectivity*

My life-act-incarnate-in-my-organico-environmental-structures is characterized by a temperamental disposition. This disposition, as we know, does not express itself at every moment in the same way. My life-act incarnate lives in various ways the different situations in which it finds itself. These various affective states are various ways in which my temperamental inclination expresses itself.

I have shown that my act-project may be characterized as the personalization of my fundamental affective disposition and that this basic affectivity expresses itself in some way in all the particular initiatives by which my act-project realizes itself. This phenomenon must be connected with the fact that these initiatives are carried out in organico-environmental situations which my life-act "experientializes" in the form of affective motions which are also expressions of my temperamental disposition.

When it experiences in itself these affective movements, the personal act incarnate may "react" in different ways which are comparable to the different ways in which it can react to adventitious thoughts and imaginations:

(1) The personal act may take up the situation in which it finds itself incarnate and make of it an authentic expression of its tension towards its end. In this case, the emotion which has begun to be aroused in it by the fact of its being involved in this situation is converted into a transcendental affect. This conversion often implies a real re-creation of the affective state which was trying to invade the whole psychological make-up. Indeed, affective motions tend by their own dynamism to develop into articulate behaviours; they are ordained towards particular aims. But, in order to be transcendentalized, these emotions must become variations of the movement by which the personal act tends towards its end. Therefore the authentic personalization of these affective states entails their integral sublimation.

It must be realized that it is not by eliminating or annihilating feelings and desires that a true spiritualization of the personal structure can be achieved. Affectivity and life are one; killing one's emotivity is a way of killing oneself. This means that, as a rule, the personal act incarnate transcendentalizes its affective states not by refusing or stifling them, but by accepting them in an "intelligent" manner. Let us explain this.

As it actuates its life intention through a particular course of action, the personal act finds itself involved in various situations in which it vibrates in various phenomenal ways. Now, in these particular occurrences, the personal act cannot reject the circumstances in which it finds itself, since these circumstances are the very modalities of its incarnate existence. But the non-rejection, or the acceptance, of these circumstances implies that the act must take up a positive attitude towards the affective states which it experiences in itself, since these affective states are the very way in which the act lives, animates, these particular circumstances. This positive attitude, however, does not mean a surrender of the act to the emotional urges which condition it, but a creative integration of these urges in the movement by which it tends towards its end, in the particular activity by which it actuates this tension. This integrating process enriches and disciplines these affective motions, transforms them into new potentialities, into liberating forces.

Once more, it must be noted that the act of submission which is at the heart of this personalizing activity is fundamentally obedience to the Creator: the personal act incarnate integrates the various motions which take place in it to the degree to which it takes them up in the reflective consciousness and in the positive acceptance of its own existence as act-created-for-an-end.

(2) The personal act may "let itself go"—that is, allow the affective urges which it experiences to express themselves freely and develop into definite behaviours. In this case, as we know, the act incarnate allows itself to be "decentralized", depersonalized; its freedom, and therefore its reflectiveness, decrease; its world shrinks and loses much of its transcendental meaning. The more often the personal act surrenders to emotional tensions, the more it reduces itself to a succession of disconnected motions, of fitful initiatives, of meaningless comportments. This disintegration, no doubt, can never be complete, because the act, even though it allows itself to be carried along by the stream of emotivity, receives its existence from Above, and therefore remains a radically transcendental reality.

(3) In most circumstances, the personal act neither fully transcendentalizes the affective motions which it experiences, nor allows itself entirely to be carried along by them: very often, its self-actuating initiatives are both volitivo-reflective activities and emotional behaviours. This can easily be understood, since we know that the personal act always remains self-given and deeply involved in the structures of its expressive field. As a rule, it may be said that the various initiatives and behaviours of the personal act incarnate are always conditioned and, to some extent, motivated by the affective states which it experiences in itself. Some organico-environmental situations may be experientialized by the personal act incarnate in the form of paralysing tensions, of overwhelming emotions. In such circumstances, it seems as though the act-volition is entirely absorbed by the disturbances of its existential field, by the forces which are at work at the various levels of its cosmico-biological system.

These observations show the central role played by affectivity in our personal life. The personal act cannot abstract itself from the conditions in which it lives, nor ignore the emotional values which these situations have for it: each meaningful peculiarity of the spatial field in which it is incarnate tends to be lived by it in a characteristic way, and thus to develop into a dimension of its existence. A bodily infirmity is not an indifferent phenomenon, or a pure "physical" detail; it is an element which affects the whole psychological setting of the personal act incarnate, conditions all its initiatives and the way in which it constitutes its world. Poverty is not simply an accidental factor in the life of a man; it is an obsessing reality which invades the whole field of his volitivo-reflective behaviour, and influences his whole personality and the way in which he makes the world exist for him.

Let us conclude with a few words about the relation between affectivity and thinking. It is often said that our intellectual knowledge of reality is by itself "objective", but that this knowledge may be vitiated by "subjective" elements which are of an emotional or affective character. This position is based on the intellectualistic notions of the intellect as a cognitive faculty whose object is the "external world", and of affectivity as an activity which is exercised entirely within the knowing subject. From the analyses contained in this chapter, it is clear that this position cannot be accepted as it stands. Our intellect is not a power which enables us to know "objectively" outward reality; affectivity is not a phenomenon which takes place merely in our body, it is not a mere derivative of knowledge (even though many affective states are, indeed, provoked by our perceptions and intellections).

The life-act incarnate in the body, in the environment, in the whole world, is *always* characterized by a certain affectivity, since affectivity is the existential vibration of the act in the expressive structures which it occupies and animates. As the life-act actuates itself into an act-volition, an act-project, and, through this act-project, into a particular course of action, it is the whole phenomenal field, and therefore the whole affective life, which is personalized, transcendentalized. Now intellectual knowledge is nothing but the luminous presence of the personal act incarnate to itself. This means (1) that knowledge is always self-knowledge, (2) that affectivity is an essential element of knowledge (there is no such thing as an "act" of knowledge which is not "coloured" by affectivity).

Does this mean that knowledge is never "objective"?

The answer to this question depends on the meaning we give to the word "objective". I have shown that objective knowledge must be defined as understanding of oneself and of the world in relation to the Creator. This understanding, as we know, takes place in the personal-act-incarnate-relating-itself-to-its-Creative-Source-through-obedience; it is a personal and luminous realization of the intention by which we are constituted as creatures. Such a self-understanding, it is clear, develops within a certain affective climate (a climate which is not made up of phenomenal emotions but of transcendentalized affects). Therefore objectivity and affectivity are not mutually exclusive but concretely one.

However, the fact remains that emotivity may and does often give our knowledge a "subjective" character. This happens when, influenced by some feeling or passion, we give our world a character of inauthenticity by failing to build it in accordance with the Creative Intention. When I give way to anger, the objects which surround me, my whole world, reflect this feeling: I live my environment, I see it as an expression of my irritation; this irritation inspires the way in which I think and judge about it; my anger is the atmosphere in which my world exists. When this happens, my knowledge of the world is "subjective" not simply because it does not "correspond" with reality, but because the world to which my anger gives existence—a world which is a reality—is not in harmony with the world as intended by the Creator, with the world-existing-without-me. We shall have occasion later to return to this point.

Conclusion

In the first chapter of this study, I showed that the world as I perceive it is a unity expressed in a great diversity of elements, of aspects. No element of this totality has any meaning apart from the other elements, from the whole: each element is essentially a particular expression of the whole system in which it is included. This means that a study of reality which aims at defining with precision what particular objects are "in themselves"—that is, isolated from one another and from the totality—is doomed to failure: objects have no being "in themselves". The only fruitful analysis is that of particular objects in relation to each other, to the whole system of which they are parts and from which they receive their meaning and their existence.

Examining the nature of the unity-meaning constitutive of the universe, I discovered this fact: my personal life-act is the unity-meaning of the world. Later, I realized more and more vividly the interpenetration of the various aspects which I tried to bring to light: the various parts of my body and of my environment are essentially related to each other; my organism is nothing apart from the surrounding world; the world—my world—receives its existence from its relation to my body; the different elements of my personal life—such as perception, affectivity, imagination, intellection, will—are various aspects, each one of which expresses the totality of my personal structure. None of them, therefore, can be studied in isolation: such notions as pure feeling, pure desire, pure knowledge are meaningless fictions.

The complementariness of the various aspects of my act-world has brought to light the importance of a continual experiential contact with living reality in order "to know what we are talking about". Speech tends to atomize reality, that is, to reduce it to a system of solidified and mutually exclusive substances. It is only through a vivid intuition of the inter-relation of the different elements of our existential field that we can give full meaning to the words we use to describe this field. Life has priority over knowledge: reality must be luminously lived in order to be correctly expressed.

As has been shown, the interpenetration of the various aspects of reality is by no means a fusion into a single undifferentiated totality. Each aspect of my act-world has a unique meaning, a unique function with regard to the whole in which it is included. Moreover, my personal structure is, so to speak, a hierarchical system: it has a definite centre to which all its different elements are related; it is constituted by a guiding force which must organize and integrate the diversity in relation to an end.

A last point must be emphasized. My personal act-world has revealed itself as a reality which does not stand by itself: the fact of my createdness is at the heart of all my activities, of all my initiatives, of all my perceptions, of my self-understanding—it is my very being. The reflective acceptance of this fact is the very condition of my personal realization. Correlative to my createdness is the fact of my coming to existence in an already existing world, of my being continually conditioned, supported, generated, by this sphere of being which is in some way transcendent to me. What is this universe in which my world is immersed? How can the existence of this transcendent world be reconciled with my existence as act-world? Further enquiry, I hope, will throw light on these problems.

Note on Thomist Psychology

In my Introduction, I tried to characterize in a few sentences the "intellectualism" of St Thomas. I said there that the "intellectualistic" passages abounding in the writings of Aquinas are at times counterbalanced by other texts which seem to be inspired by a completely different attitude. This, I said, inclines me to think that the experience which gave birth to Thomism is in reality deeper and more genuine than the basic experience of intellectualism. I shall now substantiate this opinion by analysing in a few pages the structure of human personality as it appears from a certain number of texts of the *Summa*. My interpretation of these texts will, perhaps, be considered "subjective", or "coloured" by my vision of reality. It will be remembered that I am writing not as a historian of St Thomas's philosophy but as a philosopher who has found in Thomism the initial inspiration of his personal thinking.

First of all, the concrete aspect of St Thomas's philosophy of man should be emphasized. St Thomas is keenly aware of the incommunicable individuality of each human being. He knows that "man in general" must be at once soul and body, but that this man whom I meet in the street is not "man in general"; he is this particular and unique person, he is this soul, this flesh, these bones.[20]

1. *The Soul, its Nature and Activity*

(a) **My Soul constitutes My Body, makes it Live.** The soul of man is not a vague entity separate from his body; it is present in the whole body and in each part of the body; it is the form, the act, the life, the very *esse*, of the whole body, and of each particular limb and organ. It is my soul that makes my body to be a real human body, acting and living; it constitutes my hand and my eye; it makes my flesh real flesh, and my bones real bones; it gives each part of my body its proper function.[21]

[20] "Sicut enim de ratione huius hominis est, quod sit ex hac anima, et carnibus, et ossibus: ita de ratione hominis est, quod sit ex anima, et carnibus et ossibus." (*Summa Theologica* I, LXXV, 4, ad Resp.)

[21] "Si anima uniretur corpori solum ut motor, posset dici quod non esset in qualibet parte corporis, sed in una tantum, per quam alias moveret. Sed quia anima unitur corpori ut forma, necesse est quod sit in tota et in qualibet parte corporis; non enim est forma corporis accidentalis sed substantialis. Substantialis autem forma non solum est perfectio totius, sed cuiuslibet partis. Et ideo recedente anima, sicut non dicitur animal et homo nisi aequivoce, quemadmodum et animal pictum et lapideum; ita est de manu et oculo, aut carne et osse. . . . Cujus

(b) **The Life of My Body is not Mere Awareness but a Manifold Activity.** In a number of passages, St Thomas identifies the soul with the intellect. However, he is far from making it an arid principle of knowledge and from reducing the whole of human activity to a certain "act of consciousness". In *Summa Theologica*, I, LXXVI, 1, ad Resp., which I have quoted above, St Thomas affirms, no doubt, that the intellect, which is the principle of intellectual operations, is the form of the human body, but in the very same passage he adds that the soul is the reality which gives life to the body—this life is not mere awareness but a manifold activity. My soul is what makes me feel, feed myself, move from one place to another, just as it is the principle which makes me understand.[22]

(c) **My Soul is One and Therefore My Body is One.** Some philosophers have maintained that man has a threefold soul: a rational soul by which he is a real man, a sensible soul by which he is an animal, a vegetative soul by which he is a mere living thing. St Thomas rejects this position because it destroys the unity of man. The body is not like a single container which holds the three souls together by the fact that it is one; the real container is the soul, the intellective soul, which makes the body one as it constitutes it as a human body.[23] This soul is the reality which makes man exist, which makes him body, which makes him a living thing, an animal, a man.[24] This means that man is not a beast to which rationality is superadded.

---

signum est quod nulla pars corporis habet proprium opus anima recedente." (*Ibid.*, I, LXXLI, 8, ad Resp.)

"Anima illud esse in qua subsistit, communicat materiae corporali, ex qua et anima intellectiva fit unum; ita quod illud esse quod est totius compositi, est etiam animae." (*Ibid.*, I, LXXVI, 1, 5um.)

[22] ". . . Primum quo corpus vivat, est anima. Et cum vita manifestatur secundum diversas operationes in diversis gradibus viventium, *id quo primo operamur unumquodque horum operum vitae est anima*. Anima enim est primum quo nutrimur, et sentimus, et movemur secundum locum, et similiter quo primo intelligimus. . . ." (*Ibid.*, I, LXXLI, 1, ad Resp.)

[23] "Quia animal non esset simpliciter unum, cujus essent animae plures: nihil enim est simpliciter unum nisi per formam unam per quam habet res esse: ab eodem enim habet res, quod sit ens, et quod sit una. . . . Si igitur homo ab alia forma haberet quod sit vivum, scilicet ab anima vegetali, et ab alia quod sit animal, scilicet ab anima sensibili, et ab alia forma quod sit homo, scilicet ab anima rationali, sequeretur quod homo non esset unum simpliciter. . . . Et non potest dici quod uniantur per corporis unitatem: quia magis anima continet corpus et facit ipsum esse unum, quam e converso." (*Ibid.*, I, LXXVI, 3, ad Resp.)

[24] "Una et eadem forma est per essentiam, per quam homo est ens actu, et per quam est corpus, et per quam est vivum, et per quam est animal, et per quam est homo." (*Ibid.*, I, LXXVI, 6, 1um.)

Animality and rationality are not two real parts of man. The soul of man, the "intellective soul", contains in itself and sublimates all the properties of the "sensitive" and "vegetative souls"; it contains them not as real elements which are distinctly present in it, but as potencies which it realizes in the very process by which it informs the body.[25]

(d) **The Soul Rules the Body and Transcends it.** Not only does the soul inform the body, but it rules it, sets it in motion[26]; it does so as intellective soul, giving to the body a truly personal direction. The sensitive forms obey the intellect and serve it.[27] This shows the transcendence of the soul in relation to the materiality of the body. The main activity of man, intellectual activity, is not *exercised* by any particular organ, but by the soul as a transcendent reality[28]; however, this activity takes place in the body in so far as the soul is the form of the body and the term of human generation.[29]

(e) **The Powers of the Soul.** The texts of St Thomas that we have quoted describe the body as a reality constituted in existence by the soul which informs it and communicates to it its own *esse*; they describe it also as a movement, an activity, whose principle is the same intellective soul; but St Thomas explains that the soul does not move the body by its *esse* but by its potencies.[30]

What is the nature of these operative potencies?

25 "Nulla alia forma substantialis est in homine, nisi sola anima intellectiva . . . ipsa, sicut *virtute sua* continet animam sensitivam et nutritivam, ita *virtute* continet omnes inferiores formas et facit ipsa sola quidquid imperfectiores formae in aliis faciunt." (*Ibid*., I, LXXVI, 4, ad Resp.)

26 "Anima intellectiva administrat corpus et movet per suam potentiam et virtutem." (*Ibid*., I, LXXVI, 6, 3um.)

27 "Intellectus inter caetera quae ad homines perinent, principalitatem habet; obediunt enim vires sensitivae intellectui et ei deserviunt." (*Ibid*., I, LXXVI, 2, as Resp.)

28 "Quanto magis proceditur in nobilitate formarum, tanto magis invenitur virtus formae materiam elementarum excedere: sicut anima vegetabilis plus quam forma metalli; et anima sensibilis plus quam anima vegetabilis: anima autem humana est ultima in nobilitate formarum; unde in tantum sua virtute excedit materiam corporalem, quod habet aliquam operationem et virtutem, in qua nullo modo communicat materia corporalis. Et haec virtus dicitur intellectus." (*Ibid*., I, LXXVI, 1, ad Resp.)

29 "Intelligere enim est actus qui non potest exerceri per organum corporale sicut exercitur visio: sed in materia est, in quantum anima, cujus est haec virtus, est forma corporis et terminus generationis humanae." (*Ibid*., I, LXXVI, 1, 1um.)

30 "Anima non movet corpus per esse suum secundum quod unitur corpori ut forma, sed per potentiam motivam, cujus actus supponit jam corpus effectum in actu per animam; ut sic anima secundum vim motivam sit pars movens, et corpus animatum sit pars mota." (*Ibid*., I, LXXVI, 4, 2um.)

It is unfortunate that some manuals of so-called Thomist philosophy describe them in a way that does much to discredit Thomism in the eyes of many authentic philosophers. Some interpretations are more akin to geometry than to sound philosophy. Their authors appear to believe that the chief task of metaphysics is to establish distinctions and define clear-cut entities. They describe man as an immutable and transcendental substance to which accidents are added. These accidents are the *potentiae operativae*—really distinct from the substance, and from the different activities of man—really distinct from the potencies which produce them and from the substance. Thus man is a cascade of entities which (in spite of their relationship) must be thought of in terms of mutual exclusion.

In my opinion, such an interpretation does not give a true picture of the philosophy of St Thomas. No doubt, St Thomas is far from simply identifying the potencies with the soul, but his views seem to me to be very different from this "geometricism".

Let us start from *Summa Theologica*, I, LXXVII, 1, ad Resp.[31] In this text, we are reminded that the soul is, by essence, the form of the body—that is, the reality which makes us live (a life-act). *As such*, the soul is not *actus primus* but simply act: it gives us a certain perfection of being, it has not to be perfected. However, the soul *is* ordained to a further actuation; not the soul considered in its totality, in its essence (*secundum suam essentiam*)—that is, as the form of the body—but the soul considered under a certain aspect (*secundum suam potentiam*). *As such*, it is *actus primus* ordained towards an *actus secundus*. This actuation is effected through the operative potencies. These potencies are not entities somehow superadded to the soul; they *are* the soul itself ordaining itself towards different vital operations, giving movement to the body and ruling it,[32] differentiating itself as it pervades the body,[33] they are

[31] "Anima secundum suam essentiam est actus. Si ergo ipsa essentia animae esset immediatum operationis principium, semper habens animam actu haberet opera vitae: sicut semper habens animam actu est vivens. Non enim, in quantum est forma, est actus ordinatus ad ulteriorem actum, sed est ultimus terminus generationis. Unde, quod sit in potentia adhuc ad alium actum, hoc non competit ei secundum suam essentiam, in quantum est forma, sed secundum suam potentiam; et sic ipsa anima, secundum quod subest suae potentiae, dicitur actus primus ordinatus ad actum secundum."

[32] *Ibid.*, I, LXXVI, 4, 2um. This passage has just been quoted. It suggests that the soul itself considered under a particular aspect is the immediate principle which gives movement to the body.

[33] *Ibid.*, I, LXXVI, 8, ad Resp.: "Anima tota est in qualibet parte corporis secundum suam totalitatem perfectionis et essentiam, non autem secundum

powers of the soul (*virtutes animae*), functions of the soul. Among these, the intellect is the most important—so much so that it is sometimes identified with the soul.[34] The exercise of the intellect, though independent of any bodily organ, takes place in the body in so far as the soul is the form of the body. The other powers—the sensitive faculties—are essentially functions of the soul-incarnate-in-the-body. They belong to the soul, they flow from its essence,[35] but they are exercised through bodily organs: the visual power through the eye, the auditive function through the ear, etc.[36]

In conclusion, we may say that the vision of St Thomas is a vision of unity. He maintains, no doubt, the plurality of the operative potencies as powers of the soul; his chief concern, however, is not to explain that the one is not the other, but to show that, through all of them, the same soul, the same act, moves the body, operates, realizes itself.

(f) **Intellect and Will.** The intellect and the will are the two spiritual potencies of man. They are not two parallel and independent faculties but two complementary functions.[37] The will needs the intellect in order to see the end towards which it must tend, but the intellect and all the other powers of the soul need the will as their motive agent. Thus the will is the act which gives to the whole man its unified and personal impetus.[38]

---

totalitatem virtutis: quia non secundum quamlibet suam potentiam est in qualibet parte corporis, sed secundum visum in oculo, secundum auditum in aure, et sic de aliis." Therefore sight, a particular power, *is* the soul-itself-as-present-in-the-eye, hearing, the soul-itself-as-present-in-the-ear, etc.

34 "Anima intellectiva quandoque nominatur nomine intellectus quasi a principaliori virtute." (*Ibid.*, LXXVII, 1, 1um.)

35 "Omnes potentiae animae, sive subjectum earum sit anima sola, sive compositum, fluunt ab essentia animae, sicut a principio." (*Ibid.*, I, LXXVII, 6, ad Resp.)

36 "Quaedam sunt animae quae exercentur per organa corporalia sicut visio per oculum, et auditus per aurem, et simile est de omnibus aliis operationibus nutritivae et sensitivae partis. . . ." (*Ibid.*, I, LXXVII, 5, ad Resp.)

37 ". . . ratio, quare hae potentiae suis actibus invicem se includunt: quia intellectus intelligit voluntatem velle, et voluntas vult intellectum intelligere." (*Ibid.*, I, LXXXII, 4, 1um.)

38 "Movere dicitur dupliciter. Uno modo per modum finis: sicut dicitur quod finis movet efficientem: et hoc modo intellectus movet voluntatem, quia bonum intellectum est objectum voluntatis, et movet ipsam ut finis. Alio modo dicitur aliquid movere per modum agentis . . . hoc modo voluntas movet intellectum et omnes animae vires. Voluntas per modum agentis movet omnes animae potentias ad suos actus, praeter vires naturales vegetativae partis quae nostro arbitrio non subduntur." (*Ibid.*, I, LXXXII, 4, ad Resp.)

(g) **Perception as a Function of Life.** The way in which St Thomas describes perception often tends to reduce it to a purely cognitive process. However, attempts are made on occasion to account for its complexity and to make it a real function of life. In *Summa Theologica*, I, LXXVIII, 4, ad Resp., St Thomas explains that, in order to live, an animal must apprehend not only things which are present before it, but also things which are absent. How could it search after these if it had no apprehension of them (the motions and actions of an animal always follow an apprehension)? Through its sensitive soul, an animal must not only receive the impression of sensible things when these things actually move it, but must also retain and keep them—this requires a special potency. Moreover, if only objects which are attractive or repugnant to the senses could move an animal, it would need a sensitive faculty which apprehends pleasant or unpleasant things but nothing more. In fact, an animal seeks or avoids things, not only because they are good or bad for the senses, but also for other advantages or disadvantages. For instance, a sheep who sees a wolf coming runs away not because it does not like the colour or the shape of the wolf, but because it *sees* it as its enemy. In the same way, a bird will gather pieces of straw not because they please its eyes, but because they are useful for building its nest. Thus an animal *perceives* things not only as material objects but also as *intentions*. In other words, perception is concerned with life and action and must be understood within the general movement of an animal's existence. In man, there is a special function called *ratio particularis* which is entrusted with the gathering of such "intentions".

2. *The Dependence of the Soul on the Body*

The passages I have examined so far consider the soul as the constitutive aspect of man: it informs his body, takes various shapes and manifests different virtualities as it actuates itself.

There is another aspect of the human structure alluded to by St. Thomas which I must mention now, namely, the dependence of the intellective soul on the body.

Considered under this aspect, the soul is, as it were, the crowning of the body. It appears to me that St Thomas considers this dependence from two main points of view:

(a) As I have mentioned above, the intellect needs the body not as an organ through which it acts, but as a stimulus, as a sensory apparatus by which the "phantasm" is prepared. In this context, the union of the body and the soul is effected *per speciem intelligibilem*. This *species*—the world apprehended by the intellect through the senses—resides both in the body and in the soul; through it there is continuity between the body and the soul.

This union, it must be noted, cannot *by itself* make the act of the intellect a personal action; thus it is not *by itself* a personal union—that is, the factor by which man's personality is constituted. In other words, this union, *considered in itself*, pertains to a nature and not to a person. However, the act of the intellect *is* personal, and so the union of the sensory apparatus and the intellective soul *is* also personal. This is due to the other aspect that we examined first, namely, the fact that the intellect is united to the body as its form. This aspect of informing is the reality by which a man's personality is constituted.[39]

(b) It is also as "term of human generation" that the soul crowns the body and depends on it. The order of generation, St Thomas explains, which is a temporal order, proceeds from the imperfect to the more perfect. In this view, the nutritive potencies of the soul precede its sensitive potencies and prepare the body for them; in the same way, the sensitive potencies of the soul pave the way for the intellective potencies.[40]

3. *Conclusions*

Before drawing conclusions from this brief study, I should add that

39 "Relinquitur ergo quod intellectus aliquo modo corpori Socratis uniatur. Hanc autem unionem Commentator in 3 de Anima (comment. 36) dicit esse per speciem intelligibilem; quae quidem habet duplicem subjectum; unum scil. intellectum possibilem; et aliud ipsa phantasmata quae sunt in organis corporeis. Et sic per speciem intelligibilem continuatur intellectus possibilis corpori huius vel illius hominis: sed ista continuatio vel unio non sufficit ad hoc quod actio intellectus sit actio Socratis. . . .

"Sic se habent phantasmata ad intellectum . . . sicut colores ad visum. Sicut ergo species colorum sunt in visu, ita species phantasmatum sunt in intellectu possibili. Patet autem quod ex hoc quod colores sunt in pariete, quorum similitudines sunt in visu non attribuitur parieti: non enim dicimus quod paries videat, sed magis quod videatur. Ex hoc ergo quod species phantasmatum sunt in intellectu possibili, non sequitur quod Socrates, in quo sunt phantasmata, intelligat, sed quod ipse, vel eius phantasmata intelligantur. . . .

"Relinquitur quod hic homo intelligit, quia principium intellectivum est forma ipsius: sic ergo ex ipsa operatione intellectus apparet quod intellectivum principium unitur corpori ut forma." (*Ibid.*, I, LXXVII, 1, ad Resp.)

40 "Secundum ordinem generationis et temporis, prout ex imperfecto ad perfectum venitur, e converso se habet. Nam potentiae animae nutritivae sunt priores in via generationis potentiis animae sensitivae; unde ad earum actionis praeparant corpus; et similiter est de potentiis sensitivis respectu intellectivarum." (*Ibid.*, I, LXXVII, 4, ad Resp.)

there is of course no question of simply identifying the position of St Thomas with the views that I have expressed in this book. Such an identification would be mere anachronism. However, in spite of differences that derive chiefly from historical circumstances, the intuition at the base of this study is, I think, derived from the intuition of St Thomas and at the same time develops it. I have constantly been trying to discover reality as it is, to express it as I experience it. Any success I may have had is, for me, the best guarantee that the views I am trying to express are close to the teaching of St Thomas.

(a) **The Soul, Act of the Body.** I have shown that our personality is an act which expresses itself in space and is conditioned by the structures in which it incarnates itself. This act is a certain "I live" which gives existence to our body (with all its parts) and to our world as it unfolds itself.

According to St Thomas, a person is a soul, an act, which informs a body and makes it exist as a real human body by communicating to it its own *esse*. St Thomas does not say anything about the informing of the world by the soul (though an allusion to it may be seen in those passages in which he says that *anima humana est quodammodo omnia*). His affirmations stress the all-important fact that our body has no reality and no existence apart from our soul. Considered in itself, our body is a mere abstraction; it is not even a human body, it is nothing at all.

The soul is evidently one; it constitutes the body as a unified structure the parts of which are essentially integrated in the whole. It is present in each one of these parts *secundum totam suam essentiam, sed non secundum totam suam virtutem*. So far, there seems to be agreement between the position of St Thomas and the views expressed in this book.

(b) **The "Intellective" Soul and the "Act of Understanding".** Now St Thomas calls the soul intellective soul (sometimes simply intellect), because it is the principle of intellectual activity, which is the essential activity of man.

I have shown that, in order to realize itself, the life-act actuates itself into an act-volition and that it expresses itself in many different activities. This implies that the soul is really the principle from which the whole of our human life proceeds. In a true sense, it may be called intellective soul, for thinking, knowing, and understanding are indeed essential aspects of our personal existence: our act-volition actuates itself through the mediation of knowledge. However, I must acknowledge that, in this respect, the views which I have presented differ from the position of St Thomas.

According to St Thomas, the act which characterizes man as man is intellection; the soul of man is essentially the principle from which this act proceeds. In other words, man, as a rational being, is first of all an intellect whose function is to understand and to know. In conformity with this view, St Thomas describes the relation between the world and man mainly as a relation of knowledge.

In my view, there is, strictly speaking, no such thing as an "act of understanding". I have shown that the soul of man is essentially a life-act (I live), that every activity which takes place in man is a manifestation of this act, an expression of life, that man as a living person is co-extensive with the whole universe; in consequence, the relation between his body and the world has from the very first a vital and personal meaning (vital because we live it and are, in our very existence, conditioned by it before knowing it; personal because it pertains to us in an incommunicable manner). In this view, knowledge, or understanding, is a modality of human life; it pertains to the personal act as one of its essential properties, but "in itself" it is not an act. The act is the life-act actuating itself into an act-volition and expressing itself in a particular activity which may be an act of writing and thinking, but which is never an act of knowing or of understanding—though knowing is present in this particular activity and is required to make it a real human activity.

(c) **The Life-Act.** However, the equation which St Thomas establishes between soul and intellect, between human activity and intellection, is not absolute and exclusive. I have shown that, according to St Thomas, the intellective soul rules the body and sets it in motion. Such an activity is surely more than mere intellection; it is produced by the intellect to the degree to which it is one with the will. The will is indeed the agent which moves the intellect and all the other powers of the soul; it is the soul considered under its dynamic aspect. From this we can see that the intellective soul gives life to the whole body, a life which is not mere awareness but a manifold activity.

In conclusion, I can assert that my views concerning the life-act and its various manifestations are a legitimate development of St Thomas's philosophy of man. No doubt, the vision of St Thomas is not yet unitary and his expression could sometimes be more adequate; yet his explanations, because they are attempts at expressing what we experience in ourselves, always point to something real. We may reach a vision of reality more integrated than the vision of St Thomas, but we always find that his observations retain a true meaning. They can be understood and made use of even if they cannot be accepted as they stand.

(d) **The Potencies of the Soul.** I have explained that our life-act giving existence to our body and our world, and incarnate in them, is the fundamental reality from which our act-volition, our life intention and our whole activity proceed. This activity has many facets, because the life-act, as it spatializes itself, diversifies itself into a number of functions. This position is close to the teaching of St Thomas concerning the relation between the body and the soul and the nature of the operative potencies.

According to St Thomas, the soul communicates its own *esse* to the body as it informs it; the whole soul is present in every part of the body, but not everywhere in the same way: it is vision in the eye, hearing in the ear, etc. Thus, as it incarnates itself, the soul manifests different virtualities; these are called functions or potencies.

(e) **Perception and Life.** St Thomas's allusion to the perception of "intentions" shows us that, in his mind, the world is not simply an assemblage of substances and objective qualities which a subject must apprehend, or an intellect conceptualize, but a field of life made up of values which have a personal character, a variegated reality which provokes concrete behaviours as it offers itself to be perceived. This view leads naturally to the discovery of what I have called my world, my personal universe—that is, a reality made of my individual life, constituted by my personal act.

(f) **The Dependence of the Soul on the Body.** All these considerations deal mainly with what I have called the "aspect a", or centrifugal aspect; they describe the unfolding of the act in space, its constitutive function with regard to our body and even to the whole world (this can be asserted even though St Thomas does not describe this centrifugal movement as I have described it).

The other aspect—the dependence of the soul on the body—is described by St Thomas mainly in reference to knowledge. This is in agreement with the Thomist view that the "act of understanding" is the human act *par excellence* and that the intellect is the soul of man. By itself, this position implies that reality is first of all a process of knowledge; it is a strong argument for those who favour an intellectualistic interpretation of St Thomas's philosophy of man.

However, here also the emphasis which is laid on knowledge is softened. This happens chiefly in those passages in which St Thomas describes the soul as the term of human generation—that is, as the crowning of a vital process which cannot be identified with the preparation of the phantasm by the sensory apparatus. Would it be forcing the thought of St Thomas to see in this generative activity not simply the beginning of human life, but a continuous process by which man is kept alive and by which his personal act is at every moment conditioned?

Whatever it may be, this centripetal process is not "by itself" constitutive of our personality: the union of our senses with our intellect is not by itself a personal union, generation does not *give existence* to our soul. Our soul is created as an act expressing itself in space. This is the fact which constitutes our personality, activates the centripetal aspect, and makes of it a personal aspect.

CHAPTER V

Temporality

At the beginning of the previous chapter, I proposed to make a careful study of the structure of my world—that is, of the different aspects of my personal act incarnate. This study, I remarked, would elucidate the observations gathered in the second chapter of this book. Now, in that second chapter, I said explicitly that the meaning which the world and all the objects of the world have for me is constituted by my life experience. I pointed out also that my life is essentially a time process: each moment of my life actualizes the past and is orientated towards the future. These are aspects of my personal structure which my study of my act incarnate has not covered. I shall examine them now, taking into account the facts so far brought to light. The first part of this investigation will be a general description of the personal act as temporal act, the second part an analysis of the various aspects of temporality.

I. THE TEMPORAL ACT

Past, present and future are often spoken of as the three "dimensions" of temporality. However, *the present is the only temporal "ekstasis" which actually exists.* I shall accordingly begin my study with a description of the present, that is to say, of "my present".

1. The Present

I am engrossed in my work. My eyes are fixed on the white sheet of paper on which I am painfully trying to express what I have in mind. This is my present—a particular form of the self-actuation which my personal life-act, my act-project, assumes while tending towards its ultimate realization. This present is a certain disposition of my body: the present condition and functioning of my biopsychic system, my state of awareness, the disposition and movements of my limbs, the expression of my face, my whole attitude; this present is also the particular relationship in which my body stands to my environment and my environment to my body; the way in which my hand grasps the pencil and makes it run on the paper, the arrangement of my table, of my room, the atmosphere I breathe, this summer weather, the geography of Calcutta, of Bengal, the political, economical, social, cultural, religious situation of India, of the world at large; in short, my present is my world as it exists today, being both the actual unfolding of my personal act (aspect a) and the existential field in which I find myself incarnate (aspect b).

2. The Present and the Past

Let us examine now the relation between the present and the past. For this purpose, I must analyse the way in which my life develops—that is, the way in which my personal universe evolves.

I consider a certain moment of my life soon after my birth. I call it moment Z. At that moment, my organism was still undeveloped and my personal initiatives were therefore extremely limited. However, I was already in possession of a world, raised to a certain level, from which I had to start in order to build my personal existence. Let us explain this.

At moment Z, just as much as today, my organism was linked with my environment, with the whole world. The whole universe was already converging towards my brain, endowing me in this process with those vital structures the development of which would enable my personal act to expand more and more freely. Owing to this centripetal movement, I existed from the beginning of my life as a product of my milieu. This milieu was in particular my family and social environment, with its racial and cultural characteristics. Thus I was from the start in possession of a more or less determined biological and cultural deposit, a deposit which was given to me together with my own existence.

This original accretion was itself the result of a long historical process. At moment Z, all the years and centuries that had gone before were not dead; they subsisted in the present which they had prepared and brought about; they were living in Z more real than ever because in it they reached a higher point of maturation. Thus my life-act, rooted from the beginning in my organism and in my surroundings—that is, in spatial structures—was also conditioned by history. In fact, the centripetal process by which the world converged towards my brain in order to become my world *was* identically the process by which the whole past made itself my present: history did not offer itself to me as a vague totality without relation to space, but as the very stuff of which my body and my environment were made. All the past of the universe, all the experiences, the endeavours and aspirations of mankind from its origin down to Z were there, fused with Z, one with my surroundings and with my biological apparatus, giving substance to my own life, a store from which I could always draw; an inner urge which I would have to master, take up and personalize more and more; sometimes a burden that I would have to carry; in any case a possession with which I could never part without disowning my very nature and destroying my existence.

Let us analyse now the way in which my life has developed. This growth was a synergetic process. At Z, my life-act, conditioned as it was by a still rudimentary biological apparatus, could not yet take up my organism and my environment and, in them, the whole of history in a very integrated and personal way. I was at that time being carried by the world and history much more than imparting to them a definite orientation. However, my personal act was already there and at work. Under its thrust, thanks to the multiple influences which were pressing upon me, I began to develop. In this forward movement, each moment was preparing its following moment and unceasingly merging into it. Everything contributed to this growth: the air I breathed, the food I ate, the heat and light I received from the sun, the education I was given, the contacts I made, all the actions that I carried out, and all the events that took place in the world. Little by little, thanks to the use I was trained to make of the objects which surrounded me, to the different impacts they made on me and to the attitudes I began to take towards them, all the things of the world, charging themselves with my experience, acquired definite meanings and values for me. In this way, the world was more and more integrated in my life, it became more and more my world. Through the development of all the vital structures which conditioned it, my personal act attained emancipation; in me the whole universe and the whole of history took a more and more personal orientation. In this way, I reached the moment I live now, a moment in which the whole past—my personal past and, in it, the whole of history—is present as a totality which I have partially built, a sum of experience immanent in my world, in my organism, constituting my culture, inspiring my decisions, giving substance to my present activity.

But am I not contradicting one of my previous assertions? I wrote not long ago that the present alone exists. If this is true, how shall I account for this permanence of the whole past at every moment of my life?

The first fact which I have to acknowledge is that the past *as such* does not exist any more. All the events of history do not persist today as they happened formerly. Considered in their historical modalities, *as particular occurrences*, these events are no more. However, as has just been explained, the past is not dead; it lives in the present, not as present—not as this or that particular event persisting today as it happened a week, a year, a century ago—but *as present: it is one with the world as it exists today*, a world which it contained "in embryo". Thus we may understand in what sense I can affirm both that the present—my present—is the only temporal reality which exists for me, and that the whole past—my past and, in it, the past of the whole universe—is today more real than ever.

3. The Present and the Future

My present takes up the whole past and realizes it, but it is not the end of history. At every moment, I look forward to a future which will give the present its full meaning. I am working at my table. This occupation—my present—does not stand by itself; it is essentially orientated towards the whole book which I wish to write, the whole task to which I wish to devote my life. To put it in a more comprehensive way: the universe-in-me is a totality in a state of genesis; through my personal activity, it tends towards its ultimate realization, a realization which is identical with my personal end.

These observations lay new emphasis on two complementary aspects of the structure of my world which I have already mentioned several times: the aspect of incompleteness and the aspect of tension. These aspects do not manifest themselves when I look at the things which surround me: my table, my books, my fountain pen, my bed, the walls of my room. . . . The meaning of all these things seems to me very clear and definite. What more do they need if they are to be themselves? These aspects begin to appear when I understand that the meaning of each thing is a particular expression of the meaning of the whole universe and that this unity-meaning is made up of the experience of men integrated, individuated, in my own experience: a growing reality. But it is only when the whole movement of the universe becomes self-transparent in me that I realize the essential incompleteness of my world and its inner tension. My personal act actuating itself through my present occupation, taking up the whole past, tending towards a more and more perfect self-realization, is the reality which constitutes my world. This world of which I am the *esse*, the things which surround me, must realize themselves in me: their full meaning lies neither in the past nor in the present, but in the future. The table on which I am writing is not a mere piece of furniture consisting of a flat board fixed on four legs—as such, a solid "in-itself" the whole meaning of which is in its being what it is—it is a utensil which my work, my life, has to transform more and more into what it is meant to be; it is a reality which has to "find itself" in the very use I make of it, in the process by which I make it mine, by which I realize and find myself through it. So is the world in which I live: a totality which I build with my own life and bring to completion in the very movement by which I tend towards my end.

The relation between the present and the future must be rightly understood. My present—my world as it exists today—is the realization of the whole past. This means that all the events which have already taken place are still real today, not as they happened in their historical setting, but identified with the present situation of the universe-in-me, reaching in it, in what I do and in what I am, a further stage of maturation.

But, as has been said above, my present is essentially ordained towards a future in which it will attain a more perfect realization of itself. I consider a certain moment X which, I suppose, will take place in the future. That moment, *considered in its particularity*, is not yet something real: it will occur one day, but that day is still to come. Thus in the same way as the past *as past* is no more, the future *as future* is not yet: the present is the only temporal reality which actually exists. However, it is not true to say that the future in no way pre-exists: just as the past persists today, not as past, but as present, so also the event X is already real, not as it will take place one day, but in the present situation of the universe.

From this, it must not be concluded that past and future are contained in the present in exactly the same way. When a seed germinates and develops into a sapling, I can say that the seed is *still* present in the sapling, not as seed however—the seed, as seed, is no more—but as sapling—that is, as a partial realization of what it was meant to become; I can say likewise that the tree is *already* present in the sapling, not as tree—the tree, as tree, is "not yet"—but again as sapling. However, the presence of the seed in the sapling and the presence in the sapling of the tree are two different modes of presence: the seed is *more determinately* present and, thus, more real in the sapling than "in itself"; the tree, on the other hand, pre-exists in the sapling, not as a fully developed reality, but as a potentiality, as something which the sapling is meant to become but is not yet: the tree is not present in the sapling in a determinate, but in an embryonic, inchoative way.

Similarly, my present is, on the one hand, a further realization of what the universe was one day, one year, one century ago, it is the past made more real, more determinate, more "itself" than itself (the past "in act"); on the other hand, my present is the embryonic existence of the future, the germ of what the universe will be tomorrow (the future "in potency").

This last assertion means that the future moments of my life and of history will be further realizations of what the universe is already today in me. Each of these future moments will bring something new, but this new element will always be a development of what is already present now.

Can we already say something about the aim towards which my life is tending, the final reality which already now gives their meaning to all my actions, to my projects, to my world? According to some contemporary philosophers, the end of human life is death understood as a complete annihilation of self. But this is an absurdity. Indeed, the goal towards which I tend is the attainment of my full personal stature, the perfect realization of what I am already today "in embryo". Now, if to become really myself I must become nothing, my life is absolutely meaningless and absurd, and the whole of reality is monstrous nonsense. If nothing is the fulfilment of my personal destiny, the end towards which my world is in progress, my present—the present of the universe-in-me—is less than nothing. To affirm that the annihilation of self in death is the term of human life is to profess absolute nihilism—it is to adopt a completely self-destructive position.

We must therefore acknowledge that our personal immortality, our personal existence, and the existence of our world, are essentially linked together: to exist is fundamentally to exist in a personal way, to exist in a personal way is to be immortal. From this it follows that death cannot be considered as the end of our personal existence; it must be understood as the transformation of our present earthly existence into another type of human existence; consequently, it must be understood as a transformation of our world: in order to realize itself—that is, in order to become in fact what it already is embryonically—our act-world must transcend itself into a new structural ensemble (the nature of which will be studied later on). Thus we realize the essentially transitory character of our present existence: it has no meaning in itself; its whole reality consists in its being a preparation for, a way towards our future existence. Our world is essentially a prefigurement of the world to come.

Because our world is imperishable, it should not be concluded that all the objects that we see around us are individual substances destined to persist for ever. From the beginning of this study, it has been made clear that the various objects of the world have no meaning, and therefore no existence, apart from the totality in which they are included. Thus "in themselves" they are nothing—in other words, they have no selfhood which must realize itself in an independent manner; they have no individual destiny; their existence is of a purely relative character; they are destined for the self-realization of the totality of which they are parts. Now this totality, as described so far, is my act-world—that is, my personal act incarnate. Thus the finality of all the things I perceive around me is identical with my own finality: things must be used, transformed, destroyed; they must merge into one another and reappear in new forms in order to attain their own realization *in the totality to which they are essentially relative*—that is, in my act-world-tending-towards-its-end.

All these observations enable us also to determine in some way the value of each particular happening, of each moment of history. My personal act, as has just been recalled, is the *esse* of my world. Now this act does not exist simply as the "form" which constitutes space, but—while being this form—it exists also as a temporal act—that is, as an act which takes up the whole past as it tends towards its future realization (in fact, spatiality and temporality are complementary aspects of one and the same reality: my act-world). Now, to say that my act-world is *essentially ordained* towards an end in which it is to attain its supreme realization is to affirm that *the very existence of my act-world consists in its dynamic relation to its end.* If this is true, each particular event of my life, of history, has no definitive value "in itself"; it exists essentially within the movement of my act-world towards its end—that is, in so far as it is ordained towards the full realization of the totality which it expresses, of which it is a constituent element. This suggests that there are two radically different ways of looking at any particular happening:

(1) I may consider it "in itself"—that is, in its very particularity, as a restricted fact distinct from the spatio-temporal totality in which it occurs (i.e., distinct from the rest of the universe, and from all the events that have taken place before it). The more I thus remove the event from its historical context, from the integral movement of my act-world, the less I understand it: it becomes meaningless and, finally, dissolves into nothing. The event has no individuality which can be understood independently of the spatio-temporal whole of which it is an expression.

(2) I may consider the event in its relationship to the past, to my whole world, as a particular moment of the movement by which my act-world tends towards its end. Looked at in this way, the event reveals its particular meaning—which consists in its particular and unique manner of expressing and determining history. The more I thus integrate it in the whole and the more I live it as a concretion of the totality, the more also I understand it, the more meaningful it becomes for me.

These facts show us that an event, considered merely in its particularity—that is, as distinguished from the whole of history—is of no abiding value. As a particular happening, the event is ephemeral: it takes place, fills a moment of time, and then vanishes for ever. On the other hand, considered in its integrity—in its relationship to the totality—the event does not pass away: it abides for ever, because it is one with the whole of history, because, in the movement of my act-world, it exists essentially as an anticipation of the end.

This view should not induce us to dismiss the particularity of an event, its uniqueness, as of no importance. Just as my personal act, to the extent that it constitutes my world as a spatial reality, exists only as act-incarnate-in-a-diversity-of-structures, so also to the extent that it is a temporal act, it subsists *in* the particular moments and events which make up the web of history. Now in the same way as each particular object of my world (1) is a particular expression of the unity-meaning of the whole, (2) conditions the whole, determines it according to its modalities, so also each event (1) is a particular concretion of the totality of history, (2) influences, determines the course of history, the movement of my act-world towards the end according to its particular vital significance. In saying this we stress the fact that each moment of history, in so far as it is integrated in the totality, brings something new, and has a positive influence on the movement of my act-world towards its end. Some events may be so full of meaning that they modify the course of history strongly and decisively.

4. The Movement towards the Future as the Realization of the Past

First, let us recall the central perspective which the study of the act incarnate has brought to light:

Phase a: My personal act comes to existence in an already existing world, unfolds itself from a definite centre and, in so doing, recasts the world into its own expressive field, into the concretion of its self-actuating movement.

Phase b: Simultaneously, from every place which it occupies and animates, my act incarnate returns to its source and, in this regressive movement, conditions itself-continuing-to-unfold-from-this-source. Thus, while taking up and personalizing itself-already-realized and, through itself-already-realized, the world-already-constituted, my personal-act-realizing-itself is continually dependent on, conditioned by, these pre-existing vital structures. Fundamentally, as we know, this dependence of my personal act (my existence) upon itself (my essence) is identical with my createdness—that is, with the fact that, while positing itself as act-of-the-universe, my act is transcendentally given to itself.

The following points should be noted:

(1) My personal-act-unfolding-itself is the "element" constitutive of the whole system. Therefore my existence has absolute priority over my essence: it is in my act-continuing-to-realize-itself that my act-already-realized-in-the-form-of-a-world and, in it, the world-already-constituted are kept in existence, continually vivified and activated—in other words, my act-already-realized (and, in it, the world-already-constituted) exists by, in, and for my act-continually-transcending-itself-incarnate.

(2) However, my act-already-realized-in-the-form-of-a-world and,

in it, the world-already-constituted, have a real anteriority in relation to my personal-act-continuing-to-unfold-itself to the extent that the latter is conditioned by them. But we must be quite clear that this conditioning of my personal-act-actuating-itself by the structures in which it incarnates itself is itself existentially dependent on the centrifugal movement of my act. The solution of this apparent tangle consists in the fact that, as I posit myself as act-of-the-universe, I am ontologically dependent on the Creative Act—that is, I exist as a personal act transcendentally given to itself in the very world which it constitutes as concretion of itself.

All that I have said about the temporality of my act-world should be integrated in this unifying perspective:

(1) The whole system just described is *my present:* my personal act *actually* unfolding itself from its expressive centre, *actually* taking up itself-already-realized and the world-already-constituted, being *actually* conditioned by itself and the world—in other words, my personal act *being actually created* as it posits itself as act-world.

(2) The movement by which my personal act unfolds itself from its expressive centre, by which it constitutes my world and realizes itself—my existence—is identically the tension of my act-world towards the future.

(3) The process by which my act-already-realized and, through my act-already-realized, the world-already-constituted condition my act-continuing-to-realize-itself is identically the process by which my past and, through it, the past of the whole universe, shape and condition my present, i.e., the movement of my personal act towards the future.

From these facts, I can draw the following conclusions:

(1) My concrete essence is made up of my whole past and, through it, of the past of the whole universe: it is the totality of the past individuating itself in me, realizing itself in my present. Thus, in a true sense, I can assert that I am a product of history—of my personal history and of the history of the whole world.

(2) However true this may be, my personal individuality is not *actually constituted* by my past realizing itself in my present; it is constituted by my personal act actually tending towards the future—that is, by my personal-act-continually-ahead-of-itself (my existence). It is my act-in-tension-towards-the-future which realizes my past as it constitutes my present.

(3) As it gives existence to my past (to itself-already-realized) in

the movement by which it tends towards its future realization, my personal act is nevertheless conditioned, fashioned, by the past: my act-project is a concretion of my experience; my present is anticipation of the future to the extent that it is realization of the past; my future will be built on my past; my movement towards the future is my past continually projecting itself ahead of myself. The fact that, in the very process of realizing my past, my personal-act-in-tension-towards-the-future is actually conditioned, is so to speak generated by the reality which it constitutes, is due to the fact that, at the very moment it posits itself as the act-of-history, it finds itself created as act-having-a-past-and-conditioned-by-the-past. Thus my dependence on my past in the movement by which I give myself a future is fundamentally my ontological dependence on the Creative Act.

A Final Remark

To some philosophers, time is a mere flux, a succession of moments each of which sinks into nothingness as it is replaced by the next; the present emerges precariously between two abysses: the abyss of the past—the non-existence of whatever has taken place—the abyss of the future—the non-existence of whatever has still to take place. In this view, there is no such thing as a real becoming, there is nothing permanent, there is only a succession of disconnected "now", of temporal atoms.

The position which our analysis of facts has forced us to adopt is in agreement with this view in so far as it asserts that the present is the only temporal reality which actually exists. However, this present does not posit itself by excluding the past and the future but by including them in a certain way. The present is the whole universe as it exists now; time or history is the process by which this universe tends towards its completion, it is genesis, it is the coming into existence of something which is already present in some way, it is growth. In this movement, nothing is ever annihilated. Whatever has taken place continues to exist in the universe as we live it today—the past is the substance of the present. Therefore time is not a mere flux; it is duration, persistence of the old in the new, or rather continual re-creation of the old in the new.

II. TEMPORALITY AND INCARNATION

From the analyses made in the previous sections, it is clear that temporality is not something which pertains to my personal act in an accidental way: it is the very existence of my act incarnate, the movement and the life of my world. In this section, I shall analyse the various aspects of my temporal act—in other words, I shall examine the way in which my temporality specifies itself at the various levels of my personal structure. In this study, it will be remembered that my personal act incarnate is a living unity which cannot be dissected into independent components and, therefore, that each aspect of my act-world is a particular expression of my whole historicity. In keeping with the method followed in the previous chapter, I shall analyse first the temporality of my life-act-incarnate, then my "transcendental" temporality—that is, the temporality of my act-world-tending-personally-towards-its-end.

A. The Temporality of My Life-Act-Incarnate

To a large extent, I experience my life as a process which takes place without being controlled by my will, a stream from which I emerge, which I try to direct, yet by which I am borne along until the end in an apparently impersonal way. All around me in the world, forces are at work, events take place, changes occur, life bursts out in many forms, various tendencies and conflicting currents manifest themselves. All these phenomena, as we know, occur within my own life sphere, yet they appear to me as "third person processes" which condition my life, which force themselves into it, which affect me more or less intensely without being brought into action by any conscious initiative of my act-volition. In my body also, I experience evolutions, tensions, various phenomena which occur without any positive intervention of my will. All these cosmico-biological activities are modifications of that life stream which is constituted by my life-act-incarnate-in-tension-towards-the-future. Some of these modifications have a cyclic character: to each day succeeds a night and to each night a new day; each day and each night belong to a certain lunar month which will be followed by another lunar month; each lunar month falls in a certain season after which there will be another season; each season takes place during a certain solar year to which another solar year will succeed. These cyclic modifications of my life stream, the evolutive process of which these rhythmic phenomena are the frame, are "accompanied" by characteristic transformations of my surroundings and of my body. Other modifications of my life stream are sudden and unexpected (which does not mean that they are not connected with its cyclic modifications): a sudden storm, the sudden passing of a jet plane in the sky, an accident, an unexpected sickness, etc.

I shall now analyse my life-act-modified-by-these-phenomena from the angle of temporality. This study will be made first from the "biophysical" point of view, and then from the "psychological" point of view.

First Approach

At this moment, my life-act-unfolding-itself-from-its-centre constitutes the different organs and functions, the present disposition, the various activities of my body-situated-in-my-room; it constitutes all the details of my room, the trees and houses which I see through the window, the birds flying among the trees, the traffic of the street, the brightness and heat of this summer morning; it constitutes the earth rotating and revolving around the sun, the solar system with all its peculiar properties, the vast expanses which separate the different stars, the various galaxies which form the universe and the dynamic relations which bind them together. This "creative" unfolding of my life-act, this centrifugal wave which gives existence to the totality of my world and to its diversity is, as we know, identically the "natural" movement of my act-world towards the future, its fundamental self-orienting towards its final realization; the whole system which this movement constitutes at this moment is, in its concrete dynamic actuality, the seed of the world to come.

This whole reality is my present, my existence. Considering its different elements from the point of view of temporality, I shall not describe them simply as spatial structures which express in various ways the potentialities of my life-act, but as events which are various concretions, various hypostases of its existential tension towards the future. In this perspective, the different organs of my body, their present functioning, the dynamic relationship in which they stand to each other, are various events subordinated to, included in, this central event which is constituted by my body at the present moment of its existence; the peculiarities of my environment—these pieces of furniture scattered around me, those trees shaken by the wind, those houses lit up by the morning sun, those figures moving on the pavement—the whole earth as it exists today, the various elements of the universe and the relations which they have to one another—are also happenings integrated in this global event which is formed by the totality of my act-world at the present moment of its progress.

But my life-act is not a purely creative principle. While giving existence to my world, while constituting my present as the incarnation of its tension towards the future, my life-act is conditioned by the world-already-existing, by the past-realizing-itself-in-my-present. Therefore all the particular events which take place within the unity of my integral present are not simply concretions of the centrifugal movement of my life-act but also parts of the centripetal process formed by 'my-act-already-realized'-determining-'my-act-continuing-to-realize-itself', or my past-determining-my-present. Seen in this light, each particular event included in the totality of my present offers itself as a particular realization of the past, a particular hypostasis of history. The various organs which form my body are not simply expressive realities which my life-act improvises as it unfolds itself: each one of them in its particular place, in its present constitution and functioning, in its relationship to the whole organic system, is a particular resultant, a particular actualization, of whatever has taken place in the past in my body, in my environment, and in the whole universe. Similarly, the peculiarities of my environment, of my whole world, the structure of the objects which surround me, the changing relations which they have to one another (whatever occurs around me in the world) are the fruit of a long evolutive process; they are the product of my individual history, of the history of Calcutta and Bengal, of the history of the earth, of the whole universe.

As a rule, I must affirm that whatever takes place in my world, to the extent that it conditions my life-act-unfolding-itself, is a certain way in which the past of the whole universe realizes itself in my present *through the mediation of my personal past*. In other words, all events, whether they occur in my body or in my environment, determine my present first of all as crystallizations of my personal history and, mediately, as condensations of the totality of history. To understand this, we must remember that my life-act is never conditioned by anything other than itself: as it unfolds itself and constitutes my world, it is continually determined by itself-already-realized-in-the-form-of-a-world and, through itself-thus-realized, by the world-already-existing—in other words, it is determined by my past and, through my past, by the past of the whole universe. Therefore, in order to realize itself in my present, in order to influence, guide, and subtend the centrifugal movement of my life-act, the history of the world must first be taken up in, be identified with, my personal history.

Prima facie, it may be hard to understand how events which take place in my environment—those birds flying among the palm trees, those houses lining the street in the heat and glare of this summer morning, etc.—may present themselves as crystallizations of my own past. This difficulty arises from the fact that we consider them as "realities-in-themselves" rigidly localized in their proper places; thus we do not understand how such extraneous occurrences, even though they are charged with a whole history, can condition my life-act through the mediation of my own history.

Once more, we must change our outlook. A careful observation of reality shows us that the events which take place in the world exist for me, influence my life, *to the extent that, converging towards my expressive centre, they develop into modifications of my organic substratum*—that is, to the extent that they are modalities of 'my-act-already-realized-in-the-form-of-a-world'-conditioning-'my-act-continuing-to-realize-itself': they condition the centrifugal movement of my life-act not as realities-in-themselves but as realities-for-me, not as "physical events" taking place in the "physical world" but as biological events pertaining *from the first* to my individual life structure. Thus it is clear that, to the degree to which they are history-realizing-itself-in-my-present-in-various-ways, these events must be first of all concretions of my individual history and, mediately, concretions of the history of the world.

This becomes even more evident once we realize that the way in which particular events condition the centrifugal movement of my life-act *is itself conditioned by my biological individuality*—that is, by the fundamental way in which my life-act-unfolding-from-its-centre constitutes my body and my world. In fact, it is by and in my life-act-unfolding-itself that these events are constituted as realities-for-me; it is by and in my act-tending-towards-the-future (my existence) that the past—my past and the past of the whole world—is crystallized in the form of these particular-events-determining-me-in-particular-ways.

Let us now describe in more detail the relation between incarnation and temporality.

The various elements of my life field have different vital meanings. Each of these elements, in so far as it means something, is characterized by a certain destination. As such:

(1) It is a particular concretion of the movement of my life-act

towards the future, a particular embodiment of its potentialities (aspect a).

(2) It is a particular way in which my life-act-tending-towards-the-future is conditioned by the past (aspect b).

The meaning of this last assertion is that each part of my world is a particular way in which the history of the world realizes itself in my present and carries me towards the future, through the medium of my individual history. Thus each element of my world, while being a more or less definite modification of the spatial field in which my life-act is incarnate, is also a more or less definite temporal current running within the broad stream formed by my act-world moving towards the future. This view shows that the temporality of my life-act incarnate, though it is fundamentally unitary, has a great variety of aspects. Each element of my life field is in a way a particular history because it is a particular way in which the whole movement of history flows into my individual history, because it is a particular way in which my own history determines my life-act-in-tension-towards-the-future.

The various temporal currents, it is true, running within my whole life stream are essentially interconnected, since each one of them in its proper channel is continually fed by all the others, by the whole movement of my life-act incarnate. No spatial reality, as we know, has any meaning or existence apart from the environment in which it is situated, apart from the totality of which it is a part—in other words, each element of my world, in its very particularity, mirrors its surroundings, is an expression of the whole system in which it is included. This means that each detail of my life field, as a particular history, is charged with many other particular histories, is a condensation, a product of the history of the environment in which it has taken shape, of the history of the whole universe.

The historicity of my body and its relation to the temporal flow constitutive of my whole life field call for special notice.

Aspect b: My life-act came into existence in a definite centre which presented itself as the crystallization of a family, regional, national, history and, through the medium of this narrow temporal channel, as a particular hypostasis of the history of the universe. This original accretion constituted what I call my heredity; taken up and vitalized by my life-act, it became the very substance of my biological and temperamental individuality. This shows us how, from the very beginning, my life-act, while being conditioned by the elementary organism which it animated, was truly generated and moulded by the whole stream of history flowing into it through the medium of particular temporal currents.

Aspect a: It cannot, however, be maintained that my life-act came into being as a mere product of history in general and of various particular histories; the truth is that, from the very beginning, it derived its existence from the Creative Act. I shall not, therefore, consider my original biological and temperamental individuality as a mere hereditary accretion, but as the original way in which my life-act incarnated itself at the moment it came into being. It was created from the very beginning as act-of-the-universe: unfolding itself from my organism, it constituted the world as the concretion of the primitive and inarticulate mode of being which it had at that early stage of its existence—that is, as the extension of the elementary organism which it fashioned as its original expressive centre. In this centrifugal movement—which was already its tension towards the future—my act recast into its own life stream all the various temporal currents which formed the movement of history. Thus the temporal flow constituted by the whole field in which my life-act expressed itself began to exist for me in a way that had a strict relation to the original way in which my act animated my organism.

It is my createdness that reconciles these two aspects: in the very process of creating its world and of originating history in its original way, my life-act found itself created in relation to a world co-created—in other words, it found itself conditioned by itself-already-realized-in-the-form-of-a-world-having-a-history and, through itself-thus-realized, by the world-already-existing—that is, by the whole of history. My life-act-unfolding-itself-in-dependence-on-the-Creative-Act was the existence of this whole system. This explains why, from the very beginning, the way in which I made history shape me was strictly dependent on the way in which I made history exist for me; it explains also why the vital meaning which the various temporal currents flowing within my whole life stream had for me was from the start essentially relative to the modalities of the temporal stream constituted by my body. In fact, the essential dependence on my whole life stream of the various temporal currents just mentioned was from the beginning—and remains today—identical with their dependence on the temporal flow constituted by my organism, since my body is the place from which the whole of my world derives its existence—that is, the original temporal stream of which my whole life stream is the overflow.

As years passed, the temporal accretion which, from the beginning of my life, constituted my biological individuality was never obliterated. Nor did it remain unchanged. My organism developed and manifested its potentialities; my life-act-in-tension-towards-the-future continually took up in itself the various circumstances in which it found itself incarnate. A growth took place during which the old was continually kept alive and integrated in the new. The temporal stream constituted by my body as it exists today is the continuation of the tiny current formed by the organic centre in which my life-act came to existence; the very way in which my act unfolds itself today, and the way in which it tends towards the future, remain substantially what they were at the first moment of my existence—thus my biological individuality persists. However, this original accretion as realized in my present has grown into a whole which actualizes in itself whatever my personal life has been. This dynamic totality—my life stream at the present moment of its flow—is the principle which gives to the various temporal currents, to the whole movement of history, the existence and the meaning which they have for me as biological realities.

Second Approach

I shall now study the temporality of my life-act incarnate from the "psychological" point of view.

i. *Temporality and Temperament*

My temperamental inclination is the fundamental way in which my life-act animates its field of existence and faces the world, the fundamental way in which it ordains itself towards the future. Originally, this basic attitude was not self-conscious. However, by the mere fact of living and acting, I became aware of my fundamental affective disposition—in other words, my temperamental inclination became self-transparent.

As it exists today, my temperament is not a mere "hereditary factor". I have just pointed out that my life-act incarnate, in its present state, realizes in itself not only my pre-personal past but also the totality of my personal history. My present attitudes, reactions, initiatives, are largely determined by the influences which I have undergone, the experiences I have had, the type of existence I have led in the past. Thus, phenomenally speaking, my temperamental individuality, as it exists today, is a product of my personal history as well as a hereditary accretion: it is the revelation of what was latent in my original biologico-temperamental deposit, the accentuation of its tendencies in accordance with the way in which they have been exercised and acted upon.

In the concrete movement formed by my temperamental inclination at the present moment of its actuation, no legitimate distinction can be made between "inborn" and "acquired" dispositions—in other words, in my concrete individuality, there is no such thing as a superimposition of new elements upon old elements. This is clearly so, because we know that the past does not persist in the present *as past* but as present, and that the present is the only temporal reality which actually exists. My act-unfolding-itself—as it lives now, that is, as it at this moment constitutes my body and my world—is, in its unity and diversity, at once the realization of my pre-personal past, the actualization of my individual past, and an individuation of the whole movement of history.

ii. *Temporality and Perception*

I have pointed out more than once that my whole experience—that is, my personal past—is present in the way in which I look at the world and in the way in which the world reveals itself to me. Some philosophers see in this a contamination of direct perception by subjective reminiscences: through sensation, they say, we are in touch with the object, but this original contact is "vitiated" by the fact that we project in the object memories that arise from our own subjective deposit.

We recognize at the root of this interpretation some of the basic postulates of intellectualism: man is a subject-in-himself facing a world-in-itself; perception is a synthesis of "objective" and "subjective" elements.

Let us analyse our experience. My eyes are fixed on the houses which stand there along the street, on the palm trees waving in the evening breeze.

Aspect a: This perception takes place within the movement by which my life-act unfolding from its centre constitutes my body, my environment, my world, as the incarnation of itself, as the concretion of its tension towards the future; it is this movement-illuminating-itself-in-a-particular-manner.

Aspect b: In the very process of making those houses and those trees exist as luminous expressions of its self-actuating movement, my life-act is conditioned by those-houses-and-those-trees-already-constituted-as-particular-expressions-of-itself-incarnate—that is, by those-houses-and-those-trees-already-existing-as-particular-crystallizations-of-my-past-and-of-the-past-of-the-whole-world.

Therefore those houses and those trees, as they exist for me, as I perceive them, are *from the first* constituted by my own life experience and, through my own life experience, by the totality of history. This whole past—my personal past and the past of the universe—is not contained in those houses and in those trees in the form of memories, but first of all as a living presence which forms their very substance—that is, what they are for me: my historicity is the historicity of my world because my existence and the existence of my world are one. No doubt, the perception of an object may at times be accompanied by some definite reminiscences; however, this is not due to an association of "objective" data with "subjective" elements, but to the fact that this object presents itself to me from the first as a particular concretion of my life.

The presence of my whole past in the objects which I perceive does not eliminate the internal diversity of my world. My life-act expresses itself in each element of its field of existence according to the modalities of this element; this means that each object realizes my past and the past of the universe in a particular and unique way. In the way in which I look at an object, in the way in which this object reveals itself to me, there is present whatever this object has meant to me from the beginning of my life. Thus, if each object does indeed offer itself to me as a crystallization of my whole past, this does not prevent it from constituting a particular temporal current, from embodying a particular aspect of my life experience.

Following Husserl, phenomenologists stress the fact that our perception of an object is always apprehension of it from a definite standpoint. The way in which I see those houses along the street is determined by the position and attitude of my body, and is therefore perception of them in a determined profile. From the place which I occupy, I perceive only the façades of those houses, I do not perceive their roofs, their backs, the different rooms inside them. It would not, however, be correct to say that my present perception is nothing more than the apprehension of flat surfaces which stand erect at a certain distance from my body. In each of those façades, it is really a whole house which offers itself to my perception—in other words, I see each of those façades as a concrete expression of the whole house to which it belongs. Moreover, I do not perceive those houses as isolated entities; I see them against the background of the entire city: those houses, as they appear to me, are essentially parts of Calcutta, each of them reflecting in its own way the living totality in which it is integrated.

This all-embracing character of my perception derives in the first place from the fact that my perception takes place in the movement by which my act, unfolding itself from its centre, constitutes my body as the first concretion of its potentialities, constitutes those houses, their surroundings, the city, the whole world as the continuation of my body, as the actuation of my initial potentialities. (This movement, as we know, is identically my tension towards the future.) It derives also from the fact that, while unfolding itself in this way, my act is continually conditioned by itself-already-realized and, through itself-already-realized, by the world-already-constituted—that is, by my past and, through it, by the whole of history. It is because my act-unfolding-itself is charged with my whole experience—not in the form of memories, but in the form of a living accretion—that my perception of those façades is really perception of those houses and, in them, of the whole of Calcutta. It is the whole of my past living in my present which gives to the movement of my act towards the future, to the world which this movement brings into existence, to each element of this world, its articulations, its expressiveness, its evocative power.

In my previous study of perception, I have already pointed out the continuous character of my perceptive life. There is no more possibility of resolving the life of my senses into a succession of distinct "acts of perceiving" than of reducing the world to a collection of independent substances. Each object is a particular concretion of the totality of my act-world; thus it has no existence by itself—it is constituted by its relation to the other objects which surround it, by its inclusion in the whole system of which it is an expressive element. Similarly, each of my perceptions is essentially a moment of the integral movement of my act towards its final realization; it does not subsist by itself—that is, as a particular event which can be abstracted from my whole life stream and studied "in itself"—it receives its meaning, its particular *esse* from the totality of my temporal-act-in-tension-towards-its-end (in the same way as each particular event which takes place in the world receives its meaning, its existence, from the totality of history). This is the light in which the relation between the successive moments of my perceptive life must be understood. From the terrace of St Xavier's College, I gaze at the city which stretches all around. At this moment, my look is directed towards the twin steeples of St James's Church. This perception, understood as the self-revelation of my act incarnate at the present moment of its existence, is the only temporal reality which actually exists for me. It is not, however, a temporal atom whose whole existence consists in its being "just itself". Before fixing itself on St James's Church and its surroundings, my attention had been wandering over other sections of the city and been caught by other conspicuous landmarks. All these past perceptive moments are actualized in the present moment: in my way of looking at the steeples of the church, in the way in which the church and its surroundings reveal themselves to my view. This persistence of my previous perceptions in my actual perception—*together with the presence in it of my whole experience*—contributes towards making my present act of looking a particular apprehension of the spatio-temporal totality formed by my act-world-in-tension-towards-its-end: in the same way as St James's Church, while reflecting its surroundings, expresses in a particular way the whole of Calcutta, the entire world, so my perception of St James's Church, while realizing my previous perceptions, totalizes my experience of Calcutta, my whole life experience. In fact, these two perspectives are one and the same reality: the spatial totality of which St James's Church is the expression *is* the sum total of experience which my present perception actualizes, because my life-act—which gives its existence-for-me to St James's Church as it stands there among the houses and the trees and which constitutes my present perception of it—is at once the "form" of space and the act of history—in other words, because the movement by which the whole world converges towards my body and my eyes fixed on the church is identically the process by which the whole past is actualized in my present perception, because the centrifugal expansion of my life-act which makes my surrounding exist for me (of which my present perception is a modality) is identically the tension of my act towards the future.

i. *Temporality and Imagination*

Like my perceptions, my thoughts and imaginations take place in the movement by which my life-act tends towards the future; like my perceptions, they are charged with the totality of my experience. There is, however, a great difference between the way in which my perceptions actualize my past and the way in which my imaginations contain it. The way in which this difference must be conceived may easily be gathered from what has already been said about the existential status of my life-act-incarnate-in-my-perceptual-apparatus-in-relation-to-my-environment and the existential status of my life-act-incarnate-in-my-brain, about perceptive and imaginative consciousness. In our present study, there is no need to dwell further on this point.

A few words must be said about the experience we have of the flow of our imaginative consciousness as a "third person phenomenon". Thoughts and imaginations present themselves in the form of reminiscences, of mental conceptions charged with our past experience. At some moments, these thoughts flock to our mind and invade the whole field of our mental activity; we feel so to speak carried along by them and by the emotional current in which they are immersed. This phenomenon shows how much our life-act is conditioned by itself-already-realized and by the world-already-constituted: as we lose ourselves in the stream of our thoughts and imaginations, we feel the incessant flowing of our past and of the past of the world into our present; we experience our life as a tide whose waters continually rise from the depths of our biopsychic history and of the history of the universe.

I have already referred to the link between my imaginative consciousness and my perceptive consciousness. This relation, as has been explained, must not be understood as a necessary dependence of my thoughts and imaginations upon my *actual* perceptions, but as a movement taking place within the temporal flow of my life-act incarnate. At every moment of its progress, my act incarnate takes up my whole past and realizes it; this totality which forms my present includes the whole of my perceptive experience, not in the form of images, but in the form of vital determinations identified with the present state of my life-act-in-tension-towards-its-end. This experiential deposit together with my affective motions and preoccupations expresses itself in many ways in my thoughts, imaginations, memories. This phenomenon shows how my mental representations are in a real way "products" of my perceptive experience without being necessarily derived from my actual perceptions.

iv. *Temporality and Affectivity*

Our affective motions are modifications of our life-act incarnate which, while expressing and revealing our temperamental inclination, bear striking testimony to the persistence of our past in our present. The way in which we live the various situations in which we find ourselves is largely due to the vital meaning which these situations have acquired for us in the course of our existence. This fact is so obvious and has been so often emphasized that it would be tedious to labour the point. What has escaped the notice of most philosophers and psychologists is the fundamental perspective in which this phenomenon must be understood—the perspective which has been the leading thread of this study: if all the situations through which I pass, all the events which take place in my body and in the world around me, have for me vital meanings which depend on my temperamental disposition and on my personal past, the world as it exists for me, as I live it, is a unique reality constituted by my individual *esse*, a reality which cannot belong to anybody else than myself; it is even a reality which, radically, cannot *be* anything but myself. This fact must be accepted as the very foundation of psychology.

My feelings and emotions cannot, any more than my perceptions, be abstracted from the temporal current in which they are immersed. As has been pointed out in the preceding chapter, the way I live a certain situation in which I am involved depends not only on my temperament but also on the particular mood in which I find myself when meeting this situation. Thus the affective disposition which I experience at a given moment is never entirely determined by the circumstances in which I am placed. On the one hand I live each particular situation according to the meaning which it has acquired for me in the course of my existence, but on the other hand this experiential deposit conditions myself-placed-in-this-situation according to the particular affective climate in which I find myself at the moment of meeting this situation. This fact is parallel to what I observed earlier in my study of perception. Each of my perceptions actualizes my whole life experience through the medium of the particular perceptive current in which it takes place. Each concrete perception, as well as each particular emotion or feeling, is a deeply individualized phenomenon. There is no possibility of reducing any of my concrete affective states to an abstract pattern. No doubt, I can define my various sentiments by referring them to invariable categories, but this definition leaves out what is most intimate in them, namely, their concrete insertion in the stream of my individual existence.

Conclusion of the Two Approaches

The various descriptive attempts contained in this study of the temporality of my life-act incarnate are sufficient to show that each aspect of my biological and psychological existence is a certain way in which my temporality expresses itself, a certain way in which my past and the past of the world model my present, condition the movement of my life-act towards the future.

It should be borne in mind that the whole temporal movement analysed so far is not a self-controlled process: it is myself existing as a stream which feels itself carried in a certain direction, a stream continually fed by the broader stream formed by the world-existing-without-me. This temporal movement includes such realities as are usually called physical time, biological time, psychological time. The notion of physical time designates the forward movement of the system formed by the so-called physical universe; the notion of biological time refers to the vital processes which take place in my body-in-relation-to-the-world; finally, the notion of psychological time points to the whole stream of my sentient life. Now these three times must not be understood as three distinct parallel currents, but as three different aspects under which the movement of my life-act incarnate can be studied. As we know, there is no such thing as a physical universe subsisting independently of me. The universe as it exists concretely, as I study it, is in its entirety the expressive field of my life-act, a system constituted by its relation to my body, to my brain. Each modification of this system is from the first a biological phenomenon; it has a meaning in relation to my personal existence. Therefore the physical universe and physical time are, *as such*, non-existent entities; the concrete totality from which they are abstracted is my act-world-in-tension-towards-its-end.

Another point must be mentioned. Our study of temporality has been in fact a first approach to the problem of memory. From what has been observed, it is clear that memory cannot be considered as a special "faculty of the soul" entrusted with the retention and the re-presentation of the past. The actualization of the past, as has been shown, is effected by the whole life-act incarnate. It is not a purely mental or cognitive operation but a vital process which, in fact, is identical with the movement by which the life-act constitutes its field of expression while tending towards the future. Thus the phenomenon of memory must be understood first of all as the living persistence of the past *in the present*. From this we see that memory, like temporality (of which it is but an aspect) must be studied at the various levels of the personal structure: it is not simply the "mind" which retains the past, it is the whole body, the whole life-act incarnate; each aspect of the personal structure is a particular mode in which the past persists in the present and conditions the movement of the act towards the future.

B. The Temporality of My Act-World-Tending-Personally-Towards-Its-End

I have more than once described the way in which my life-act incarnate actuated itself into an act-volition, and so began to tend towards its end in a truly personal way. I have shown also that, while taking more and more luminous possession of itself, my personal act expressed its tension towards its end in the form of a definite life project which inspired my daily decisions and undertakings and so gave its meaning to my whole existence. I shall now study this transcendental sphere under the aspect of temporality. The first part of this study will be an analysis of the relation between the reflectiveness of my personal act and its temporality, the second a description of the temporal structure of my personal-act-tending-towards-its-realization, special attention being paid to the relation between temporality and liberty.

1. Temporality and Reflectiveness

My transcendental activity is essentially reflective—in other words, my personal-act incarnate is luminously present to itself at every moment of its progress towards its end. This self-transparency of my personal act manifests itself in many ways: in the fact that it determines reflectively the way in which it must realize itself; in the fact that, while actuating itself through the pursuit of various particular aims, it is continually aware of the various modalities of its expressive field; in the fact that it continually tries to understand itself more deeply in order better to possess and realize itself. I shall now analyse the link between these three aspects of my reflectiveness and my temporality.

My Temporality and My Act-Project

In the second chapter of this book, when examining the nature of the principle from which my activities receive their impulse and their meaning, I came to the conclusion that my life-act-realizing-itself-through-my-act-project is the "I live" to which all my actions refer. In that passage, I pointed out that my life project had been formed gradually, that it came to existence in the movement of my act towards the future *in dependence on the past.* At a certain moment of my life, my personal act reflecting upon itself-already-realized and, *in this light,* becoming conscious of its destiny and of the destiny of the world, gave to this dynamic self-awareness a more or less definite expression. The concrete way in which my personal-act-reflecting-upon-itself moulded itself into a life project, the particular form which this project assumed when it came into existence, were essentially related to the degree and type of self-understanding I had reached at that stage of my life. The characteristics of this self-understanding—which reflected the existential disposition of my personal act at that moment of my childhood—were themselves related to the way in which my life had developed during the previous years (owing to my temperamental inclination, to the education I had received, the geographical, social, cultural, religious environment in which I had moved, the various influences which I had undergone, the decisions and initiatives I had begun to take in the various situations in which I had been placed, etc.). In short, my life project manifested itself from the first as a more or less definite concretion of my life experience, as the concrete way in which my personal act reflectively took up itself-already-realized (i.e., my past and the past of the world) in order to determine the way in which it would continue to actuate itself.

As years passed, my personal act became more and more reflectively conscious of itself—of its potentialities and limitations—of the end towards which it was ordained, of its relationship to the whole universe; consequently, its progress towards the future became more and more "intelligent" and "realistic". As it exists today, my life project reflects the way in which my environment, the various situations in which I have been placed, have influenced me, in short, the whole of my life experience. In its present state, my life project manifests the understanding of myself-incarnate to which the concrete way in which I have actuated myself has led me.

All these observations show how my temporality—i.e., the fact that and the way in which, my personal act is, in its progress towards the future, determined by itself-already-realized (that is to say, by my past and, through it, by the past of the world)—conditions my reflective predetermination of what I, and my world, and the whole universe must become and of what my future must be.

Now, in the same way as my personal act exists only as act-incarnate-in-a-multiform-spatial-field, my reflective tension towards the future is essentially a progressive movement which takes place within a changing world and varying situations. The consequence of this is that my life project cannot remain in existence unless it expresses itself in particular projects, decisions, and actions. The forming of these particular projects into expressions of my life project implies that my personal act must accept the situations in which it finds itself incarnate in the light of its integral finality; thus it presupposes in my personal act a relatively high degree of reflectiveness—that is, a transcendental understanding of itself-incarnate, a vision of the situations in which it is involved as modalities of its movement towards its ultimate realization. This self-understanding, it must be noted, is not supratemporal as would be that of a pure consciousness without relation to history. It is achieved by the fact that my personal act, in the movement by which it tends towards the future, lives the various situations in which it is incarnate as luminous concretions of its integral life experience, and is therefore able to shape them into prefigurements of its end. Thus my temporality is the very stuff of which my reflective taking up of myself-incarnate-in-particular-situations is made. It is by living the particular circumstances in which I find myself not as realities-in-themselves but as dynamic concretions of my personal history and of the history of the world, that I make my particular projects into expressions of my integral life project.

This reflective taking up of the various situations I meet in the movement of my transcendental existence does not destroy their singularity; on the contrary, it confirms it. As we know, the singularity of a situation or of an event does not reside in its isolation, but in its relationship to the whole spatio-temporal reality: it consists in the unique way in which this situation expresses the whole universe, the totality of history. Therefore, by integrating *reflectively* the circumstances in which I find myself in the movement of my personal act towards its end, by taking them up in the light of my integral finality, far from reducing them to undifferentiated moments of a continuous flow, I allow them to be in me really "themselves".

There is, of course, a way of forcing all particular situations into the pattern of a certain idea, or leading intention, which tends to eliminate all difference between them. But this is due to a lack of genuine reflectiveness, of deep self-understanding, on the part of the personal-act-incarnate-in-these-situations: its movement forward is not a real transcendental self-realizing endeavour but a sort of blind impetus. As we know, true reflectiveness implies the acknowledgment of the situations in which we are involved as various expressions of our createdness, and hence the discovery of each situation—in its very singularity—as a reality intended for the end. But only a person whose life project tends to coincide with the intention by which he is constituted as creature—that is, who, through the act of transcendental obedience, has attained the realm of freedom and genuine self-knowledge—can make this discovery.

Abstracting a situation from the whole context which gives it its meaning is another way of dealing with it in an unreflective manner. According to some philosophers, each situation in which we find ourselves, because it is a unique conjuncture, has *in itself* its own law: it must be lived according to its concrete requirements, in a deeply particular, individual, original manner—in other words, we must live each situation we meet without referring ourselves to anything other than that situation.

No doubt, by stressing the unique character of each concrete situation, those who hold this view emphasize a reality which generations of essentialist philosophers have too often overlooked. Their position, nevertheless, is vitiated by their lack of perspective, their failure to understand human existence as a whole, as a process ordained towards a goal. According to their conception, human life is but a succession of moments each of which has its value in itself, independently of the end towards which this movement is ordained. This is a fallacy. Each situation we meet, each moment of our existence, cannot be understood "in itself", and so cannot be lived "for itself". As we have just said, it is the whole movement of our life, the totality of our act-world-in-tension-towards-its-end which gives their meaning and value to all the circumstances in which we are placed: the singularity of each situation consists in the unique way in which it expresses the whole, in which it prefigures the end. Therefore, to deal with a situation in a truly reflective way, we must see it in the light of our final destiny. To abstract a moment of our existence from its reference to our end is to reduce it to a meaningless temporal atom, to prevent ourselves from discovering the intention by which it is constituted.

My Temporality and My Knowledge of the World

In the previous chapter, when analysing the reflectiveness of my personal act, I pointed out that my personal-act-illuminating-itself-in-the-modalities-of-my-brain is identically the world-illuminating-itself-in-me—in other words, that the consciousness I have of myself and my knowledge of the world are radically one. This consciousness of myself-qua-world may be described as my personal-act-already-realized-in-the-form-of-a-world illuminating itself in my personal-act-continuing-to-realize-itself. Now, my personal-act-already-realized-in-the-form-of-a-world, in so far as it is an existing reality, is my past and the past of the world conditioning my present (i.e., my personal-act-continuing-to-realize-itself) and actualizing themselves in it. Therefore my consciousness of myself and my knowledge of the world are a vision of the present in relation to the past (in relation to my past and, through it, to the past of the whole world). This, we should note, does not tell us anything new. I have already shown (in my second chapter) that my experience living in my present activity gives the world its meaning, its reality-for-me. From this it follows that my understanding of myself and of the world is conditioned by my temporality; it is a dynamic, growing reality, because, as I continue to actuate myself, the experiential store through which I discover myself and the world continually increases.

What exactly are this "self" and this "world" which I understand more and more profoundly as my life experience increases?

As we know, the reality which my personal-act-tending-towards-the-future continually actuates is itself-already-realized-in-the-form-of-a-world. Now my personal-act-already-realized-in-the-form-of-a-world is the whole history of the world (i.e., the world-already-constituted) crystallized in my present through the mediation of my personal history. Thus the world which I understand better and better as I go on living is really the world-formed-without-me (i.e., the world existing as the actualization of the whole of history). But I do not understand this world "in itself": I understand it as identified in my present with my personal-act-already-realized (i.e., shaping my individuality through the mediation of my personal history), as living qua myself (i.e., existing by, in, and for my personal-act-continuing-to-realize-itself). More deeply, the reality which I understand better and better as my life experience increases is the one intention by which I and the world-in-me are constituted: as my experience increases, I discover the creative Idea from which I and the universe proceed, from which my life and, in it, the whole of history receive their basic meaning, their dynamism.

From the consideration of my knowledge of the world as a whole, let us pass now to that of my knowledge of particular objects. I pointed out earlier that my transcendental consciousness is never consciousness of myself and of the world as pure indifferent being, but always consciousness of myself-already-realized-in-the-form-of-a-pluralized-world—that is, consciousness of the world-already-existing-in-the-form-of-many-objects-intentions. Now, as we know, the particular meaning which an object has for me is constituted by my life experience: as a particular intention—that is, as a more or less determinate "towards-which"—each object manifests itself as a particular crystallization of my past, as a particular concretion of the movement by which my act-world takes up itself-already-realized while tending towards the future (towards its ultimate realization). This throws light on the connection between my knowledge of things and my temporality. This connection is based on the fact that the objects which surround me, to the extent that they exist for me, are parts of the system constituted by my personal-act-conditioned-by-itself-already-realized-while-continuing-to-realize-itself.

It must be remembered that, as parts of the world-existing-without-me, the various objects which surround me are already meaningful realities; they are already objects-intentions. As such, they are not crystallizations of my personal past but particular condensations of the whole human history and of the whole history of the world. The process by which I make them into realities-for-me is identical with the process by which I take up the whole of history in my present through the mediation of my own life experience, of my personal past. This shows once more that the meanings which I give to the objects I perceive are not arbitrary. Independently of me, things are already constituted as meaningful realities because they are already charged with a whole history (their "quiddity" is nothing but their specific manner of individuating, of containing history). By the fact of living in the world, of making it mine, I let this history become my personal history—thus, as my life experience grows, I let the objects of the world realize and manifest in me their particular destinations.

My Temporality and My Thinking

The reflectiveness of my personal act incarnate manifests itself not only in the fact that, while tending towards the future, it is continually aware of the modifications which its expressive field undergoes, of the meanings which these various modifications possess within the whole temporal stream, but also in the fact that it tries constantly to understand itself more deeply in order to master itself more fully. I shall analyse now the temporality of this thinking activity.

I am engrossed in my study. My personal act tries deliberately to express itself to itself in a luminous and penetrating way. This present effort is not a pure beginning, a sudden initiative which stands entirely by itself; it is conditioned, guided, illuminated by the whole thinking activity which I have carried on up to this day: my present thinking is the realization and the fruition of my past thinking. Thus it is on the basis of itself-already-luminously-realized that my personal act continues to discover and realize itself.

This thinking activity requires a continual self-transcending. To be authentic, the effort I make to understand myself cannot be the mere repetition in my present of the self-discovery I made in the past; it cannot be the mere restating of what I have already expressed to myself yesterday; it cannot be the mere apprehension of myself-already-realized—that is, of myself-qua-essence. To be authentic, my present thinking must be a grasping of myself in the very act by which I go beyond myself; it must be a luminous realization of my existence—that is, the self-reflective presence of my personal act in the very movement by which it tends towards the future.

These two aspects of my thinking activity—its "essential" aspect (i.e., its continual dependence on what is already achieved, the fact that I think by continually taking up myself-already-thought) and its "existential" aspect (by which my "essential" thinking is continually vitalized, "experientialized")—are complementary. To the extent that it loses its direct, intuitive character, my thinking depersonalizes itself, it tends to become mere relation to the past, mere verbalism; to the extent that it refuses to take up what is already acquired, it loses sight of the very "what" which the movement of my life continually carries ahead of itself. On the one hand my authentic self-understanding takes place in the very act by which I go beyond the present moment, on the other hand it is understanding of my present as the realization of the whole past and projection of this totality into the future.

Let us now, with the help of these considerations, describe the temporal movement of my thinking as it takes place concretely. At this moment, taking up and actualizing all my past thinking, basing my reflective effort on the totality of myself-already-thought, I try to progress in my self-understanding and to put in writing what I experience. In doing so, while giving expression to the present consciousness I have of myself, I reinterpret all my previous discoveries, I recast in a new form the whole stream of my past thinking. The words which I write on the paper are for me a means of progressing in my self-understanding, they feed and support my intuition, they help me to make it more vivid. At the same time, they tend to fetter me: as I express myself, I bind myself, I become the prisoner of the written words. I must question them continually, I must go beyond myself-already-expressed in order to keep my thinking free, dynamic —that is to say, authentic.

This does not mean that my reflective effort must tend to become a purely creative process. As we know, true self-mastery always implies self-acceptance. Thus the very effort I make in order to grasp and realize myself, even though it transcends my past, remains deeply conditioned by it. My present self-understanding cannot break its essential relation to what I have previously experienced and expressed of myself, because my present in all its modalities offers itself as the realization of my whole history, because my self-consciousness—in its present state—is intimately dependent on the way in which I have lived up to this day, and it depends, therefore, on the way in which my personal act has gradually realized and illuminated itself. However, just as my personal-act-tending-towards-the-future is not *constituted* by its dependence on itself-already-realized, so my present self-understanding (which is nothing but the presence of my personal act to itself) is not the mere result of my past thinking. The acceptance of myself on which my self-discovery is based is not a mere surrender of my present thinking to the world of thoughts already formed in my mind (such a surrender, far from authenticating my present thinking, would, on the contrary, devitalize, depersonalize, "essentialize" it); it is a conscious relating of it to the Transcendent Source of my temporal existence. In the light which emanates from this Source, I discover myself as transcendentally given to myself; my acceptance of my past becomes a liberating and illuminating submission to the Act which creates me *in the present* as personal-act-world-conditioned-by-itself-already-realized (my past)-while-tending-towards-an-ever-more-perfect-self-actuation (my future).

What we have just said about my philosophical thinking may legitimately be applied to any kind of intellectual pursuit.

The physicist tries to determine with increasing accuracy the structure of the "material universe". To do so, he studies carefully all the discoveries that have already been made and all the theories and explanations which have been proposed. Thus he acknowledges that, as a scientist, he depends on the past. But the past to which he is related is not a series of happenings which persist unchanged in their own places in the chain of history. It is through the lectures he attends, through the books he reads, through his experiments and research (or through the memory he retains at this moment of his earlier studies and reading)—that is, through events which take place here and now—that he links himself with the past. In other words, the data on which he now depends in his scientific study are historical facts which subsist not as past occurrences but as present realities. Moreover, we should note that the way in which he assimilates all this material depends on the way in which he has formed himself, on his own experience as a physicist: it is through the mediation of his own past that history shapes his present scientific knowledge, and conditions his present study and research.

However, it is not the mere reliance of the physicist on the experience which he *has* acquired, on the formation which he *has* received, on the data which he *has* assimilated—that is, his dependence on himself-already-realized and, through himself-already-realized, on the world-already-constituted—which enables him to be an authentic scientist. What makes him a real scientist is the power he has of continually reinterpreting, remodelling, experientializing the knowledge he has acquired in the movement of his present study, of his present research, of his present teaching, in his present contact with the reality which he wants to grasp and to express to himself; what makes him a real scientist is the vigour with which he transcends and masters the scientific world which is already formed in him, the energy with which he leads this world (which is himself) towards new forms of self-expression.

Nevertheless, the research of an authentic scientist is not a purely creative endeavour: his mastery over the field which he explores is continually based on an act of submission: the scientist transcends his past to the extent that he accepts as they are the facts in which his past and the past of the world are actualized. This acceptance of reality which liberates and authenticates the research of the scientist is not a mere identification of his intellect with a scientific world already constituted; fundamentally, it is an acknowledgment of his createdness: it is by surrendering his mental endeavour to the light which emanates here and now from his Creative Source that the scientist apprehends dynamically the scientific *esse* of the field which he studies (a field which is nothing but himself-under-a-certain-aspect). This certainly does not mean that he rejects whatever has been established in the past; it means that he revivifies and re-creates the whole scientific world in the act of his own scientific research: by allowing himself to be illuminated from Above, by linking himself to his Creative Source in the effort he makes to penetrate into the core of reality, he gives real existence and life to a universe which otherwise would be reduced to a system of notions, concepts, abstract laws, and stereotyped formulae.

The case of the historian is of particular interest in this analysis of the relation between temporality and thinking.

In this context we should recall a number of points made in the first part of this chapter:

(1) The present is the only temporal reality which exists here and now.

(2) The past, as past, is no more. However, the past is not dead, it lives in the present which it has prepared, and towards which it was ordained.

(3) No historical event has any existence "in itself", that is, as an isolated fact, as a temporal atom. Each event reflects the period in which it takes place, expresses in a particular manner the totality of history, is a prefigurement of the end towards which history tends.

From this we may see that history as a science is not the study of events which have their full meaning "in themselves", in other words, which are complete and perfectly determined at the moments they take place. No event can be studied independently of the historical setting in which it occurs, of the past which it fulfils, and of the future it contains potentially; no event can be fully understood apart from the totality of history. Now this totality, as an existing reality (i.e., identified with the universe at the present moment of its progress towards its completion), is a still unfinished system. Therefore, in the present circumstances, no definitive meaning can be attributed to any event which has taken place in the past or takes place in the present: the past must be continually reinterpreted in the light of the present, and it is only in the future that the present will reveal its significance. Thus history as a science can never claim to have provided a definitive account of the past, to have discovered definitively the meaning of any epoch or of any historical event.

These are facts which all historians acknowledge in their own way. They know that a synthesis of the past is always imperfect, that today events take place and tendencies manifest themselves which require a new interpretation of circumstances which formerly were considered as definitively classified. They know that to appraise facts a certain distance is always required: only time can reveal the meaning of an incident, the value of a work, the way in which a man influences history. More precisely, historians know that to grasp the meaning of a historical phenomenon they must study the earlier events of which this phenomenon is the fulfilment; they must study the general setting in which it takes place and which it reflects in its own way; they must study also whatever follows it, that is, the different circumstances in which this historical phenomenon lives on and realizes its potentialities.

Let us illustrate this by two examples taken in turn from the history of philosophy and from political history.

To understand Descartes, the historians of philosophy go back as far as St Augustine and then follow the whole current of medieval philosophy. St Augustine himself cannot be studied apart from the Christian and Neoplatonic traditions. Neoplatonism is linked, through the Academy, to Socrates and the Eleatic philosophers. On the other hand, the work of modern and contemporary philosophy enables present-day historians to see Descartes in a new light, to give new interpretations to the various aspects of his thought. Thus historians acknowledge that the work of Descartes is not something which stands by itself in its historical setting, something which requires nothing but itself in order to be what it is; they acknowledge that even today the work of Descartes is not complete; they are continually discovering *in the developments of contemporary thought* elements which make Descartes' philosophy more genuinely "itself" than it was at the time of its formulation (elements which prolong

Descartes' thinking and actuate the potentialities of his philosophical endeavour).

Political historians find the same in their own field of research. Historians know that the French Revolution is not a historical event which can be strictly localized and has its own explanation "in itself". In order to grasp its meaning in the development of history, they must first "replace" it in its historical setting: France and, more broadly, Europe at the end of the eighteenth century; further, they must see it as the fruition of a long historical evolution: they must study the way in which the *Ancien Régime* gradually ran to seed, the way in which political trends manifesting themselves in England, in other European countries and in America influenced the mentality of the French people, the decisive role played by a number of leading personalities—more generally, they must have a certain understanding of French and European history as a whole—ideally, they should have a vision of the way in which the whole world, in the course of its becoming, "engendered" the French Revolution,[1] of the way in which the French Revolution actualizes and expresses the history of the whole universe. But this understanding of the French Revolution as a particular reflection of the whole historical setting characterizing France and Europe in the last decade of the eighteenth century, as a particular realization of the history of the world before 1792, still does not give to historians a satisfactory knowledge of what the French Revolution means for history as a whole. If they are to judge its significance more accurately, they must look at the way in which it has influenced and shaped the subsequent history of France, of Europe and of the whole world. To do this, they must study the way in which the world has evolved from the end of the eighteenth century until our own times. In so doing, they will find out what the French Revolution contained—at the moment it took place—in a potential and latent form. In other words, it is in the world of the nineteenth and twentieth centuries that they find the realization, the actuality of the French Revolution.

This introduces the further question of whether history as a science can be defined as the study of the past.

The expression "study of the past" may be taken to mean the study of facts (events, persons, philosophical systems, etc.), of

[1] In writing so, it may seem that I exclude all "free agency" from the process in which a historical event is brought about. Later chapters will show clearly that this is not so.

historical developments, fully intelligible "in themselves" because fully realized and determined at the very time they took place. In this case, the effort of the historian must be once more to link himself from his own place in history to the portion of the past which he wishes to describe in order to grasp it in its very historicity. This, of course, is an impossible undertaking. As we know, the present is the only temporal reality which actually exists. Thus the very notion of a past event persisting in its own place in the chain of history, offering itself as an object to be studied and fully understood "in itself", is an absurdity. In fact, this notion implies the very negation of time as the progress of the universe towards its completion or as a real genesis; it is a product of the geometrical mentality which considers history as a succession of independent temporal atoms just as it considers the spatial universe as a collection of co-existing substances.

However, in a certain sense, history may rightly be understood as the study of the past. As we know, the past is not dead but realized *in the present*. History as a science is the study of the past as realizing itself in the present and the study of the present as actualizing the past. Therefore we should not wonder whether the science of history allows us to grasp the meaning which past events had "in themselves" at the moments they took place, but realize that it allows us to know the *reality* of those events by revealing the particular way in which they are actualized in the world of today (the only existing world); we shall understand also that the science of history allows us to discover more fully the world in which we live by showing us how it realizes the various events of the past or the different epochs of history. From this point of view, we must say that the French Revolution which historians study is not and cannot be the French Revolution as it took place at the end of the eighteenth century; we must say that the French Revolution as understood by contemporary historians is the French Revolution that has grown into the world of today—this is the only French Revolution which has any meaning, because it is the only one which offers itself as a reality.

We may finally confirm this view by analysing the way in which an authentic historian pursues his research.

First, we must acknowledge that, the aim of the historian being the understanding of the past, he is really conditioned in his study by events, by temporal developments, by ideological trends, which *have already taken place:* his work calls for a continual scrutiny of the world-already-constituted and a continual acceptance of the facts which this totality includes. Moreover, we must acknowledge that it is always through his own experience as a historian that the past reveals itself to him: it is through himself-already-realized that the world-already-constituted conditions the act of his research.

In order to progress in his discovery of the past, the historian studies all available documents: manuscripts kept in libraries and archives, monuments and stone inscriptions, works dealing with the various questions in which he is interested. He also visits the countries in which the various events which he wants to bring to light have taken place. In this environment, he tries to rediscover the mentality of the past and to acquire a personal and dynamic experience of it. In all this activity, it must be noted, the historian deals with present realities: through them, he tries to penetrate more deeply into the reality of the historical facts which he studies; he tries to understand better the stuff of which these modalities of his life field are made.

However, it is not the mere dependence of the historian on the various elements of the world-already-constituted-in-him, his "passivity" with regard to the data which he collects, which *constitute* him as an authentic historian. To be a real scholar, the historian must continually transcend the whole field of his research and re-work it, in the act of his historical study, through real creative thinking. This means that the historian must discover the past in the very movement by which he leads the world towards its completion—that is, in the act by which he personally tends towards his final realization. If, instead of taking up dynamically the various aspects of his field of research in his drive towards the future, he allows his thought to lose itself in facts and documents, and to be entirely moulded by what he reads, his historical knowledge tends to become a mass of lifeless material, an amalgam of reminiscences, of historical events reduced to static essences.

This does not mean that the work of an authentic historian is a *purely* autonomous endeavour, or that, in the act of his research, he gives the past an arbitrary meaning. The creativeness of a historian—like the creativeness of a scientist, of a philosopher—is entirely based on an act of submission: it is to the degree to which he lets himself-incarnate-in-his-field-of-research be illuminated by the light which proceeds from his Creative Source that the historian discovers in a dynamic and synthetic way the authentic meaning of the facts which he investigates. Through the identification of his reflective endeavour and of his incarnate will with the intention constitutive of his world, he unifies the various elements of his field of study and experiences, even if indistinctly, the way in which the past precontains the future —in one word, he discovers, by *living* it, the meaning of history.

A few words may be said about political thinking. Politicians set forth the principles according to which a state must be governed and organized, and the rules to be followed in international relations. Before framing their theories, they try to acquire some experience: they study the various political systems which have been tried in the past, the methods and policies followed by successful statesmen, the programmes of the different political schools, etc. Thus, in formulating their own ideas, politicians are very much influenced by the past; their position is, so to speak, a particular crystallization of the political experience of mankind. Expressing this fact in our philosophical language, we shall say that, in his own thinking, each politician is deeply conditioned by the world-already-constituted individuated in himself-already-realized.

However, it is not this subjection of himself to a political world already in existence which makes a politician into an authentic statesman. What makes him such is the power he has of taking up in a personal dynamic way the experience of the previous generations and of re-creating it forcefully in the movement of his own existence as a leader of men. If, instead of mastering the various aspects of his world and of giving them continually new life, he is himself carried along by the political ambiance in which he lives, he will be regarded not as a farsighted statesman, but as a mediocre politician. The political world is full of personalities who are the prisoners of ideologies, who follow blindly the "party line", who reduce their political thinking to the formulation of slogans, who are captives of their own ideas and their past thinking, who, in presence of new situations, cling to old policies because they are unable to free themselves from the world of theories with which they have identified themselves. . . .

These considerations, however, do not justify the conclusion that the authentic statesman is the politician who, throwing off all connection with the past, takes independent and arbitrary initiatives and accepts no law other than his own autocratic will. The reflection through which an authentic political leader matures his decisions is no more an autonomous process than is the research of an authentic historian, of an authentic scientist, or of an authentic philosopher: like any thinking worth the name, it is entirely based on an act of submission. An authentic statesman is a man who sees and accepts facts and who adapts his policies—that is, his thinking and acting—to the demands of the various situations in which he finds himself. This submission which liberates him is fundamentally an act of transcendental obedience: the authentic statesman acknowledged—at least implicitly—the circumstances in which he is placed as the expression of his createdness; in the light which emanates from his Creative Source, he discovers the intention by which these facts are constituted; in so doing, he transcends his situation and takes it up—at the same time, he takes up the whole past and re-creates it in his reflective act, in the decisions which his thinking inspires him to take.

What has emerged from these various analyses may leave us with the impression that every thinking is either purely authentic or completely inauthentic—in other words, that there is no intermediate between perfectly authentic thinking and totally inauthentic thinking. In fact, there is probably no human thinking which ever attains pure authenticity and no human thinking which may be qualified as completely inauthentic. The reason, in the latter case, is that complete inauthenticity implies a total alienation: it implies that a person must have been completely overtaken by his past and by history, that he must have surrendered the *totality* of himself to the influences which condition him. This is an impossibility because a person, *as person*, is not produced by any sort of evolutive process but brought to existence and kept in existence by a Transcendent Initiative: he holds his being not from below, but from Above. However, the human condition is such that, in many circumstances, man is much more a person carried along by his ambiance and his temperament, by his past and by history, than one leading his life and guiding his world in a distinctly personal manner (a fact which does not necessarily imply a moral connotation).

To conclude this study of the relation between temporality and reflective consciousness, I shall indicate briefly the role played by imaginative consciousness and affectivity in the process by which our past conditions our thinking.

Towards the end of the previous chapter, I showed the relation existing between reflective consciousness and imagination. I expressed this relation in these terms: the act-illuminating-itself-reflectively is both conditioned and supported by itself-already-thought and by itself-illuminating-itself-imaginatively. In the next paragraph, I pointed out the way in which thinking is influenced by affectivity.

In this chapter, I have indicated the way in which our thoughts and imaginations contain our past; in particular, I have mentioned that, at those moments when our mental faculties are filled with the stream of our imaginations, we feel the incessant flow of our past and of the past of the world into our present. In this chapter, I have referred also to the relation which our affective motions have to our past experiences.

Taken together, these two series of observations show that it is often through our imaginations and affectivity that our thinking is conditioned by our past. Our thinking is authentic to the extent that it takes up creatively, and sublimates, the temporal streams which our imaginations and emotions represent; it is inauthentic in so far as it allows itself to be carried away by these phenomenal currents. But, as we know, in ordinary life, we neither fully master and integrate the flow of our imaginative consciousness and of our affectivity, nor allow our thinking to be entirely drowned in it. Many of our mental states may be characterized as both transcendental acts and as phenomenal processes: in them our past is reworked by the movement of our personal act towards the future, and at the same time it lives on in the form of thoughts, imaginations, emotions, which tend to absorb our reflective endeavour and decrease the transcendental impetus of our will.

2. Temporality and Freedom

My life-act-actuating-itself-through-my-act-project is the "I live" which gives its existence and its meaning to whatever pertains to me in any way. I have shown the relation between my temporality and my act-project in general, and also the relation between my temporality and the particular decisions in which my act project expresses itself. We must now study the temporal character of the voluntary activity through which my act-project and my various decisions are carried out.

As I pursue my daily activities, I am conscious that the stream of my life runs within another broader stream. This broader stream, which I call history, is formed by the whole past assuming new forms as it actualizes itself, moving towards a future which it contains in a potential way.

History is the very being of the world in which I live. It constitutes all the processes which take place in the universe, all the events occurring in the world, and all the objects which I see around me. History constitutes the meaning of every worldly reality: every object, every happening, in so far as it contains in itself an intention—in so far as it *is* an intention—is a particular way in which history expresses, realizes, or crystallizes itself.

At this moment, I am absorbed in my work. This work—my act of thinking and writing—is a particular activity through which my act-project actuates itself, a particular moment of my personal progress towards my end—as such, it is a self-determined, self-possessed endeavour.

However, my work is not a purely autonomous, self-creative initiative. Indeed:

(1) My present thinking and writing is based on my past thinking and, through it, on the whole of history.

(2) It takes place essentially within history, in dependence on and in conformity with history. It is the actuation in a certain direction of those intentions which were already constitutive of my pencil, of my paper, of my table, of my chair, of my room, of the whole world, before I started my work. My present activity, while fulfilling these intentions, leads history towards its completion.

(3) As I express myself in writing, I depend very much upon habits ingrained in my right hand grasping the pencil and making it cover the paper, in my left hand holding the paper, in my arm, in my eyes, in my whole body bent over the table. This dependence of my personal activity upon dispositions and aptitudes which I have acquired makes of it a partly "mechanical" process. These habits are a certain way in which my past persists in my present, conditions my work, and enables it to progress smoothly. They are not definite entities produced in my biopsychic organism by previous exercises and giving me "pushes" at the required moments; they are the whole system formed by 'my-body-in-relation-to-my-world'-existing-presently-as-the-incarnation-of-my-thinking-activity considered under a certain aspect.

We should be careful to note the relationship in which (2) and (3) stand to each other: the fulfilling of the intentions constitutive of the objects which surround me is effected largely in a "mechanical", non-reflective manner. In other words, in my act of thinking and writing, I do not make these intentions mine in a vividly conscious and heedful way but out of habit: while I concentrate my attention on the way in which I must express what I have in mind, habits, which are parts of myself-engaged-in-this-work, look after a multitude of details such as the way in which my pencil and my paper must be used, the way in which words must be written and sentences be formed. . . .

All these facts, which are various aspects under which my act-world takes up the past and depends on it at this very moment of its self-realizing movement, are elements without which my present activity would be unthinkable, non-existent.

Let us take another example. I have to go to St Teresa's Church to preach a sermon. I come out of St Xavier's College and proceed towards the east, walking on the pavement of Park Street. As I arrive in Lower Circular Road, I move a few yards towards the north until I reach the tram-stop. I wait there for the first tram going to Sealdah Station, taking care not to board one bound for Wellesley Street. In the tram, I sit down next to a window and buy a ticket from the conductor. I follow with my eyes the traffic of the street, I look at the tombs dotted about the cemetery, at the portico of St James's Church, at the incredibly rickety and rusty municipal trucks standing under the trees on the broad roadway. As soon as the low structure of Entally Market appears, I leave my seat and move towards the platform of the tram. All these movements and actions are the carrying out of my intention of going to St Teresa's Church to preach my sermon; thus they are a voluntary, self-determined activity. However, they are not purely spontaneous, totally self-creative initiatives:

(1) As I go from St Xavier's College to St Teresa's Church, I make mine and fulfil in a certain way intentions which are already present on the pavement of Park Street, in the tram-stop of Lower Circular Road, in the tram, in the small coin which I give the conductor, etc. These various objects, in so far as they are constituted by these intentions, are different ways in which history is crystallized in my surroundings, in the little world of my journey to St Teresa's Church.

(2) The activity by which I fulfil these intentions, far from being a succession of continually reflective and deliberate operations, is to a large extent a routine process: while actuating itself, my intention of going to the church to preach my sermon is supported by habits present in my body-related-to-my-world. The exercise of these habits

within my intention-actuating-itself is a particular way in which my past—and, in it, the whole of history—lives on in my activity, conditions, subtends, and facilitates it.

These observations may be extended to the whole stream of my daily activity. It is my custom to get up every day at 5 a.m. and kneel down for my morning prayer; after getting up, I shave, wash, and dress myself in accordance with a certain routine; following my habit, I then spend some time meditating, say Mass, take my breakfast, recite my breviary, start working. . . . In performing all these actions *out of habit:*

(1) I make mine and fulfil intentions present in the world around me: the night is *meant* for rest and the day for work, my prie-dieu is *meant* for my daily meditation, and the altar in the chapel for the offering of the Sacrifice, the food prepared on the table is *meant* to be eaten, my room, my chair, my table, my paper, my pencil are *meant* for my work. . . . In fulfilling these intentions, I lead history towards its completion.

(2) I actuate in a personal manner my act-project. In fact, fulfilling in a certain manner—largely by force of habit—the intentions present in the objects which surround me (1), and actuating my life project (2), are one and the same act.

Therefore, in my daily activity:

(1) I am carried along by history, I take up history, I lead it towards its fulfilment.

(2) I am carried along by my past actualized in the form of dispositions, of facilities, of automatisms.

(3) It is largely through the exercise of these habits in my personal activity that I fulfil the intentions constitutive of the objects of my world—intentions which are nothing but history expressing itself in various ways.

Do these facts contribute to the emancipation of my act, or do they tend to depersonalize me, to reduce my life to a succession of "mechanical" processes? This is the problem which I must now examine.

Fundamentally, I am a life-act incarnate in a definite centre—unfolding itself from this centre and, in this process, constituting the world as the realization of its potentialities, as the actuation of its being-towards-an-end—being conditioned, while unfolding itself, by itself-already-realized and by the world-already-constituted (i.e., by the totality of history). As we know, this living system—which is myself—does not, originally, move itself in a self-determined, self-possessed manner.

However, at a certain moment of its existence—which, of course, cannot be strictly delimited—my life-act actuated itself into an act-volition, and thus began to tend towards its end in a personal, reflective manner. My freedom resides in this transcendental self-actuation of my act-world, in the movement by which it determinedly goes beyond itself-already-realized, by which it leads itself towards new forms of existence, towards its final realization. With respect to my free activity, the following must be noted carefully:

(1) This activity is the authentic self-actuating movement of my act-world. It cannot be simply identified with the whole movement of my act incarnate, of my world, towards the future. My personal act remains life-act even after it has perfected itself into an act-volition; therefore, even then, its tension towards the future remains to a large extent a "third person process".

(2) To master the field in which it expresses itself—that is, to be authentically transcendental—my personal activity must concentrate itself, it must direct itself attentively towards particular aims which it envisages as prefigurements of its end.

(3) My personal-act-tending-freely-towards-its-end, even though it emerges from the stream of its phenomenal existence, even though it continually transcends itself-already-realized, remains deeply conditioned by the various currents above which it rises, by the various modalities of the expressive field which it must continually re-create. However, my free activity is not *constituted* by its dependence on the flow of my biopsychic existence, by its dependence on vital structures which are already constituted—in other words, my personal act, as a free act, is not simply generated by my life-act incarnate; it is not a mere product of history, the result of a "natural" growth. As a self-determined principle, my personal act is constituted by its relation to the Creative Source. This means that the essence of human freedom consists in dependence: not in dependence on impersonal realities, but in dependence on the Transcendent Personal. From this, it should not be concluded that, to be authentically free, my personal act must break its relation to the stream of phenomenal existence. My free act is created from Above as the transcendental actuation of my life-act incarnate, as an act-in-tension-towards-an-

end continually conditioned by itself-already-realized. Therefore, to remain authentically self-determined, my personal act must accept itself-incarnate, itself-already-there, in obedience to the Creator.

(4) It requires a continual effort, a tension of the will, to remain authentically free, to increase one's personal freedom. As recalled above, my freedom is in the act by which I go beyond myself, by which I tend personally towards the future. Now, in the very movement by which it throws itself forward, my personal act must continually incarnate itself—that is, "take shape", express itself in a concrete, practical, tangible way. This continual self-materialization of my act is the very process by which it re-creates, transforms, the world. My act, however, has no sooner assumed a particular form of self-expression than it finds itself conditioned by the reality to which it has given birth: it must continually go beyond its own productions, beyond itself-incarnate, in order to keep its creative impetus—that is, in order to remain authentically free.

These various considerations—some of which relate to facts mentioned earlier—will enable us to answer the question of habit and freedom.

First, it cannot be maintained that my freedom consists merely in the exercise of those habits which are ingrained in my body-related-to-my-world. It is not simply by performing actions out of habit that I actuate myself as a free person. Considered "in itself", the "mechanical" aspect of my personal activity is part of the "natural" movement of my life-act incarnate towards the future; it is a "third person process".

As we have just seen, my freedom is in the act by which I transcend myself-incarnate, by which I tend self-determinedly towards the future. Thus my free activity is, as such, a "first person process". However, there is an intimate connection between this transcendental endeavour and my "instinctive" activity. As has been explained, my personal act, in order to master its field of expression, must concentrate itself—that is, it must at every moment tend towards its end through the attentive pursuing of some particular aim. This implies that my act, while actuating itself in a particular direction, must at the same time set in motion many habitual dispositions and automatisms on which it can rely. The exercise of these habits and my reliance on them are factors which contribute immensely to the liberation of my act. Let us imagine what my act of thinking would become if, while expressing myself in writing, I were suddenly obliged to pay attention to the way in which my pencil must be used, to the way in which each word must be spelt and each sentence be formed. . . . It would be the end of my philosophizing. The presence of automatisms in my body-related-to-my-world is not only an assistance to my act of thinking; it is an element without which this act would be simply non-existent. Thanks to these habits, I have the freedom I need to pursue my philosophizing.

This shows once more that my freedom—as a human freedom—can never claim to be absolute. To be and remain authentically free, my personal act must accept itself as an act-conditioned-by-itself-already-realized—in other words, to actuate itself as a "first person process", it must accept to be also a "third person process"; to realize itself creatively, it must accept its createdness.

Now, I have pointed out that there is always in my free activity an aspect of effort: as a "first person process", it is not something which "goes by itself". It is only through a sustained effort that I can transcend *personally* myself-incarnate. This means that my reliance on automatisms, to be really liberating, cannot, as a rule, be a mere surrender of myself to them. If my life becomes a succession of instinctive reactions, of routine activities, it is no longer an authentic human life. It is an existence without struggle and, thus, without real freedom.

However, even here some qualification is necessary. My condition as a human being is such that my personal act cannot maintain itself in a state of perpetual tension. Intervals during which I adopt a less strenuous manner of living—moments of relaxation and rest—are indispensable. Without these, my personal act incarnate loses the energy required for carrying out steadily and effectively its life project. These intervals of relaxation, even if "in themselves" they can be described as moments during which the effort of the will is allowed to relax, are moments of a general movement which, in its entirety, is self-determined. They are by no means moments of self-indulgence during which the act "forgets itself", and practically ceases to tend personally towards its end. On the contrary, they are essentially meant for the end, motivated by the knowledge which the act has of its human condition and by its acceptance of its limitations—as such, they are moments of submission to the Creator. This shows that, even at the time of rest, the act-tending-towards-its-end remains in a true way self-determined and free: as parts of a whole movement which is essentially a personal endeavour, moments of relaxation—

even moments of sleep—remain under the influence of the will and receive from it their concrete destination.

From what has been said about the relation between our personal activity and our "mechanical" activity, it should not be concluded that any and every habit can contribute to the liberation of the act. There are dispositions ingrained in the body-related-to-the-world which tend to slow down or even to divert the progress of the act towards the future. Such habits cannot be relied upon at moments of greater effort since their exercise does not help the concentration of the will but hinders it; they cannot be brought into play at moments of relaxation since the very fact of setting them in action disorientates the movement of the act. Faced with such tendencies, the only way to prevent a self-depersonalization is self-mastery: the personal act incarnate must, in the light which emanates from its Creative Source, rediscover its fundamental destination and integrate its past by re-identifying the whole of itself with the intention which constitutes it.

CONCLUSION

Let us conclude this study of temporality by considering the various ways in which the persistence of the past in the present is analysed by the different scientific disciplines, and the relation between these various approaches.

Studying the world from his own point of view, the physicist describes it as a system of more or less regulated phenomena the determinations of which pertain to the physical order. These determinations, in their present state, are representative of the particular stage which the material world has reached at the present moment of its evolution. They are the actualization "in a physical form" of the whole history of the world.

The biologist's interest is in living organisms. He describes them in terms which are strange to the physicist because the modalities of the former's field of study belong to the vital order. These modalities, in their actual condition, express the degree of development which the "organic" world has attained today. As such, they are the crystallization "in a biological form" of the whole history of the world.

The various branches of anthropology study man in terms of physical character, racial, geographical and social relations, culture, etc. The determinations which anthropologists classify and interpret belong to phenomena observable in the realm of human life; they are modalities which pertain essentially to a certain area of the human world. In their present state, these determinations represent the particular stage which the world of men has reached at the present moment of its progress towards the future. They are the realization in human form of the whole past.

The philosopher considers man as a whole and tries to determine the structure of his personality and the fundamental meaning of his existence. Again, the human reality which he studies, *as he sees it living*, represents a particular historical moment and, as such, is a particular concretion of the whole history of the world.

(The fact that the modalities of the various areas studied by the different sciences are, in their present state, expressions of the stage of development which the world has reached today does not imply that the conclusions reached by the different scientific disciplines are of a purely relative, ephemeral character. Through their scientific intuition—that is, through a living contact with the reality which they study—scientists and thinkers discover to some degree the intentionality constitutive of the objects they analyse. This intentionality though crystallized in a particular manner in each element of the world at every moment of the evolutive process, is a persistent reality which, no doubt, reveals itself more and more adequately as history progresses towards its fulfilment, but which never obliterates at a certain stage of its self-actuation and self-manifestation anything of itself that it has expressed at earlier stages.)

Now, the tendency of each researcher is to consider the field which he investigates as a whole, complete in itself, and to envisage the various orders of reality as distinct and, so to speak, superimposed entities. In this perspective, the "passage" from one order to another is effected by a sort of jump.

In fact, as we know, the only world which exists concretely for us is our personal world. The other worlds—the physical world, the biological world, the world of social relations, etc.—are contained within this fundamental totality and have no existence and no meaning apart from it. This means that the temporal accretion which constitutes the determinations of a given order of reality is *fundamentally* identical with our personal accretion—that is, with the history of the world actualized and individuated in our own history.

Anyone engaged in a particular field of research might object to this as follows: It is a fact that, millions of years ago, at the "beginning" of its evolutive process, the stuff of which the world was made was of a purely "physical" nature. There was then no life, no consciousness, no freedom in the world. Therefore there was once a time when the world existed *by itself* as a reality pertaining merely to the physical order. But, if the physical order has been *in the past* a reality-in-itself, there is no reason why it should not go on existing *today* as an independent entity. The fact that the notion of a merely physical world makes sense, the fact that the temporal accretion by which the present is formed is to a great extent the actualization of a purely "physical" evolutive process, point to the present existence of such an order. Now, if the physical order does exist as a self-contained sphere of being, the reality of an independent biological or vital order—that is, of an order which is the realization in the present of a purely biological evolution—must also be acknowledged. Finally, the vision of the universe to which we are led back is that of a system formed by the co-existence of various particular worlds each of which subsists by itself and in itself.

We may answer, briefly, by saying:

(1) It is an undeniable fact that the "physical" order and the "biological" order, in so far as they exist for me, are part and parcel of my world—that is, of the world constituted by my personal act incarnate, by my own life. Thus they are not in themselves and by themselves, but in me and for me. Even the "purely physical order" which is supposed to have been in existence so long ago, in so far as it is a reality-for-me, is made up entirely of my own experience, of my temporality. In this connection, let me quote a passage from a fairly recent work, often profound and penetrating, but not completely satisfactory in as much as its author has not succeeded in overcoming the subject-object duality:

"Against the assertion that there is no world without man the objection is often raised that the findings of the empirical sciences show the contrary. Geologists, geophysicists, and astrophysicists have established the fact that the world is much older than man and that the world was prior to man, i.e., without man. According to Laplace's theory, our earth resulted from a primitive nebula, and the physical conditions of this nebula were such that no life—*a fortiori*, no human life—was possible. The appearance of subjectivity in the infinite evolution of the cosmos is of a fairly recent date. What, then, is the sense of claiming that there is no world without man?

"Of course, there is not a single phenomenologist who even thinks of throwing doubt on the results of the empirical sciences. All accept that the earth is much older than Adam, and none wants to raise any difficulties against Laplace's primitive nebula. (Incidentally, contemporary empirical scientists now raise serious objections against it.) It must be admitted, of course, that certain empirical sciences speak of a world dating from before the first man. However, does this mean that, say, geologists speak of a world-without-geologists? This is the point at issue, and an affirmative reply to the question does not make any sense. What would be the meaning of Laplace's primitive nebula, of his formulas and calculations without the presence-in-the-world of the subjectivity of Laplace or of those who took over his viewpoint?"[2]

(2) The picture of evolution which the empirical sciences gives us does not reveal to us the "within" of things; it does not make us understand the deep meaning and the inner structure of the whole cosmogenesis. Whatever the appearances, there has never been a universe which was a mere "physical system" (excluding life, consciousness, freedom), there has never been a universe in which life was reduced to what is called vegetative and animal life (excluding true intelligence and freedom)—in short, there has never been a universe leading a merely impersonal existence. The idea of such a universe is a perfectly meaningless, absurd notion. The world-before-me and the world-before-man, *by the very fact that everything in it meant something, revealed a more or less definite finality*, was a world constituted and moved by personal acts. *There is in the world no meaningful determination, no meaningful form of existence, which has not its origin in free decisions, in personal endeavours.* The notion of purely physical or biological determinism is completely unintelligible.

The remaining chapters of this book will, I hope, convincingly substantiate these assertions.

[2] William A. Luijpen, O.S.A., Ph.D., *Existential Phenomenology*, Duquesne University Press, Pittsburgh, Pa., 1960, p. 30.

CHAPTER VI

The Community

Throughout this study, I have shown that my personal life-act is the *esse* of the world; I have shown that every object, in so far as it exists for me, is constituted by my life-act-unfolding-itself-from-a-centre (my existence)—in other words, I have shown that my world *is* myself-incarnate.

However, at almost every step of my investigation, I have been forced to admit that my world is not the whole of reality. Over and over again, I have experienced the presence around me of a world which does not owe its existence to me; I have realized that my world is continually related to this transcendent totality: I came into existence in an *already-existing-world*; at every moment of my life, my personal-act-realizing-itself is conditioned by itself-already-realized and, through itself-already-realized, *by the world-already-constituted*; as I progress towards the future, I am continually conditioned by my past and, through my past, *by the whole of history.* It is the nature and the structure of this world-without-me and the way in which I am related to it that we must study now.

But is such a study possible?

I cannot grasp and understand any reality unless I live it—that is, unless I integrate it in my world, unless I identify it with my own field of existence. How then shall I be able to penetrate into a sphere of being which is essentially distinct from me?

To this question the following answer can already be given: It is evident that I shall not be able to study the world-without-me *in itself.* If I did so, I would reduce it to myself, convert it entirely into my world, and it would then cease to exist *in itself*—that is, as a reality distinct from me—it would exist purely and simply in me;

moreover, I would cease to be myself, since in very existence implies the presence around me of a transcendent world to which I am related. I shall study this world *in so far as it expresses itself in me.* This study will give me a real but analogical knowledge of the world-without-me: real, because, in my personal-act-unfolding-and-realizing-itself and in my act-already-realized, it is really the whole world-already-constituted, the whole of history, which is actualized, individuated, which expresses itself; analogical, because the whole world expresses itself in my world according to the way in which I live it; it reveals itself to me according to the way in which I allow it to realize itself, to take shape in me.

What is the nature of the world-without-me?

Let us try, from what we already know, to give this question a general answer.

First, it must be clear that this world does not present itself to me as an object to a subject. There is no question of re-introducing at this stage of our investigation the dualism which we rejected at the beginning of our enquiry. The analyses of many contemporary phenomenologists are still deeply influenced by intellectualistic prejudices. They often make of consciousness as such an act which stands by itself, and then, repeating what they have learned from Husserl, they stress the intentional character of consciousness—that is, its essential "directedness to what itself is not" (i.e., to an "objective reality").[1] Phenomenologists, it is true, are careful to emphasize the opposition between their view and that of the idealistic monists which also affirms that consciousness is consciousness of something, but for which this "something" is nothing other than consciousness itself.[2] In fact, both the phenomenology inspired by Husserl and idealism make the same mistake of defining man as a subject of consciousness, and of describing consciousness or knowledge as an act. In so doing, they fail to see that man is not first an "I know" and then an "I live", but essentially an "I live", even when he is also an "I know"—more precisely, they fail to realize that man is a personal life-act which constitutes its world as the concretion of its self-realizing movement, and that consciousness is the self-transparency, the luminous presence to itself, of this existential endeavour. Once this is understood, it is no longer reasonable to define consciousness as a "directedness to what itself is not" (i.e., to an "objective world"

[1] Cf. W. A. Luijpen, *op. cit.*, pp. 92–3.
[2] Cf. *ibid.*, p. 20.

distinct from it). This is because, *in itself*, consciousness is nothing, and because the reality of which man is conscious—the object of his knowledge—is always a particular aspect of himself-incarnate. Nor is it reasonable to describe human consciousness (i.e., man himself) as an act of pure self-awareness, since consciousness, *in itself*, is not and cannot be an act, and the personal act to which consciousness belongs always apprehends itself as an "I live" ahead of itself, which realizes itself through continual self-unfolding from a centre in which it comes into existence.[3]

The world-without-me is not a world-object. Neither is it a chaotic whole which, in itself, is unintelligible,[4] an impenetrable *Seiendes* in which my personal existence is grounded, which I transcend in the process by which I build my world, a "natural world which presents itself as existing in itself over and above its existence for me".[5] On several occasions, I have pointed out that the various objects which surround me, as parts of the world-existing-without-me, are already meaningful realities: as I integrate them in my world, I make mine and fulfil the intentions by which they are constituted. From this it is clear that the world-without-me is not a chaos or a nature deprived of any intelligibility. Were it so, it would have no meaning, no finality—it would be simply non-existent.

We have to accept that *the world-without-me is already a personal world*. It is because this world is constituted by personal life-acts essentially distinct from my act, that the objects which make it up

[3] Human consciousness is never the realization by the human mind of its identity with itself and the realization of the pure identity between the whole universe and the human mind. Human consciousness, as the luminous presence to itself of the personal act in the movement by which it tends towards the future, is the negation of pure identity. It is literally true to say that the personal act always apprehends itself *from a distance*. In perception, it apprehends itself from its centre in the objects which it constitutes as various concretions of itself; in thinking, it apprehends itself in the spatial modalities of the cerebral apparatus which, while unfolding itself, it constitutes as expression of the totality of itself. That the personal life-act always perceives itself from a distance becomes clear once we understand that the very existence of the act is in the movement by which it tends towards the future and *this movement is identically the process by which the act spatializes itself*—that is, by which it constitutes its variegated expressive field, by which it gives existence to its world. It is this "self-exteriorization" of the personal life-act which gives rise to the notion of the subject-object duality and leads to the conception of consciousness as a "directedness to what itself is not"—in other words, it is this self-exteriorization of the personal act which engenders the geometrical mentality.

[4] Cf. W. A. Luijpen, *op. cit.*, p. 127.

[5] M. Merleau-Ponty, *Phenomenology of Perception* (tr. Colin Smith), p. 154.

are already objects-intentions. Thus my relation to the world-existing-without-me is neither that of a subject to an object, nor that of *Dasein* to *Seiendes*, but that of a person to other persons. This shows me that the world in which I live is essentially a world of persons; it is a community of which I am a member. We must now consider in what way this interpersonal world is structured.

A. A Plurality of Worlds

There are few realities which appear to me more evident than the presence around me of other human persons. I am intimately convinced that there are in the world other men who are constituted as I am. Let us try to understand the implications of this.

I am sitting in my room. My person is not simply this body which occupies a definite place in a definite environment; it is an act incarnate co-extensive with the whole universe. This act comes into existence in the modalities of my brain, which it constitutes as its first expressive centre; diffracts itself in my body as it manifests in it its various potentialities; it unfolds itself in my environment and in the whole world, constituting them as the continuation of my body, as the concretion of its tension towards its end. Throughout this movement by which it gives the world its existence-for-me, by which it leads the world towards its completion, my act is continually conditioned by itself-already-realized and, through itself-already-realized, by the world-already-constituted, by the whole of history.

Through the open window, I see a figure standing at the bus stop some fifty yards from the place where I sit. This is another human person, a life-act unfolding itself from a centre distinct from my expressive centre. Let us analyse this in some detail.

Prima facie, it appears to me that the world in which that man lives and the world in which I live are one and the same world—in other words, that the *same* spatial universe is both his field of existence and my field of existence; it is the unfolding both of his life-act and of mine. If, however, we study this more closely, we shall see:

(1) The body of that man, which is the centre of his world, and my body, which is the centre of my world, are never situated in the same place. Therefore the point of view from which that man looks a things and the aspect in which he sees them can never be identified with the point of view from which I look at them and the aspect in

which I see them—in other words, the world-for-that-man and the world-for-me can never coincide.

(2) It may, however, be argued that this difference is somewhat superficial. In spite of our different situations and attitudes, it is really the same world which we see from our respective points of view. If that man comes into my room and sits on my chair, he will see the world exactly as I see it now; if I go to the bus stop and stand in the place which that man occupies now, I shall see the world exactly as he sees it at this moment. Thus the difference at a given moment between the world-for-that-man and the world-for-me is without practical significance: the fact that we look at things from distinct points of view does not destroy the substantial unity of the reality we perceive.

At the root of this argument, there is, of course, the conception of the world as an objective and essentially immutable spectacle which offers itself to be perceived by subjects who are "ontologically" distinct from it and outside it. This conception, we know, is a product of the geometrical mentality and is incompatible with the facts.

Let us carry our analysis further.

That man standing there at the bus stop is a life-act essentially distinct from my own life-act. His life-act comes into existence in his brain, which it constitutes as its first expressive centre; it diffracts itself in his body, which it moulds into the concretion of its fundamental inclination, into the expression of its various potentialities. In this process, the life-act of that person is conditioned by itself-already-realized, by the past of that man and by the whole of history. From this it is already clear that the individuality of that man is basically different from my own individuality: with his body, he has his own temperament and affectivity, his own propensities and aptitudes, his own experience and habits, his own manner of facing the world, his own fundamental reactions.

Now, just as my life-act unfolding from my body constitutes my environment, my world, as the actuation of my central potentialities —as an existential field in which it expresses in various ways its individuality and its tension towards its end—so also the life-act of that man, unfolding from his body, moulds his environment, his world, into the living concretion of his fundamental affective disposition. In this movement, his life-act is continually conditioned by itself-already-realized, by the world-already-constituted, by the whole of history. These facts make it clear that the world in which that man lives—his world—and my world cannot be one and the same world. Objects and events cannot have for him and for me exactly the same meaning, the same existential value. Were his world and my world to coincide, we would no longer be two different persons with two different individualities: we would be one and the same act.

(3) The role played by our personal and pre-personal past, by the whole of history, in shaping our respective individualities (and, therefore, in giving to our respective worlds their particular physiognomy) can hardly be overemphasized.

In order to realize itself in the present of that man standing at the bus stop, the history of the world has, so to speak, canalized itself in various ways: that man is a member of a community, of a family—thus he has a particular heredity—he has lived in a definite geographical, social and religious environment; he has received a particular education; he has accustomed himself to a particular way of life; he has formed himself in a particular way; he has acquired a definite experience. All these realities live in the act by which, at this moment, that man gives existence to his world; all these realities express themselves in his organism, in his environment, in his whole field of existence.

The temporal accretion which forms my present is completely different. It is made up of different national, geographical, social, family and personal modalities. Through these, the history of the world individuates itself in me—in my body, in my world—in a manner which is essentially personal to me.

Thus we see even more clearly that the world in which that man lives—his world—and my world cannot coincide. They are two different worlds, because they are two different realizations of history.

The fact that, as different human persons, we are different temporalities, different worlds, accounts for the difficulty which we often have of agreeing among ourselves, of understanding each other. Because of our different historical backgrounds, we do not see things and events in the same way; we have different mental outlooks, different conceptions of life, different cultures, different affective reactions, behaviours, customs.

(4) My life-act actuates itself through my act-project. My act-project, realizing itself through my present philosophizing, is the reality which constitutes and animates my body, my hand holding a pencil, my eyes fixed on the white sheet of paper, my chair and my table, my room, my environment, my whole world. This act-tending-

towards-its-realization is the reality in which and by which my past and the whole of history are actualized in my present; it gives my world its actual existence, its personal destination.

The life-act of that man waiting at the bus stop actuates itself through his act-project. This act-project, realizing itself through his present intention of going to his office, is the reality which constitutes and animates his body standing on the pavement, his look turned in the direction from which the bus is expected to come, his environment, his whole world. This act-in-tension-towards-its-goal is the reality in which and by which the past of that man, the whole of history, is actualized in his present; it gives to his world its actual existence, its concrete destination.

In the light of this the world of that man and my world are seen to be two unified systems *which tend towards their completion along two different lines.*

(5) Finally, let us consider the most fundamental reason why the world of that man and my world cannot be reduced to one.

As we know, what gives to my world its individuality is not in the first place the dependence of my present on my personal past, or the way in which the history of the world actualizes itself in me; it is not even the unique way in which my world progresses towards its completion. It is the unique intention by which I am constituted, my unique relation to the Creative Act.

Similarly, what constitutes the world of that man as an individual reality and what differentiates it from my world, is *fundamentally* his unique relation to the Transcendent Source of his existence.

Therefore the irreducibility of our worlds is not due to any accidental factor but *to the Transcendent Initiative which creates us as two different persons.*

All these facts lead us to the conclusion that the universe is not one world but many worlds, it exists in the form of many individual persons, it *is* a plurality of persons. History as a totality is the progress of all these individualities towards their ultimate realization; it is not a simple, homogeneous, unitary movement, but a stream made up of many currents, a tide constituted by a great number of personal lives progressing along different lines towards their end.

B. Interdependence and Interpenetration of the Different Acts-Worlds

The personal acts-worlds which constitute the universe, however distinct they may be from one another, are essentially interrelated; they are united by vital bonds which can never be broken.

We shall now study this interdependence from various angles.

1. Study of the Way in which a Particular Person comes into Existence, Develops, and Forms himself in the Community

Each man comes into existence through the mediation of an act performed by two other persons. These two persons do not perform this act as isolated individuals. Each one of them is a personal life-act which, while unfolding itself from its centre, constituting its world and tending towards its end, is at every moment conditioned by itself-already-realized and, through itself-already-realized, by the world-already-constituted, by the whole of history. Now, the world-already-constituted is not an impersonal field of presence; it is a human world, a community of persons. Therefore the two persons who perform the generative act are, while uniting themselves, vitally related to, dependent upon the other personal acts-worlds—in other words, while procreating, they are in a true sense actually generated by the human community of which they are members. This means that, when a human being is engendered, it is really the whole family of men which gives him life through the generative act performed by his parents.

This, of course, does not eliminate the preponderant and unique role which the parents play in the procreation of their child. They are not impersonal channels through which the family of men propagates itself; they act as free persons. The generative operation by which they give life to a new human being takes place in the movement by which their personal life-acts unfolding themselves from their centres constitute their worlds and tend towards their realization; thus it is a particular actuation of their personal existence. Now their personal life-acts, in spite of the vital relation which binds them to the other acts-worlds, are not produced by the action of the community—as transcendental realities, they proceed directly from the Creative Act. This means that the generative act which they perform is theirs in an incommunicable way, even though, through it, it is really the whole human community which operates. Thus the new child is in a unique way indebted to his parents for the life which he receives, even though he is in a true sense generated by the whole family of men.

This indebtedness, however, has its limitations. It is true to say that, when performing the procreative act, the father and the mother unite themselves in order to produce a new living being out of their own substances; but it is also true that, without a Transcendent Creative Initiative, the embryo to which they give existence would remain themselves and it would never become the centre of a new personal existence. Just as the parents of the new child receive their *personal existence* directly from the Creator—not from the community of which they are members—so also the living being which they procreate is constituted as a personal life-act distinct from them by the Creative Act—not by their own initiative. No doubt, the tiny organism in which the new personal life-act incarnates itself is drawn from the biological substance of the father and the mother, but, from the moment it becomes a new personal centre, it is re-created into the concretion of the life-act which takes possession of it and which, from it, gives existence to a new world in order to begin a new human adventure.

Even this way, however, of expressing the whole process is still very imperfect. I have already said that it does not make much sense to say that the Creator gives existence to a human person *with the help of some pre-existing organic material.* As has just been pointed out, the two persons who procreate are themselves created in the very act by which they transmit life. Moreover, all the other acts-worlds to which they are vitally related at the very moment they perform this act also receive their existence from the Transcendent Creative Source. Therefore it must be said that every new human being is created as an individual act-world essentially related to other acts-worlds co-created—in other words, that the Act by which one person is brought into existence is identically the Act from which the whole community of persons (i.e., the whole universe) proceeds, and that this Act is a Transcendent Reality for which there is no yesterday and no tomorrow, but only Now.

From our human point of view, accordingly, it is perfectly good sense to affirm that each new human person comes to life with a definite historicity. Every child receives his human nature through a particular channel; therefore he has a particular heredity; his organism is history in general crystallizing itself in a particular centre through the medium and modalities of a particular history—the new child belongs to a particular family, to a particular nation, to a particular race, he comes to life at a definite moment of history. All these factors condition and shape his individuality from the very beginning of his human existence.

As soon as the embryo is a new personal centre, the life-act which animates it exists in the form of a new act-world-ordained-towards-an-end. Thanks to the dynamism of this act, the embryo grows into a more and more elaborate human organism. This development enables the life-act to actuate its latent potentialities, to manifest its individuality. From this it is apparent that the growth of a child in the body of his mother is not due first of all to extraneous "physical" or "biological" causes, but to the impetus inherent in the principle which from the beginning constitutes him as a human being meant for an end.

However, it must be acknowledged that at the beginning of his existence the child is in a state of helplessness and total dependence. As an act incarnate proceeding from the Creative Act, he is, no doubt, a personal being which no created force can destroy, nevertheless, the life which he possesses *as a member of the earthly community* is still welded to that of his mother and in a true sense continually derived from it. This flow of life from the body of the mother into that of the child must not be understood as a mere "natural" phenomenon. It may, it is true, be described as a biological process which takes place according to a regular pattern, an operation independent of man's will; we must, however, understand that this phenomenon is not simply a modification of the life-act of the mother (as such, a "third person process"), but an actuation of her whole personal act—that is, of her life-act-realizing-itself-through-her-act-project, a concretion of her personal tension towards her end. Indeed, it is through her free initiative that she has conceived a child; therefore the setting in motion of her generative faculty has been the direct expression in her body of her personal option. Moreover, even though the flow of life from her organism into that of her child takes place as it were "by itself", it is her desire that the embryo present in her womb should develop as perfectly as possible and, to this end, she takes the necessary precautions and offers her daily prayers. This means that the operation by which the mother communicates to her child her own substance is not a mere "third person process" but the incarnation of her constant solicitude and aspirations. When the child converts her flesh and blood into his own, he assimilates love, he re-creates into modalities of his own life those desires and intentions which are immanent in the organic bonds which unite him to the body of his mother.

Let us now consider another aspect. While giving life to her child, the mother is herself continually "vitalized" by the other acts-worlds to which she is existentially related. The closer her union with a person, the more vital her dependence on him. Now, of all human persons, the child present in her womb is undeniably the one with whom she is most intimately united. Therefore, while communicating her own life to her child, she herself is in a true sense re-generated by him. This re-generation may be seen in particular in the fact that her whole psychological make-up—her existential attitude, her personal structure—is transformed by the presence in her of the growing embryo. This transformation must not be understood as a mere "biological" phenomenon, but as the expression of the fact that, in the very act of giving life to her child, she is created in essential relation to, in dependence upon, the human person co-created in her. Thus the exchange of life between the mother and the child is a human dialogue rooted in the Creative Act.

After his birth, the child must be reared and educated; his organism must develop so that his life-act may actuate its potentialities, may transcend itself into a real act-volition, may express itself in free decisions and in a life intention which will give his existence a self-determined unity and a personal destination. The growth and human formation of the child must be understood as a process which takes place essentially within the human community. The growing child is continually fashioned by the other persons to whom he is vitally related; he forms himself through the influence which he himself exerts upon the other members of the community.

During his first years, it is mainly through his parents and his family circle that the child is linked with the life-giving community. As he grows older, the channels through which the other personal worlds influence and feed him multiply; he becomes more independent of his family, more "universal". Yet, it is always through a determined milieu, through particular events, that he receives his concrete nature, his human life, his culture, his ideas—in other words, it is always through particular temporal currents that the whole of history shapes his individuality, and conditions the movement by which his personal act, unfolding itself from its centre, constitutes its expressive field, tends towards the future.

The operation by which the community gives life to the growing child, feeds and forms him, is the unbroken continuation of the same process by which it cared for him when he was in his mother's womb. Its modalities, no doubt, have changed, because the milieu through which the community now reaches the child is quite different, and because the way in which the child assimilates the various influences which act upon him, and makes them exist for him, is much more elaborate, versatile, and personal than it was at the beginning of his human existence.

If we are fully to understand the interpersonal world there is an important fact that we must be careful to appreciate. It is impossible to make a sharp distinction between care and nourishment of the child's body, and the fashioning of his affectivity, of his culture, of his mental outlook, and moral character. These are not two independent processes. The child does not make his own any human value which does not present itself to him in a concrete form,[6] and does not assimilate any "material substance" which is not impregnated with human intentions and human life. We must always remember that the world in which the child lives has no existence, no reality whatsoever, apart from the personal life-acts which constitute it, that this world is essentially a community of persons, a human world. Therefore whatever reaches the child, whatever feeds and influences him, has a human "exponent", it *is* human life presented to him in some form or other. We must remember, too, that a human person is a unitary structure the "elements" of which intercommunicate. Whatever the way in which the child is approached or acted upon, whatever the mode in which human life and human experience are imparted to him,[7] his whole personal act incarnate is conditioned by the influences which he undergoes. This fact, of course, does not prevent each of these influences from having a definite relation to a particular aspect of his personal structure.

Let us take an illustration of this. It is not a mere metaphor to say that the child's home and the school which he attends are characterized by two different "atmospheres". The air which the child breathes when he is at home, while playing its allotted role in the maintenance and development of his biological system, contributes

6 The reason for this is that no human value can be separated from the personal life-acts in which it comes into existence and that every personal act always exists as an act incarnate.

7 These modes may differ widely. There is no question of reducing everything to a single, uniform process: feeding the child and teaching him to talk are by no means the same thing.

to the fashioning of his psychological make-up, of his personality, in a way that is determined by the particular human significance which the family circle has for him. The school atmosphere has another human "exponent". Therefore, while penetrating into his lungs and oxygenating his blood, it shapes his individuality and conditions his progress towards the future, in a different way. The plate of rice, the cup of *dal*, the dish of curry, which the child has for dinner have been prepared by his mother. She offers them to him not as meaningless material substances, but as various expressions of her solicitude for him. When the child eats his food and so strengthens his body, he is forming his whole personality by assimilating those human intentions of which the food is the concretion. If the child is sent to a boarding school, the food given to him there may be "as good", it may even be "more nutritious"; even so, it has not the same human meaning for the child nor, accordingly, the same formative value, as the food he receives at home. These facts show that, even if a medical verdict says that the atmosphere of the boarding school and the food prepared in its kitchen are healthier for the child than the air he breathes and the food he eats at home, it does not mean *necessarily* that the *actual breathing* of the school atmosphere and the *actual eating* of the food served at school are more conducive to the harmonious development (both physical and psychological) of the child than the *breathing* of the home atmosphere and the *eating* of the food prepared by his mother. It is undoubtedly a mistake to rely *only* on the verdict of biology to judge whether one ambiance is healthier for a child than another. The mistake consists in considering the child as a mere organism which can be fed with abstractions such as oxygen, calories, vitamins, and not as an integral human person who, no doubt, is in need of such biological elements, but who, through them, communicates with a concrete human environment from which he receives life.

In considering the child's education, we must realize the importance of the law of incarnation. There are no human values, no truths which exist in the form of ideas preserved in an immaterial world. Human culture and knowledge, therefore, will never make their appearance in the mind of the child from above or from no matter where. As we know, whatever the child learns or assimilates, he must first live as a modality, an aspect, a dimension, of his incarnate existence. A human value or a piece of information which is presented to the child in a visible, tangible way, which is inculcated in him through the performance of concrete actions, which marks him physically and biologically, naturally becomes a value or a truth for him: it penetrates into his field of existence and, thereby, becomes part and parcel of his personality and of his culture. To teach the child the first elements of arithmetic, his mother does not simply repeat to him that two and three make five; she makes him lay out on the ground first two little sticks, then three little sticks, and then makes him add them. By doing so, she makes the child feel and live the solution of the problem with his eyes, his hands, with his whole body, before making him realize it "mentally". To teach him piety and the truths of religion, she does not simply tell him that he has a Father in heaven or that Christ died for him on a cross; she shows him the crucifix, makes him touch and kiss it; every night she makes him kneel down and say his prayers. By such means, much more than by any theorizing, the mother develops the religious life of her child: she makes him believe with his knees, his hands, his eyes, his tongue, his whole body; she fills his whole life field with the spirit of religion, before leading him to a reflective act of faith.

These educative actions are one of the ways in which the mother continues to feed the child with her own life, and thus to transmit to him the life of the community. The mother cannot communicate anything to her child which she does not possess as her own; she cannot make him accept any value or any truth unless it has first become a value-for-her, or a truth-for-her. When the child assimilates what his mother teaches him, when he makes of it a value-for-him or a truth-for-him, it is the very life of his mother which passes into his own life; it is her individuality which he transforms into his own individuality.

These considerations make it clear that practical attitudes, concrete actions, are the vehicles which transmit human life, human values, human culture and knowledge. We understand this fact when we remember that the act by which the members of the human community are constituted are not "acts of knowledge" but life-acts, and that reality is not a collection of ready-made ideas but human life existing in various forms. This means that, before transforming any reality into a personal conviction, before he can convert it into a truth-for-him, man must first assimilate it by living it, and by living it intensely; he must make it part and parcel of his field of existence, and experience it as such.

We should not conclude from all this that theoretical teaching has no influence on the formation of personality. We know the importance of reflectiveness in the life of a human person. If a reality is to become a truth-for-him, he must not simply possess it as a modality or a dimension of his life field, he must live it *in a luminous way*. Man cannot assimilate any reality in a truly personal manner unless he takes *conscious* possession of it. Thus authentic self-realization must needs be *reflective* self-realization; the progress of man towards his final destiny entails a continual self-illumination. In this light, we can understand the indispensable role which the formal imparting of knowledge plays in the formation of human personality.[8]

It is important to realize that theoretical teaching—just like practical teaching—is a channel through which *human life* is communicated from person to person. The imparting of knowledge by the teacher to his students, or by the master to his disciples, does not take place in the realm of "pure thought", above the realm of existence; as a human activity, it is essentially an incarnate activity. It is immanent in the words and gestures of the teacher, in what he writes on the blackboard, in the atmosphere of the class-room which he animates with his presence. Each one of the students apprehends the gesticulating figure of the teacher, the words he utters, the signs he draws on the blackboard as modalities of his own field of existence. In the very act of constituting these realities as luminous expressions of himself, he is conditioned by himself-already-realized (i.e., by his past, his experience); he is generated by the whole human community reaching him through the act by which the teacher communicates himself to him. Thus, while what each student discovers when he understands his teacher is nothing but himself-incarnate, at the same time he understands himself as existentially related to the person of the teacher; he progresses in learning by allowing his own potentialities to be luminously actuated by the teaching of the master.[9]

8 This formal teaching, it is obvious, can be given only to persons who are able to assimilate it. It must be continually adapted to the degree of human development attained by those to whom it is addressed; it must be proportioned to the human experience which they have acquired. These are realities to which modern psychology and educational science are fully alive.

9 In this section, I am analysing the way in which a person develops and forms himself in the community. This is not the place for a complete study of the relationship in which teacher and students stand to each other. However, it may be noted that, in the very act of teaching, the master himself is stimulated, actuated, generated, by the whole human community reaching him through the students who listen to him. Looked at from this angle, the imparting of knowledge by the teacher is seen to be formative to the extent that his own life flows into the

Books also are channels through which human life is luminously communicated from man to man. The books which a student reads —with all the words, sentences, paragraphs, chapters it contains—is a reality pertaining to his field of existence; as such, it is constituted by his personal life-act unfolding itself from its expressive centre: it receives its concrete existence-for-him from his act of reading it. However, this act is not a purely creative initiative. While studying the book, the student is continually conditioned by, dependent upon himself-already-realized (the meaning which he gives to the words and the sentences he reads is essentially related to the way in which he has formed himself in the past—that is, to his own experience); he is generated by the whole human community reaching him through the particular person who communicates himself to him through the pages of the book. Of course, the personal relation established between the student and the author of the book is not of the same type as the relation which unites the student to his teacher, and has not, therefore, the same formative value. However, it is really the life of the person who has written the book which passes luminously into the life of the person who studies it in order to understand its message. No doubt, when the student discovers the meaning of the sentences he reads, it is himself-incarnate which he actuates and realizes in a more reflective way; nevertheless, in order to actuate and discover himself in this particular way, he must be actuated, vitalized, illuminated, by the writer-communicating-himself-to-him.

---

lives of his students and their lives into his. The first condition required to make this movement a true personal exchange is that the teaching of the master be authentic. This is so when the master puts himself personally into what he tries to impart to his students—that is, when he identifies his teaching with the movement of his personal existence, when he re-creates vividly the learning which he communicates in the act by which he tends towards the future. When a student listens to an authentic teacher, he becomes aware of his own potentialities (because these potentialities are actuated by the teaching he receives), he is trained to personal thinking and to the leading of a true personal existence.

It is regrettable that the system of education prevailing in some places does not stimulate authentic teaching. So much emphasis is laid on syllabuses, textbooks, ready-made answers to stereotyped questions, so much importance is attached to examinations in which the individuality of the teacher who has formed the students is completely neglected, that the personality of the master hardly counts: the teacher is continually obliged to withdraw into the background in order to make way for an impersonal machinery. This develops in him a sense of frustration and reduces to a minimum the personal relation which he should establish between himself and his students through his teaching. Such a system tends to thwart personalities instead of allowing them to mature and reach their full stature.

Thus, while reading the book, the student understands himself-qua-existentially-related-to-the-person-of-the-writer; he progresses in learning by allowing himself to be luminously actuated by the author of the book (and, through him, by the whole human community).

In all these analyses, I have shown that the growth of a human being and the formation of his personality are conditioned by the community of which he is a member; I have shown how the life of the community continually flows into his life. Now, it must be noted carefully that the very way in which a person is vitalized by other persons is itself determined by his individuality, by the way in which his personal life-act constitutes his world, tends towards the future.

From the facts observed so far, it appears already that the process by which a personal act-world is fed by the other acts-worlds is concretely identical with the process by which, while actuating itself, it is conditioned, moulded, by itself-already-realized. This means that the way in which a person is energized, generated, by the other members of the community is determined by his own past, by his experience—that is, by the way in which he has formed himself. This implies that a personal life-act, however much it may be influenced by the other acts-worlds, is *strictly speaking* never conditioned by anything but itself: it is conditioned by itself-qua-permeated-by-the-other-acts-worlds-while-continually-regressing-to-its-source.

But this is not yet the real point. As we know, a person's individuality is not *constituted* by his past, or by his experience; it is constituted by his personal-life-act-unfolding-itself-from-its-centre,-constituting-its-life-field,-tending-towards-its-end-in-an-original-and fundamentally-incommunicable-manner. The way in which his own experience and the other members of the community influence him is determined by the basic existential attitude of his personal-act-actuating-itself. Thus what actuates the potentialities of a person, what forms him, is not *primarily* the way in which he is fed and carried by the community, but the personal way in which he realizes himself: much more than the actions of others, it is his own actions which form him. No doubt, a person's actions—the movement of his personal act towards the future—are modelled, subtended, by his past, by his habits, by his experience, by the influence of the community, but what makes them *his* actions, what gives them their existence as self-determined initiatives, is his own existence as a personal-life-act-proceeding-from-the-Creative-Act. In so far as he thus exists as an original act incarnate, he continually re-creates his own history and all "external" influences in the movement by which he tends towards his final destiny.

Now, it must be noted that in so far as a human being acts in a personal way, he influences those with whom he lives. This means that, through his own actions, a person forms himself in a way which corresponds to that in which he acts upon the other members of the community. At home, a child influences his brothers and sisters; his presence and the way in which he develops condition the life of his parents and contribute towards shaping the family atmosphere. At school, he influences his companions and also his teachers—especially if he has the temperament of a leader—he contributes towards forming the "spirit" of his class. These influences which the growing child exerts upon the human environment in which he lives play a very important role in his own formation. This fact, together with the facts pointed out earlier, shows that, from whatever angle they are studied, the development and formation of a human person appear as processes which take place essentially in and through the community of which he is a member.

To conclude, let us indicate the perspective in which all the facts analysed in this section must be integrated.

A person is a self-determined act incarnate which *as such* proceeds not from the other acts-worlds to which it is related, but from the Creative Act: a person's freedom—his existence as a *personal* life-act—is constituted by his ontological dependence upon the Creator. Thus man forms himself in a truly *personal manner* not simply by allowing himself to be fashioned by the other members of the community (by all the influences which he undergoes), not simply by acting in conformity with the will and desires of his fellow-men (whether his subordinates, his equals, or even his superiors and educators), but first of all by surrendering his will to the will of the Creator—that is, by identifying his life intention with the intention constitutive of his transcendental individuality.

This does not contradict what has been pointed out above. As we know, each person is created as a personal life-act continually conditioned by itself-already-realized and, through itself-already-realized, by the other acts-worlds. Thus the relationship in which a person stands to the other members of the community is fundamentally identical with his createdness: he is created as a personal act-world essentially related to other acts-worlds co-created. This means that in order to actuate himself as a self-determined principle, in order to form himself in a truly personal way, man must accept his dependence upon his fellow-men, he must allow himself to be fed, guided, educated by them. However, this submission of himself to the others, in order to be truly formative, cannot be a mere alienation of his will and freedom: to form himself as a truly *self-determined* act-world, man must reflectively make his relation to his fellow-men be subordinate to his ontological relation to the Creator —in other words, his acceptance of his dependence upon the other members of the community must be an actuation of his dependence upon the Creative Act; it must be an act of transcendental obedience. If, instead of identifying his submission to other men with his submission to the Creator, man blindly surrenders his will and his personality to the influences which act upon him, far from forming himself, he depersonalizes and, so to speak, bestializes himself. (This alienation, of course, can never be complete, because man, however deeply influenced he may be by other people, remains a personal act-world which derives its existence from the Creative Act.)[10]

2. Study of Interpersonal Relations

I have already pointed out that the phenomenological descriptions of W. Luijpen, penetrating and valuable though they are, are nevertheless unsatisfactory in as much as they are still an explanation of the way in which the "objective reality" is related to men. Luijpen points out, it is true, that the world which I perceive, in so far as I perceive it, is essentially a world-for-me—that is, a world which holds its meaning and its existence from my subjectivity—but in several passages he still refers to a world existing in itself (i.e.. without me) as *Seiendes*, i.e., as brute reality. From his guarded references to this reality void of meaning and intelligibility, it is apparent that he is uncertain what to make of it. Moreover, when he comes to the study of intersubjectivity, Luijpen, following Heidegger, asserts that "my world is our world".[11] This assertion implies that the

[10] These considerations show that education must always be permeated with respect. The authentic educator is not the one who imposes his will autocratically, who dominates those whom he is supposed to form; it is the one who seeks resolutely and perseveringly to ensure that those entrusted to his care shall develop harmoniously according to the will of the Creator—that is, who wants his charges to become what the Creator intends them to be.

[11] *Existential Phenomenology*, p. 178.

world of my existence, however mine it may be, can exist without me since it exists also for others. But if my world is for everybody, it is, strictly speaking, for nobody, since no one can claim it as *essentially* his own. This brings us back apparently to the crude opposition between subject and object which intellectualism considers as the experimental datum from which philosophical thinking must take its start.

In the first part of this chapter, I have shown that, *fundamentally*, my world is unique and exclusively mine, because it is constituted by my personal life-act, and that the universe, therefore, is not one world but many worlds. However, it is clear that these worlds, far from being locked up in themselves, are essentially interrelated, that they interpenetrate. This intercommunication has already been brought to light in the study we have just made of the way in which a person comes into life, and forms himself in the community. But the fact that the different acts-worlds are thus interdependent does not allow us to affirm the existence of a *Mitwelt* which belongs equally to all. We shall now study in more detail the way in which the interpenetration of the different worlds which constitute the human universe must be understood.

i. *Mutual Involvement of our Incarnate Existences*

I am working in my room. My personal life-act gives my body, my environment and my whole world their existence-for-me: it constitutes my brain as its first expressive nucleus; my organism as the unfolding of my cerebral potentialities, as the dynamic concretion of my present concern; my room with all the objects it contains, the house of which my room is a part, the city, the whole world, as the continuation of my body, the realization of my possibilities, the total incarnation of my life project, of the present endeavour through which my life project actualizes itself. At every moment of this self-actuating movement, my personal act is conditioned, moulded, by itself-already-realized (by my past) and, through itself-already-realized, by the world-already-constituted. Now, considered in itself, the world-already-constituted which my personal act continually takes up, identifies with itself, is not an impersonal static reality; it is a universe constituted by other personal acts which unfold themselves from other expressive centres and tend in various ways towards their ultimate realization; thus it is not only a reality which is *already constituted* but also a totality which is *in the process of constituting itself*; it is a stream made up of innumerable personal currents which interpenetrate even though each one retains its individuality. These various currents, or these various worlds, may be considered from different angles:

(1) I may consider them in so far as they form a universe which does not receive its existence from me, a human totality which is transcendent to the life field constituted by my personal act. At every moment of my life, I am vitally aware of the presence of this transcendent universe: there is in the objects which surround me a wealth of meaning and of life which does not come from me, which is not due to their lying within my field of existence—in other words, things are not only in me, by me, and for me, but also in, by, and for others. This field of presence is a field of *personal* presence in so far as it is constituted by personal life-acts distinct from my act; however, considered in its totality, it is for me an anonymous reality in so far as it does not reveal itself to me in the form of this or that particular person. This human universe, it must be noted, though it does not receive its existence from me, is essentially related to me. Indeed, all the personal life-acts by which it is constituted, from the centres in which they come into existence and throughout their world-constituting, self-actuating movements, continually take up, re-create in themselves, and identify with themselves my act-world, and, at the same time, are conditioned by it (in a real though often indeterminable way). Thus the concrete way in which the human universe exists is, to a certain extent, relative to the way in which my personal act realizes itself and constitutes its world.

(2) I may picture to myself what each one of the particular worlds which form the human universe is in itself. Each of these worlds is constituted by a personal life-act which is centred somewhere. As it comes into existence, unfolds itself, and tends towards its end, this act recasts in itself all the other acts-worlds (including mine); *ipso facto*, it is conditioned by them. Thus the whole human community does not exist in each particular person in a general, anonymous way; it exists in him in an individualized way, as identified with his incarnate existence.

(3) I may consider the human universe in so far as it is individuated in me. As we know, my personal act, while unfolding itself from its centre and constituting my world, continually re-creates in itself the world-already-constituted. To the extent that it is thus integrated

in my world, the human universe is no longer transcendent to me; it is identified with the life field in which my personal act incarnates itself. This identification, of course, is always relative, because the various acts-worlds which form the universe continue to exist in themselves (i.e., transcendentally) however much they communicate themselves to me.

Let us now consider how I am related to another particular person.

Through the window of my room, I look at an old woman working in the courtyard of her little house. This stooping figure moving to and fro, in so far as it exists for me, is constituted by my personal life-act unfolding itself from my body; it is a particular actuation of my central potentialities, a particular concentration of my act-project-realizing-itself-through-my-present-occupation. Thus the body of that old woman is inhabited and, in a real way, animated by my personal act. I give it the existence which it has *for me* at this moment. Moreover, it is my life experience which makes me see the stooping figure of that woman as the carrying out of a definite intention; it is my experience actualized in the present movement of my personal act which gives to her posture and to her gestures the meanings which they have for me. Thus my own life is immanent in the body of that old woman and makes of it a living form which materializes and expresses my historicity, my present endeavour, my existential tension. In short, the gesticulating figure which I see in the courtyard of that little house, as I see it and live it, is part and parcel of *my world.*

Now, I am perfectly aware that this figure is not a mere concretion of my personal life, a mere modality of the movement by which my act tends towards its realization. I know that this stooping figure is primarily the embodiment of a personal life-act other than my act, and that it is therefore a reality the fundamental *esse* of which is not derived from my personal *esse.* As the first incarnation of a personal act distinct from my act, this figure is the centre of a world different from my world, so radically different that its existential dimensions will for ever remain beyond my grasp.

Now, in spite of the fact that the body of that old woman (1) in so far as it exists for me, is animated by my personal act, is included in *my world,* (2) in so far as it is truly her body, is constituted by her personal life-act as the centre of *her world,* there is a vital communication between my personal-act-existing-in-the-form-of-her-body and her personal-act-constituting-her-body-as-the-project-of-her-world. Let us explain this briefly.

In the very movement by which the personal act of that woman incarnates itself in her body, makes her body exist as the centre of her world, it is conditioned by her body-already-there—that is, by itself-already-incarnate-in-her-body and, through itself-thus-incarnate, by other personal acts which animate her body while constituting their worlds. My personal act is one of these acts. Thus, while expressing itself in her body in a unique and incommunicable way, the personal act of that woman is to some extent moulded and vitalized by my personal act present and living in the spatial modalities which the act of that woman constitutes as its expressive nucleus.

Let us now consider this structural ensemble from the point of view of my body.

My body is constituted by my personal act as its expressive centre, as the *fons et origo* of my world. As such, my body is inalienably mine: it is my incarnate existence, it *is* myself. Thus I own my body; I inhabit it in a really exclusive manner.

As I am looking at that old woman working in the courtyard of her house, I realize that my body is also her possession and that the life which animates it at this very moment is in a real manner her life in me.

Let us make this clear.

My eyes are fixed on that stooping figure moving to and fro. I live this peculiarity of my existential field as the carrying out of a certain intention, the actualization of a definite purpose. We have seen that, as lived by me, this figure-intention is a particular way in which my personal-act-realizing-itself-through-my-present-occupation expresses itself. Now I realize clearly that the gesticulating figure which I see there through the window of my room, *as the incarnation of an intention*, is constituted, principally and substantially, by a life-act distinct from my personal act. What is more, I realize that the life which *I* infuse into this figure is in a real way the life by which it is originally animated.

How is this possible?

At this moment, my personal act, while expressing itself in my body and, from my body, in my surroundings, and in the stooping figure of that old woman, while constituting this setting as the living concretion of its existential tension, is conditioned and modelled by itself-already-incarnate-in-this-expressive-field and, through itself-thus-incarnate, by the world-already-there—by the personal act of that old woman incarnating itself in her body, in her environment . . . in my body, constituting this setting as her field of existence, as the dynamic expression of her vital tension. Thus the act by which, from my expressive centre, I constitute her stooping figure as a meaningful reality, as a concretion of my life experience, is identically the process by which her own presence in her body, in her world, *in my body* transforms itself into my presence in them. It is by living in a personal way—i.e., according to my own experience, historicity, preoccupation, temperament—the intention with which she animates my body related to her body that I discover and, at the same time, create this intention. Thus the life which *I* infuse into the stooping figure of that woman, while being inalienably my life, is also her life; the intentions which I put into her posture and gestures, even though they proceed from me, are in a true sense her intentions: they are her intentions merged into my intentions through the mediation of my body, revealing themselves to me within my own life experience.

This examination of a particular instance introduces us to a universal fact: my personal act is immanent in the bodies of all the persons who form the human community; it makes them live as extensions of my own body, as realizations and revelations of my own central potentialities; conversely, there is in my body a physical and dynamic presence of all the persons who live with me "on earth": they animate my body, they inhabit it and, in a true sense, they own it. This immanence of my personal act in the bodies of other persons and of their personal acts in my body strikingly brings out the mutual involvement of our incarnate existences.

The dynamic presence in my organism of the other personal acts which, together with my act, constitute the human universe—their "influence" upon me—is a constant phenomenon. This is evident since, at every moment, my personal act, while constituting its world as the realization of its own potentialities, is conditioned by itself-already-existing-qua-world and, through itself-thus-existing, by the world-existing-without-me—i.e., by the other-personal-acts-constituting-their-worlds.

Let us take a concrete illustration of this constant animation of my own body by the other personal acts present in it.

I come out of my presbytery with the intention of visiting some people who live on the other side of the canal. I walk alongside the church till I reach the gate of the mission property. From the gate, I proceed along the canal towards the bridge. As I pass in front of the neighbouring house, I stop for a while and tease the five little girls playing with their rickety tricycle. I cross the bridge and take a path which, through a paddy field, along a pond, leads me towards the house which I can see through a curtain of plantains and coconut palms. This whole activity, the world which it creates, is the expression of my personal-act-realizing-itself-through-a-particular-initiative; as such, it is my creation. Now, as it actuates itself in this particular manner, as it creates this particular world, my personal-act-incarnate-in-my-body is continually conditioned, set in motion, by the other personal acts—in other words, my organism (as the first incarnation of my act) is continually enlivened, moved, by the other persons who are present in it, possess and inhabit it.

Indeed:

(1) My present initiative, and the various actions by which I carry it out, take place essentially within the context of my life intention—they are the actualization of this intention. This intention—incarnate in my body, realizing itself through the present movements of my limbs, constituting these movements, living in them—is, no doubt, my own decision: it is the self-determined, self-transparent actuation of my personal act. Nevertheless, it is not a pure self-creative endeavour. In its present mode of existing, within the actions and movements which it constitutes now as the realization of itself (i.e., within my body as it exists at this moment of my walk to the house on the other side of the canal), my personal act is energized, subtended, quickened by the whole community present in this dynamic setting, and in particular by the human environment in which I am at this moment living and acting. As the living thing which it is now, my body is, no doubt, the incarnate existence of my life intention, but it is also the immediate, inspiring, spell-binding, compelling presence-for-me of the human world which "surrounds" me. My body gesticulating and moving is myself tending in a concrete way towards my end, it is myself acting—it is also myself driven forward, myself acted upon. These persons among whom I live—leading their own lives, experiencing their own needs, having their own aspirations, thinking in their own ways, creating their own worlds—constitute my body as the dynamic concretion of themselves; they move it according to their own preoccupations, impulses, desires. My personal act makes these human aspirations its own, it is conditioned,

modelled, by them in the very movement by which it incarnates itself in my body, actualizes itself in my present initiative, expresses itself in my environment, in my whole world.

Let us illustrate this still more concretely.

Before leaving the presbytery, I was sitting in my room reading a book. Suddenly I experienced the presence of that house on the other side of the canal, its particular human significance, as a certain urge, an ill-defined anxiety—that is, as a particular disposition of my biological being. This phenomenon was the action in me of the human world centred in that house. My decision to go and visit it was nothing but the personal taking up by my act of that presence by which it found itself physically conditioned.

(2) As I proceed on my way towards the house, I make my intentions present in the road along the canal, in the bridge, in the path across the paddy field, in the whole setting in which my movement takes place. These intentions are nothing but human life pervading in many ways my existential field, shaping my body, transforming itself in it into various actions. These actions are identically the steps which *I* take in order to carry out *my* intention of visiting that house. Thus, as I walk towards the house, I move myself by continually taking up myself-already-moved—at every moment, I make mine the human presence by which my limbs—as parts of the world-existing-without-me—are animated.

These reflections make us even more vividly aware of this fundamental fact: the presence of other persons is an essential dimension of *my* presence in the world. It can be traced at the various levels of my personal structure:

(1) There is in me vegetative life. This life is *my life-act incarnate* considered under a certain aspect. It is also the re-centralization in me of a biological flow coming from other centres. While diffusing itself from its centre and canalizing itself, my life-act is continually fed, energized, and conditioned by the life of the community, by the human environment in which I am situated.

(2) There are in me impulses, feelings, desires. These are various aspects and fluctuations of *my* incarnate existence—as such, motions and reactions of *my* life-act, modifications of *my* world. They are also vibrations in me of that life wave which, coming from "outside", occupies and models my field of existence, my body. *My* impulses, *my* feelings, *my* needs, *my* desires are the taking up by my act

incarnate of a world of impulses, feelings, needs, desires constituted by the living community, by the particular social environment in which I live.

This truth can be illustrated in many ways. X wants a Parker fountain pen, a transistor radio, a car, *because* his colleagues possess such things. He must go to the cinema once a week and wear "drain-pipes" because he sees his friends going to the cinema and wearing "drainpipes". Y takes bribes, drinks, leads a licentious life *because* other people do so. Sitting in a train, Z yawns *because* he sees other travellers yawning; at a station he buys an ice cream *because* other people buy one. The children of my parish school feel together that they must drink water, that they must leave the class-room to satisfy their needs, that they must chase a goat, that they must wade in the school pond. Considered from a particular angle, the various attractions, repulsions, feelings, which I experience in me are various ways in which the human world which surrounds me moves me through the medium of organs and faculties with which it endows me. This is the fundamental perspective in which the old adage "verba volant, scripta manent, *exempla trahunt*" must be understood.

(3) My sensations, as has been shown, are various ways in which my life-act incarnate illuminates itself while diffusing itself from its expressive centre and constituting its world; they are also various ways in which my life-act finds itself already illuminated in its expressive field. This fact must be understood in this way: while illuminating itself through visual, auditory, tactual, perception, my life-act is continually conditioned, moulded, by itself-already-illumined-in-these-various-modes and, through itself-thus-illuminated, by the world already constituted as a diversely illuminated reality. Now, the world already constituted is nothing but the world existing by and in other personal life-acts. Thus, considered under a particular aspect, my sensations are nothing but expressions in me of the way in which the persons who surround me see, hear, and feel. *While* seeing the road on which I walk, the palm trees along it, the mud houses of the Bengali peasants *with my own eyes*, I see them also *with the eyes of the people* who live around me. *While* attending a musical performance and listening *with my own ears* to a particular item, I listen to it also *with the ears of the whole audience* present in the concert hall. The photo at which I look appears to me in a new light since my sister has written telling me how much she liked it. I had often looked

at it before, but never as I do it now: I see it now with the eyes of my sister and, thus, discover in it aspects which so far had not struck me (aspects which are nothing but concretions of my new manner of "living" it). All these examples show that there is among us a real community of sensations. This community is rooted in the interpenetration of our incarnate existences—that is, in the interfusion of our worlds—it is a particular aspect of this interpenetration.

From these considerations, we may understand how erroneous is the conception according to which we see things in the same way because, from our various "subjective" standpoints, we perceive the same "objective reality". The truth is that each one of us, while constituting the world in his own original way, is conditioned by all the other acts-worlds. Therefore, while seeing things in a strictly personal way, each of us sees them also with the eyes of all the other persons: he sees them with their eyes because *his life* is to a great extent *their life in him.*

(4) In the modalities of my brain, my life-act, before transcending itself into an act-volition, remains in a state of indetermination. At this level of loose integration, it illuminates itself in the mode of imaginative consciousness. Considered from a particular point of view, my dreams, imaginations, thoughts, are a certain way in which the world-already-constituted becomes, in me, aware of itself. This means that the flow of my imaginative consciousness is to a great extent fed by the human environment in which I live. The ideas which cross my mind, the dreams and thoughts which succeed each other in the background of my mental world, though inalienably mine (they are modes in which *my* life-act incarnate illuminates itself, they reflect *my* past, *my* temperament, *my* tendencies and aspirations), are different ways in which the human world which surrounds me expresses itself in me.

At the level of imaginative consciousness, the presence in us of others manifests itself most strikingly. We experience the stream of our thoughts and dreams as a third-person process, a movement which takes place in our mental world without being controlled by our will. Our imaginations and our thoughts act as forces which take possession of us and move us—sometimes violently and arbitrarily.

I am working in my room. Suddenly an idea crosses my mind. I am aroused and soon after find myself walking along the canal towards that house hidden among the plantains and coconut palms. That idea, no doubt, was mine—rising up from the depths of *my* incarnate personality, reflecting my individuality—yet it moved me as a force, an appeal coming from outside. It was the expression in my mind of a need felt by another, of a certain void affecting a world both transcendent to my world and deeply immanent in it.

(5) My knowledge, my culture, are undoubtedly personal to me: they are the "result" of my studies, of my past undertakings, of all the experiences I have had in my life; they are conditioned by the way in which my mental world has developed. They are also, however, the expression in me of the knowledge, the culture, the mentality, of the time in which I live—that is, of the human environment in which I have grown and in which I am at the moment situated: it is the whole human community that knows and understands in me and through me.

It is also the whole human world that thinks in me and through me. If my philosophizing develops as it does, it is because I live in this century among people who have an existential bent of mind. From the beginning, my philosophical research, while reminiscing my personal effort, was the expression in me of the interests and anxieties, of the intellectual preoccupations, of my contemporaries: my thinking was their thinking in me, my philosophical experience was the actualization in me of their experience, my frame of mind was the expression in me of their frame of mind, of their manner of living.

(6) It is in the realm of my daily activity that the interpenetration of our incarnate existences reveals itself most significantly. The first point to be noted is that my initiatives, however personal to me, are in a true sense initiatives of the whole community of which I am a member. While acting in a self-determined manner, I continually take up myself-acted-upon; while taking free decisions, I am continually determined, conditioned, by myself-already-decided. This "myself-acted-upon" and this "myself-already-decided" are to a great extent "myself-possessed-and-moved-by-others".

There are various ways in which this compelling presence in me of other persons may be taken up by my personal act. Sometimes my activity is almost entirely motivated by the human environment in which I live; social pressure, the "social imperative", seem to influence my whole behaviour. In such cases, it cannot be said that I take up in a truly personal manner the strange world by which I am possessed. No doubt, the activity which I exert pertains inalienably to me, but it is carried along by the social stream: the flowing of the life of the community into my life takes place at a level of loose integration, in a region of myself where my life-act has not yet become a true personal act. (This may be due to a definite surrender of my personal act to the social influences by which it is conditioned. Such a surrender often entails a depersonalization, an alienation of my freedom.) At other times I act more reflectively and autonomously, I take up personally, creatively, the influences by which I am moved. In such circumstances, the integration of the life of the community into my life takes place at a transcendental level. While effectively conditioning my existence, the active presence in me of other persons is re-created into original initiatives, into free and "intelligent" decisions.

But there is more to say. I have shown earlier that my personal activity takes place in a reality which has already reached a certain degree of perfection but has still to be further actuated in order to become fully what it is meant to be. Through my personal initiatives, I lead this world towards its completion. What exactly does this mean?

The world which surrounds me, in so far as it exists without me, is constituted by other personal acts from various centres different from my personal centre. As such, it is a world which has reached a definite stage of self-development even though it tends towards a more perfect realization of itself. When I act in a personal, self-determined way, I take up the human environment in which I live and lead it towards the end which I have in view. Thus, while perfecting myself, I perfect the other members of the community; while building my own future, I build the future of the whole human family.

Let us take a concrete example of the way in which my activity brings to fulfilment the potentialities of the human field in which it exerts itself. As I am working at my table, I realize in a particular way the intentions immanent in my chair, my table, my pencil and my papers, my whole room, in all the objects which surround me. Now these objects-intentions, in so far as they belong to the world-existing-without-me, are entirely constituted by the other personal acts; they are nothing but modes in which these personal acts express themselves while tending towards their final realization. Thus, in my present activity, while actuating myself, I perfect all the other persons with whom I am vitally linked. By making use of the various objects which surround me, I lead the human world towards a certain goal which, through them, communicates itself to me.

Let us note carefully that this is not something purely "accidental": it pertains to the very essence of a human person that his potentialities and his projects should be realized not merely through his own initiatives and endeavours but also through the activity of the other members of the community. The human aspirations constitutive of the objects which surround me *need* my present efforts in order to attain fulfilment—in other words, the persons who communicate themselves to me through these objects *need* me in order to perfect themselves. Similarly, the desires and intentions which I embody in the book which I write *need* the patient and indulgent attention of those who will peruse it in order to attain their realization. Thus this book can be completed only by its future readers. *I* need them in order to reach my goal, in order to find my own perfection. All our creations are invitations or appeals which must be answered by others. The members of the human community are so vitally linked that none of them can attain by himself alone the realization of his own potentialities, the fulfilment of his own existence. Every human person must lose himself in other persons in order to find himself.

From this we may see what "human nature" is in its concrete reality.

According to many essentialist philosophers, human nature is an "essence" which is characterized by immutability, by constant self-identity, even though it is individuated in many particular persons. Each particular person, in so far as he possesses "human nature", is a "substance" which, in itself, remains unaffected by the vicissitudes of life: nothing "essential" can be added to it or subtracted from it; by "nature", man is above change; he is outside time and outside history, he is above existence.

Some contemporary "existentialist" philosophers take a diametrically opposite view. In their opinion, there is no such thing as "human nature". The essence of man, they say, is in his very existence and his existence is entirely measured by the historical situation in which he finds himself. To affirm that man has a "nature" which is not affected by change is to overlook the historicity of man and to deny his condition as an incarnate being.

Let us briefly sum up the conclusions to which our phenomenological study has led us.

I am a life-act which unfolds itself from a definite centre and constitutes a world in the process of tending towards its realization. In this movement—which is identically my *existence*—my life-act is continually conditioned, structured, by itself-already-existing-qua-world (my *essence*) and, through itself-thus-existing, by the other acts-worlds (my essence considered in so far as it thus includes all the other acts-worlds *is* my *nature*).

Thus:

(1) Against the "essentialists", we affirm that man is first of all a self-transcending act, a personal *esse*—therefore we affirm that man's existence is absolutely prior to his essence. (Man is not a certain essence to which existence is added, but a personal act—an existence —which has a definite structure, an essence). Moreover, we affirm that man's essence or nature (the two are concretely identical) is not a suprahistorical and immutable entity. Finally, we affirm that "human nature" is not an abstraction but a community of vitally related persons. In other words, we affirm that the "system" formed by all the mutually dependent acts-worlds is the only human reality which exists. "Human nature" has no meaning at all apart from it. In so far as I possess "human nature", I am not an "individuated essence", but I depend upon, I am actually generated and conditioned by, the living persons who together with me form the human universe.

(2) Against the "existentialists", we affirm that man, though he is always immersed in a particular historical situation, transcends the narrow limits of this situation in so far as he actualizes in it the totality of the past and prepares in it the whole future. We affirm that man is a subsistent reality because whatever man has been since his appearance "on earth" is realized in what he is today. Therefore the notion of "human nature" is a meaningful "concept", even though mankind is a continually growing, evolving reality. This notion expresses the fact that the human community of today is the *actualization* of the human community of yesterday and the preparation of the community of tomorrow—thus there is unity, continuity, subsistence—whatever is implied in the "concept" of nature.

In spite of their different outlooks, "essentialists" and "existentialists" have a common presupposition: they consider the movement of history as a succession of situations which are loosely linked together (because they fail to see that history is *the genesis of a totality*, that history is a movement which has a sense, a direction, a goal). But here the agreement stops. In their anxiety to safeguard the unity of mankind, the essentialists make of it a supratemporal entity, a static essence characterized by self-identity, immutability. Thereby they deprive history of all value and of all significance. Convinced of the reality of history (as they understand it), the existentialists plunge man into it. In doing so, they reduce man to the situation in which he finds himself, and dismiss the notion of "human nature" as a mere fiction of the mind.

In fact, history is much more than a stream of disconnected events. As we know, it is constituted by the personal acts which form the human universe. Each of these acts takes up the whole past and is conditioned by it. Thus far from "transcending" history, concrete human nature is made of it. And far from being imprisoned within the limits of a narrow situation, man transcends his situation by actualizing in it the whole of history—in other words, each particular circumstance of a man's life exists only as an expression of the totality of history and as a prefigurement of the end.

To these considerations, a very important complement must be added. I pointed out earlier that man's existence *on earth* is not a purely accidental fact, that it is something which pertains to his very essence. I am a life-act which comes to existence in a particular centre "on earth" and constitutes the world while diffusing itself from this earthly centre (aspect a). While thus positing itself as act-world, my life-act is continually conditioned by itself-already-existing-qua-world and, through itself-thus-existing, by the world-existing-without-me (aspect b). This fact must be understood in a very concrete sense. The world-already-existing by which my life-act is conditioned is the world-converging-towards-the-earth,-towards-a-particular-centre-on-earth; it is the human community whose dwelling-place is the earth.

This assertion points to two different facts:

(1) There are cosmic forces which, from the very confines of the universe, conspire to build the earth (with its atmosphere, its seas and continents, its physical characteristics . . .) and to "humanize" it. The centripetal aspect of my personal structure (i.e., my whole personal structure considered as a centripetal reality) is to a great extent constituted by these forces. My personal act is conditioned and fed by them, it takes them up, integrates them, in the very movement by which it constitutes the earth, and the whole world, as its expressive field. From this angle it is apparent that, as a human being, I am, through a "conspiration" of the whole universe, constituted as an

earthly being. In the following chapter, I shall study the nature of these cosmic "forces" which collaborate to make the earth what it is.

(2) The other persons which, together with me, form the earth "humanized" conspire, from their various expressive centres, in an "earthly" way, to build my own biological structure, my own expressive centre. My personal act takes up these human influences while it constitutes the earth, the world, as my field of existence (in the same way as it takes up the "cosmic" forces just mentioned).

These facts show that the human community is the personalization of the universe to the extent that the universe exists as a system centred in the earth.

The earthly character of man is an evident reality which only a philosopher lost in a world of essences can fail to grasp. Man is not "on earth", he is not simply "of the earth", he is the earth in its full sense—man is the earth personalized, the earth exists as a community of human persons. There is no need to explain at length how our body is fed by the earth, by the atmosphere we breathe, by the general ambiance in which we live. The important point to understand is that no value can become a real human value unless it is earthborn, unless it takes an earthly shape, expresses itself in an earthly language. Our whole human culture is conditioned by, made up of, earthly realities. The rotation of the earth, the alternation of days and nights, the movement of the sun and of the moon in the sky, the succession of months, seasons, years, the physical, climatic, biological characteristics of the earth, of the environment in which we live, earthly sights, earthly sounds, earthly smells are the very substance of our existence as men. There can be no human life apart from the earth.

This fact should be pondered by those who dream of extensive travelling in space. I do not deny that it will ever be possible for man to reach the moon and spend a few days there (what is a day, an hour on the moon?) provided he remains closely linked with the earth and, so to speak, takes the earth with him (scientists know in their own ways what this means and the problems it raises), but it is vain to think that man will ever be able to settle in another part of the universe and keep his manhood. The "obstacles" which man has to overcome in space travelling are simply indications of his essentially terrestrial conditions. There is only one earth in the universe because there is only one mankind: the two are concretely one.

We come now to a final consideration. I have pointed out that our sensations, our thoughts, our decisions and actions—our life—are in a true sense the sensations, thoughts, decisions, and actions—the life—of the other people in us. In this connection, Heidegger affirms that the selfhood of the everyday mode of being-man is the selfhood of the anonymous everybody and that this selfhood constitutes the inauthentic, non-genuine man. The truly genuine man, he says, is the one who, through the realization of his own potentialities, has freed himself from the dictatorship of others and taken personal control of his life.

Can we accept this view?

I have shown that my dependence on the other members of the human community is not an accidental factor but an essential dimension of my personal existence. This dependence is concretely identical with the fact of my being continually conditioned by myself-already-there (i.e., by the world-already-constituted, by my past, by history), a fact which I cannot dismiss without annihilating myself. Therefore I cannot cease to depend on others without ceasing to exist. It pertains to my very condition as a human being that my life (in all its manifestations) should to a great extent be the life of others in me. The notion of a human existence independent of the "anonymous everybody", far from being the definition of an authentic human existence, is an absurdity.

This truth must be clearly understood. I cannot express myself without using the language of everybody (i.e., without letting everybody speak through me), I cannot cross the canal without using the bridge as everybody does, I cannot see the paddy fields without looking at them with the eyes of everybody, I cannot buy a pound of sugar without going to everybody's shop and paying with everybody's money. Thus, in order to lead my life in a human manner, I must allow myself to be carried along by the human world in which I live and allow it to realize itself through me. This "allowing to be" is a constitutive element of the very freedom of my actions (even though it may at times be exercised in a way that destroys freedom).

However, my vital relation to the other members of the community is not the reality which constitutes me as a free person; it is not simply by letting other persons realize themselves through me that I actuate myself in a self-determined manner (Heidegger is right when he affirms that an existence entirely ruled by the "anonymous everybody" is not an authentic human existence). As we know, a Transcendent Initiative is the origin of my existence; it is through my ontological dependence on the Creator that I am myself. Therefore I possess my freedom not simply through my subjection to the other members of the human community, but primarily through my obedience to the Creator.

This does not mean that, in order to lead my existence in an authentically personal manner, I must live in isolation (whatever we have said above still holds good). As has been explained earlier, I am created from Above in essential relation to other human persons actually co-created—in other words, I am created as a person having a human nature. Therefore, in order to actuate myself as a free man, I must accept my dependence on the other people with whom I live "on earth"; I must bind myself to them in many ways. But, to be truly personalizing, this subjection of myself to others must be fundamentally an act of transcendental obedience: I must let the others possess me and realize themselves through me according to the will of the Creator. If, instead of living my relation to them in a transcendental way, I simply surrender myself to their influences, I alienate my freedom, I let my life become a third-person process. Such an existence would indeed be an inauthentic human existence.

This picture shows that the different persons who together form the human world are bound into an authentic community by their relation to the Creator. It is only by accepting and living his createdness and by acknowledging the createdness of others (i.e., their presence as transcendental beings different from himself), that each member of the community, while realizing himself as a free person, while respecting and actuating the freedom of his fellow-men, unites himself with them in a truly human way.

I remember the story of a maidservant. She was humble, polite, respectful in her dealings with all. She faithfully carried out her duties, she was attentive in doing what her masters wished and in anticipating their needs. At the same time, there was nothing servile or obsequious in her ways. People felt that, should circumstances require it, she would hold her own and not give way; they felt that, while serving them, she was in fact at the service of Someone Else; they felt that, in the very performance of her duties as a maidservant, she possessed a freedom of which nobody could rob her.

A concluding remark: According to the "essentialists", man is a "substance" which can be perfectly defined without any reference to his concrete existence. In other words, man's *esse* is not part of his manhood; it does not give him anything definite which he does not already possess "by essence", or "by nature". Thus what makes man is not the *fact* of his existence as a particular and unique person, it is not the relation which *actually* binds him to the Creator, it is his "quiddity", i.e., the ontological principle which constitutes him as a representative of a certain class of beings and gives its "essential" value to his entire activity.

The analyses we have made have led us to a radically different view. Experience and reflection tell me that I am a personal-life-act-tending-towards-an-end—that is, an *existence*, a person proceeding from the Creator and facing him in a unique manner. Thus, what matters first for me is the fact of my being-here-for-an-end, my relation to the Transcendent. My existence, however, is a conditioned existence: while positing itself, my act is continually moulded, determined, by itself-already-posited—that is, my organism, the world, my past, history, the other personal acts—all these realities are concretely one and form what I call my "essence", my "nature".

Therefore I shall not say that my *esse* pertains to my essence; I shall not say that I am a substance "endowed" with existence, or an essence which exists in a personal manner; I shall say that my essence, or my nature, is the conditioning of my *esse*, that I am a person endowed with a human nature, that my existence is prior to my essence and that it is constitutive of whatever pertains to me in any way.

ii. *Presence*

The word "presence" is often used to mean simply the fact of being-there. I speak of the presence of my table, my bed in my room, of the presence of trees in the garden, of houses along the road. But, from what has come to light in this study, it is quite clear that the real presence which fills every portion of space is the presence of persons. I am present in this table, this bed, those trees, those houses, even in those figures moving on the road, in so far as I animate them. But, in so far as they are there, given to me, charged with meanings which I do not put into them but discover in them and make mine without ever exhausting them, other persons are present in them. Therefore my presence in the world is "presence to" others, and every object I perceive, every situation in which I find myself is, as it were, the sacrament of this mutual presence.

Now it is evident that we are not present to each other everywhere in the same way: there are different modes of presence. This is first of all because each personal act, though co-extensive with the whole universe, is centred somewhere, that each person animates the world and communicates with others through the mediation of his body: therefore he is present first and foremost in his body and his immediate environment. We shall study first this presence of somebody in his body (which we shall call here "physical presence") and then other modes of presence.

The presence of somebody in his body is so manifest that people are accustomed to identify a person with his body, the presence of somebody with his physical presence. This identification is to a large extent justified. The relation between a person and his body is so intimate that we consider any harm done to his body, any indiscreet appropriation of it, as a serious offence against him. We know that his body belongs to him in an inviolable and incommunicable manner. The reason for this strict right is quite obvious: a person's body is the first expression of his personal act; it is through his body that he owns his world, animates, and shapes it; his body is his world in potency and his world is the act of his body.

When we are in presence of somebody, we discover his personality through his body because we see it living in it, expressing itself through it. The process by which two persons become really acquainted with each other is a process of intercommunication through the mediation of their bodies. When I meet somebody for the first time, it is as though I were entering into a foreign and unknown country; it is a world into which I have not yet penetrated, which I have to discover and understand little by little.

Let us analyse this "first contact".

A is there before me. Before we met, my life-act already pervaded the modalities of his body, and his life-act pervaded the modalities of my body; but, most probably, this mutual relation had still a character of indetermination and generality.

Before me stands a figure characterized by definite features, gestures, a whole attitude. This is a texture of spatial modalities. "By itself", it does not differ much from those other figures which I call a tree, a chair, a statue. Yet, in the presence of this figure, I feel estranged. I am aware that behind it, in it, there is a person distinct from me; I feel that I am on the threshold of an unknown world—a sentiment which fills me with a certain fear.

Now this first contact with A creates in me a certain impression—my first impression of A: his features, his gestures, his way of expressing himself, his whole attitude, are immediately *lived by me* as a complex which has a more or less definite meaning.

Is this meaning something of him, or something of me?

In so far as the spatial modalities which form A's body are lived by me, they are a variation of my field of existence, a part of "my world"; the meaning which I discover in them is derived from my experience, my temperament, my affective dispositions: it is made up of my own life. This kind of appropriation of A's body is simply a personal realization of the fact which was already there before we met: my life-act pervading the modalities of A's body. Therefore my "first impression" of A is not a real discovery of A as he is *in himself* but simply a modification of my own existence.

Nevertheless, however subjective it may be, it has an essential relation to him as distinct from me, because the modalities of A's body are an expression of his personality and are necessarily lived by me as such. My life, however mine it may be, is largely derived from the community (of which A is a member); my experience, though essentially personal to me, is a participation in the experience of all. Therefore my "first impression" of A, though a modification of my own life, is already a penetration into A, because this modification, however mine, is already A living in me.

Now, as we live together, the feeling of estrangement which characterized our first contact gradually fades away; we become acquainted with one another, our mutual relationship becomes more and more personal. This is because, as we meet one another more and work together, we continually communicate with one another; A's life flows into mine, and my life flows into his; our fields of existence tend to fuse into one (perfect fusion is, of course, an impossibility); there is between us a growing community of ideas, of aspirations, of experience. A's body, his features, his gestures, words, attitudes, are now familiar to me and immediately mean a world. His physical presence has grown from something unfamiliar, intimidating, hostile, into something warm, rich, meaningful.

In some cases, no real community of life can be established. Instead of a growing familiarity, there is a growing hostility or antipathy. I meet B for the first time. The first impression may be good or bad. But after a while I realize that his world simply does not fit into mine. His presence provokes in me a sort of irritation—which is a modification of my existence; I develop a feeling of antipathy to him. This attitude makes me incapable of real communication with him, of discovering and understanding him; there is no genuine exchange: everything which comes from him is immediately distorted, coloured, by my feeling. His physical presence is not really the presence of another person acknowledged and respected as such, but simply an unpleasant disturbance of my field of existence with an essential relation to another individual whom I would like to eliminate.

These examples show us the essential role of physical presence in social life. To get rid of that generality in which A was first lost, I had to see him acting and reacting, to hear him speaking, to work with him; our lives had to flow into one another, not in a sort of impersonal way but through the mediation of this mutual physical presence. Only thus has A become a definite and almost indispensable part of my daily life.

An absence of physical contact always creates a kind of estrangement. When somebody who has been abroad for many years comes back home, he is received with great and genuine joy by his friends, but after a while he realizes that a gap has opened between him and them, and that he and they no longer live in the same world; he will see that the persons whom his former friends are most at home with are those with whom they have been living and working every day and that he no longer means to them what he meant before. He is now enclosed in a kind of generality which only a renewal of contact will dissipate.

There are some substitutes for physical presence which are in fact ways of extending it. When I am abroad and receive a letter from a friend at home, this letter is something in which he is to a great extent physically present. The reading of this letter creates a quasi-contact between him and me: I see him as though he were there before me. This is because the letter of my friend receives its existence as letter from the very intention of my friend who has written it and addressed it to me, and to me alone; it is the sensible expression of the relation which unites us. Similarly, a souvenir which my mother gave me at the moment we parted keeps her almost physically present to me. I feel that to destroy it would hurt her. Again this is because the object, as souvenir, is the incarnation of my mother's love for me; because it is something-of-her which is at the same time something-for-me; it is her-in-me.

The way in which a person is present in something depends on the kind of relationship in which this thing stands to him. The important fact that we must keep in mind is that *all modes of presence are modes of real presence* ("real presence" and "physical presence"—as understood here—are by no means synonymous).

A symbolical presence, for instance, is a kind of real presence. A picture has a definite relation to the person whom it re-presents. Through its medium, in it, we reach this person in a real and definite manner.[12]

Ownership is another mode of real presence. We believe that somebody is present in a very special way in his house, his garden, his fields, in whatever belongs to him. A tool which he has used for many years has become almost a part of his body. When we touch and handle something which belongs to him, when we penetrate into his own sphere of action, we feel that we intrude on foreign ground. We feel also that to deprive somebody of something which he rightly owns is to tear something away from his very life.

The difference between the symbolical mode of presence and the mode of presence created by ownership may be understood in this way:

The symbol is for us a meaningful reality; as such it is part of our existence; it is made up of our own life. However, the real meaning of the symbol (which re-presents somebody else) is not us but another person. Therefore it makes this person present-as-living-in-us; it re-presents him through his immanence in our own life; it actuates the unity which exists between him and us.

On the other hand, a thing owned by somebody else, when it is considered as such, is lived by us as a reality which transcends our own sphere of life. No doubt, in so far as it is really for us an object of experience, it is a modality of our own life, yet this is not the aspect on which emphasis is laid: the thing owned by another places us in the presence of him, not as one with us, but as essentially distinct from us. It makes us feel the rightful presence of another as other.

Besides these different modes of personal presence, there is what we may call impersonal presence. The word "impersonal" does not imply of course the absence of all human presence, but simply the relative absence of any definite presence as the presence of A or B.

[12] The error of idolatry is not the belief that God is present in the symbols and images that are used to worship him. God is intensely present everywhere and leads his own personal life independently of the signs which remind us of his presence. The error of idolatry is the belief that God needs symbols in order to *become* personal and, therefore, that symbols not only represent him but personalize him.

There are also different modes and degrees of impersonal presence. When I find myself in a deserted area, I do not feel the presence of any definite person, yet I am encompassed by the human community, I live in it. This mode of presence is extremely general and indefinite. Even there, however, the generality may at any time be broken and a definite personal relation be established. Suddenly, for some obscure reason, the perception of a tree reminds me of a particular person by creating in me a certain complex of which this person is the centre. This tree has become the medium through which this person has suddenly emerged from the ocean of human existence in which he was lost. The tree is really that person manifesting himself to me in a certain way; the countryside is now alive with his presence.

The presence of the community in its undifferentiated totality is of course much more immediate in a city. In Calcutta, I feel it everywhere as a vivid reality, intense and anxious, sometimes almost desperate. I see it like a stream when I push my way on Bowbazar Street in the morning or in the evening. This presence, though physical, at times oppressively immediate, is still impersonal because, to a great extent, it remains indefinite and more or less uniform. But here more than anywhere else, the uniformity may break down at any moment and the presence of all suddenly individuate itself in the presence of a particular person, or of a definite group of persons. This individuation may not always reach clear consciousness in me, as for instance when I am passing in front of my friend's house and, without really thinking of him, live his presence through a certain variation of my field of existence. But it will often express itself in reflections such as: "This is where Professor N. . . lives", "I have seen this man before", "Here is my friend Ojoy coming". Finally, the individuation will at times perfect itself still more and become a dialogue, a mutual exchange, which, for a few minutes, will fix the great human stream and express in a definite way my insertion in and my solidarity with the community of men.

iii. *The Historicity of the Human Community*

We must study now the genesis and the development of the human community.

I am created as a personal life-act co-extensive with the whole universe. This act originates in a particular centre. It constitutes this centre—my brain, my body—as a dynamic nucleus in which it expresses embryonically its fundamental tendencies. From my organism, my act unfolds itself and, in this movement, constitutes the world as the realization of its central potentialities, as the total incarnation of itself. While thus positing itself, my personal act is continually determined by itself-already-posited—in other words, it is conditioned by the very structures which it constitutes as the expression of itself as though these structures were in existence before it. This paradoxical reality, I have pointed out, is fundamentally the fact of my createdness: in the process of constituting my world as the expression of myself, I am ontologically dependent on a Transcendent Being—I find myself cast in the form of a body, of a world, which I do not actually create. As has been shown, this fact, considered on the phenomenal level, is identically:

(1) the fact that my personal act is, in its fundamental way of existing and in all its operations, determined by the cosmico-biological structures in which it expresses itself;
(2) the fact that I am continually conditioned by my past;
(3) the fact that I am vitally dependent upon, generated by, all the other persons existing "in the world";
(4) the fact that I am a "product" of history.

All these facts, concretely considered, *are one and the same reality*.

Let us analyse the implications of facts (3) and (4).

It pertains to my condition as a human person that my present (i.e., myself as I exist now) should be the actualization, the fruition, of a whole history of which I am not and have not been the actor. This history is the very substance of which my body, my whole world—my nature—are made. Moreover, it pertains to my condition as a human person that history should condition me largely through the links which unite me to the other members of the community: while being generated by them, my life-act incarnate is fed, moulded, by the whole of history. These facts imply first that I came to existence one day within biological structures which, in some way, were already present in the human community before my appearance "on earth". In other words, as a human person, I am essentially somebody-who-has-been-born-on-a-particular-day-in-history. I analysed earlier the way in which my birth was prepared and the development which took place after it.

Before I appeared on earth, there was already in existence a community of persons conditioned by a whole history. All the members of this community had been brought to life by other persons, each of whom was also born on a particular day.

Can we follow up this stream of human existence without ever reaching a source?

Emphatically, no.

The essentially historical nature of man implies that mankind is a totality-which-began-to-exist-one-day. Let us explain this.

At the present moment of its existence, the community of persons actualizes in itself the whole past—thus it has reached a certain degree of development, of perfection, of self-realization. But the present is not the end of history: each member of the community ordains himself, tends, towards a future in which he will attain a more perfect realization of himself. Thus the present is not a thoroughly satisfactory state, it is full of wants and deficiencies. This shows that the moment which the community lives now is the actualization of a finite past. It is absurd to consider history as a progress towards an end and to maintain at the same time that it never had a beginning. Once we understand that history is the genesis of a totality, we realize that the world originated on one particular day. A world which has "always" existed is not a temporal reality, it is not a self-developing totality, it is not history.

Now then the question arises: did the human community come into existence at the very beginning of the world?

In the concrete order of things this is an impossibility. Indeed:

The first men who appeared on earth, just like those who live today, were personal life-acts which, in the very process of constituting their worlds from definite centres, were conditioned by the cosmico-biological structures in which they incarnated themselves. Now, considered phenomenally, these structures, like the structures in which my act expresses itself, were made up of history: *they were the actualization of a long past, the term of a long evolutive process.* Thus the "humanization" of the world was preceded by many centuries during which the advent of man was prepared, during which human organisms were gradually fashioned.

This raises two further problems:

(1) We know that the universe is a community of persons. How could it already be in existence long before the appearance of man?

(2) Our incarnation within cosmico-biological structures which we

do not create is concretely identical with our vital interdependence. The biological links which unite us are the channels through which the whole human history feeds us. What about the first men who appeared on earth? There was no human world to give them life, to educate them, to provide them with a human nature and a human culture. . . .

I hope that the following reflections begin to suggest a solution to these problems.

(1) In my study of temporality, I have shown that each moment of history is essentially ordained towards further development, towards a future in which the universe will reach its full realization. With that in mind, how shall we conceive the relationship in which two moments of history stand to each other?

(a) Moment A (the universe considered at a particular stage of its progress) is ordained towards moment B (the universe at a further stage of its evolution). In other words: moment A *is* moment B announced, prepared, anticipated; it is to moment B what the sapling is to the tree.

(b) Moment B *is* moment A realizing its potentialities.

Therefore: The universe, as it existed before the appearance of man, was essentially ordained towards its "humanization"; it was the human community prepared, expected, aimed at. Thus, from the beginning, man was present as the very intention of the world; the universe had to become human in order to realize itself, in order to reach its full development. This means that the world was never completely without man; in its initial simplicity, it was already a human body in formation.

This is still not yet a completely satisfactory answer. I have shown that the universe *is* a community of persons, that it exists by and in different personal acts. Now I may argue as I please, but there *was* a time when no human life-act was in existence, *and yet the world existed.* Moreover, the appearance of men "on earth" was not simply the culmination of an evolutive process (my personal act does not emanate from my body, from the world; it is the reality which *activates* my whole organism even though it is conditioned by it), but the product of a Transcendent Initiative. Thus the problem of the existence of the world-before-man remains largely unsolved.

Let me indicate briefly the direction in which the solution will be found:

I have mentioned on several occasions the presence of "forces" which, from the confines of the universe, work together to build the earth and "humanize" it. This means that my continual dependence upon the world-existing-without-me is not only dependence upon the other *human* acts-worlds but also dependence upon mysterious influences which are not of an earthly character, even *though they pertain to the universe.* These "forces" were already in existence before the appearance of man: the world-before-man subsisted in and by them.

We shall examine the nature of these forces in the next chapter.

(2) To answer the second question, I must again emphasize the constitutive character of the act. As a human person—this fact has just been restated—I am not a mere product of the various influences which act upon me; I am not a creation of my environment (the human community), or the term of an evolutive process (history); as an individual person, I hold my existence from the Creator. My personal life-act—proceeding from Above—is the reality which constitutes, quickens, whatever pertains to me in any way: it constitutes and animates the cosmico-biological structures in which it is incarnate, by which it is actually conditioned; it actualizes in itself the whole past—the very past by which it finds itself determined; it gives their concrete existence to all the earthly and cosmic influences which it undergoes—in so far as these influences, taken up by it, become part and parcel of its own incarnate existence.

Let us now examine the situation in which the first man found himself. He did not come into existence in the midst of a community which was there before him—that is, in an already humanized world. However, at the moment he appeared on earth, there were already existing biological structures which were *meant* to become human, though they were not yet quickened by any human life-act. As soon as a personal act was created in them, they acquired a new vital meaning and were raised to the dignity of a human organism; thus they began to condition the act in a truly human way. This elevation was in fact a new creation, a "humanization" of the whole world. From that moment, the world began to exist in and by man. From that moment also, the whole past—in so far as, actualized in man, it was kept alive by and in his personal act—*became human history*, human experience, human culture (however rudimentary).

But has there ever been a time when mankind was limited to a single individual?

I have shown in this chapter that, as a *human* person, I am conditioned by, I receive life from, the other persons who live with me on earth. Therefore I cannot be a man without being actually related to other men, without being a member of a community: I possess my manhood through the vital links which unite me to other human persons. This means that the advent of man, the "humanization" of the world, must have been from the very first the appearance of a human community—which in its primitive form *may* have been only two persons.

Note: Many philosophers hold that the essential unity of mankind —which is a fact—postulates that all men should descend from a single primitive pair. If all men did not proceed from a common stock, they could not form a single species; there would be on earth several types of intelligent beings which would remain specifically distinct. The members of one family of intelligent earth-dwellers could not have any procreative relations with the members of another family.

Theologians echo these views when they assert that the doctrine of original sin—according to which our "first parents" committed sin and, subsequently, transmitted their sinfulness to their descendants by way of generation—implies that one primitive pair must be the origin of all mankind. If all men did not issue from the same ancestral pair, all of them could not possibly have inherited original sin by way of generation. It would then be wrong to affirm that all men are born in sin.

These assertions call for some remarks:

(a) I have pointed out that the human community is the personalization of the universe in so far as the universe exists as a system centred in the earth. From this it is clear that every personal act whose expressive centre is on earth is essentially a human life-act. What constitutes mankind as a definite species is not the fact that all men proceed from a single primitive pair, but the particular (earthly) relationship which unites all the life-acts centred in this part of the universe.

(b) The common idea of generation as an operation narrowly circumscribed in time and space implies that human nature (and original sin together with it) is a static reality which is transmitted once for all. Each man possesses it independently of any actual relationship to other persons. But this view is contrary to facts; it is empirical, narrow, and superficial. As has been shown, generation

—that is, the procession of man from man—is not simply the procreative process, but it is the fact that each member of the earthly community continually receives life from and gives life to the other members. No doubt, in each individual case, the whole process begins with a particular procreative act; however, it must be understood that, through this act of two particular persons, the whole community transmits life, that the whole community feeds and generates the child while he is in his mother's womb, that it continues to give him life after birth. These facts make us realize that, even if human life had emerged on earth in various places within different biological groups, there would still have been from the first a communication of life between the members of each primitive community, between the various communities. Thus, even in this case, the links uniting men would have been from the very beginning generative links; even in this case, each man would have transmitted the whole of himself within the stream of life flowing continually from him into the others. This implies that the transmission of sin by way of generation would have taken place even if the first human community had consisted of more than one "pair", even if only one of these pairs had betrayed their trust.

Can we conceive the way in which the advent of man took place? I have said that, at the moment man appeared on earth, there were already present in the world biological structures which were meant to become human; let us be more matter-of-fact: there were in existence several organisms which had reached an advanced stage of development. Now to say that one of them became human is to say that, from a certain moment, it became the expressive centre of a human life-act, the *fons et origo* of a human world. This act, from the centre in which it was created, took possession of the whole universe. (This movement of expression should not be considered as a progressive expansion, like the diffusion of gaseous matter. The act was from the very first co-extensive with the whole universe, yet centred somewhere. This is the idea behind my metaphor.) In this process, it was continually conditioned by itself-already-existing-as-world and, through itself-thus-existing, by the world-existing-without-it. The latter, as we know, is the world-existing-by-and-in-other-personal-life-acts. This means that the appearance of mankind on earth was the simultaneous infusion (at a certain moment) of at least two human life-acts into two different living organisms and, through the mediation of these organisms, and of the whole spatial field which they "occupied", their being bound together by a mutual relationship which they could not break without ceasing to exist.

Let us now briefly examine the way in which the human community developed after its appearance.

The advent of man was a decisive step in the march of the universe: the universe-centred-in-the-earth became what it was destined to be, namely: a world of human persons. To a large extent, the progress of the whole towards its end became a human affair; it was identified with the aspirations, endeavours, struggles of man—in one word, with human history.

The first men who came to existence had very little human experience and culture; their psycho-somatic apparatus was not "charged" with human "accretions", their world—the world of their daily preoccupations and aspirations—was limited to a few elementary structures.

Starting from this primitive stage, the human universe had now to grow and to realize itself more and more; man had to take progressively firmer possession of the world—that is, of himself. To visualize the way in which this process took place—and continues to take place—we must always keep in mind that mankind is a living community whose members are vitally interdependent, "flowing" into each other: each man receives life from his fellow-men, each man communicates to his fellow-men what he is and what he has. We must also remember that the past is continually kept alive, realized, in the present, and that each moment of history, while actualizing the whole past, brings something new and is essentially turned towards the future.

This development has by no means been a uniform and homogeneous process. As the universe-community grew, it also split into various groups which were vitally interrelated and yet had marked personalities. Because of these divisions, various trends manifested themselves, different cultures came into existence. . . .

This diversity, even though it helped to manifest the tremendous potentialities of the human world, was not an end in itself. From a certain angle, these divisions indicated that the human universe had not yet "found" itself; they pointed to its lack of self-realization.

Can we in any way determine the end towards which history is tending?

I pointed out in the preceding chapter that the goal of my life cannot be the self-annihilation of death. My present life is the preparation and the anticipation of my future life; my world, as it exists now, is the inception of the world-to-come. Therefore it is only by transforming itself into a new mysterious totality that my act-world can realize its destiny.

These facts must now be studied within a broader perspective: I do not exist as an isolated individual but essentially as a member of a community from which I receive life and to which I give life. The following points must be noted carefully:

(1) While exercising my daily activities, I progress towards my end and, at the same time, lead towards it all the other persons to whom I am vitally related. Thus, while preparing my "beyond", I build the sphere in which the other persons will lead their future lives. Thus, to a certain extent, the other persons will be for ever what I shall make of them.

(2) While living and acting, the other persons tend towards their ends and lead me towards them. In this way, they determine what kind of existence I shall lead after I die. To a large extent, I shall be for ever what the other persons make of me.

(3) Nevertheless, each person remains the author of his own destiny. My situation after death will not be the mere resultant of the way in which my fellow-men live; neither will their future state of existence simply derive from my way of spending my time "on earth". The reason for this is that each personal life-act receives its existence from Above: each person is *fundamentally* independent of the others even though he is continually conditioned by them. Thus, in the last resort, *I* shall decide the way in which my fellow-men will influence my future life; each of them will determine for himself the way in which I shall make him be for ever.

(4) Just as my present existence is in tension towards a future existence, so history is in tension towards a fulfilment. This fulfilment can only be the formation of a community in which the limitations and deficiencies of the present world are to a large extent overcome. It is only when this future community is complete that my personal existence will reach its ultimate realization. This means that, even after I die, I shall still wait for a final consummation, for the attainment by the whole universe of a definitive state of existence.

(5) The present human community does not include only the persons who live presently "on earth", *it is chiefly made up of the multitude of those who, after leading their earthly existence, have attained*

a more definitive manner of being man. This "heavenly" community[13] is the "real" human community; in its members, the universe exists in a new and mysterious way. With regard to it, the following facts impose themselves:

(a) In the heavenly community, the end towards which we tend in this life offers itself in some way as an existing reality. Thus there is a vital tension between it and us—this tension is an essential dimension of our present existence.

(b) The heavenly community, though incomparably "larger" than our earthly community and transcendent to it, has still to be completed and perfected by us. As we exercise our daily activities and tend towards our heavenly goal, we continually build the definitive community. Thus our earthly endeavours and struggles have a meaning with regard to the "departed". They need us in order to reach the fullness of their heavenly existence.

(c) These two facts show that there is a dialectical relation between the earth and heaven: heaven attracts the earth, polarizes it; the earth builds heaven, completes it. The community of the "departed" and the earthly community are not two separate communities: both together form a structural totality the parts of which are vitally interrelated.

(d) In my study of temporality, I have shown that each moment of history is the realization of whatever took place before it. Now the whole past which the present actuates is made up of personal happenings and undertakings, of human achievements. At every moment of history, the universe existed as a system of interrelated acts-worlds; whatever occurred was entirely immanent in the movement by which the various personal acts constituted their fields of existence while unfolding themselves from their respective centres and tending towards their goals. Now the various acts-worlds which have appeared in the course of time and have engendered the universe of today (the present moment) continue to live now and to exert their influence. It is in them as well as in us that the past is kept alive; it is through my relation to them as well as through my relation to the other persons whom I see living around me that the whole of history conditions the present moment of my existence.

[13] "Heavenly" does not mean "detached from the earth". The "departed" still belong to the earth—since they are men—but in a new mysterious way about which very little can be said.

Let us illustrate this by an example. A lived "on earth" a few centuries ago. While leading his earthly existence, he formed himself and built his own destiny, he also influenced his fellow-men and contributed to the building of their respective worlds. A is alive today. Whatever he was and did during the earthly stage of his existence is realized first of all in what he is and does today; it is also realized in the way in which at the present moment the other personal acts which form the universe live and are structured.

These facts show that no "objective" study of the events which take place today and of their historical antecedents can give an exhaustive knowledge of the time in which we live. To understand it fully, we should penetrate into the secrets of the "other world" and bring to light the mysterious vital relations which bind us to it.

There is an immense sphere of personal presence which continually envelops and penetrates me, which conditions our interpersonal relations (i.e., our relations as members of the "earthly" community), and of which we have no clear awareness in our daily dealings. We feel its existence in a confused way, we feel ourselves immersed in it, but we cannot precisely describe the way in which it influences our lives and shapes our destinies.

iv. *Mutual Knowledge and Mutual Love*

Can I know somebody other than myself?

At first sight, it seems that I cannot. My knowledge of things is the luminous presence to itself of my personal act in the movement by which it actuates itself and constitutes my world. Thus whatever I know is but an aspect, a modification, of myself-incarnate. I cannot be aware of any reality without first living it—that is, without first making of it a dimension of my own existence.

These facts cannot be denied. Do they really imply that I have no knowledge of any person other than myself?

In the course of this chapter, I have shown that the different acts-worlds which form the human community are interrelated, that they interpenetrate. There is in me a vital presence of all the other persons with whom I live on earth. I am to a certain extent possessed by them. This means that, while knowing myself, I have also a real knowledge of others. My self-knowledge is in a true sense knowledge of them-in-me.

But is this knowledge a real knowledge of others *as others*—that is, as transcendent to me?

I know another person in so far as his existence flows into mine, and mine into his, in so far as there is between us a community of life. But the other-in-me is not the other-in-himself since, in himself, the other is radically distinct from me and transcendent to me. Therefore the other as other remains beyond my grasp: his transcendent individuality will never become for me an object of knowledge.

Let us consider how I can progress in the knowledge of another. As has just been pointed out, the fact that we can to a certain extent know each other is due to the interpenetration of our incarnate existences. There is a continuous flow of life between us; therefore I know the other in me and he knows me in him. Intensifying our existential "exchange" is the way of increasing this mutual understanding. A few examples will help us to see how this can be achieved:

(1) Every morning A comes from the city with a bundle of newspapers tied to the handlebar of his bicycle. He goes from house to house and distributes his newspapers to his various customers. Daily, at about half past nine, he comes into my office and, without a word, puts a copy of *The Statesman* on my table and walks out. Sometimes when I go out in the morning, I meet A. He cycles past me looking straight ahead. I have never seen him talk with people or stop for a while to watch some particular scene. A is a newsboy on his round; this seems to be the whole of him.

A is a person distinct from me. Of this I am, no doubt, conscious. However, do I know him?

To a great extent, no. Even now I do not know his name. I have never asked where he lives, whether he is married and has children. Thus, up to this day, A has remained for me an anonymous entity; he has not really become for me a living and transcendent individuality in which I am personally interested.

This unconcern may go on for years. For years, the stream of life which flows from A into me may remain a purely "natural" process. If so, A will never become for me more than a particular function of my daily existence; he will never be a world distinct from mine and, yet, familiar to me—in one word, I shall never know him.

The correlative is no doubt true also. If our connection remains what it is now, I shall never be for A more than a particular landmark in his daily round—that is, more than a modality of his daily existence; my world will remain outside his sphere of interest, he will never know me.

Thus mutual knowledge supposes a certain living-together which rises above our "natural" relationship—that is, above the links which bind us by our membership of the same earthly community—it supposes our being-interested-in-each-other.

(2) B is a retired school teacher who acts as a broker. I have entrusted him with the task of finding around the church some plots of land for the Christian Housing Co-operative Society and one for a girls' school. B comes to see me three or four times a week. He gives me an account of whatever he has found, mixed up with a great deal of reminiscence. Sometimes I go to his house and talk with him and his wife while sipping a glass of green coconut water.

B is a friend of mine. I am interested in him and in his family. I appreciate his devotedness and his honesty. Yet, what brings me close to him and conditions my feelings towards him is chiefly his usefulness to me. To a great extent, it is because I need him that I appreciate him; I may truly say that I have sympathy for him to the extent that he is the realization of my desires, the fulfilment of my needs. This is clear from the irritation I sometimes experience when he indulges in too many reminiscences.

My knowledge of B is largely the expression of this attitude. I know him as a devoted and reliable helper, as a hard-worker, but also as an endless talker who has frequently to be brought back to the point. Thus, in spite of all the sympathy I feel for B, the way in which he exists for me is to a large extent a function of my own preoccupations. The B who is familiar to me, who interests me, is mainly B-for-me—that is, a particular dimension of my own existence, an aspect of my world—it is not B-in-himself (transcendent to me) with all the riches of his own aspirations and potentialities, with his own needs, his joys and his fears.

It goes without saying that so long as my appreciation of B remains so egocentric, my knowledge of the world of B will hardly progress. I may continue to meet him for years and, yet, fail to raise my connection with him to the level of a fully personal relationship.

(3) C is a young man whom, at the beginning of my stay at Krishnanagar, I employed as a gardener. For two or three weeks, I was pleased with his work. One day, however, I noticed that he had appropriated two or three bundles of plantains. I promptly dismissed him and forbade him ever to set foot on the mission garden again. Since that time, I have occasionally met C and talked with him. Though I abstained from any allusions to the past, I could not help

distrusting him and doubting the sincerity of what he said. I interpreted his words, his actions, his whole personality in terms of the unfortunate circumstances which had taken place in the past and of the affective complex which these circumstances had created in me. Suspicion was the atmosphere in which I made C exist for me.

My attitude towards C, it is clear, has, so to speak, dammed the stream of life flowing from him into me; it has prevented me from communicating with him in a truly human way. This means that C-in-me is to a great extent a distortion of the real C and, consequently, that my knowledge of C is a caricature. Far from being a re-creation in me of the existing C, it tends to be a mere product of my particular psychology.

It is evident that so long as this affective complex persists, I shall not reach an authentic understanding of C's own life.

All these examples show that my knowledge of a person is a function of the manner in which I make him live for me and in me. This is an undeniable fact.

In general, I may assert that the way in which I look at people, the way in which I know and understand them, is intimately conditioned by my basic existential attitude, by my status in life. I realize that this old woman whom I see washing clothes, the doctor who came to see me an hour ago, those school-children playing under my window, look at their fellow-men and understand them in quite a different way. I realize that each person I meet knows people in a unique and incommunicable way: he knows them according to what he is—that is, in him.

These observations suggest, moreover, that authentic love is the key to authentic knowledge. Let us analyse the nature of true love and the way in which it makes us discover people.

I pointed out earlier that I need other people in order to attain my own perfection, that other persons present themselves to me as the realization of my own potentialities. This means that the movement of my life carries me towards the others, projects me in them. However, other persons do not reveal themselves to me merely as concretions of myself but also as independent individualities: while finding myself in them, I am vitally aware of their existence beyond me, of their irreducible transcendence—another person, as other, can never be the mere expression or realization of my existential propensities and aspirations, he must remain in himself and for himself. Acknowledgment of and respect for this transcendence is an essential aspect of authentic love. In other words, true love always implies a distance. Its aim is not to absorb other people but to promote their being. It is never tired of them, it never rejects them, but welcomes and benefits them.

This love transforms the human multitude into an authentic human community. Men do not simply make use of each other but respect each other as persons and work for each other's good. While doing so, they perfect one another, strengthen the vital bonds which unite them and lead one another towards their final goal. True love is creative.

It makes us discover others. When we love people authentically, we allow them to live and reveal themselves in us. True love makes us identify our lives and, thus, makes us know each other intimately and luminously. Such a knowledge is not simply the static acknowledgment of "objective" data, but the discovery of others in the act by which we make them to be authentically themselves. We know those whom we love not only as they are, but also as we wish them to be.

This knowledge, however, can never be exhaustive. First because others are continually "in the making"; they are continually in process of realizing their potentialities, of manifesting what they are; secondly and chiefly because other persons, however intimately we know them, remain irreducibly transcendent to us and beyond our grasp.

Authentic knowledge is aware of its limitations; it is prudent, free from hasty conclusions and prejudices, open to revision and correction.

A few words must be said about the distinction between "benevolent love" and "concupiscent love".

There is concupiscent love between A and B when the movement of A towards B takes place on a lower level, in an impulsive or "instinctive" way. Such a love may be called phenomenal because it is essentially a third-person process and implies a certain surrender of A's freedom to impulses and functional desires. It does not tend to the good of B but merely to the realization of potentialities latent in A. A does not love B as a person who must be promoted and respected for himself. He loves him simply as the fulfilment of his biological cravings. By surrendering himself to these urges unreasonably, A depersonalizes both himself and B.

Benevolent love, on the contrary, is a personalizing force. What interests A is not simply B as the complement of himself but B-in-himself—that is, B as a person distinct from him, transcendent to him, B as the product of a unique Creative Initiative. A wants B to be fully himself—that is, to be fully what the Creator wants him to be. By loving B in this way, A perfects himself and perfects B; he actuates his own freedom and B's freedom. Thus benevolent love is a self-controlled force of union which rises above biological impulses; it is both an act of transcendental obedience and an act of human liberty.

It is sometimes asserted that the difference between concupiscent love and benevolent love consists in that the former seeks the good of the lover whereas the latter seeks the good of the beloved. This is misleading. Concupiscent love perfects neither the lover nor the beloved since it depersonalizes both; benevolent love, on the contrary, perfects both the lover and the beloved. However, there is some truth in the assertion. It is a fact that B as the object of A's concupiscent love is a particular self-realization of A, however imperfect; it is a fact also that A, to the extent that he loves B authentically, forgets himself in order to serve B—thus what he wants first of all is the good of B.

Nevertheless, it is benevolent love, rather than concupiscent love, which provides the lover with what is truly good for him. Thus benevolent love, while tending explicitly to the good of the beloved, is also directly ordained towards the good of the lover. Man finds himself to the extent that he forgets himself, to the extent that he sacrifices himself for the good of his fellow-men. Your good and my good are indissolubly linked.

Now, from what we have just said it might appear that concupiscent love and benevolent love are mutually exclusive. In fact, there is no concrete human love which is purely concupiscent (because man, however much he surrenders himself to his biological impulses, remains a transcendental being; because B, even when made into the object of A's concupiscent love, remains transcendent to A and must be acknowledged as such). Moreover, there is probably no human love which is purely benevolent. Every human affection is at the same time partly more or less benevolent and partly concupiscent.

Moreover, the "passage" from concupiscent love to benevolent love does not imply the rejection of all natural attachment. In order to love B in a benevolent way, A does not have to kill all the attractions which he experiences in himself, but to sublimate them—that is, take them up in the act by which he desires the good of B, and so raise them to the dignity of transcendental affects.

But, if concupiscent love may be "transcendentalized", benevolent love may at times lower itself. A may work for the good of B and little by little allow his zeal to be carried away by his feelings: his benevolent love may degenerate into a phenomenal attraction.

v. *Human Communities*

To close this chapter, we may say a few words about the different human communities and the relations which exist between them. There are many different human communities; we shall confine ourselves to national communities.

I am conscious of belonging to a definite national community and of living by its life. This community occupies a definite territory which it claims to be its own. When I speak of it as a member of this community, I call it my country.

The geographical and climatic characteristics of this territory have left a deep mark on the bodies and souls of its inhabitants: we are all people of the soil; the clay of which we are made is the clay of our country. This national community has also a definite history which fashions its individuality and expresses itself in all the different aspects of its existence. It is present in the cities and villages, in the monuments, roads, fields, and rivers of the country; it is present in the whole culture of the community, in its religious beliefs, in its ways of thinking, in its customs. . . .

The national community is characterized by a certain emotivity; it has aspirations of its own, a more or less definite will—in one word, a distinctive personality. This personality is not superimposed upon the different members of the national community. Indeed, it does not exist apart from the individuals; it exists in them, it is in them as united by common bonds, as sharing the same joys and sorrows, the same aspirations, as thinking, feeling, willing, acting, living together.

This nation, of which I am a member, is surrounded by other nations, each of which has also a marked personality. Now, all the people who constitute these different national communities belong to the same great human community and are, therefore, vitally related to one another. However, it is to a great extent through their national community that the members of one nation are related to those of another nation. Even when they are abroad, they remain essentially the representatives of their own country, in virtue of their heredity, their physical constitution, their national and religious background; even abroad, it is to a great extent their national community which thinks, feels, and reacts in them, which speaks through them. In this context, we can see that the meeting of individuals belonging to different countries is in fact the meeting of different nations (that is to say, of different histories, emotivities, aspirations.)

Let us now look more closely at the relations which unite the members of different nations.

A, a member of a certain national community, meets B who belongs to another country. They are vitally related to each other by the very fact that they are men. Now there is in their mutual relationship something special which may be expressed thus: the relation between A and B is essentially the relation between A-member-of-one-nation and B-member-of-another-nation. This means that in their mutual exchange the life of A's national community flows into B, and the life of B's national community flows into A. Therefore their mutual contact, however restricted, is of national significance: it unites not only two individuals but two countries, fusing them into one.

Let us suppose that A and B, instead of becoming friends, conceive a mutual antipathy and live in a state of hostility. This split has also a national significance: it disunites the two nations of which A and B are members.

The relations between different nations are relations of interdependence. As one person, while influencing those with whom he lives, is vitally dependent on them, so also each nation as a whole, while affirming its own personality and exercising its influence on other nations, is shaped and kept alive by them. This shows that, *in order to remain itself* and to play its role, each nation must accept its dependence on other nations. Pure independence is a dangerous utopia. It does not promote but destroys the personality of a nation by drying up the source from which this personality draws a great part of its life and vigour.

The existence of different nations is a relative necessity. As history goes on, the progress of mankind, in spite of many disrupting elements, is towards a greater and greater unity. The flow of life which constitutes the whole universe is individuated in many different persons—this is something essential and definitive; it is split into different currents—this is something unavoidable; however, it tends more and more to gather into one: as the means of communication between the different countries multiply and perfect themselves, the different national communities exchange what they have with increasing eagerness, and are thus in process of passing into one another, or of fusing into one. This process of unification goes hand in hand with another phenomenon: the spatial expansion of men. These are in fact two complementary aspects of one essential reality: the growing humanization of the universe which is, as we know, a centrifugal process.

All this concerns man as living on earth. But, as we have seen, the real and definitive human community is not the earthly community. History has to transcend itself in order to attain its fulfilment. This means that each man, *while* living in his country, working for its progress, and building the human world, is on his way towards his true home. Therefore the national aspirations of a country can never become an absolute. A person can never be compelled to subordinate the attainment of his final end—the only thing which really matters for him—to the furtherance of national aims. This is not the place to develop this point. It is enough to realize that the problem implies a whole conception of the rights and duties and of the role of the leader of a nation.

Part Three

REACHING THE FOUNDATIONS

CHAPTER VII

Beyond the Human World

Is the universe nothing but a human world—that is, a community of human persons, an earth-centred system?

This is the question which we shall try to answer in this chapter.

1. There is a "Natural World"

First Approach

The things which surround me, to the extent that they mean something to me, are correlative to my existence; they are concretions of my life, parts of the world which my personal act constitutes as its field of expression. However, there is in things more meaning, more purpose, more life, than I put into them. Things are not only in me and by me, they are also in others and by others. To a very large extent, the meaning which I give them is derived from the meaning which they have as parts of the human world by which I am encompassed and from which I receive life.

Are things nothing but human life in various forms?

I look at the objects which surround me. Once more, I am struck by the fact that they are human intentions crystallized.

Are they no more than that?

This lamp burning on my table. It fulfils its purpose, it is here and now what it is meant to be. Meant by whom? By the engineer who designed it, the craftsmen who made it, the shopkeeper who sold it, all the people who, through it, are in communication with me. There is something more. This lamp is made of brass, its tank is filled with paraffin. The brass of which it is made is an alloy of copper and zinc. These substances are, no doubt, meant for some definite purposes, and are therefore constituted by some basic intentions.

Whose intentions?

Our intentions, assuredly, since we use them for specific ends and, therefore, give them definite finalities. But to reach *these* ends we have to make use of *them*—we cannot use *any* substance such as wood, earth, water. . . . Therefore, while making of them concretions of our intentions, we take up and fulfil finalities, serviceabilities which are in them *independently of us*. The whole of science and technology may be described as a continued effort to unveil and realize these original intentions.

What does this imply?

I know that, while using my lamp to dispel the darkness and enable me to carry on my work, I make mine and fulfil the human intentions by which my lamp is constituted. In doing so, I am conditioned, generated, by the life-giving community which surrounds me. Now I understand that, while working at my table in the light which comes from my lamp, I also take up, carry out, make mine pre-human intentions which form the very "substance" of my lamp—in other words, in the act of using my lamp, I allow a pre-human life, of which my lamp is a particular concretion, to flow into me, inspire me, become my life.

This phenomenon is a constant process. At every moment, my life-act is conditioned, fed, carried, by a life-field which is not of human origin; my world rests on a natural world which is older than me, and older than the whole human world.

I call this pre-human sphere a life field because I discover it not as crude reality, not as impenetrable *Seiendes*, but as an interplay of intentions, and therefore as a system pervaded, animated, moved, by personal living forces.

Second Approach

Night is falling. The sky is overcast. The earth, the grass, the trees, the houses are soaked with rain. Through the window of my room I see the long leaves of the plantain trees waving in the evening breeze. Frogs are croaking in the church pond. This setting, as I perceive it, as I "live" it, as I make it exist for me at this very moment, is a variation of the existential field formed by my personal act unfolding itself from its centre; it is made up of my own life. But this setting exists also without me. As such, it is constituted by other human life-acts unfolding themselves from other earthly centres. These facts have already been firmly established.

Is this particular monsoon landscape in its totality a man-made reality? In other words, are the intentions, the life, by which it is animated nothing but human intentions, human life?

The answer seems obvious. The meaningful activity which constitutes those frogs croaking in the church pond, those plantain leaves shaken by the monsoon wind, is not entirely of human origin; it does not proceed entirely from human expressive centres. This implies that there is in the world, in the objects of the world, much more life, much more consciousness, much more purpose, than we men put into them. In other words, the world-without-man is already a system full of meaning and finality. It is with this world that we build the human world.

Third Approach

It is essential to each human person to have been born on one particular day; it is essential to the human community to have come to existence at a particular moment of history, in an already existing universe, in a specially prepared environment. These truths, which have emerged in the course of our investigation, point to a highly significant fact with which I shall now deal.

Before man's advent, there were "on earth" living organisms which were *meant* to become personal centres. These organisms were not isolated entities. First, they were the outcome of a long "evolutive process"; secondly, they were the crystallization of a world-wide activity—two expressions of the same reality. The meaning of this is that the world-before-man was a purposeful system; it was not a chaos, it was not impenetrable *Seiendes*, it was an intention—or a sheaf of intentions—elaborating vital forms in order to realize itself.

The pre-human aspirations which constituted and animated this structural ensemble attained a definite stage of fulfilment when man appeared on earth. This shows that the coming into being of the human world took place *within a living totality* which was already a sphere of personal existence; that it was vitally inserted in and, in a way, engendered by the self-actuating movement of this totality; it shows, at all events, the degree of self-elaboration which the cosmos had actually reached made it concretely possible. Thus the human world came into being as a reality hinged on an older and much broader living system, a system to which it found itself linked by a vital relation which it could not break without destroying itself. This encompassing totality continued to feed and energize the world of men even as the latter began to follow its own course and grew into a more and more elaborate, a more and more original, personal structure.

It continues to influence and vitalize the human community of today. I have referred to this action on several occasions, in particular when I wrote of the existence of cosmic "forces" which, from the confines of the universe, conspire to form the earth, to make it the abode of men, to fashion this body of mine, to build it into the expressive centre of this original totality which I call my act-world.

2. The Natural World is a World of Persons

What is this mysterious sphere of being referred to under these three aspects?

a. *It is neither an infrapersonal physico-biological system, nor a world of "substances", but a personal life-field.*

The pre-human world is a system the totality and each element of which reveal themselves as *constituted*, pervaded, *animated*, by a living intention, or by living intentions. I affirm this because I realize that my personal life (*under all its aspects*) is, to a large extent, the taking up, the re-energizing, the re-orienting by my act, of a pre-human life—of the life which is the movement, the very *esse*, of the "natural" world into which I feel myself continually thrown; I affirm this, in particular, because I realize that, in whatever I do, I make mine and carry out finalities which are in things even before things are in men. I affirm, therefore, that the world-before-man is a living, personal system. The whole of my reflective analysis leads me to this conclusion: it is a fact which forces itself upon me.

The following considerations may help us to see this point clearly:

The picture of the world which science gives us is that of a totality existing as an infrapersonal physico-biological system, of a nature governed by impersonal physico-biological laws. Science, as such, does not tell us that this system, as so described, exists *in itself*, that is, independently—such an affirmation would not be "scientific"—but, without making any metaphysical pronouncement and remaining within the limits of its investigation, it establishes a certain order among things and determines a certain part of their utility.

Now it must be borne in mind that the world of natural sciences *has no existence independently of man*; that this world *is* the human world (i.e., the world *constituted* by human life-acts) revealing itself to itself under particular aspects; that it is, therefore, a reality entirely abstracted from that concrete totality which we call *our world.* This human world, existing *de facto* as a plurality of mutally involved acts-worlds, is the only entity which we are entitled so far to describe as *ens-in-se* (and we may add incidentally that the "inseity" of this reality has been discovered as concretely identical with, inseparable from, its "personality": my world exists in itself because it *is* my act incarnate, because my act is a personal, transcendental hypostasis).

However, the fact that the world of natural science does not exist in any way outside the human world and is, therefore, fundamentally constituted by human life-acts, does not imply that the elaboration of this world is an entirely autonomous human undertaking. As has been hinted above, the whole of science and technology asserts that the world is older than man, that this pre-human world is already an organized system, a meaningful interplay of forces, that the taking up, the illuminating, the mastering by men, of these living energies which continually flow into his sphere of existence "from outside" is a condition for the successful building of the human world. Science, however, does not assert that these forces exist "in themselves" as it described them. What these forces are in themselves must be grasped, not from the point of view of science, which is a restricted point of view, but from that of our integral experience—the all-embracing point of view from which we discover:

(1) the role which science and technology play *within* the movement of the human acts-worlds towards their end;
(2) the fact that science and technology do in fact point to the existence of a pre-human world;
(3) the inability of science to assert anything about the ontological status of this world.

The view of the world which realistic philosophy gives us is a rationalization of our direct perception. Because we see around us objects which are clearly "distinct" from one another (do we?), it is supposed that the world is *in itself* a conglomerate of radically independent substances.

In fact, realistic philosophy does not present us with anything that exists *concretely* outside man. The objects-substances of which it speaks are in reality nothing but variations of our existential field, aspects of our personal acts-worlds; moreover, the mental process of erecting these forms into supposedly self-subsisting entities does not contain anything, either in its "noetic" core, or in its "noematic" expression, which is not entirely made from human life. Clearly, to make "objective reality" exist concretely as a world of independent substances, we should do more than just think and affirm it to be so.

However, it should not be concluded from this that realistic thinking is completely out of touch with the *de facto* existing pre-human world. Its assertion of the existence of a sphere of being which subsists independently of man, is no doubt based on a genuine intuition of facts—however clumsy its manner of interpreting this fundamental experience. From the point of view of our integral experience, while grasping the ontological status of the pre-human world, we see the authentic nature of the central facts of which realistic thinking is basically aware; at the same time, however, we see the inability of this thinking to investigate these facts and to make any statement that can authentically be related to them.

From the beginning of this study, I have realized that the objects of the world, to the extent that they have existence and meaning for me, are *concretions* of my personal life, are *constituted* by the life-act which I am. Therefore, from the beginning of this study, I have realized that the world is the unfolding, the expressive field, of my personal life-act. My discovery of this fundamental act has been continually confirmed, my experience of it continually revived and enriched, as I progressed. This discovery, it must be noted carefully, did not take place on a so-called phenomenological level contra-distinguished from a higher metaphysical level at which the whole intellectualistic approach would have to be introduced. Progressing in the same line, remaining continually in the same perspective, my analysis, going down to the very heart of things, has unveiled the ontological core of the facts which it described: I am *created* as a personal life-act constituting the world as its expressive field, from an expressive centre; the world is *created* as the multiform unfolding of the central potentialities of my act. This discovery demolished the notion of the world as a totality existing *in itself* as a physico-biological nature, the notion of the world as a conglomerate of self-subsisting material beings, and that of the world as impenetrable *Seiendes*. It is essential to realize that there is now no room at all for such entities. This must be forcefully emphasized because the idea continually crops up that the world does exist *in itself* in an infrapersonal manner. The conclusion to which a careful and vigorous study of facts leads us is that such an idea is not only erroneous, but fundamentally absurd: if the meaningfulness of things—i.e., their very *existence-for-me*—is in their being constituted by and in the self-realizing movement of my personal act, it is absurd for me to speak of any object which exists *in itself* outside me.

It would be a mistake to say that the principle here posited is of a purely relative value, or that, since there *is* a whole sphere of existence which is transcendent to me, the world *may* exist outside me as an infrapersonal system. The fact is that there is nothing in the world which is not in some way in me and by me; the fact is, therefore, that my knowledge of things *as they are in me* is already an authentic perception of what they are, of what they *must* be, *without me*. My assurance of this fact enables me to assert that the world-without-me is not an impersonal nature, but a personal system. So far, this personal system has been identified with the earthly community in which I find myself inserted. Now it appears clearly that the human world is not the whole universe—there is such a thing as a world-without-me, as a world-before-man. Looking at it from the point of view of my integral experience, keeping before my eyes the fundamental perspective which my study has brought to light, I affirm that this antehuman sphere is a personal life field.

Objection. The line of argument leading to this conclusion runs as follows: whatever exists is for consciousness—if the cosmos exists before man, there must exist a non-human consciousness for which it is, before being for man. Up to this point, the principle enunciated in the major has been presented as a *phenomenological* principle (it is the fundamental principle of phenomenology and of all philosophies of consciousness). This principle refers not to consciousness in general, but to human consciousness and, in particular, to philosophical consciousness. But, in this chapter, it is taken to mean: nothing can exist independently of consciousness *in whatever form*. This is no longer a phenomenological principle used as the starting-point for a method rooted in experience, but a speculative principle which must either be presented as self-evident (this raises problems), or be justified in some way or other.

Answer. For Merleau-Ponty, the world is the prolongation of man's corporeity, the structure of the world is vitally related to the structure of the human body; Heidegger describes the world as the realization of *Dasein*'s possibilities; Luijpen's view is that the world is radically human, that the idea of a world-without-man is as meaningless as that of man without a world.

Whatever the differences between these authors, there is no doubt that in their view whatever exists is essentially related to human consciousness. This idea is at the very heart of their philosophies. It is not a principle which they affirm *a priori*, but a truth which they discover experientially.

Let us now consider the next steps in their philosophizing.

These philosophers have a manifest desire to keep in touch with concrete reality. Nevertheless, their phenomenological analyses remain too abstract and too distant: they describe man in general, and the world as related to man in general. As a result:

(1) a real duality is maintained between man and the world, in spite of their efforts to link the two inseparably,

(2) the world is described as a *Mitwelt* which belongs to all men in a more or less uniform manner.

From their point of view, let it be noted, duality cannot be eliminated. It is impossible to lay constant stress on the unity of man in general and the world without doing away with the idea of man as a member of a community. On the one hand these philosophers affirm that the world and man are united by a vital link (because they know from experience that they themselves are one with the world), on the other hand they sever this link so that the world of one man may also be the world of other men. Finally, we are left with a world-in-itself which belongs strictly to nobody and which, therefore, is not for consciousness. In this context, there will never be any question of the existence of non-human persons in whom the world subsists before subsisting in men. The reason for this is not that the positing of the existence of such persons could be effected only from a speculative point of view alien to the phenomenological point of view, but that the link between the thinking of these philosophers and living reality is too loose to enable them to grasp all that experience contains.

In this study, I have proceeded quite differently. My first step has been to show that the world is *mine*, and to describe the structure of *my world*. Neither at the starting-point of this reflective undertaking, nor at its conclusion, have I posited the principle that all existing reality is for consciousness. From the outset, I had the *experience* of the vital link which united the world to *me*; my whole analysis has developed within this experience. My conclusion is that the world exists as a unified system constituted by my personal act, that every object exists as an element of this system. I affirm this as a fact.

Now, I realize that the world constituted by my personal life-act is not the whole universe; I realize that the objects of the world, while pertaining to the system formed by my personal act incarnate, belong also to other systems; I realize that the meaning which things have in me is, to a large extent, derived from a wealth of meaning which they have outside me, before me; I realize that, while "creating" my world, while giving existence and meaning to things, I am conditioned, possessed, generated, by transcendent "forces" which are constitutive of the world-without-me, which are in things independently of me. Thus I discover *in me* the presence of other persons, I discover my existence as essentially related to other personal existences.

These other persons are first of all other human persons, the whole community of men.

But the human world is not the whole cosmos. I experience myself, I experience the human world, as inhabited by a *presence* which is older than man. I affirm this presence to be a personal presence because the consideration of my existence and, in me, of human existence, allows me to discover this as a fact (a fact which cannot be brought to light by any "speculative principle").

Exception may be taken to the use I make of the word "experience". Experience always means *my* experience: the self-revealing of my personal act incarnate. When my act reflects intensely upon itself, it experiences vividly facts which it does not notice in everyday life.

b. *It is not the "body" of the "Evolving Absolute"*

According to some philosophers, the Absolute is the substratum of the universe, all worldly objects and events are its modifications, and each human person is a concrete appearance, an embodiment of the Divine Spirit.

There is a great deal of loose thinking in these speculations about the One existing as Many and about the Many manifesting the One, in these mystico-philosophical doctrines according to which man's *summum bonum* is the dissolution of his limited personality in the nameless and limitless Absolute, in these pantheistic explanations of the world and of evolution.

From our earlier analyses the following points have emerged:

(1) While constituting its expressive field (my world) and actuating itself, my personal act is conditioned by itself-already-realized and, through itself-already-realized, by the world-already-constituted. This world-already-constituted is the human world into which I find myself continually thrown: more fundamentally still, it is a *sphere of personal life* anterior to, encompassing, supporting, the human world.

(2) I am not a self-creative being. In my very existence as a personal, self-determined act-world, I experience myself as created. I am the product of a Transcendent Creative Initiative, I am the work of a *Creator*.

It must be clearly understood that these are two *radically distinct* facts. The Creator and the pre-human personal universe are by no means the same "reality". Indeed:

(1) I am conditioned, energized, inspired, generated, by the pre-human personal universe, but I am not *constituted* by it. However much older than me it may be, however much greater, I, as a personal, self-determined hypostasis, am transcendent to it. In other words, its action upon me is essentially intramundane.

(2) In my very being as a personal, self-determined hypostasis—that is, to the very extent that I am transcendent to all other personal acts-worlds—I am dependent on the Creator. The Creator, therefore, is *absolutely* transcendent to any cosmic being: he is the Supramundane, Absolute Act.

From this it is clear that it is nonsense to consider the Absolute as the substratum of the Cosmos, and each person as a manifestation of the Absolute. The Absolute is in no way involved in any cosmic process (this will become clearer still in our next chapter). Therefore, we shall not say that the intentions which are *constitutive* of things as parts of the pre-human world are partial expressions of the Great Intention constitutive of the whole; we shall not say that things and events—in their ante-human status—are evolutions of the Great Cosmic Spirit; we shall not even say that the finalities of pre-human worldly realities are immediate expressions of the Creative Will—and this because the Creator is not a cosmic agent who makes the world exist as the variegated expression of his self-realizing endeavour.

c. ***It is a world of finite persons.***

We shall affirm that the world-before-man exists by, in, and for *created personal acts* which unfold themselves from cosmic centres different from our earthly centres; we shall affirm that things, qua constituted by pre-human intentions—that is, to the extent that they exist without us as meaningful realities—are essentially parts of living systems formed by the self-unfolding of personal acts distinct from, older than, our human life-acts. Thus the world-before-man is already a "consortium" of mutually involved acts-worlds. A close scrutiny of our experience, of reality living in us, establishes this beyond doubt.

We shall now examine the nature of these pre-human, or supra-human, persons and the way in which we are related to them.

3. The Cosmic Persons

This study of the pre-human acts-worlds will not show me what the cosmic persons are in themselves—that is, in their own individualities; it will not even make me encounter experientially any particular one of them (as daily life brings me face to face with this or that particular human person). The reason for this is that the cosmic persons do not belong to the earthly community (i.e., to the system formed by the earth-centred acts-worlds); therefore I cannot meet them *bodily*, I cannot penetrate into them as I penetrate into a person whose physical presence, whose actions, gestures, speech, are lived by me as manifestations of his inner being. I shall, however, be able to know something about the cosmic persons. They are in a real way present and living in me; therefore, my understanding of my own existence will give me a certain understanding of their existence; I shall distinguish experientially—by reflecting on the totality of my personal structure—something of their mode of being.

This knowledge will remain an approximation. I shall not grasp their existence as transcendent to my existence; I shall grasp it as immanent in my own existence; I shall grasp it analogically, interpretively, conatively.

Will this knowledge be of a speculative type?

Maybe—but it will not be "above" my experiential knowledge: it will develop entirely *within* my integral experience.

The world came to existence "one day". It was created *from the beginning* as a personal world, that is to say, as a plurality of mutually involved acts-worlds. Let me explain this.

M is, by supposition, a primitive act-world. As a finite created act-world, he is centred "somewhere". This must be so: if he had no centre of expression, he would exist intensely "everywhere"; he would then be pure act without limitation. The fact that M is a finite personal act-world implies that he exists first and foremost in a definite centre of expression.

There is something more. As a created person, M—however powerful—"finds" himself *already there*—in other words, he is continually conditioned by the modalities of the existential field in which he expresses himself, i.e., by himself-already-existing-in-the-form-of-a-world. The implication of this is that, in the very process of constituting the world as the concretion of himself, M is, so to speak, generated by the structures to which he gives existence—in other words, he receives life from one or several other acts-worlds. Therefore M is, from the very beginning, created as a cosmic person vitally related to one or several other cosmic persons co-created. The universe existed from the first as a "system" of interrelated personal acts-worlds.

This does not mean (and it is important to appreciate this) that the primitive universe was a community of persons similar to our earthly community. Our human community, we know, is the presonalization of the universe to the extent that the universe exists as a system centred on the earth. Now the earth does not form a single personal centre: it is divided into an ever increasing number of interrelated centres which, together, constitute a single community: the human community. This community, as has been explained, could not have appeared at the very beginning of the world: its formation presupposed centuries of preparation during which organisms capable of becoming human had to be gradually developed. This means that the primitive cosmic persons could not have been built on the human pattern: the expressive centre of each original act-world had to be a single cosmic centre built on a unique pattern (in accordance with the unique personality of the life-act created in it, unfolding itself from it). Therefore the primitive universe was a "consortium" of *specifically* distinct persons; it was a system of interrelated acts-worlds unfolding themselves *from different cosmic centres.*

From these facts a number of conclusions may be drawn:

(1) The cosmic persons are much more powerful (i.e., much more perfectly personal, much more creative, much more self-transparent

and luminous) than we. This is clear from the fact that each of them, as he posits himself, constitutes a unique cosmic nucleus as the first expression of himself and concentrates in this nucleus all the potentialities which are latent in his "type" of personal being. From an extrinsic point of view, this may be expressed as follows: the cosmic centres in which the cosmic life-acts are created and from which they unfold themselves are so structured that each one of them can be personal without being divided (which is not true of the earth).

(2) It follows from this that the cosmic persons have no bodies similar to our bodies. Through our bodies, we are inserted in the earthly community. My body is myself as member of the human family. But the cosmic persons are not members of a "local" community; each of them is the totality of his existential sphere.

How then are their expressive centres structured?

This is a question which it is hardly possible for us to answer. No doubt, we can in some way experience the presence of the cosmic persons in our field of existence, but we have no direct awareness of the manner in which they are constituted. We can only say that the structure of their expressive nuclei is such that it enables a high degree of concentration.

Even this, however, is a most unsatisfactory way of expressing it. It is not *because* the cosmic centres of expression are of a hyperactive type that each one of them may be fully possessed and animated by a single cosmic life-act; it is *because* powerful cosmic personal acts are created in them that they exist as hyperactive cosmic centres.

(3) Is there "intelligent" life outside the earth?

This is a question which is continually being asked. To answer it, scientists try to find out whether the conditions prevailing upon earth—conditions which are required for the proliferation of human life—can exist and do exist somewhere else.

At the root of this enquiry, there are a number of erroneous presuppositions:

(a) It is wrongly assumed that life is a phenomenon localized in "organic substances" and absent from what is called "inorganic matter". This assumption is a product of the geometrical mentality which divides the world into zones which exist in themselves, and are thus ontologically distinct from one another, and hardly communicate with each other. In fact—this is by now quite clear to us—everything exists in persons: only persons exist in themselves. Each person is a life-act unfolding itself from an expressive centre and constituting the whole world as the concretion of itself, of its self-actuating endeavour. Therefore life is present everywhere, it is the substance of everything. My life is not merely the life of my body, it is immanent in all the objects which surround me, it animates my environment, my whole world. In the light of this we can see that the life which manifests itself in "organic substances" is not a self-contained reality, that it is a particular crystallization of the vital flux which springs from personal centres—a vital flux which is immanent in and constitutive of every object even though it expresses itself in an especially significant way in organic substances.

(b) It is wrongly assumed that all "intelligent life" is necessarily built on the pattern of human life, and that the greatest part of the universe is hostile to any form of life.

We must completely change our mental outlook. Earthly life is not the prototype of life in general but, phenomenally speaking, the condensation and also the weakening of vital flows issuing from other more powerful centres. The "physical conditions" prevailing in these centres are the expression of the dynamism, strength, and luminosity of the personal acts which come into existence in them. If these conditions do not exist and could not exist in human personal centres, it is because the latter, *as the first expressions of the human life-acts which are created in them*, are necessarily of a more static and more opaque nature. The ardour of the cosmic centres consumes our centres not because it destroys all life, but because it is made of a life much more intense than our weak human life.

(4) Is the existence of the cosmic persons temporal, as are our human existences?

At first sight, it would seem that they are: the universe in which we live is essentially a temporal reality, and therefore whatever is part of it must be "in time".

A closer examination of facts will show us the meaninglessness of this proposition. In the course of my study, I have pointed out that time is the movement, the very substance, of our human existences. My existence—and the existence of my world—is temporal in so far as I am a personal life-act centred "somewhere on earth" and conditioned by the specific setting in which it is incarnate. Thus the movement of the earth around the sun (the succession of months, seasons, years), the rotation of the earth (the succession of days and nights), my inclusion in the earthly community through membership in a family, a nation, the situation of my body, etc., are part and parcel of my concrete temporality. My existence "in time", the temporality of my world, are unthinkable without these elements. In general, the universe as a temporal reality is essentially the universe existing as a personal system concretely centred in various interrelated earthly nuclei—in one word, it is essentially the human universe.

Quite different from our human temporal existence is the existence of a personal act-world whose centre is a specifically unique cosmic centre. This act-world is no doubt continually tending towards its full self-realization and, in this process, continually taking up and actualizing itself-already-realized; but the rhythm of this movement, the way in which it is structured, cannot be assimilated to the modalities of our temporal existence measured by our astronomical, physical, biological, social, situation. In order to progress towards my end, I have to work with my hands, my feet, my whole body, to transform my surroundings and express myself in them, to make my way painfully through earthly obstacles and overcome them. Through this mastery of my earthly abode, I build and conquer my world, and I realize my destiny. Throughout this life-long struggle, I must continually submit myself to the conditions imposed upon me by my existential setting. I must work during the day and rest at night; I must adapt my way of acting to the climate of the country in which I live, to the various seasons of the year, etc. All these factors are modalities of my existence as a temporal process, of my time-made psychological make-up.

For a cosmic person who is originally the totality of a cosmic centre, there is no question of building the world and realizing himself by affirming himself first of all in a restricted environment. A cosmic person does not work with hands and feet and other organs proper to an individual who "occupies" a particular place in a particular world; his milieu is from the first a cosmic setting; his action, like a wave-like self-unfolding movement, has a decisively cosmic efficacy. Throughout this self-realizing, world-constituting activity, the cosmic person is no doubt conditioned by the modalities of his existential field (by himself-already-realized, the world-already-constituted), but this determinism is not to be compared with the contingency of our earthly existence. The development of his vital endeavour, even if it takes place according to a certain rhythm, is not measured by years, seasons, months, days, hours, because these temporal units are essentially relative to earthly centres. It is the breadth of his existential milieu, the reach of his action, the manner in which his life field is structured, which fix the modalities of the movement by which a cosmic person tends towards his ultimate realization. (From this it follows that each cosmic person has a unique rhythm of existence, a unique "psychology".)

Another point must be carefully noted. It is essential for me as a human person that I should have been born on one particular day and that my earthly life should be constantly oriented towards death. This reality is at the very core of my time-existence, of my existence as a member of the earthly community. There is no such thing in the existence of a cosmic person. No doubt, I may say—anthropomorphically—that he came into being "one day" (what is a "day" for him?), but his existence is not an existence-towards-death because his life-act is not centred in and conditioned by an organism which grows old and is subject to decay. Thus a cosmic person, however intensely living he may be, has no life which may be compared to what I call "my life". Fear—provoked by the inevitability of an absolutely decisive event—does not pervade the movement by which he realizes his destiny. In one word, his existence is not a time-process because it is not the existence of a "viator".

(5) There is undoubtedly a great difference between our knowledge of things and that of a cosmic person.

I am created as a personal life-act constituting the world from a particular earthly centre; "things" are created *in me* as variegated concretions of the self-unfolding movement of my act. My knowledge of the world is nothing but the self-transparency of my act incarnate within its existential setting. I know things as they exist in me and for me; I know them from the point of view of my body; I know them according to my individuality, according to my particular status in the human community, in the world of persons. Papaias dangling on umbrella-like trees, sun-hardened Bengal clay, wood-peckers climbing on mango trunks, dry coconuts falling heavily into the pond, moon shining in the cloudless sky, breeze blowing across the fields, Darjeeling mist-clad mountains, earthquake in Chile, dark spots on the sun, all exist in me humanly, earthily, in my own unique way, all tell me what I am, speaking the language of my body, of my situation, of my relations, of my world, of the universe-in-me—my own unique language.

(Is this not pure "relativism"?

Relativism, it is, undoubtedly. I assert that things as I know them are always and necessarily things-for-me, things-in-me, things as related to me. But this relativism is not a closed and sterile subjectivism which paves the way to scepticism and destroys knowledge. My understanding of things-in-me is a real understanding of things-in-others, because my world is an expression, an individuation, of the whole created reality. Authentic self-knowledge gives me a knowledge of all.)

M (a particular cosmic person) is created as a personal life-act constituting the world from a cosmic centre other than the earth; "things" are created *in him* as variegated expressions of the self-unfolding movement of his act. His knowledge of the world is nothing but the self-transparency of his act within its existential setting. M knows things as they exist in him and for him; he knows them from the point of view of his cosmic situation, according to his individuality, and to his relationship to other cosmic persons and to human persons.

Let us be quite clear about what this implies. M does not "live" and know things as I do because he has no body like mine, because he is not a member of the earthly community: he does not constitute his field of existence as the variegated expression of a human experience, of a human temporal accretion, of human needs, human fears, human feelings, human concerns, human aspirations, human projects—of a human life. This frog jumping across the path in front of me is not for him what it is for me, it does not live for him as it lives for me; this canal to be crossed on a bamboo bridge is not for him what my body, what my emotivity, what my present activity, what my life intention, makes it be for me. They are for him, in him, altogether different realities, parts of a different life system, expressions of a different style of existence, they exist for him in a totally different world setting. M's personal act comes into existence in a unique cosmic centre and affirms itself from the first as a cosmic power. His understanding has breadth, he fills everything with light.

(It should not be concluded from this that our knowledge is false whereas the knowledge of a cosmic person is true. As far as it goes, our knowledge—our science—is true, but it is *essentially human*, ordained towards the building of the human world. This knowledge is aware of its limitations: we know that there is in things much more substance, much more purpose, much more light and consciousness that we put into them.)

In this context, we can see that the intentions which are in things as parts of the pre-human world are not and cannot be in their original sphere what they become once they are taken up by our personal acts and luminously realized in our human undertakings. In their original sphere, these intentions exist as parts of cosmic life projects; once they are integrated in us, they exist humanly. The operation by which we make them ours is an interpreting process, a humanizing process, a re-creating process, the laws of which are the very articulations of our earthly existence.

In this light let us revise what we said at the beginning of this chapter.

When I make use of my lamp to dispel the darkness and enable me to carry on my work, I make mine and fulfil pre-human intentions which form the very "substance" of my lamp. This must not be taken to mean that the finalities, or serviceabilities, revealed by the copper and zinc of which my lamp is made, by the paraffin with which its tank is filled, exist in the pre-human sphere exactly as I see them. Lived and discovered by me, these intentions are human intentions, human life—my intentions, my life. In their original sphere, they are modalities of cosmic life systems, expressions of cosmic personal projects—something quite different. Therefore I shall not imagine that my lamp, the substances of which my lamp is made, exist pre-humanly as *this* lamp, *these* substances; they exist pre-humanly in a way commensurate to the dynamism, luminosity, sweep, of the cosmic personal life-acts.

From this we may see that the unveiling and realizing by science and technology of the "natural" structure and destination of things is not the mere bringing to light and actuating of a well-determined "towards-which" which exists in things independently of us, but the interpreting and re-creating on the human scale, according to human laws of acting and living, according to human needs and projects, of the dynamic *esse* which belongs to things as parts of the pre-human sphere.

4. The Cosmic Persons and the Earth

We shall now study the relationship between the cosmic persons and the human world.

The world of science is a physico-biological nature in which phenomena are ruled by stable laws. This nature, it is said, is the realm of blind determinism. There is in it no freedom, there is no place in it for any free agent.

From what we have seen before, it is clear that the world of science is an entirely human entity—it exists by, in, and for the human personal acts, it has no independent being. This means that human freedom cannot be absent from it. In fact, this world, far from excluding freedom, implies it, nay more, is *constituted* by it. Indeed, it is *constituted* by personal acts taking luminous possession of themselves, it is, therefore, an embodiment of man's transcendence. From this, it must be concluded that the determinism which characterizes the world of natural sciences is an expression of freedom rather than the negation of it.

How should this be understood?

I assert that, given a certain number of conditions, the phenomenon A will take place. This truth is for me a principle of knowledge and a directive for action. I discover and posit it in this way: In the process of constituting the world, my act realizes that, when it finds itself modulated in this or that way in its expressive field, or when it induces this or that modulation of its expressive field, a further definite variation of this field takes place in a constant manner. This unveiling by my act of some particular modalities of its incarnate existence is a reflective operation through which my act takes luminous possession of itself. I express this operation in the form of a law. This law stands as an embodiment of my reflective power, of my freedom. Further, I let my action be guided by this law (which does not exist outside the exercise of my freedom). My action is self-determined and self-determining; the modification of my expressive field which this action induces is the concretion of this personal initiative, the living manifestation of my transcendence. Thus the world of science—a world of phenomena "ruled" by laws—exists by, in, and for the self-determined and self-determining movement of my personal act incarnate; it *is* my act taking up luminously, re-creating, personalizing, in a certain way, the field of its incarnation, the structures by which it finds itself conditioned.

It may be objected that laws exist independently of my reflectiveness and freedom, since the phenomena which they explain and "rule" take place independently of the act by which I bring them to light (they take place even when I am asleep, even when I do not think of them at all).

I answer, first, that anything which takes place in my world is an earthly event, and has, therefore, a human exponent; it is a modulation of my act incarnate, and in a real way an expression of my freedom. But this is still not the point. The fact that phenomena do take place in my existential sphere in a determined way does not imply that the laws by which I "explain" these phenomena exist before I posit them in the form of "objective" entities which "rule" nature.[1] The fact that my effort to understand phenomena takes naturally the form of a law-positing activity does not imply that the laws which I formulate exist in nature in the form of ontological principles (laws are not ontological principles but instruments of knowledge). The occurrence in my life-field of *determined* phenomena which I do not personally induce points to the two following facts:

(1) My freedom, though real, is radically limited. I determine myself, I build the world by continually taking up, repersonalizing, recreating myself-already-determined, the world-already-constituted (two expressions of the same reality). Thus my law-positing activity, though essentially free, is never purely autonomous. It realizes itself as free activity; it perfects itself in a climate of dependence and obedience.

(2) The world-already-constituted (qua pre-human world), to the extent that it is an "organized" system, is a life-field constituted by cosmic personal acts which are in process of determining themselves. This world, once taken up, inventoried, illuminated—"*scientifically*"—by my human, earth-centred personal act, becomes a nature "ruled" by physico-biological laws. In itself, it is much more than this: it is a personal sphere which no set of laws can express adequately.

From this we see how mistaken is the view according to which there are in the world two kinds of determinacy: the determinacy of physico-biological events due to the existence of "objective" laws, the determinacy of human actions and decisions rooted in freedom. In fact, there is in the universe no determination which is not fundamentally constituted by and expressive of the self-determining endeavours of free personal acts.

[1] By describing the world of nature as a system ruled by "objective" physico-biological laws, intellectualism, once more, puts the cart before the horse. It assumes that our ideas and mental conceptions are the essence of things instead of acknowledging that living reality is prior to and much richer than any knowledge we have of it.

(Let us remember, in this context, that the cosmic personal acts are created acts. This means that they are not purely self-positing and self-determining hypostases. They limit and, to a certain extent, determine each other, while depending ontologically on, and therefore being radically determined by, the Creator. Thus there is in things a fundamental determinacy—their substantial *esse*—which comes not from any created agent but from the Transcendent. This does not mean that things exist fundamentally in themselves before existing in created persons. M *is created* as a cosmic personal act constituting the world from a cosmic centre. Things *are created in it* as expressions of its centrifugal, self-actuating movement. I *am created* as a human personal act constituting the world from an earthly centre. Things *are created in me* as expressions of the centrifugal, self-actuating movement of my act. Thus the fundamental determinacy of things—their substantial *esse*—is concretely identical with the *actus essendi*, the "being-towards" of the created acts-worlds. It is by realizing and determining themselves according to the will of the Creator that created persons fulfil the fundamental "towards-which" of things. This "towards-which" is nothing apart from the "being-towards" of the personal acts in which the world is created. We shall treat this more fully in the next chapter.)

These considerations bring to light the relationship between the earth and the pre-human sphere. It is a relationship of persons to persons. As human personal acts-worlds, as free, self-determined hypostases, we find ourselves linked to cosmic persons by a vital bond which we cannot break without destroying our existence. Our human liberties are, in their very essence, conditioned by trans-human liberties; they are not only limited by these liberties, but also internally fashioned by them. We cannot act in a truly self-determined, authentically human way without carrying out deliberately pre-human intentions; we cannot build the human world without taking up and making ours the building activity of the cosmic persons, without studying and adopting—*humanly*—their ways of building; in short, we cannot lead human existences without allowing pre-human existences to reflect and perfect themselves in us.

Our common view of the world must be radically transformed. Things are not opaque and static realities; they are instinct with personal presence, personal life, constituted by intentions proceeding from personal centres; they are full of consciousness and light.

They are media through which we are in communication with a preterhuman world (just as they are channels through which we communicate with one another). This communication is a constant process. Through all the parts of our world, we continually receive life, movement, inspiration, from the cosmic persons. The world-already-constituted, by which our world-building activity is constantly conditioned, which our self-realizing endeavour constantly re-creates, is to a very great extent the world-existing-by-and-in-the-cosmic-personal-acts.

Not only the objects which surround us, but also our bodies are possessed, moved, fed, by the cosmic personal acts. The cosmic persons are truly present at the heart of all our perceptions, impulsions, feelings, desires, imaginations, thoughts, decisions. Whatever constitutes our concrete nature—our biological make-up, the various "determinisms" which subtend and condition our personal life, the various forces which we experience in ourselves, which drive us to action, which sometimes hinder our efforts, paralyse us or carry us away, the various psychological states in which we find ourselves—all this is not simply the active persistence of our past in our present, or the active presence-in-us of the living community of which we are members, but is to a very large extent the individuation in us of the living streams which proceed from the cosmic personal centres. In short, our bodies-already-constituted (i.e., the centres to which our worlds-already-constituted refer), which our personal acts continually take up and re-animate while positing and expressing themselves, are to a great extent our bodies-existing-by-and-in-the-cosmic-personal-acts.

Our bodies, it is true, do not exist in us and by us in the way in which they exist in the cosmic personal acts. They exist in each of those in a way conformable to its fundamental dynamism, as a part, a modality of its specific world. They do not exist in them humanly, but angelically, or demoniacally. "Once" they are taken up and animated by our personal acts, they exist in us not only in a human way, but also in a way conformable to our respective individualities. My body-animated-by-my-life-act *is* this unique reality which I call "myself".

From this we can see the very important role which the cosmic persons play in our human existence. We are continually in their sphere of action, under their influence. They feed our bodies, our faculties and, in a true sense, fashion them. We need them in order to lead our human life. Our world is their creation to the extent that the earth depends on the rest of the universe in order to be what it is and to evolve as it should. They are those cosmic "forces" which, from the confines of space, conspire to build the earth and to humanize it.

It does not follow from this that the cosmic persons are the creative sources from which our human life-acts draw their being and their fundamental dynamism. Whatever their role in our lives, however powerful their influence upon us, we are not at their mercy, but remain truly the masters of our lives. In fact, while we are conditioned and driven to action by them, it is in the last resort by ourselves alone that we are moved. Let me make this point clear.

From the centre in which it first expresses itself, my personal act unfolds itself. It constitutes my body, my environment, my whole world, as the concretion of this self-realizing movement. While thus positing itself and tending towards its end, my act is continually conditioned by itself-already-posited and, *through itself-already-posited*, by the world-already-constituted. Now, my body and my world already constituted are to a great extent my body and my world constituted by cosmic personal acts. Thus it is *through the mediation of my act-already-realized* that cosmic persons move me. The cosmic-persons-conditioning-my-personal-act-unfolding-itself are the cosmic-persons-identified-with-my-personal-act-already-unfolded. This is why the way in which they act upon me, the way in which I am influenced by them, is always conformable to my individuality—that is, to my unique manner of being, of facing the world, of tending towards my end. Fundamentally, it is my personal-act-realizing-itself-in-its-unique-manner which constitutes the cosmic-persons-influencing-me.

As we know, the fact that my personal act, while determining itself, is itself already determined, the fact that, while constituting the world, it is conditioned by the world-already-constituted, is identically the fact of my ontological dependence on a Creative Source. This fact indicates that the cosmic persons, in spite of their all-pervasive dynamism, are unable to force themselves into us and to reduce us to mere variations of their existential field. Our personal acts, in spite of their native weakness, cannot be subjugated by any other created power.

So far, I have shown how our personal life-acts are influenced, conditioned, by the cosmic persons. To conclude this chapter, I shall indicate briefly how cosmic personal acts, while unfolding themselves from their centres, while constituting their worlds, while influencing us, are themselves conditioned by us. Indeed, as they posit themselves and "create" their worlds, they find themselves determined by themselves-already-posited, by the world-already-constituted. Now, in relation to each of them, the world-already-constituted is the world-constituted-by-other-personal-acts; it is to a certain extent the *world-constituted-by-our-human-life-acts*. Thus, *to the extent that we are transcendental life-acts*, we contribute to the shaping of the cosmic acts-worlds, we have them under our influence.

It is not *humanly*, of course, that the cosmic personal acts are themselves conditioned by us. It is *through their acts-already-posited* that they are influenced by the world-already-constituted—in other words, it is we-assumed-in-them, we-identified-with-them, who determine them: we do not condition them in our own earthly way, but angelically, or demoniacally.

CHAPTER VIII

The Creative Presence

The universe is not an immense receptacle "containing" persons (among many other things), like a box containing jewels which are and remain "distinct" from their container. The universe *is*—and was from the beginning—a system of interrelated acts-worlds.

The demonstration of this truth is a refutation of materialism. According to materialistic philosophers, the universe, in its original form, was matter alone. By its own internal dynamism, matter generated life and, finally, in man, became self-conscious. This view, we know, makes no sense at all: the notion of the universe as a purely physical or biological system, and the notion of man as a mere product of evolution, are absurdities. In reality, spirit is first: from the beginning, the universe existed by and in personal acts. It is within the movement by which these acts-worlds tended towards their perfect realization that the earth has evolved, that the human world has come to existence and developed.

Now, in spite of this fact, in spite of the fact that the various personal acts are vitally interdependent, it cannot be maintained that we draw from each other our existence as persons. Throughout this study, it has become increasingly clear that as transcendental life-acts, as personal beings, we receive life from a Transcendent Creative Source.

I am at work in my room, conscious of the presence about me of many other persons to whom I am vitally related. Together with these persons, I *constitute* this world in which we live: we make it exist as a human world. Nevertheless, my act does not experience itself as a pure creative act positing itself and the world in a perfectly spontaneous, independent way. The fact is that, at this moment, in the very process of giving existence to my world, I find myself already living in it; I am "there" before I take any personal initiative: *my act is given to itself in the very process by which it gives itself a world.* I can express this experience in these words: I, personal act, am simultaneously act-intention and life-act.

Now the fact that, in the very act of constituting the world, I experience myself as constituted is not simply the fact that I am vitally dependent upon other persons. It is precisely *as transcendent to them*, as transcending the structures in which I am incarnate, that I experience myself as created, given to myself and given to the others. This experience reveals to me a *Creative Presence which constitutes me as person*, which gives me my personal existence and, therefore, gives existence to the world, a Creative Presence *which constitutes us as a community of interrelated acts-worlds.*

This Creative Presence is a Personal Presence—indeed, the unique Source of all personal existence and of all life: the Act by which it communicates itself creates us as living persons—our existence as personal acts-worlds is entirely and continually derived from it.

This fact has very great significance. Not long ago, we were still identifying personality with our human way of being persons. This was unavoidable. We have now, however, realized that our true, definitive personality is still something to be won: we begin life in a state of utter powerlessness and have to be raised from childhood to manhood; we arrive at self-consciousness only to discover that we have to realize ourselves through daily painful labour and struggle, and that our aim will not be realized on earth; we live for a Beyond in which our human existence, our human personality, will attain its full stature. This tensional character of our life is linked with all the other aspects of our personality: our incarnation—that is, the dependence of our act on the spatio-temporal structures in which it expresses itself—our "localization", our insertion in the community (different ways of expressing the same reality). All these facts point to the fundamental imperfection of our human existence. There is in us a want which will never be completely filled, for, even after death, whatever be our mode of existing, we shall remain a community of persons vitally related to one another, limiting each other. Therefore our human way of being persons is essentially defective; to attain the full stature of manhood is still to remain a finite person.

In the preceding chapter, we discovered the existence of cosmic persons. This discovery has forced us to broaden our "concept" of personality. To be a man is but a weak and defective way of being a person. There are "in the universe" personal acts which surpass us in perfection and power. Before we came into existence, the world existed in them; from the beginning of time, it was constituted by them. However, to the extent that they are *cosmic* beings, centred "somewhere", these personal acts remain finite beings, dependent on one another and limiting each other.

This limitation of created personality is, of course, relative to the One who is the Source of all personal existence, the One who, though creating all persons distinct from each other, binds them together in an immense unified system. This Being is not a cosmic being: he is absolutely transcendent to all created persons, and therefore absolutely transcendent to the universe; he is not centred "somewhere" and, therefore, exists "everywhere", intensely, with the fullness of his creative power.

He is God, the Perfect, Infinite Person.

This is a truth that calls for a profound examination. There are many thinkers and religious people who deny the personal character of the Absolute. They do so because in their minds the very notion of person (somebody to whom we can talk and pray, who "listens" to us and loves us) entails a kind of internal multiformity (*namarupa*), an imperfection incompatible with the very notion of Absolute. The Absolute, so they say, is supra-personal; he makes himself personal in relation to the devotees, in the deities through which he manifests himself, and in which, therefore, he becomes an object of worship. In himself, however, he remains above them, pure undifferentiated Being without personal attributes. True religion, therefore, must go beyond the devotional stage and arrive at the realization of our identity with the Absolute, or the dissolution of our personality in the Absolute.

This belief, however exalted, is based on an erroneous assumption. It has become clear to us that impersonality may only mean absence of being, and that to grow in perfection is to become more and more personalized. Taking this principle to its logical conclusion, the Absolute Being will be the Infinite Person, the Unique Source of all personal existence.

I. GOD

We must try, so far as we can, to discover something of God's own way of existing.

I can know another man in so far as there is community of life between him and me—that is, to the extent that he communicates himself to me and becomes a part of my own life. This knowledge is really positive and may, at times, become very intimate. Moreover, this knowledge is connatural to me. As a human person, I am open to the world and, so to speak, spreading myself in it. This impetus carries me towards other persons and throws me among them. I experience them as the very complement of my own life; they are there before me, in me, sharing with me the same universe. However, in spite of this communion, other persons remain essentially distinct from me, and their own interiority therefore always escapes me.

I cannot hope to meet God in the same way as I meet my fellow-men. The prospective look which I direct upon the world does not reveal to me his presence as it reveals to me the presence of other human persons (though something more will have to be said about this matter). Quite naturally, I let myself be involved in these human relations and feel tempted to make of them the whole of my life. It is by reflecting on the fact of my existence (on my essential "facticity") that I have discovered myself as created. It is by a regressive movement opposed to the natural movement of my life that I have discovered the Source of my existence, the Creator of the universe. Therefore my knowledge of God cannot have the same immediacy as my knowledge of my fellow-men. I do not meet God as an equal, as one among those who share with me the possession of the earth, as one who discusses worldly matters with me. I meet him in silent meditation as the Hidden One from whom my existence flows.

Nevertheless, to the extent that he communicates himself to me in the very act by which he makes me exist, to the extent that my life is derived from him, and is thus a reflection of his own life, I catch a glimpse of his own mode of existing. This knowledge, of course, will remain extremely imperfect because there is hardly any proportion between my limited being and his infinitude .If, already, the interiority of my fellow-men is not accessible to me, how much more will God's own internal life remain veiled to me. Even so, my knowledge of God will not remain merely negative; it will have some positive content, chiefly because of the aspiration it will contain and express.

I am an act incarnate—that is, living in community with other acts incarnate. In so far as I am act, I am myself—a personal being; in so far as I am incarnate, my personality is limited.

God, who is One, is also perfectly personal: he is Pure Act, without any limitation whatsoever.

Though my personal act is both life-act and act-intention, there is no absolute identity between these two aspects. As life-act, my act is given to itself in the very process of constituting the world. As act-intention, my act realizes itself consciously and freely, is master of its own destiny, self-determined, creating its world.

In God, there is no such distinction. Because he is One and perfectly personal, he is also pure self-determination, pure creativeness, never given to himself, but always giving himself to himself with perfect consciousness and spontaneity: he is plenitude of personal life.

As a being incarnate, I find myself situated in my body and acting from this centre within a certain environment more or less effectively. My act has to realize itself through particular decisions and actions; my consciousness is always focused on some particular point; it is never purely universal. I always look at the world from my restricted standpoint.

God has no standpoint. He is present everywhere in a fully actual manner; his presence is not diffusion, but intensity and concentration. His consciousness is absolutely universal, not by spreading over all things uniformly but by creating them all in the perfect simplicity of one Act. God fills every place on earth with his presence and acts everywhere with unrestricted efficacy. God is in me, infinitely more real, more present, more active, more alive than myself. Nevertheless, God is nowhere contained; he is not in space, he does not act here and there; he simply IS, and everything subsists in him—in himself as himself—though in me as myself.

As a member of a community, I am continually dependent on my fellow-men, I receive life from them. In everything I do, I am determined by my body and my environment. My act is at every moment conditioned by the modalities in which it expresses itself; I have no sooner created something than I become a prisoner of my work; I must continually tear myself away from what I produce in order to remain free and maintain some real impetus.

God is one, not one among many. He does not depend on anybody else. God has no body, no environment, determining his course of action; he acts with pure self-determination. God is never tied by what he creates; he is never the prisoner of what he does; he remains perfectly independent, the Supreme Master of his work.

My life is a time process, a genesis. My act totalizes in itself the whole of history, very imperfectly. It takes up the whole in its own way and continually projects itself into a future which it already contains in itself as a potentiality, an aspiration. In this movement of self-realization, my act is continually dependent on the whole past which it takes up; it is with the substance of the past that it must build the future. This dependence is not absolute. As a free person, I control my life and the course of history, I *am* history progressing towards its fulfilment in a self-determined way. However, because my act is incarnate, its autonomy is limited; even my most spontaneous initiatives are still to a great extent imposed upon me by the very fact that they somehow emerge from the temporal current by which my act is carried.

In God, there is no trace of determinism. He is not in a state of genesis, because he is pure self-realizing Act. God has no past—he has never been less than he is now; God has no future—he will never be more than he is. God is pure self-constituting Present; in him, the totality of the past and the whole future are perfectly realized in the absolute simplicity of One Act. From my earthly standpoint, I say that God began "one day" to create the world, that "day by day" he keeps the world in existence, and will "in the future" bring it to fulfilment; I say that God was "yesterday", that he is "today", that he will be "tomorrow". These are human ways of speaking which are unavoidable. They try in their own awkward way to express God's ineffable mode of being. But for God there is no "one day", "day by day", "yesterday", "today", or "tomorrow", no past and no future, but only the present, a pure, infinitely rich, intensely luminous NOW, plenitude of bliss, eternal and all-consuming Presence.

God's knowledge of the past and the future is not like a very perfect human knowledge. God is not a Great Historian (any more than he is a Great Mathematician, or a Great Physicist . . .), but the Author of history. He knows the whole past and the whole future in the very Act by which he creates them, not progressively, but NOW. What is for us, in us, a genesis, a time process, is in him Pure Act, a perfectly realized Present.

How is this possible?

If the whole past and the whole future are in God Pure Present, must I not conclude that my present also contains the whole time to come in a definite way and, therefore, that history is perfectly and definitely realized in me?

The answer to the second question is without doubt that, if this is so, I am not an act incarnate but Pure Act: there is in me no past and no future, no genesis and no history; there is simply an all-totalizing NOW, and this NOW is myself.

This is surely not supported by experience (if I were God, the answer would be obvious). No consideration relating to God's own Being and Acting can make me deny my condition and the existence of my world, since these are the very ground from which I raise myself in order to form some idea of God, and since the idea I form is always relative to this human standpoint. The only valid conclusion to which my reflection can lead me is: God, whom I discover as Pure Act, Pure NOW, is the Source from which the world of my experience draws its being; he alone, the Supreme Person, gives existence and meaning to this world and to my life. Now, if I dismiss experience and say: God, the Creator, is Pure Act, Pure NOW; therefore the world-in-me is also Pure Act, I make a completely absurd and illegitimate assertion. It is evident that, in affirming such a thing, I assume that my knowledge of God is so perfect that, from the idea I form of his mode of being and acting, I can draw any conclusion which seems to me implied in it. By doing so, I simply deny the essentially relative and limited nature of my knowledge and refuse to be tied to my situation in the world, the very standpoint from which I discovered God and continue to discover him. I may not understand too well how the world, which is for me and in me a temporal reality, may be in God and for God Pure Act, but I should not therefore deny existence to the world of my experience, since that world is the only reality of which I have adequate and immediate knowledge and is the very ground from which I can catch a glimpse of the Creator. It is enough for me to realize *that I do not have to understand.* The world-in-God-and-for-God is far beyond my grasp and must remain for ever hidden to me: it is God's own secret. This World is the foundation of my world: but how it is, is the mystery of creation before which I must bow in awe and adoration. I know for certain that my world is what it is precisely because God is what he is and acts as he acts in his own ineffable manner. This may be faith that goes beyond understanding. I can accept that—but at least I understand clearly that to make this act of faith is for me the only *reasonable* attitude.

Thus we have discovered God, the Creator, as both absolutely transcendent to the world and intensely immanent in it.

(1) God is transcendent because he is the Supreme Person in whom there is no limitation whatsoever, no unrealized potency—whereas our universe is a community of limited persons who are trying painfully to realize themselves.

In this connection, we must avoid considering God's omnipotence as a kind of potency—saying, for instance, that, in creating this world, God has actuated one of the potentialities latent in him, and that the number of these potentialities remains infinite. We must say that God is so perfectly self-determined that the act by which he posits something is always the act by which he posits himself as perfectly identical with himself. Therefore there is never any potentiality in God which remains non-actuated. The act by which the world is created is identically this Pure Act. It is the universe, as it springs from the hands of the Creator, which contains innumerable worlds in potency. This pregnancy of the thing created points to the perfect actualness of the Creator.

(2) God is immanent because he is everywhere present in his work, not in a spatial—that is, a diffuse, imperfect—way, but with pure actualness, self-identity, in a perfectly concentrated way.

These two attributes of God—transcendence and immanence—must not be conceived as two different aspects of God. In fact, God is transcendent to us by the very intensity of his immanence. He is more present in me than myself, more myself than myself. In so far as he is in me, he is immanent; but the very intensity of this presence makes him infinitely transcendent to me: he is present as Pure Act, whereas I am a mere act incarnate.

II. THE WORLD IN RELATION TO GOD

Having raised our minds to God, the Creator of the universe, and having tried to discover something of his transcendent mode of being, we must now look again at the world of persons and contemplate it in its relation to God. We shall thus be able to understand better the modalities of the movement by which the universe progresses towards its full realization, and to discover the deeper meaning of our life and of history.

A. Preliminary Considerations

1. The End towards which We Tend

When we studied the problem of time, we first realized that the present is the only temporal reality which actually exists. At that stage of our study, we had not yet discovered our insertion in the community; consequently, the present of which we then became aware was essentially "my present": the world as it exists today in relation to my body—that is, integrated in my activity, living by my life. While this perspective still remains true, we now realize that it must be broadened. The present is not merely the world-now-in-me, but also the world-now-in-A, the world-now-in-B, the world-now-in-C . . ., in short, the human community as it exists today within the universe actually constituted by the cosmic personal acts. No doubt, this totality, to the degree to which *I* live it, experience it, know it, is integrated in my life: it is my world; nevertheless, I am aware of a transcendent presence which surrounds and pervades me at all times, I am aware that the world is much more than my world (this awareness is a constitutive element of my experience, of my personal life) and, consequently, that the present is much more than my present: it is *my* present, but it is also *their* present.

This total present—which I always contemplate from the point of view of my present—may be considered from various angles. Looking at it from one particular angle, I call it the political world of today; from another angle, the economic world; from a third angle, the religious world. . . . There is the world-of-science-today, the world-of-art-today, the world-of-philosophy-today. . . . Each of these worlds is the whole universe, the total present, considered under a certain aspect. This total present owes its existence to the Creative Presence which pervades it, yet remains absolutely identical with itself, undivided, and non-extended. This present, as we said, is the only temporal reality which exists—in other words, the world exists only as present; whatever is, is actually created by God, a participation in his eternal NOW.

The total present, however, is not meant for itself, it is not a complete reality. The present is essentially oriented towards a future in which it will become fully itself; it has a real meaning to the extent that it already pre-contains this future. My knowledge of this fact is grounded in the experience I have of my present and of my life as a whole. What I do now is not an end in itself, its meaning is not simply today: it is tomorrow, it is the great Tomorrow, the Beyond in which my life will attain its fulfilment, in which my present will be definitively realized, in which the world-in-me will achieve its supreme consummation. But my present is essentially a part of the total present, my world a part of the great world of persons, my life a part of history as a whole. Therefore what I do now is not simply meant to prepare what I shall be Tomorrow, what the world will be in me Tomorrow; it is meant to prepare what the whole universe will be Tomorrow, to prepare the ultimate world, the eschatological community.

Can we determine what that end will be?

My life is the movement by which the world-in-me tends towards its supreme goal; my personal act is the act-of-the-world-in-tension-towards-the-end. The world-in-me wants to perfect itself, to become the reality of which it is the prefigurement; it wants to overcome its present limitations and reach something definitive.

To understand the nature of this final realization, let us analyse the movement of our life. The situation from which I start is the "natural" world, the world constituted by my life-act. This world, as it is given to me, is not a virgin land, an untamed jungle. It has been built by the cosmic persons; it has been cleared and cultivated by all the generations of men which succeeded each other before I came into existence; it is already intensely humanized. Now, I have to take up this world and to carry on the process: I have to integrate it—the whole of it—in my daily preoccupations, I have to build it more fully, to personalize and spiritualize it more and more. To this end, I open myself wide to the world—the movement of my life is essentially centrifugal; I try to grasp the universe in my consciousness, to live it in its totality, to coincide with its inner dynamism, to make it intensely, deliberately mine. In this effort of totalization, I am continually bent on transcending my spatio-temporal limitations, but this liberation cannot be achieved without a radical change in the structure of the human world; therefore *the world-in-me aspires to a new creation which will both transform and perfect it.*

This whole movement of the world-in-me must be understood in essential relation to God: the Creative Act is its Transcendent Source and gives it its direction. God, as we know, is the Transcendent Person from whom every personal act receives its existence. Therefore to exist is for me to be from God, to be related to God, to be in God—*as Creative Presence God is the plenitude of my present.*

All the other persons on whom I depend, to whom I am vitally related, also proceed from God. The very Act by which they are created unites them with me and, thus, shapes me through them. Now, this relationship I have with God through the other members of the community is identically my dependence on the whole past: God shaping-me-through-the-other-persons is God-actualizing-in-me-the-whole-of-history. Therefore, *as Creative Presence, God is, in the present, the plenitude of my past;* God is the *Alpha.*

But the whole past-in-me, the world-in-me, is essentially ordained towards its consummation in the future. In the very Act by which he creates me, God urges me ahead; he creates my act as an insatiable will in tension towards a Beyond. This Beyond is the ultimate realization (or personalization) of the world-in-me. Now, to be a person is "to wear God's own image and likeness", to participate in God's own manner of existing. The more intensely, the more perfectly personal I shall be, the closer I shall be to God. Therefore *God is, in the present, the plenitude of my future*—that is, the pole of all my aspirations, the fulfilment of history. God is the *Omega.*

(Let us note carefully that, in our movement towards the future, we are not tending towards identification with God, towards absorption of our personality in the Absolute. Our realization as individual persons cannot be the loss of our identity; it is the supreme discovery of it through the actuation of our relation to God. The closer I am to him, the more I shall find myself.)

To this, we must add that the universe-in-tension-towards-the-end wants to realize itself as a world-of-persons. All the members of this personal system, progressing towards their final goal, build and personalize the world together. In this common enterprise, they are vitally united, dependent upon each other, helping each other. Each person, while realizing himself, actuates his union with all the others: he receives more and more from them, and gives more and more to them. In this process, he in no way tends to absorb the other persons into himself; on the contrary, he promotes them as persons: the more he unites himself with them, the more also he realizes himself as person and contributes towards shaping their personalities. The ultimate universe will be a community of persons eminently distinct from each other *because* supremely united with one another.

Again, this movement of unification must be understood in essential relation to God. He is the One who creates persons distinct from one another, binds them together, and promotes their unity while exalting each of them in particular. For each person, self-realization means actuation of his relation to God, finding himself by "finding" God. In fact, the proximity of each person to God and the union of all persons among themselves are one and the same reality. The former is the foundation of the latter: there can be no real nearness to God without a deep union with all men and with the cosmic persons. The latter cannot, however, be effected authentically without the former: authentic union with men and with the cosmic persons brings us closer to God.

2. The Fact of Sin

To understand the concrete modalities of the movement by which the various acts-worlds realize themselves, it is not enough to indicate the end for which the persons are created. A very important fact which affects in some manner every created reality must now be considered—namely, the fact of sin. Without a deep understanding of this fact, there can be no understanding of the "evolution" of the world, of history, of any cosmic happening.

The universe is created by God as a totality ordained towards an end. This means that the whole cosmos is constituted by an intention; to realize itself harmoniously, to attain its full development, it must fulfil this intention.

The universe is essentially a plurality of interdependent personal acts-worlds. Therefore the finality of the universe expresses itself concretely in the form of vitally interrelated personal destinies: each person *is* a particularization of the intention constitutive of the whole.

This fact is clear. Let us look at it from our human point of view. I am a personal life-act constituting the world from a particular earthly centre. I am "surrounded" by other human persons, my existence is linked with their existences. We help, influence, promote each other; together, we work "on earth", or rather, we "work" the earth; we prepare each other's future.

This living-together is ordained towards a goal. As we have just pointed out, while struggling on earth, we build the community of Tomorrow, we determine what we and all the other members of the human family are to be in the world to come. This future world, to be an authentic realization of the present world, will have to be a community whose members are supremely close to God while intensely united with one another. This indicates that the progress of the human world towards the future, in order to be an authentic personalizing movement, *must* be of a definite type, that it *must* be effected in a definite direction. The foundation of this necessity is in the Act which, while creating the world, gives it an impetus, a finality, which impresses on it the pattern of its ideal mode of being.

My personal-act-in-tension-towards-an-end is a particular and unique individuation of the intention constitutive of the world; to realize itself in an authentic way, it *must* fulfil this intention in its own appointed way. As a life-act endowed with consciousness and freedom, it does so in a self-determined way: I live the various situations in which I find myself, I organize my field of existence, I actuate myself, *in accordance with the Creative Will operative in me*. In doing so, I lead the whole community towards its authentic realization.

Let us now consider how this is achieved in practice.

While constituting my world as the concretion of its self-realizing endeavour, my personal act, by the very fact that it occupies the expressive field in which the other personal acts unfold themselves, carries the latter in its own impetus. Influenced by me in this way, other persons tend to adapt the movement of their own existences to that of my existence. While taking up in themselves the vital stream which proceeds from my personal centre, they feel themselves carried in the direction in which this stream flows. This fact can make itself apparent in a very concrete way. As I tend towards my end in my own way, I make my body, the things I use, my environment, into concretions of my intention, into prefigurements of the end which I have in view. Thus I charge them with meanings which are nothing but dynamic reflections of my life purpose; I give them a driving force commensurate in intensity and value with the determination of my will. With regard to the other persons who penetrate into my sphere of existence, the fact of seeing me gesticulating, acting, of hearing me speak, of reading what I write, of using for their own purposes the objects I fill with my own presence—in short, the fact of living with me, in me, of being under my influence—acts as a determining power which drives them in the direction in which I go.

Now it cannot be denied that, as a personal act endowed with self-determination, as an act-world whose potentialities are largely unactuated, I have the "power" to deviate from what I know to be the way of authentic self-realization, the power to refuse obedience to the Creator and, therefore, to refuse help to my fellow-men; I have the power to actuate myself and, therefore, to actuate the world in a wrong direction, i.e., in an inauthentic way—the more so in that authentic self-realization (in conformity with the Creative Will) implies a continual self-transcendence, and is therefore a strenuous process. When I thus fail to conform to the intention by which I am constituted as God's creature, I make my body and the objects of my world into forces which prompt the other members of the community to turn aside from the way of righteousness, which lead them towards an inauthentic mode of self-realization.

Let us go one step further. It is evident that a great number of human persons fail to actuate themselves in an authentic manner, to live the various situations in which they find themselves, as prefigurements of the end for which they are created; they do not build their world in accordance with the Divine Will. We live, in consequence, in a world in which evil is rampant. Its presence is, no doubt, manifest in many things which we see around us, in many occurrences and circumstances (in the political, economic, social, cultural spheres), in many customs, fashions, productions, etc . . ., but in a more general way, it must be affirmed that in every single object of the world—in our very bodies—there is a human presence which lures us, which pulls us downwards, which hinders our efforts towards authentic self-realization. This must be so, because the whole world—especially the earth—is the field in which every member of the human community—whether he leads an authentic or an inauthentic human existence—expresses his purposes and his various interests. It follows from this that the progress of our personal acts towards their ends takes place among many obstacles, in an atmosphere of struggle, failure, and tension, and that human history is by no means a smooth progression revealing a unity of meaning but an adventure in which conflicting tendencies, ups and downs, and false starts abound (even though its movement is in fact ordained towards a glorious fulfilment).

Nevertheless, human sinfulness, however great, is not at the root of all evil. There are in the world many harmful things which are not simply the embodiment of the perversity of human wills. The concept of "physical evil" is commonly used to designate these harmful phenomena. They are of very many types: harmful events taking place in "nature" (earthquakes, floods, droughts, avalanches, periods of excessive heat or excessive cold, destructive storms, etc. . . .), harmful places, substances, and environments, harmful events of a "biological" type (epidemics, diseases, etc. . . .), harmful plants and animals, harmful defects in our organisms, harmful physio-logico-psychological processes which we experience in ourselves. In a general way, there seems to be, throughout "nature", a hostility towards us which is ready to manifest itself at any time in some way or other.

(We should note that it is entirely in relation to us—that is, in so far as they affect us—that these phenomena exist as "evils". A storm on the planet Mars is not an evil, neither are viruses present on it harmful creatures; conversely, most phenomena which are harmful to us are not likely to be evils in relation to Martians. In other words, phenomena cannot be harmful to us unless they have a concrete meaning for our human, earth-centred existences, unless they *are*, in a full sense, human realities.)

The notion of "physical evil"—as opposed to that of "moral evil"—implies that the phenomena to which it refers are due to the action of "natural causes" subject to physical or biological determinism—not to the intervention of human liberties or, for that, of any created liberty. These natural causes are found in the "material world"—that is, in a universe existing *in itself* as an infrapersonal physico-biological system.

This philosophical view is a rationalization of scientific observations. Studying the various phenomena which are harmful to men, science tries to make out their structure, to establish their connection with other phenomena, to determine the laws of their appearance and behaviour. This is, we know, an analysis of a purely descriptive type; its concern is not with the ontological status of the facts which it studies, but with their observable characteristics and liaisons.

What we have just said holds good in this context:

(1) Science does not deal here with realities-in-themselves, but with modifications, peculiarities, of our life-field (this harmful occurrence which I study in a "scientific" manner is nothing but a particular evolution of my act-world; as I study it, it takes place entirely within *my* existential sphere). The explanations which science gives are descriptions in human terms of an order of phenomena which are entirely made up of human life, which are, thus, constituted by our human life-acts (my scientific explanation of this harmful occurrence is my personal-act-illuminating-in-a-particular-way-some-particular-conditions-of-its-incarnation, it is a particular self-revealing of my life-act incarnate—it does not deal with any reality existing independently of me, in a world-in-itself).

(2) However, the whole scientific investigation of harmful phenomena contains an implicit reference to a pre-human world with which our human world is vitally linked.

To what kind of pre-human world?

Harmful phenomena appear to us as realities constituted by hostile intentions; the dynamism which animates them reveals itself—in relation to us—as a destructive energy; we live and experience these phenomena as obstacles on our way, as efforts to weaken our will and lead us to ruin. This is no doubt a human outlook, yet the fact is that in making them exist as such, we *are* conditioned by some pre-human evil-doing: the operation by which we fill them with hostile intentions is the taking up, the interpreting, by our human life-acts of their original teleology (i.e., of the intentions by which they are constituted as evolutions of the pre-human sphere).

Thus:

(1) Among the cosmic persons who form the pre-human world, a certain number are evil powers, rebellious creatures whose will is a will of destruction, whose presence and action fill the universe with maleficence, and make the objects in the world into obstacles on our way towards our authentic self-realization.

(2) The traditional distinction between "moral evil" and "physical evil" must be abandoned. There is, in the world, no evil which does not proceed from, which is not expressive of the perversity of created personal wills. Sinfulness, either human or pre-human, is the reality which engenders, constitutes, all the harmful forces, harmful substances, harmful processes which are present in the world.

(3) We must go back to the fundamental intuitions of "primitive thought" which have been veiled by centuries of intellectualistic theorizing. There is no worldly happening which is simply the effect of a "natural cause", no "natural force" which presents itself as a mere third-person process. Whatever we see and experience in the world, and in ourselves, is but a sign which points to a mysterious reality which we do not see, but can make out and, to a certain extent, feel after an effort of careful penetration into the heart of things.

One point, in particular, is relevant in this connection. Several passages in the Gospels tell us how Christ delivered persons afflicted by "evil spirits". Nowadays exegetes and doctors tell us that many of these people described as "possessed" by the evangelists were in fact suffering from some nervous or mental disorders. These scholars argue as follows: The "possessed" of the Gospel were *either* persons tormented by the devil *or* sick people. Those in the first category were sound in body but inhabited by a satanic presence; those in the second category were not under the devil's influence but suffering from such diseases as epilepsy, schizophrenia, hysteria. These diseases were the self-sufficient *causes* of their derangements.

This reasoning is based on erroneous assumptions. First, the notion of a disease as something capable in itself and by itself of *causing* a malfunctioning is a product of the geometrical mentality. Secondly, the radical distinction made between diabolical possession and disease is untenable. In fact, there is no satanic possession which does not express itself in some organic way[1], and there is no organic malformation which is not in some way the manifestation of a diabolical presence.[2] This is why such disorders may sometimes be cured by efficacious exorcisms, and at other times by appropriate medical treatment. A modification of the expressive make-up in which the evil powers manifest themselves naturally effects a change in their mode of presence. This is why science and human efforts can do much to check malignant influences and undo the harm that has been done (not only in the "biological" sphere but also in the "physical" sphere, not only on the individual scale but also on the social scale).

The following points should be appreciated:

(1) Our discovery of the prehuman or transhuman world does not in any way decrease the value or limit the scope of genuine scientific research. Men must go on investigating the whole sphere of phenomena, they must go on studying the structure of things, the connections between the various elements of the phenomenal field, between the various experiential levels. This activity is meaningful and has an indispensable part to play: there can be no harmonious human progress without science because the world-already-constituted is the stuff with which, the ground on which, the world-to-come has to be luminously built.

[1] The devil by whom I am tormented is the devil-taken-up-in-my-own-life-structure; thus, in the last analysis, it is myself. But my personal act always exists as an act-incarnate—that is, as an act spatialized, as an organism. Therefore my personal-act-tormenting-itself must always be expressed in some organic manner.

[2] As it unfolds itself and constitutes my body and my world, my personal act is conditioned by itself-already-incarnate and, through itself-already-incarnate, by other human life-acts, by cosmic personal acts. Thus, considered from a particular angle, organic malformations are ways in which other human acts and, especially, cosmic personal acts, possess me, operate in me, live in me.

In particular, for the reasons just indicated, men must go on studying scientifically the whole range of harmful phenomena. Men have the power and the freedom required to counteract evil influences. *As it is constituted*, the world is the expressive field of the cosmic powers. This world is integrated in us, taken up by our life-acts, humanized. We must find out humanly—scientifically—what modifications of the phenomenal field have to be effected in order to repair the damage.

(2) Scientific investigation cannot discover the real nature of the forces at work in the world. *The question of the "within" of things is not and cannot be a scientific question.* To retain its validity, scientific research must remain a descriptive investigation of phenomena and of the connections between phenomena. It is both unscientific and philosophically unsound to attribute a metaphysical value to the conclusions of science. It is only from the point of view of our integral experience that we can discover the reality which underlies phenomena and can give a metaphysical interpretation to the picture of the universe drawn by science.

What we have said about prehuman sinfulness and its relation to our human world must not lead us to think that there is any place, any substance, any event—in one word, any force—on earth, in our bodies, which relates us only to a transhuman diabolical presence. Every phenomenon which we observe, to the extent that, while being part and parcel of our human world, it is also the medium through which a transhuman presence conditions or inhabits us, is the expressive field of both the "docile" and the rebellious cosmic persons. Therefore there is no force on earth, no worldly happening, which is altogether harmful (any more than there is any worldly reality which is altogether beneficial). At the heart of each event, of each phenomenon, there are both a presence which tries to lift us and a force which tends to abase us, to drive us away. From this it follows that our human lives take place at the heart of a cosmic struggle—a struggle in which our final destinies are at stake.

There is another reason why no worldly happening can be "by itself" altogether harmful to us. As a free person, I have the power to re-create into something new whatever penetrates into the sphere of my existence, whatever I integrate in the movement of my life. Thus I can give a new meaning, a new value, to circumstances which are intended to destroy me; I can live them as expressions of my faith, of my desire, of my love, and I can therefore make of them modalities of the movement by which I tend towards God. This is ultimately the only way I can eliminate from them whatever is harmful to me.

B. The Genesis and the Progress of the Universe

Having determined the end towards which we tend and indicated the interplay of influences in which this movement takes place, we may now contemplate the universe in its relationship to the Creator.

Two points have been established:

(1) The appearance of man on earth did not take place at the very beginning of the world. It was very gradually prepared during many centuries.

(2) The universe has always been a world of persons (the notion of a world existing in itself as a mere "physical" system is an absurdity).

Let us now raise our minds to the Creator.

God is Pure Act, pure Self-determination. In this respect, I have pointed out that God's omnipotence should not be defined as an almost pure potency. We should not say, for instance, that God is almighty because there is in him an infinite number of possibilities which he could actuate but freely refrains from actuating. We must say that God is so powerful, so perfectly actual, that the Act by which he produces something is identically the Act by which he communicates himself entirely: God's pro-ject is always the fullness of God (otherwise there would remain in God unactuated potentialities, and God would not be Pure Act).

It is within this "movement" of God's life that we must contemplate the universe and understand its finality:

(1) The Act by which God *communicates* the fullness of himself is the Act by which the world came into existence, the Act from which the world proceeds, the Act by which the present lives now as the realization of the whole past. God-*communicating*-himself is, in the present, the fullness of the past—he is the *Alpha*.

(2) The Act by which God communicates *the fullness of himself* is the Act by which God gives to the world of persons a finality. God-fully-communicated is the Pole towards which the persons tend, he is the fullness of the future—the *Omega*.

From this we can obtain some slight idea, at least, of how the acts by which, in the present, the created persons pro-ject their past (i.e., themselves) into the future, by which they posit and realize themselves, are participations in God's pure Self-Communication, pure Self-Pro-ject, Pure Act: our time-life is a contingent partaking, a pale reflection of Pure Life.

The universe was created as a system of interrelated acts-worlds. In the early stage of its existence, it was very different from what it is now. The rich interplay of influences, meanings, intentions, which we observe in it today was lacking. (This is evident, since every meaningful process is an actuation—that is, the realization—of a potentiality.)

What does this imply?

Every determination comes into existence in the movement by which the personal acts which constitute the universe actuate themselves, "determine" themselves. If the primordial universe was lacking in determination, it follows:

(1) that the personal acts which constituted it were still largely undetermined;

(2) that all the personal acts which constitute it today did not then exist.

From this we may conclude that, at the beginning, the universe was made of a very limited number of cosmic acts-worlds (were there more than two?). But these acts-worlds could never have been *purely* undetermined. To the extent that they were *acts*, they must have been from the first characterized by an elementary determinacy. Pure undeterminacy means pure non-actualness, pure unrealness, pure absence of being—therefore it means nothing. Thus the primordial personal acts must have received with their existence whatever specification enabled them to be. How shall we conceive this elementary determination? We shall soon give an answer to this question. Whatever it must have been, we can be certain that there was in the primitive cosmic personal acts a world of unrealized possibilities. "In itself", this wide potentiality of the primordial acts-worlds must not be considered as a "perfection" ("in itself", it is only a state of want) but as a mere correlative of God's pure actualness: it indicates that God's infinite perfection, God's pure self-communication, the "movement" of God's inner life could be shared by the created personal acts in an endless variety of ways. In this respect, we can understand that the self-actuating concretely effected by the personal acts (starting from their primitive state)—because it became more and more definite, because it reflected in a more and more determinate way God's infinite perfection—was self-limiting. It was not a limitation with regard to the primitive universe considered "in itself"—in this respect, it was only a perfecting—but with regard to God's unlimited "participability" to which the primitive universe was related in a very general and largely undetermined way: the direction taken by the personal acts in determining themselves, as it became more and more definite, became also *a more and more particular way of expressing God's infinite perfection.*

The primitive cosmic personal acts were no sooner created than they began to actuate themselves, to shape the world. This self-actuating, to be authentic, had to be effected in a given direction. Indeed, from the very beginning, the universe was ordained towards a certain end, it had a finality—concretely: from the very beginning each primitive cosmic person had a destiny which he had to realize in order to realize himself authentically—that is, in order to reach the fullness of his own existence (this is why we can assert that, from the very beginning, there was in the cosmic personal acts a certain amount of determinacy). This means that for each primitive person, from the very beginning, authentic self-actuating, authentic self-realizing, was identically self-submitting, personal, acknowledgment and acceptance of the Creative Will.

Can we distinguish the direction in which the primitive cosmic persons had to actuate themselves in order to realize their destiny?

In a broad way, yes. The primitive cosmic acts had to personalize themselves by personalizing the universe; they had to raise themselves to closer intimacy with God by bringing to him other created persons. To do this, they had first to develop within their own worlds conditions that favoured the appearance of new personal acts—in other words, they had to elaborate structural ensembles suitable for becoming new personal centres. Thus the striving of the primitive persons after their ultimate realization was inseparable from a cosmic mission to be fulfilled.

Now, as we know, a split occurred among the cosmic persons. Some of them, rebelling against the Creator, began to actuate themselves in an inauthentic way; they opposed the Divine Will and refused to carry out their cosmic mission. Thus they became evil powers hostile to God and to the other created persons, and self-destructive. The presence of these disruptive forces obliged the obedient cosmic persons to convert their self-actuating endeavour into a constant struggle: in fulfilling their appointed task they had continually to react against hostile influences which tried to destroy what they were building. This explains why the progress of the universe towards its ultimate realization has been and still is a slow and laborious process. We must accept this fact if we wish to understand what is at the heart of "evolution" and of history.

Let us now study the way in which the universe has progressed and continues to progress in spite of the presence in it of powerful antagonistic forces. In doing so, we shall emphasize the positive endeavour carried on by the obedient personal acts and refer briefly to the obstacles encountered.

The mission of the primitive cosmic persons was a personalizing mission. From what has been said above, we can surmise that, in their self-realizing, world-building, activity, they first developed structural ensembles suitable for becoming the expressive centres of new cosmic personal acts. They did not, of course, *give existence* to these new acts—a person receives his act of existing from God alone—but, in the light emanating from the Creative Source, they "prepared the ground" for their coming into being. This does not conflict with what we said earlier. I have explained that the appearance of man "on earth" *had* to be preceded by many centuries during which organisms "capable" of becoming human were gradually fashioned. Thus, I said, the persons in whom the universe was originally created could not have been "built" on the human pattern; each of them must have been a cosmic personal act unfolding itself from a unique cosmic centre. This, of course, does not imply that *all* the cosmic persons had to come into existence "at the same time". As they actuated themselves, the primitive persons, no doubt, brought about cosmic conditions favourable to the appearance of other cosmic personal acts. These new cosmic persons, as well as those who preceded them, worked together to prepare (or hinder) the coming of man.

We may now consider how the humanization of the earth has taken place—continues to take place. The central idea which we immediately come up against is that of evolution. From the strictly scientific point of view, this notion cannot be more than descriptive. According to the scientist, from what can be observed in the world, it appears that, in the course of centuries, there has been on earth a movement upwards from inorganic matter to organic matter, from vegetative life to animal life, from animal life to human life. In so far as he can, the scientist shows how his ascent was effected; he indicates the various ramifications of the "tree of life" and the various directions in which the movement has taken place. It is not the task of the scientist, as scientist, to tell us the profound meaning of the facts which he describes—that is, to give us a metaphysical interpretation of the whole process.

The facts which the scientist brings to light provide the philosopher with rich food for speculation. The usual process will be a direct transposition of the concept of evolution from the scientific plane to the transphenomenal plane. On this plane, the contention is that the world has existed first of all as a pure physical system, that from matter life has arisen, has spread, and has raised itself to a higher and higher level, that finally man has come into existence as the crowning of the whole evolutive process. Some philosophers "explain" this process without referring it to any Creative Source. In their view, it is by its own internal dynamism that the universe has evolved, and has "produced" man. Other philosophers see in it the development of a Creative Intention: it is the Creative Act continually at work which has raised the world from its primitive darkness and infused into it life and consciousness. Whatever their differences, these two philosophical trends agree on one point: both admit that the universe has, for many centuries, existed *in itself* as a mere physico-biological system.

In his *The Phenomenon of Man*[3], Pierre Teilhard de Chardin gives us an impressive vision of evolution in its totality. In the preface to this study, he warns us that his work does not pretend to be more than a scientific treatise: "it deals with man solely as a phenomenon, but it deals with the whole phenomenon of man". However, Teilhard's book is much more than an ordinary "scientific treatise". This is evident from the fact that the whole line of argument it develops is based on the relation which Teilhard posits between the "without" and the "within" of things. This "within" is a psychical factor; it is characterized as life, consciousness, spontaneity, love: it exists in an obscure and primordial way in the stuff of the primitive universe, in inorganic matter; in a more articulate way in living organisms, especially in animals; in a reflective manner in man. This is, no doubt, a philosophical consideration. Even if direct

[3] Translated from French by Bernard Wall, Collins, London, revised edition, 1965. The French original entitled *Le phénomène humain* was published in 1955, Editions du Seuil, Paris.

observation shows that to each degree of complexity and "centricity" reached by the elements of the universe there corresponds a particular state of development of a certain factor x present in them, the exact nature of this factor x cannot be determined through direct analysis of phenomena; it must be inferred through reflection; it must be intuitively perceived. My philosophical investigation has shown me that it is only from the point of view of our integral experience that the nature of the "within" of things can be ascertained. This investigation has led me to conclusions which enable me to integrate the scientific view of the universe in a broader totality, even though science as such is and must be completely silent about these conclusions. My conclusions show the "within" of the universe to be very different from what Teilhard holds it to be: a psychism present in some way at the heart of each cosmic element. From this it is clear that I can discuss the views of Teilhard as one philosopher discusses the views of another philosopher, but that I must not deal with them as a philosopher should deal with scientific conclusions.[4]

According to Teilhard, the primitive universe was a system from which personal life was absent. However, the elements of this system had already a certain "psychism", a finality; they had, in fact, all the attributes of personal existence *in an obscure, primordial, impersonal way*. This, Teilhard tells us, is because, "in the world, nothing could ever burst forth as final across the different thresholds successively traversed by evolution (however critical they be) which has not already existed in an obscure and primordial way".[5]

Was this "psychism" a unitary principle—that is, a factor pertaining *per primum* to the universe taken as a totality, distributed

[4] In this work, I am trying methodically to express a fundamental experience which embraces the whole of created reality. The perspective of my study is an integral perspective. It is *in it* that I must "place" and appreciate other perspectives. To grasp the meaning and the implications of Teilhard's "phenomenology", I cannot abstract from what appears to me total truth. I must understand Teilhard's position within the totality which reveals itself to me.

Within this totality, the system developed in *The Phenomenon of Man* will reveal many implications which Teilhard did not see. My criticisms will never, therefore, be directed against the personality of Teilhard, or against his personal convictions. Nowhere shall I call in question the integrity of his faith. Were my intention to give a literal account of his thought, or to make a study of his spirituality, it would be very unfair on my part to present his views as I shall do. Overwhelming evidence shows that Teilhard believed firmly in the spirituality of the human soul, in the transcendence of God, in creation. Nobody who knew him would ever think of denying this.

[5] *Op. cit.*, p. 71.

among the "elementary grains" without being divided—or was it first of all a property of each "elementary grain" as distinct from the others? (In the first case, the universe would be a diversified *unity*; in the second case, an aggregation of elements, a unified *plurality*.)

This problem is difficult to solve because Teilhard did not explicitly formulate it. In my opinion, the following answers may be given:

(1) In several passages of Teilhard, the trend is definitely pluralistic. The myriads of elementary grains of consciousness form a "dust of particles", a "disordered multitude"; evolution is a "struggle in the universe between the unified *multiple* and the unorganized *multitude*".[6] Moreover, the way in which the evolutive process (or the "cosmic process of vitalization") takes place seems to imply pluralism: the elementary grains coalesce to form better organized structures in which consciousness reaches a higher degree of concentration. The human organisms with their nervous systems are the summit reached by this synthetizing movement: in them, consciousness has become reflective because, in them, it has reached an eminent degree of concentration (proportionate to the degree of complexity attained by the human nervous systems).

The whole operation, however, is not yet complete. The various grains of thought are in the process of "becoming enclosed in a single thinking envelope so as to form, functionally, no more than a single vast grain of thought on the sidereal scale, the plurality of individual reflections grouping themselves together and reinforcing one another in the act of a single unanimous Reflection".[7] The forming of this supreme synthetic centre is the goal towards which evolution is steadily moving.

As can be seen, throughout this movement, it is always through the coalescence of distinct elements that a higher unity is obtained—in other words, unity is not constitutive of multiplicity, but multiplicity is the principle of unity: the supreme personal centre will be formed by the synthesis of many distinct personal centres.

Again and again, Teilhard tells us that it is simply through a methodical and comprehensive study of phenomena that the whole perspective which he develops has been obtained. In this context, it

[6] *Op. cit.*, p. 61. In the French text, the words "multiple" and "multitude" are not italicized as they are in the English translation, but are capitalized.

[7] *Op. cit.*, pp. 251–2.

seems to me that the movement of his thought can be described in this way.

Central Observation: The presence of a certain factor x (which Teilhard calls life, consciousness, "centricity") is always linked with a great material complexity so that x *appears* as the effect of a synthesis. Beings in which x reaches a high degree of perfection are also characterized by a great internal multiplicity. The movement of the universe is towards the forming of systems characterized by more and more complexity and centricity.

First Implication: If the organizing of elementary particles into unified systems engenders or liberates x, this factor must have been present in some way, from the very beginning, in the particles which formed the primitive universe.

Second Implication: As evolution is the gradual elaboration of more and more complex and unified systems (characterized by a higher and higher degree of x) and as evolution is still continuing, it follows that a supreme cosmic centre synthetizing all particular systems is in process of formation. In this Centre of centres, complexity and unity will reach the highest possible degree.

(2) We may wonder whether Teilhard's view is, fundamentally, as pluralistic as the above seems to imply. He tells us, it is true, that, "considered in its pre-vital state, the *within* of things . . . must not be thought of as forming a continuous film, but as assuming the same granulation as matter itself"[8], yet, when describing the movement of evolution, he often seems to make of life or consciousness a single dynamic principle which, though it realizes and expresses itself through the elaboration of more and more complex organisms, remains undivided throughout. Let me quote a few passages of *The Phenomenon of Man* in which this trend is apparent:

"While capable of supple regulating within organic bodies of the blind movement of molecules, Life seems still to exploit for its creative arrangements the vast reactions which are born fortuitously throughout the world between material currents and animate masses. Life seems to play as cleverly with collectivities and events as with atoms. . . . The impetus of the world, glimpsed in the great drive of consciousness, can only have its ultimate source in some *inner* principle, which alone could explain its irreversible advance towards higher psychisms."[9]

[8] *Op. cit.*, p. 58.
[9] *Op. cit.*, "The Impetus of Life" (*Le ressort de la vie*), p. 149.

"From the biosphere to the species is nothing but an immense ramification of psychism seeking for itself through different forms."[10]

"Above the point of reflection, does the whole interest of evolution shift, passing from Life into a plurality of isolated living beings?

"Nothing of the sort. . . . Until now it was enough to consider in nature a simple vibration on a wide front, the ascent of individual centres of consciousness. What we now have to do is to define and regulate harmoniously an ascent of consciousness (a much more delicate phenomenon). We are dealing with a progress made up of other progresses as lasting as itself; a movement of movements."[11]

"Following each anthropological line, it is the human element (*l'Humain*) that seeks itself and grows." This statement is explained as follows: "We find hundreds or thousands of facets, each expressing at a different angle a reality which seeks itself among a world of groping forms. . . . How is it that we are not more sensitive to the presence of something greater than ourselves moving forward within us and in our midst?"[12]

"Man was born a direct lineal descendant from a total effort of Life."[13]

"The passing wave that we can feel was not formed in ourselves. It comes to us from far away; it set out at the same time as the light from the first stars. It reaches us after creating everything on the way."[14]

"We are discovering that something is developing in the world by means of us, perhaps at our expense."[15]

There is no doubt that the idea conveyed by such passages is no longer that of a dust of particles organizing themselves into more and more complex systems, but that of a unitary factor as old as the world seeking itself—realizing itself—through the elaboration of more and more perfect living forms and, finally, through our personal activities. In other words, the perspective implied here is no longer pluralistic but radically monistic.

Does this antinomy derive simply from a certain inaccuracy of

[10] *Op. cit.*, p. 151.

[11] *Op. cit.*, "The Threshold of Reflection", pp. 173–4.

[12] *Op. cit.*, pp. 177–8. This passage shows us that, even though evolution as hominization is an ascent of consciousness*es*, a movement of movements, it is still the genesis of something which, although present in each one of us, is transcendent to us.

[13] *Op. cit.*, p. 189.

[14] *Op. cit.*, p. 224.

[15] *Op. cit.*, p. 230.

expression in the passages just quoted (and in other similar passages), or does it indicate a more fundamental cleavage in Teilhard's thought?

It is my opinion that, when we think dynamically of the perspective developed in *The Phenomenon of Man*, we are driven towards monism by the very movement of the whole system.

The discovery of the connection between complexity and "consciousness" takes place on the phenomenal plane; it is a fact which, to a certain extent, can be observed (I say "to a certain extent" because, strictly speaking, the "within" of things cannot be the object of a direct perception). From the discovery of this connection, we are led to conclude that, from the very beginning, the factor "consciousness" is present, in some rudimentary manner, in the particles which form the substance of the primitive universe and that evolution is the process by which this factor gradually emerges from the multiplicity in which it is lost; this it is enabled to do through the elementary grains grouping themselves into more complex units.

Either the elementary particles which form the primitive universe are *completely* independent of each other, so that the universe, in its original state, is *pure multiplicity*; or these particles are already dynamically related, so that the primitive universe is in some way a unity.

The second alternative is the only possible one, the only one which makes sense—pure multiplicity is the negation of all intelligibility, it is nothingness. Thus the primitive universe is already *a genuine totality.*

Is this totality formed simply by the co-existence of its elements and by the fact that each element relates itself actively to all the others, so that the unity of the primitive universe is a unity of composition springing from the coming-together of its parts—multiplicity being the "form", the principle of unity; or is this totality something original, so that multiplicity is but the weakening, the differentiation of unity—unity being the "form", the principle of multiplicity?

Again the second alternative is the only one which is really meaningful. This has been established in the first chapter of this study where we have shown that the parts of a system are nothing apart from the totality in which they are included and, therefore, that the unity-meaning of the whole is constitutive of all particular elements. This leads us to the conclusion that the primitive universe is a single wave materialized in an infinite multiplicity of elementary particles, that each particle, to the extent that it is a concretion of the whole wave, is co-extensive with the universe, dynamically related to all the other particles.

This is practically what Teilhard acknowledges. No doubt, he tells us that "atomicity is a common property of the Within and the Without of things", but, a little earlier, he has explained this statement in these terms: "Looked at from *within*, as well as observed from *without*, the stuff of the universe thus tends likewise to be resolved backwardly into a dust of particles that are (i) perfectly alike among themselves (at least if they are observed from a great distance); (ii) each co-extensive with the whole of the cosmic realm; (iii) mysteriously connected among themselves, finally, by a global energy (*par une Energie d'ensemble*)."[16]

The conclusion of this is that a monistic interpretation of the whole evolutive movement is, in the last analysis, the only one which really makes sense. Evolution is not the process by which a multiplicity of elementary grains endowed with a rudimentary psychism organizes itself, and so gives rise to more complex systems with a higher degree of consciousness; it is the movement by which a single psychic wave elaborates more and more perfect expressive ensembles, and so realizes itself in a more and more articulate and luminous way.

When we speak of the "within" what exactly do we mean?

I look at the world around me—my sphere of existence, the expressive field of my personal life-act. In it, I see many "living" forms—that is, organic systems in which there is "life", "consciousness".

As I know this "within", as I make it be for me, it is nothing but my own experience, my own life expressing itself in various ways. These forms, to the extent that they live for me, that they mean something to me, are constituted by my personal life-act; they are modalities of my personal life-field.

But they live also without me. True, as other than me, they are constituted by other personal acts, they pertain to other personal systems. These life-acts other than mine are either human, or prehuman. In each of them these living forms exist in a manner determined by its existential conditioning, by its luminousness, by its fundamental dynamism.

Therefore these forms have no "within" which may be character-

[16] *Op. cit.*, p. 59.

ized as a self-contained "psychism"; they are not independent "grains of consciousness"; they are not constituted by autonomous vital principles. To the extent that they *are*, they are in, by, and for personal life-acts unfolding themselves from various earthly or cosmic centres. This is what my integral experience shows me.

What about the primitive universe? It was not a single impersonal life-wave materialized in numberless elementary particles. The notion of consciousness—as well as those of spontaneity (i.e., self-determination) and love—as a reality existing *in itself* in an indeterminate manner, independently of any definite person to whom it belongs, is totally meaningless. (This point must be emphasized because in much philosophical writing this notion is used without discernment and without a real intuition of the reality which it is meant to express.) If, from the very beginning, the "with-in" of things was life, consciousness, freedom, then, from the very beginning, the universe existed in a personal way. This is precisely the conclusion to which a careful study of reality leads us. The primitive universe was a system formed by cosmic personal acts unfolding themselves from cosmic centres and expressing themselves in various elementary ways; therefore, from the very beginning, all things existed by, in, and for personal acts. The life, consciousness, freedom, which were in them were not due to the presence in them of some indeterminate, ill-defined spiritual energy, but to their inherence in personal acts-worlds. The true perspective is neither that of monism, nor that of atomistic pluralism—but that of personal pluralism.

This personal system is the sphere within which we must try to understand the meaning of evolution.

But has there ever been an "evolution"?

(1) Science tells us that ages ago there were on earth no "living" organisms; that, in the course of millions of years, vegetable life and animal life appeared, first in a rudimentary form, and then gradually in more developed and more sophisticated forms. Science tells us that animal life developed in many directions, assuming an incredible variety of forms; it tells us that the appearance of man was seemingly the term of a particular evolutive process. In all these assertions, science, faithful to itself, simply tells us what it observes; it does not make any pronouncement about the *in-itself* of the facts which it enumerates (saying, for instance, that the universe existed first as a pure physical system, that, subsequently, it developed into a physico-

biological reality . . .), but indicates an order of phenomena. This means that the scientific notion of evolution is, as such, without any ontological connotation; it is essentially a descriptive notion based on direct observation—in other words, what science tells us does not, as such, enable us to know *what* has taken place throughout the ages and continues to take place today; it does not make us see what is at the heart of the whole process.

(2) The various philosophical doctrines which describe the movement of the universe as an ascent from matter to life, and from life to consciousness, cannot be accepted as genuine explanations of the evolutive process—they are uncritical transpositions of scientific views to the ontological plane. Evolution understood as the self-development of the physico-biological universe is not only a non-reality, it is an impossibility. "Impersonal" realities do not and cannot exist *in themselves*, they do not and cannot tend *by themselves* towards definite goals. The dynamism and finality which we put in things are and can only be expressions of our own vital endeavour, of our own teleology. Things exist in us, by us, and for us. This is our fundamental discovery.

(3) Our integral experience enables us to understand in some way what is at the heart of the whole movement of the universe. The primitive cosmic persons have a destiny to realize, a cosmic mission to fulfil. Their self-realizing endeavours are the "noumenon" which subtends the whole "phenomenon" of evolution; better still, this noumenon is the struggle which opposes the obedient persons to the rebellious ones—this is why, no doubt, the whole process does not appear simple and homogeneous; everything does not reveal the same purposiveness; there is aberrance, obscurity, waste; significant gains always appear as victories over countless obstacles.

This "noumenon" can never be grasped *in itself*. We cannot know anything unless we live it first as an aspect, a modality, a dimension, of our own sphere of existence—that is, unless we humanize it, give it an earthly shape and colour, integrate it into our individual life structures. But, *in itself*, the noumenon of evolution is not of an earthly nature, it is not a human but a transhuman reality. Therefore the cosmic processes do not exist in the sphere in which they are activated in the way in which we observe them in our own sphere of life.

It is very important to grasp this point. I suppose for a while that a community of microbe-like intelligent beings is living in my body.

Each microscopic process taking place in me, each tiny element of my organic tissues is "experientalized" by them in a manner proportionate to their existential conditioning, to their needs and projects; their science is a microbial science, their technology a microbial technology—everything exists for them "microbially". These intelligent microbes perhaps think that the "things" they perceive in my body are objects-in-themselves, independent "substances"; perhaps they set up a system of "objective laws" to "explain" the phenomena taking place in my organism; they probably do not guess that, without them, the world in which they live is already a personal system in which things exist in a way very different from that in which they make them exist.

We live in a human world, we see it with human eyes, explain all worldly phenomena in a human way, we build up a human science, a human technology. Let us realize, let us admit at least—even though we do not *see* it—that all things, before being parts of our existential sphere, before existing humanly, are modalities of transhuman personal systems in which they exist transhumanly. What exactly is their transhuman mode of being? What exactly is the "noumenon" of evolution? How is "nature" alive in the cosmic persons? There is no adequate *human* answer to these questions.

But we can understand something: our knowledge will be authentic to the extent to which the cosmic personal acts really express themselves in us.

The task of the primitive cosmic personal acts was to personalize themselves further by personalizing the world—they had to bring about the humanization of the earth and to help men to realize their destinies. Some of them, as we know, submitting themselves to the Creator, strove to fulfil their mission. Others, refusing obedience, tried only to further their own ends. This struggle is co-extensive with the whole evolutive process, it fills the entire creation.

Science tells us that, at an early age, the earth was only inorganic matter. This state of things must be understood as an expression of the degree of self-development, of self-realization, reached by the cosmic personal acts at that moment of their progress towards their ultimate goal (as the scribbling of a child learning to write is the expression of the degree of human development which he has attained). As time passes, new phenomena appear. These are never entirely new creations, they are new developments, intensifications, of what was already present at an earlier stage. These new phenomena have not been "engendered" by the old any more than the handwriting of the adolescent (A) has been "engendered" by the scribbling of the child (B). In the same way as the "continuity" between A and B is constituted by the permanence of the act in which they inhere, which they express, so also the "continuity" between the new phenomena brought about by evolution and the old phenomena is due to the subsistent character of the cosmic acts in which both the old and the new belong, to the persistence in the new phenomena of the intentions which constituted the old phenomena. Just as the superiority of A in relation to B is but an expression of the human progress made as the child grew into an adolescent, so also the progress that can be seen in the realm of phenomena points to the self-actuation which the cosmic persons have effected within themselves. Everything appears as though it were going "by itself", as though it were moving itself; in fact, everything is moved by the cosmic personal acts from their expressive centres, everything moves in them.

In the course of centuries, many animal forms have appeared on earth. It is not possible to determine the meaning of each of them in the whole process. The whole process, as we know, is not a rectilinear movement but a struggle, an interplay of conflicting tendencies in which the leading elements have continually to regroup themselves in order to surmount the disruptive forces. In such an ambiguous state of affairs, there are naturally very few specimens whose meaning is simple and obvious (as there are very few tendencies in our individual natures which are free from ambiguities)—even though a directing intention is at work throughout and carries the whole system towards a definite goal.

A few words must be said about the animal world. In this respect, Teilhard remarks that each species should be defined by the particular form of instinct which characterizes it, and that the whole process of animal evolution should be considered as consciousness seeking for itself through different forms. This is why the natural history of the world should be written "from within". "It would thus appear no longer as an interlocking succession of structural types replacing one another, but as an ascension of inner sap spreading out in a forest of consolidated instincts."[17]

In these assertions, we recognize Teilhard's main ideas; the universe has a "within" which is consciousness, life; evolution is the

[17] *Op. cit.*, p. 151.

movement by which this principle hidden in things is progressively emancipated, comes to full expression; an authentic description of evolution should be a description of this movement.

These views raise many questions. How can a consciousness which is still impersonal and diluted (a meaningless notion) possess the extraordinary acumen and purposefulness required to elaborate countless intricate animal forms? Are the power, intelligence, and creativeness of such a consciousness not incomparably greater than the power, intelligence, and creativeness of man? Yet, according to Teilhard, man is the "within" of things personalized and the works of man are the *continuation* on the personal plane of evolution. How is it that by "finding itself" consciousness has lost so much of its power and inventiveness?

The truth is that the whole animal world (the whole process of animal evolution) is constituted by the self-actuating endeavours carried on by the cosmic personal acts, not blindly and hesitantly, but in a purposeful and enlightened way (the cosmic persons are, we know, incomparably more intelligent and powerful than we). Thus there is no such thing as an impersonal consciousness diffused "within" things; there are many cosmic personal acts expressing diversely and vividly their personalizing desires, and there are many cosmic personal acts filling the universe with their disruptive projects: the animal world, as it exists concretely, is the "condensation" of these various intents.

In the light of this, how should we conceive animal "psychology"?

Let it be noted first that the feelings, desires, passions, intentions, which we attribute to animals as we see them moving, acting, reacting, are nothing but projections of our own life. We cannot interpret their behaviour without humanizing it, without filling it with our own experience, our own sensitiveness, our own intelligence and purposiveness, our own temperament and individuality. This is because animals, as we perceive them, are constituted by our personal acts; they are modalities of our individual life-fields, part and parcel of our worlds.

What about *animals-in-themselves*? Do *they* really see, hear, feel, desire, intend, as we suppose them to do? The answer is obvious. *In themselves* animals are nothing, *by themselves* they do nothing, because they are not centres of consciousness, and thus have no independent, self-controlled activity. Apart from us, the animal world exists in the movement by which the cosmic personal acts actuate themselves; it is a variegated expression of this movement—thus whatever activity, life, consciousness, purpose, there is in animals proceeds in some way from the cosmic expressive centres. This activity, however, is not the activity which *we* observe in them because the animal world does not exist in the existential sphere of the cosmic persons as it exists in our human world.

How do animals exist in this transhuman sphere? What is the meaning of each of them, of the various aspects of its behaviour as parts of the suprahuman world? These are questions to which we, human persons, can give no precise answer.

Now, it is not in a purely arbitrary way that we make animals feel, desire, perceive, intend—live. To understand this, let us note the following points:

(1) As parts of the world-existing-without-us, our bodies are built on the animal pattern. They belong to those worlds which the cosmic personal acts constitute as the concretions of their self-actuating, personalizing or depersonalizing endeavours. Thus we understand that, from the very first, there is *affinity* between our bodies and the animal forms which we see moving around us.

(2) As they incarnate themselves in our bodies and constitute them as their expressive centres, our personal acts continually take up, integrate, our bodies-already-constituted. While doing so, they are conditioned by the organic structures in which they express themselves, by all the phenomena taking place in these structures; they "experientialize" these phenomena in the form of feelings, sensations, inclinations. Subsequently, as they unfold themselves in our surroundings, as they constitute our world, they animate and experientialize all animal forms in accordance with their primordial manner of being—that is, in accordance with the way in which they find themselves living in our bodies. In this process, it must be noted, there is no falsification. It cannot be said that we introduce into animals a psychological activity which, in reality, is absent from them. As parts of our worlds, animals are *really* living in us and by us; thus our life—our sensitiveness, purposiveness, intelligence—is *really* present in them as we see them moving and acting. Apart from us, they do not exist "in themselves" (thus they have no sensitiveness, purposiveness, intelligence *of their own*) but in and by other personal acts—the question of their *own independent* psychological activity does not arise.

The fact that animals do not exist *in themselves*, the fact that they are not *centres* of personal activity, explains why animal behaviour—as it appears to us—is characterized by a lack of transcendence. As Merleau-Ponty points out in all his descriptions of animal behaviour, an animal clings closely to what he does, he does not look at things "from a distance", and has no real freedom of action. The following passage brings out well the difference between animal and human behaviour:

"It is not the power of creating a second nature—economic, social, cultural—over and above his biological nature which characterizes man but rather the power of transcending created structures in order to create new structures. This power is visible in all the particular things which human labour produces. . . .

"If a monkey picks up a branch to reach something, it means that he is able to give to an object of nature a functional value. But a monkey cannot make instruments which would be used only to produce other instruments. We have seen that the branch which has become for him a stick has ceased to be for him a branch; this means that he never possesses it as an instrument in the full sense of the word. In both cases, the activity of the animal reveals its limitations: it loses itself in the real transformations which it performs and cannot reproduce them. In the case of man, on the contrary, the branch which has become a stick will remain simply a branch-stick, one and the same 'thing' with two different functions visible 'to him' under several aspects. This power of choosing and changing the points of view enables him to create instruments, not under the pressure of the situation in which he actually finds himself, but for any possible use, and, in particular, to create other instruments."[18]

Human behaviour is characterized by self-determination, freedom. This characteristic is linked with the high development of the human brain. Now, as the whole of evolution—to the extent that it reflects the endeavours carried on by the cosmic persons who submit themselves to the Creator—is the preparation of man's advent, the main line of evolution is to be traced among those animal forms which, one after the other, show a gradual development of the nervous system, a progressive "cerebralization". (This does not mean that this line reflects *only* the personalizing efforts of the transhuman persons who realize themselves authentically. In fact, the struggle

[18] M. Merleau-Ponty, *La structure du comportement*, pp. 189–90.

between the "powers of light" and the "powers of darkness" expresses itself everywhere. But the fact that there *is* such a line indicates clearly that the personalizing forces are the leading forces.) Teilhard gives the name of "Ariadne's Thread" to this line of progressive cerebralization, because it shows beyond any doubt the main direction of the whole evolutive process. "From the moment that the measure (or parameter) of the evolving phenomenon is sought in the elaboration of the nervous systems, not only do the countless genera and species fall naturally into place, but the entire network of their verticils, their layers, their branches, rises up like a quivering spray of foliage. Not only does the arrangement of animal forms according to their degree of cerebralization correspond exactly to the classification of systematic biology, but it also confers on the tree of life a sharpness of feature, an impetus, which is incontestably the hallmark of truth. Such coherence—and, let me add, such ease, inexhaustible fidelity and evocative power in this coherence—could not be the result of chance. . . . *It provides a direction*; and therefore *it proves that evolution has a direction.*"[19]

With the advent of man a sort of revolution took place. First, it must be stressed again that the humanization of the earth was not simply the outcome of evolution, the fruit of the activity carried on by the cosmic persons: it was the product of a Creative Initiative. From the moment man appeared on earth—within biological structures elaborated by the cosmic persons—the earth was no longer the exclusive "dominion" of the cosmic persons, *it became first of all the property of the human persons* (since the human community came into existence as the personalization of the earth). This does not mean that the cosmic persons were not to continue to fill the earth with their own projects and intents. They would no doubt remain actively present (as we know they are), but their presence and action would henceforth be conditioned by the presence and the action of men. Concretely speaking, the obedient cosmic persons would no longer work to prepare the advent of men, but, taking into account the fact that men existed, they would help them to reach the fullness of life, to realize their destinies, conversely, the rebellious cosmic persons would try to destroy men or, at least, to hinder their progress.

These new preoccupations on the part of the cosmic persons express themselves in particular in the fact that, since the advent of man, there is no longer in the realm of wild life the same proliferation

19 *The Phenomenon of Man*, pp. 145–6.

of animal forms. With the appearance of man, animality has somehow come into its own. The one for whom they are meant is now present in the world. Animal life loses much of its "wild" character and becomes tame; animal psychology is humanized. Under man's influence, new living forms come into being manifesting the new status of animal existence. This is no longer "evolution" but the expression in the realm of animal life of the new meaning which the earth has acquired since the advent of man. A tame animal is an animal who has found himself by finding man.

In this connection, I may quote the two passages of Genesis which narrate in a very evocative manner the creation of man and the appropriation of the earth by man:

"And God said, Let us make man, wearing our own image and likeness; let us put him in command of the fishes in the sea, and all that flies through the air, and the cattle, and the whole earth, and all the creeping things that move on earth. So God made man in his own image, made him in the image of God. Man and woman both, he created them. And God pronounced his blessing on them, Increase and multiply and fill the earth, and make it yours; take command of the fishes in the sea, and all that flies through the air, and all the living things that move on the earth. Here are all the herbs, God told them, that seed on earth, and all the trees, that carry in them the seeds of their own life, to be your food; food for all the beasts on the earth, all that flies in the air, all that creeps along the ground; here all that lives shall find its nourishment. And so it was done.

"And now, from the clay of the ground, all the beasts that roam the earth and all that flies through the air were ready fashioned, and the Lord brought them to Adam, to see what he would call them; the name which Adam gave to each living creature is its name still."[20]

The radical difference between animal generation and human generation must be clearly perceived. The generative process has been gradually developed and perfected in the course of millions of years—as a vivid expression of the world-building, self-actuating endeavour carried on by the cosmic persons. So far as the animal world is concerned, this process must be described as an activity which takes place entirely within the worlds of the cosmic persons (and within our worlds) and which does not end in the production of any new

[20] Genesis 1. 26–30; 2. 19. Translated by R. Knox.

autonomous centre of existence. With regard to human generation, the following points must be stressed:

(1) The cosmic persons and, of course, the other human persons, are at work in each particular generation. To the degree to which a particular man receives life from his fellow-men and from the cosmic persons, the process of his procreation can be likened to animal generation. This is why the study of the latter helps geneticists to understand the "mechanism" of human generation.

(2) But man does not receive his personal existence from any created agent. As a transcendental being, he proceeds from Above. Therefore human generation, in so far as it ends in the production of new centres of personal existence, is radically different from animal generation. To discover the essence of human generation, we cannot judge merely from appearances and listen only to what biologists have to tell us about it.

Let us follow the passage of time and try to understand still better what has been going on since the appearance of man on earth. We have seen that the end towards which we are tending is our ultimate realization as persons—that is, the formation of an eschatological community characterized by intimacy with God and close union of its members among themselves.

As has been pointed out, according to Teilhard the whole evolutive process consists in a rise of consciousness. With the advent of man, this movement has not come to an end; it continues until it culminates in some sort of supreme Consciousness.[21] This consciousness, because it is supreme, must contain in the highest degree what constitutes the perfection of our consciousness, it must be "hyper-reflection", or "hyper-personalization". Teilhard thinks that we are actually witnessing the birth of this Centre of centres. The scientific and philosophical activity which characterizes our time—an activity in which everybody participates—shows that an aggregation of a higher order is taking place. We experience "the birth of some single centre from the convergent beams of millions of elementary centres dispersed over the surface of the thinking earth."[22]

Whether we interpret these views in a pluralistic perspective (in conformity with Teilhard's explicit argument and belief) or in a monistic perspective (as, in some passages, Teilhard seems to invite

21 Teilhard, *op. cit.*, p. 258.
22 *Ibid.*, p. 259.

us to do, and as also we feel inclined to do when we try to disclose the implications of Teilhard's thought), these two points stand out:

(1) Throughout the whole evolutive process, until the final emergence of the supreme Centre of consciousness, there is unity of movement, unity of "mechanism". What takes place through the activities of the various "grains of thought" (human persons) is the unbroken continuation of what was taking place before the appearance of man; the law which determines the movement of the "noosphere" and gives it its destination is the very law which, from the very beginning, ruled the whole of pre-human evolution.

(2) The supreme Consciousness in which the whole evolutive process must culminate is the "within" of the universe fully brought out, fully realized, through the coming together and mutual perfecting of all the particular centres of consciousness—thus it seems to be the universe itself at the apex of its evolutive ascent.

The facts we have discovered in the course of our study make us unable to accept these views:

(1) There can be no question of a unity of movement, of a continuity between the *phenomenon* of prehuman evolution and human progress. The latter takes place in the movement by which the human personal life-acts tend towards their realization, it is a *personal striving*; the former is not a process which goes on by itself, which can be understood in itself: it relates us to other personal centres; as we see it, it is the expression in our own spheres of existence of the world-building activity carried on by the cosmic persons, an activity which goes on today (independently of our activity) even though—for reasons which we know—it no longer expresses itself in the same way. Therefore we shall not say with Julian Huxley that "man is nothing else than evolution become conscious of itself"[23], nor shall we say that "the consciousness of each of us is evolution looking at itself and reflecting"[24]. If the whole process of evolution were the rise of consciousness in matter undergoing organization and if mankind-in-progress were simply the highest point actually reached by this ascending force, such expressions would, no doubt, be meaningful. This is not so. Evolution is not *something* capable of becoming conscious of itself because it is not a self-consistent movement. The humanization of the earth is not the personalization

23 *Ibid.*, p. 221.
24 *Ibid.*, p. 221.

of an impersonal universe ("below" man, there *is* nothing; "outside" man, everything exists in the cosmic persons—not as "less" than man, but as "more" than man; man is the "lowest" of all *subsistent* beings); it is the infusion by God of new personal acts into earthly centres elaborated within the cosmic acts-worlds—the creation by God of new worlds.

Can we speak of a unity of mechanism between the evolutive movement and human progress? Not in Teilhard's sense, for the reasons just indicated.

Must we then reject altogether the law of complexity-consciousness which, according to Teilhard, underlies and explains the whole movement of evolution?

It is my experience that, when I want to create something (i.e., to actuate myself in a more perfect manner), I must incarnate my project in a certain expressive set-up. To do so, I must organize a certain diversity of elements into a meaningful totality; I must not only put together these elements, I must combine them in a purposeful way, build them suitably into a dynamic whole. This living totality will stand as the embodiment of my act-project. Now, I notice that the broader, the more vital and meaningful my project is, the more complex and elaborate will be the expressive field in which I shall realize it. This observation makes me realize that, among human achievements, those characterized by the highest degree of complexity-within-unity are also those inspired, constituted, by the broadest, the most enlightened and dynamic human intentions.

We have acknowledged that in "nature" where there is meaning, organization, finality, there are prehuman personal intentions at work. Now it must be understood that the phenomenon which science calls "life" is nothing but a certain type of organization and meaning—in vegetable life, there is less complexity-within-unity, less meaning; in animal life, there is a higher degree of both; the closer we come to man, the richer, the more meaningful life becomes. What does this imply? In conformity with the data of our experience, we shall say that this rising organization, complexity, meaningfulness, in "living nature" points to the increasing dynamism, purposefulness, breadth of the prehuman personal intentions of which the phenomenon of nature is the expression. *In this sense*, the law of complexity-consciousness holds good. In so far as the whole effort of the cosmic persons was ordained towards the humanization of the earth, the *phenomenon* of man is truly the culmination of the whole evolutive movement. This perspective makes us understand vividly that the whole of living nature is actually meant for man[25] and that man's body is nothing apart from the whole "biosphere", from the living ambiance in which it is situated, even though man is not created, brought into life, by the personal forces in which nature originally subsists.

(The difference between the types of organization, of complexity-within-unity, of meaning, produced by men and those achieved by the prehuman persons points to the difference between the existential structure, the mode, power and breadth of action, the "intelligence", of the human persons and those of the cosmic persons. What we know of living nature is but the expression *in our own existential spheres*, the translation *into human terms*, of an activity taking place originally in the existential sphere of the cosmic persons, an activity much more enlightened, much more intense, than our human activity. We understand why, by "becoming human", the "within" of things has lost so much of its creative drive. Has it?)

(2) There can be no question of an "omegalization" of the "noosphere". The task of men is not to build themselves into a Super-Consciousness, but to build the human world and the eschatological community—a community of which they will all have full membership.

As has been shown, Teilhard's idea of a Super-Consciousness to be brought into definite existence through the synergetic efforts of all the thinking elements is implied in his conception of evolution. Let us examine in more detail the development of his argument, as presented in the section entitled "The Personalizing Universe"[26].

Teilhard tells us how the process of personalization is carried on and brought to completion. The sum of the elements (the different centres of reflection) brought together in a synthesis has the same function as the elements taken separately. How will the two movements harmonize? To answer this question, we must analyse the nature of Omega, the higher Pole of evolution. In Omega, the quantum of consciousness liberated on Earth by Noogenesis will accumulate. This means that Omega will not simply gather together

[25] Let us remember, however, that there are powerful antagonistic disruptive "forces" at work and that, therefore, nature *must* appear in many respects hostile to man.

[26] *The Phenomenon of Man*, pp. 260ff.

our ideas, discoveries, artistic creations, etc. . . . but ourselves too. Therefore the concentration of a conscious universe must reassemble in itself all consciousnesses as well as the Conscious. In this supreme Synthesis, each particular consciousness will remain conscious of itself and even perfect itself. This is the application of the universal law: "In any domain—whether it be the cells of a body, the members of a society, or the elements of a spiritual synthesis—*union differentiates*. In every organized whole, the parts perfect themselves and fulfil themselves."[27] This is the natural mechanism of all unification. Thus we can picture the final state of the World: a system whose unity coincides with a paroxysm of harmonized complexity. Omega will be "a distinct Centre radiating at the core of *a system of centres*; a grouping in which personalization of the All and personalization of the elements reach their maximum, simultaneously and without merging, under the influence of a supremely autonomous focus of union. That is the only picture which emerges when we try to apply the notion of collectivity with remorseless logic to a granular whole of thoughts."[28]

Teilhard's intention, I believe, remains throughout pluralistic; however, it seems to me difficult to understand this line of argument in anything but a monistic perspective. There is no doubt that what is called here "the sum of the elements brought together in a synthesis", "the Conscious", "the All" is given a consistence of its own: it is a unitary factor subsisting within and above the particular elements, a Cosmic Consciousness which it is the task of all the particular consciousnesses to perfect, to personalize, even as they perfect and realize themselves. Teilhard, it is true, tells us that, in the final synthesis, the various elements will remain themselves, they will even "accentuate the depth and incommunicability of their *egos*[29], but this is a natural phenomenon: "in every organized whole, the parts perfect themselves and fulfil themselves"[30]. This self-perfecting of the parts in the whole, we know, far from excluding the essential dependence of the elements on the totality, implies it: in every system, each component, in order to fulfil itself, to reach the perfection of its "componenthood", *must* be integrated in the whole, it *must* be a particular expression of the entire system; thus it has no independent existence or meaning; its being is essentially being-for-the-whole.

This position is dangerous. If the relation of all the particular

[27] *Ibid.*, p. 262.
[28] *Ibid.*, pp. 262–3.
[29] *Ibid.*, p. 262.
[30] *Ibid.*, p. 262.

centres of consciousness to the cosmic totality can be assimilated to that in which, *in every organized system*, the parts stand to the whole, each particular human person is not an "end-in-himself" and, therefore, cannot be considered as a really transcendent, free hypostasis—his existence is simply the existence of the totality of which he is a particular function.

In fact, each particular person is, in a certain way, the whole: each particular person is, in a certain way, an absolute. There is no cosmic reality from which particular persons receive their existence as persons (as "consciousness") and towards the perfecting and personalizing of which their personal activities are essentially ordained. In other words, after or beyond persons, there is nothing; each person is the end of the line. The whole human progress is not ordained towards the emancipation of a "Spirit of the Earth", but to the perfecting of each individual person in close union with all other persons. In view of this, it makes sense, no doubt, to speak of the elaboration of a common seeing, feeling, suffering, thinking, in one word, of a common living[31], provided we understand that this common good will always be possessed by, be hypostatized in, each individual person in a radically incommunicable way. Teilhard does not deny this, and even seems to affirm it on several occasions; however, the value of his affirmations is, in my opinion, greatly compromised by the fact that he ordains the activity of each centre of consciousness towards the realization of a unitary principle from which each particular centre holds its existence and to which he is essentially subordinated. This would mean that, for him, the common "I live" which will characterize the future Noosphere will be transcendent to each element instead of being owned by each person in a transcendental way; it would mean that, for him, each person is not a real hypostasis.

In the passage analysed above, Teilhard tells us that the final synthesis will be reached "under the influence of a supremely autonomous focus of union". In a footnote, he adds: "It is for this central focus, necessarily autonomous, that we shall henceforward reserve the expression 'Omega Point'".

So far, the term "Omega" has been used to designate the Super-Consciousness emerging from the union of the various "grains of thought"—the Noosphere itself at the summit of its evolutive ascent.

[31] *Ibid.*, p. 251.

What is this "autonomous focus of union" to which this name is suddenly reserved? To answer this question, we must examine the function which Teilhard ascribes to love, and the attributes of the "Omega Point".

Teilhard tells us [32] that love is the force which unites the elements of the cosmos. As such, it is a universal phenomenon and constitutes the very dynamism of evolution. "Driven by the forces of love, the fragments of the world seek each other so that the world may come to being."[33] In the Noosphere, love brings together the various centres of consciousness. It is a common error to think that man is not able to love more than a few people, that universal love is an impossibility. In fact, the most fundamental form of human passion is "the one which, under the pressure of an involuting universe, precipitates the elements one upon the other in the whole—cosmic affinity and hence cosmic sense"[34]. This love for the Whole is possible because the Whole presents itself to us as a Person. It is impossible to give oneself to an Anonymous Entity. But if the Universe ahead of us assumes a face and a heart, then in the atmosphere created by this focus our hearts also will open. The presence of this personal focus is necessary for the very success of evolution. "For the concurrence of the human monads to come about, it is necessary and sufficient for us that we should extend our science to its farthest limits and recognize and accept (as being necessary to close and balance Space-Time), not only some vague future existence, but also . . . the radiation *as a present reality* of that mysterious Centre of our centres which I have called Omega."[35]

These views contain a number of great truths. Love is a powerful bond of union; the more it purifies itself, the more universal it becomes. Love is always directed to a person; we cannot love an impersonal entity.

However, it is difficult to accept Teilhard's argument without reservations:

(1) Love is presented as the force which brings together the elements of the world, whether they are "thinking" or "non-thinking" elements. This statement must be understood in connection with Teilhard's ideas about the "within" of things. As a uniting energy, the "within" of things *is* love.

[32] *Ibid.*, pp. 264ff.
[33] *Ibid.*, p. 265.
[34] *Ibid.*, pp. 266–7.
[35] *Ibid.*, pp. 267–8.

We recognize in this view Teilhard's tendency to consider human persons as "fragments of the whole" in a way comparable to that in which atoms and molecules are "fragments", and to attribute to the latter what belongs properly to persons. What is love? This is a question which experience alone can answer. There is love in me to the extent to which I effectively desire my good and the good of all my fellow-men (as being linked with my own good), in respectful obedience to the Creator's will. This love, in so far as it is identified with the dynamism of my act, is the force which holds my world together and builds it harmoniously; it is the force which directs me towards others and unites me with them while making them eminently themselves; it is the force which makes my will conformable to the Creator's will. Such an impetus pertains to my act to the degree to which it is a personal act; it originates in my expressive centre in so far as it is a centre of personal existence. These facts show that love cannot exist in anything but persons and cannot be directed towards anything but persons. The "fragments" of the world cannot love and cannot be loved because they are not personal beings. If they "seek each other so that the world may come to being" it is because they pertain to acts-worlds tending personally towards their realization. The love which I see in them is nothing but a concretion of my love.

(2) Universal love is no doubt a possibility, but the way in which Teilhard explains it is somewhat disquieting: (i) it is a force operating in the elements "under the pressure of an involuting universe"; (ii) it is a force which "precipitates the elements one upon the other"; (iii) it is a passion directed towards the whole. This must be understood in conformity with Teilhard's main line of argument. The "pressure" alluded to is the rise of consciousness within the elements of the cosmos; the falling of the elements one upon the other is their coming together in order to form new aggregates characterized by a higher degree of consciousness; the direction of love towards the whole is the synergetic moving of all the particular centres of consciousness towards the forming of a supreme synthetic Centre. Now Teilhard tells us that this great cosmic Centre (which he calls here the "Whole") is already in existence, nay more, that it already presents itself to us as a Person. The reason for it is that love is always directed towards a person (never towards an Anonymous Entity—towards a Being *in fieri*).

This is a nice problem. On the one hand, Omega has been repeatedly described as the term of evolution, a Super-Consciousness arising from the personalization of the All, and therefore a personal Centre engendered by the combined activity of all the particular centres of the whole cosmos; on the other hand, it is now characterized as the personal Summit towards which evolution is ordained: the "*Source* of love and *Object* of love at the summit of the world above our heads", "the Universe ahead of us assuming a face and a heart, and, so to speak, personifying itself", "the mysterious Centre of our centres necessary to close and balance Space-Time". Shall we, at the end, be faced by two great Persons who will have exactly the same function: that of uniting in themselves all the small persons (I say "at the end" because "Omega B" is already in existence as an object of love and, thus, draws all the elements towards himself, whereas "Omega A" is still in genesis and, therefore, not yet present as a personal Centre of all centres)? We shall soon see the answer which Teilhard himself gives to this question.

In the argument just analysed, it is the consideration of Love as energy which enables Teilhard to posit Omega as an independent personal being. Could he not have dispensed with it? In his view, love is present in the world from its very origins: it is the force which unites all the elements of the Cosmos. Thus it has from the beginning a universal significance. Is it therefore love of God?

Whatever it may be, we know for certain that Teilhard believed intensely in the transcendence and actuality of God. This vivid faith seems to me the vital factor which led him to posit "Omega B" in addition to "Omega A". This is more or less what he tells us: "God, the Centre of all centres. In that final vision the Christian dogma culminates. And so exactly, so perfectly does this coincide with the Omega Point that doubtless I should never have ventured to envisage the latter or formulate the hypothesis rationally if, in my consciousness as a believer, I had not found not only its speculative model but also its living reality."[36]

It is not my task to determine here whether Teilhard rightly understood the Christian dogma. In my sense, from the point of view of philosophical reflection (which is the point of view of this study), we shall never show that personalization, carried on in a straight line, culminates in a sort of deification of the whole cosmos. As I have shown, personalization (as carried on by human persons) is the

36 *Ibid.*, p. 294.

building of the human world; it is ordained towards the edification of the eschatological community. No doubt, this ultimate community will be characterized by "proximity to God"—in other words, the relation to God which already constitutes the universe-community of today will be further actuated. But what will be the exact nature of this actuation? This is a mystery which philosophy is unable to solve because philosophy is essentially a reflection within the limits of our experience—that is, of our present earthly condition. The only certainty we have is that God will always remain absolutely transcendent to his creation.

We must now examine the "Attributes of the Omega Point". At the beginning of this section, Teilhard remarks that the idea that some Soul of souls should be developing at the summit of the world is not completely foreign to the views of our contemporaries. However, according to the general opinion, this Soul could not form itself except in a very distant future and in total dependence on the reversible laws of energy. Thus Omega is characterized by remoteness and fragility.

For two positive reasons, one of love, the other of survival, Teilhard urges us to rid ourselves of these two restrictions. His argument from love does not bring any new element. If Omega has to be object of love, it must be more than an ideal or potential centre, it must be real and actual. "To be supremely attractive, Omega must be supremely present."[37] The other argument can be summed up in one sentence: "Omega A" would be too fragile and problematic a reality if "Omega B" were not there to lend it consistence and stability.

These two arguments are followed by an interesting consideration. Evolution and, in particular, Noogenesis lead to a progressive emergence of Consciousness from the elements of the Cosmos (the first part of *The Phenomenon of Man* introduces us to this idea). Seen from this angle, Omega is the culmination of a movement of synthesis. But "under this evolutive facet Omega still only reveals *half of itself*. While being the last term of its series, it is also *outside all series*. Not only does it crown, but it closes.... When, going beyond the elements, we come to speak of the conscious Pole of the World, it is not enough to say that it *emerges* from the rise of consciousness: we must add that from this genesis it has already

[37] *Ibid.*, p. 269.

emerged; without which it could neither subjugate into love nor fix in incorruptibility."[38]

Thus the four attributes of Omega are: autonomy, actuality, irreversibility and, finally, transcendence.

What can we say about this further development?

The arguments by which Teilhard tries to prove the present existence of Omega as a transcendent personal Centre may well be sound, yet I do not think that discussing them would lead to a very definite and useful conclusion. Let us concede that Teilhard has established the necessity of positing "Omega B" in addition to "Omega A".

Are there two Omegas?

Teilhard answers this question for us. In fact, "Omega A" and "Omega B" are not two different Omegas but two aspects, two "halves" of the same Omega. By "half of itself", Omega transcends the world and evolution; by the other half, it "emerges" from the stuff of the Cosmos, it is the fruit of a genesis.

To sum up our conclusions:

(1) From the beginning of *The Phenomenon of Man*, Teilhard points out that the elements of the Universe have a "within" which may be defined as "consciousness". Cosmic evolution is the progressive emergence of this psychic factor: the elements of the universe combine in order to form more and more complex structures characterized by a higher and higher degree of consciousness. The term of this movement is the formation of a Great Synthesis in which Consciousness will attain the highest possible intensity and perfection. This Pole of the World is called Omega. Teilhard, however, never makes it quite clear how this cosmic movement must be conceived. His expressed intention seems to be pluralistic throughout, yet it is hard to understand his system and many of his explanations in anything but a monistic perspective. We are told that Omega, the supreme Consciousness, is not only a futurity, but an existing reality and that this existing Absolute is also the great Soul which, by one aspect of itself, is emerging from the rise of all the particular consciousnesses. This last development seems finally to justify the monistic interpretation. So far, in spite of many indications, we were still uncertain whether the "within" of things should be understood

[38] *Ibid.*, pp. 270–1.

as a unitary factor or as a plural reality, but now that Consciousness is presented as an *actual reality* which by "half of itself" emerges from the rise of consciousnesses it seems clear that it cannot be understood as anything but a unitary element. From that point of view, the "fragments of the world", the particular centres of consciousness, must be understood as elements which, though differentiated, are none the less fundamentally one in so far as they are functions of the great emerging Soul (just as the organs of my body, though many, are one to the extent that they are all constituted by the same life-act, to the extent that they *are* functions, expressions, of my life-act-realizing-itself).

These conclusions show us that, *once its implications are unfolded*, Teilhard's position comes close to that of realistic monism as defined in the third chapter of this book. Everything starts with an objectification of our representations, an objectification or externalization of "consciousness". Once the relation complexity-(objectified) consciousness has been established, the whole system develops organically. I have shown that, as I see it, Teilhard's fundamental mistake is his failure to examine reflectively, to "experientialize" the true nature of the "within" of things. He tells us, it is true, that his study is no more than a study of phenomena; but in that case he was in no position to discuss the "within" of reality. If an argument based on the nature of this "within" is to be developed, it must be done in the light of our integral experience.

(2) Omega, as pictured in *The Phenomenon of Man*, is not God, but an idealization of our consciousness. God is absolutely transcendent to the universe and *in no way* involved in any cosmical phenomenon. In God, there is no genesis, there is plenitude of self-determination. God is Pure Act.

My criticism of Teilhard's position does not imply that there is no continuity whatsoever between the phenomenon of evolution and the activity of human persons.

In a true sense it can be affirmed that just as the animal forms which succeeded one another on earth before the coming of man existed by and in the cosmic personal acts and expressed the vital endeavours of these persons, so also our human organisms, our psycho-physiological structures live by and in the cosmic persons. Indeed, the life which circulates in our bodies, which constitutes our limbs, all the psycho-physiological phenomena which we experience in us, to the extent that they are already in existence before we integrate them in the movement of our personal life, to the extent that they belong to the world-existing-without-us, are modalities expressing the aspirations and tensions which form the life of the cosmic powers; they are concretions of the cosmic struggle which opposes the obedient persons and the rebellious persons. This means that, from a phenomenal point of view, our human lives may be described as the continuation of evolution; analogies can rightly be established between the "mechanism" of our personal growth and that of animal evolution, between the "mechanism" of our human activity and that of animal activity.

To close this section, let me point out once more the integral perspective in which the whole of human history reveals its full meaning.

I have shown that our earthly life is only a preparation for life-after-death, that to perfect ourselves as human persons we have to liberate ourselves from our earthly condition. Now, we know that the sphere of the Beyond is not simply a future reality, but something intensely actual. Millions of men have lived before we came to existence, thousands of them are daily departing from this world. All these persons form the *real* human community towards which our earthly community is essentially ordained. A vivid consciousness of this fact will transform completely our habitual mental outlook and our vision of the earth. Because we live in this world and are tied to our earthly condition, we are too ready to think that there is nothing beyond what we see, and we are tempted to make of the earth our true home. Thus our life becomes earthbound and we limit our ambitions to the building of a "paradise on earth". Such a narrow outlook denotes a spiritual blindness which is both tragic and comic: the blindness of a man who spends his whole life in his room and consumes all his energies in adorning it because he has made it his world. In all its dimensions, our present world is a tiny reality compared with the sphere of eternal life in which it is immersed and to which it points. This is the vision which must illuminate our earthly life as it draws nearer and nearer to its end.

Let us try to determine—in so far as we can—in what relationship the two "branches" of the great human family stand to each other. As we shall see, their exchanges constitute a real dialectical process.

We have admitted that the heavenly community[39] is the "true"

[39] The term "heavenly" means here "not of *this* world", "passed beyond". It has no other connotation.

human community. However, we must assert that it has not yet reached its eschatological dimensions. Indeed, it is continually growing, acquiring new members "daily". Thus it is a community which is still being constituted, which has not yet attained its full stature. Moreover, the human progress realized on earth has a vital meaning for its members (this is clear since they are one in nature with us—that is, forming with us one community, in spite of their being already "beyond"); therefore, even though they have reached the end of their earthly journey and enjoy the fruition of their labours, they have still something to gain from what is happening on earth. These facts show that the heavenly community is, from a certain angle, really dependent on the earthly community. From another angle, we depend on those who are beyond. The heavenly community constitutes the sphere of life in which our earthly lives will attain their fulfilment, towards which they are ordained. Thus we are essentially related to it, in tension towards it. In other words, those who are beyond continually draw us towards them; they call us and make us already share in their own manner of living.

These views show us the full meaning of our earthly existence. As we are labouring day by day on earth, we are collaborating in building a reality, a sphere of life which will be complete only at the end. This ultimate reality will be the eschatological community gathering its members in a truly definitive way.

This definitive existence is not to be conceived as a state of eternal immobility. At the beginning of this chapter, I have shown that the world of persons is created by God as a participation of the movement by which he communicates the totality of himself. Thus God-given-to-himself is the End towards which all persons are ordained. This does not mean that all persons will be finally deified—that is, completely identified with the Logos. God-given-to-himself is a Pole of attraction which can never be reached by any created being, because he is *absolutely* transcendent to the universe, infinitely above and beyond any act-world. Our definitive existence will still be a continual progress, a continual actuation of our relation to the Transcendent, a continual movement towards him. This is clear to us. We know that our very *existence* is in the act by which we go *beyond* what we are—towards an End which, while attracting us, remains for ever beyond our reach. We cannot stop tending towards it, we cannot stop transcending ourselves, without ceasing to *exist*.

III. LIBERTY

In the Act by which he created man, God ordained him towards his supreme realization in the eschatological community. This finality was from the beginning constitutive of the very existence of man.

We must appreciate all that this means. As we know, man is by nature a life-act co-extensive with the whole universe. In our present condition, this life-act unfolds itself from a definite earthly centre which we call our brain. Spreading out from this centre, it first constitutes our body—it divides itself into several functions according to the particular modalities of the organic regions in which it expresses itself. Through our body it constitutes our environment, and through our environment it pervades the whole universe. In this movement, our life-act, though it diversifies itself in many different ways, remains one and undivided. This means that each function of our body-in-relation-to-our-environment is essentially a function of the act; it *is* the act realizing itself in a particular manner—thus it has no independent finality.

This finality which constitutes us must not be understood in terms of biological determinism, as a "necessity of nature". It manifests itself in a context of relative indetermination and can be understood only as the expression in us of the Creative Initiative.

It does not actuate itself "by itself". As a human person, I am able to transcend my own actions and the influences which act upon me, I am able to think, to dominate—to a certain extent—the course of events, to live in myself. Because I am a transcendental hypostasis endowed with interiority (wearing God's own image and likeness), I am capable of self-determination, I am to a great extent master of my own life. Therefore I must actuate in a personal way the finality which constitutes me—my life-act transcending itself into a personal act must tend freely towards its supreme destiny.

This brings home to us the greatness, and allows us to glimpse the tragedy, of human existence.

I am free. This means that *I* actuate myself, that *I* lead my world towards its consummation—in other words, that nobody can live for me, that my destiny is in *my* hands. My freedom is *in the act* by which, taking up my past, my situation, the whole world, I realize myself in a determined way. But this self-determination, as a human act, is in its very essence limited. It is limited because it must actuate itself progressively. However much I transcend my situation, I cannot do away with it; my act must incarnate itself in it at the risk of becoming crystallized in it, of alienating itself. This essential limitation of my liberty expresses itself in the fact that my personal act is continually conditioned by the structures in which it unfolds itself, that it is vitally related to other personal acts by which its progress is either stimulated or hampered. A particular aspect of this finitude is the necessity I experience at every moment of following a particular course of conduct.

In this respect, we must dispel a too frequent misconception. Some philosophers say that liberty consists *essentially* in the choice of one definite line of action among many possible lines of action. That at every moment many possible courses offer themselves to me, that my decision to actuate myself in one particular direction is an act of liberty, these are evident facts. But the obligation I have to make a choice does not point to the perfection but to the limitation of my freedom. My personal act, however intensely it desires the end, and thus the whole, has to restrict itself, has to tend towards the end step by step, through limited realizations of itself.

In the following pages, I shall first characterize authentic existence—that is, human life growing in freedom—and indicate various modes of inauthentic existence; in conclusion, I shall reflect on our condition as persons living in a world where inauthenticity seems to prevail.[40]

1. Authentic Existence

God is Pure Act—that is, unrestricted Self-Determination. The Act by which God creates the universe does not proceed from a divine decision to give existence to just one world among many possible worlds, a decision which is motivated by the fact that "one has to limit oneself", "one cannot do everything at the same time". In other words, the Creative Act is not a human act, i.e., the actuation of oneself in one particular direction chosen among many. (To consider Creation in this way amounts to denying the absolute transcendence of God over the created universe; it makes of the genesis of the universe the process by which God gradually realizes himself.) The Act by which God creates the universe is in God pure unrestricted self-positing, self-communication, self-possession; it is God giving

[40] The expressions "authentic existence" and "inauthentic existence" are borrowed from Heidegger. However, they are given here meanings which Heidegger never attributed to them. This will be evident to all those who are familiar with the thought of the German philosopher.

himself to himself, not in a progressive manner, but in the absolute perfection of an eternal NOW.

The world of persons—each particular act-world—exists as a created participation in the Divine Act. Our personal acts, the acts by which in the present we take up our past and pro-ject ourselves into the future—that is, our acts of self-determination, self-realization—limited and progressive, groping and wavering though they are, bear in themselves the image and likeness of God's pure self-determination, of the Pure Act.

This fundamental reality—our existence as created participators in the Divine Act—makes us understand that our liberty is constituted *as liberty* by the Act which creates us as persons. Therefore it cannot exist as something purely autonomous and independent; to remain itself, it must be essentially an act of dependence, it must be obedience. This obedience will consist in making actively ours the intention by which we are constituted—that is, in actuating consciously, determinedly, the finality which is immanent in our natures.

Thus we see that in order to live as free persons we must first of all surrender our freedom to God; we must make his will our will. By taking this attitude, we accept the truth; acknowledging God as our Creator and accepting our condition as creatures, we conform ourselves to the real order; instead of becoming slaves, we accede to the realm of spiritual liberty, whose dimensions are unlimited.

This fundamental submission to God, because it actuates our participation in God's own manner of being, makes us more and more self-determined; therefore it develops our true human personality, ensures our self-realization, and thereby draws the whole universe towards its supreme destiny. It is the true liberating attitude, a spiritualizing fidelity which detaches us from the contingencies in which our daily life tends to lose itself, and makes us control without arrogance the influences which act upon us. In one word, through obedience to God, we realize ourselves as transcendent hypostases.

Thus we see the fundamental characteristic of authentic existence. This obedience must be understood in a very concrete way.

Each person, as we know, is an act-world possessing his own incommunicable individuality. No doubt, there may be similitudes, affinities, between different persons; there may even be close community of lives, feelings and aspirations, but there can never be identity. Each man is fundamentally irreplaceable; he is a unique world.

What is the source of a person's originality?

Shall we say that it resides in the unique make-up of his organic structures—that is, in his unique way of being incarnate? This surely makes sense, especially when we realize that a person's individual nature is the concretion of his personal history, a particular taking up of the whole of history.

However, there is a deeper answer. I am what I am first of all because God wants me and creates me as such. *I am unique because the intention which constitutes me is unique.* Thus my originality resides first of all in my incommunicable way of participating in the Divine Act, in my unique relationship to God.

From this we may see what our obedience to God must be *in concreto.*

My life will be the progressive realization of this unique design and image of God which I am. I shall make intensely mine the unique intention which constitutes me. In other words, I shall fulfil the mission entrusted to me, and to me alone: I shall identify my life with this mission. I shall play my unique part in the building of the human world and of the eschatological community. What God wants of me, he does not want of anybody else. I shall realize myself by carrying out this will.

This is authentic existence, our personal accession to true spiritual liberty by the actuation of the unique relation which binds us to God.

Can we specify further the nature of this relation?

The intention by which we are constituted is identical with our finality, our destiny; therefore it orders us towards our ultimate realization in the eschatological community. We may call this end our supreme good because it is our highest perfection, the fulfilment of all our personal aspirations. Thus we discover the Act which creates us as a Supreme Benevolence; we exist as the products of a Creative Love.

But, as we have just seen, each one of us participates in the Divine Act in an incommunicable way. This means that God loves me with a unique love; in my own individuality, I am the "object" of a unique Divine Benevolence.

This realization will of course influence my obedience. I shall not obey like a slave, but rather like a son, in a fully spontaneous and grateful way. My "yes" to God will be a return of love, it will be adoration. Thus it will be a real act of liberty. Love by which I surrender myself gratefully to my Creator, and self-determination by which I realize myself as a transcendent hypostasis, are one and the same reality.

Authentic existence means loving personal fidelity.

We must still go one step further. As we know, our supreme realization will be characterized by "nearness to God", thus it will be our accession to a way of living in which we shall discover fully what God's love means to us. Now this supreme good cannot be won "through our own efforts"; it is the summit of a long ascent each stage of which can be reached only through the Creative Love at work in us. Thus the success of our journey, however much it may be the result of our daily struggles, must always be expected as God's gift; it depends entirely on the Divine Liberality. Consequently, we shall pray God to guide our steps and make us reach the end. This prayerful attitude will keep us from autonomous self-affirmation, from excessive self-reliance, and develop in us the awareness of our total dependence on God.

This prayer must be trustful. We know that the Act which creates us is Love, Benevolence. God desires our supreme good much more than we desire it because he desires it in his own Divine Way. Thus our prayer will be animated by faith in the Divine Fidelity.

This concludes our analysis of authentic existence considered in its immediate relation to God, our Creator. It is loving, grateful, prayerful and persevering obedience; therefore liberating self-realization.

We must now examine how this fundamental attitude will incarnate itself—without losing itself—in the world of our daily tasks and of our relations.

First of all, it must express itself in a general life-intention by which we take up in a personal manner the finality of our existence. This general intention will be a broad sketch, a project fixing beforehand the main lines of our life.

But how can a person know whether his life-project is in conformity with the intention constitutive of his own individuality?

Put in these terms, the problem is insoluble because it is presented in an artificial way. Remembering that a human life is essentially a genesis, a history, we shall try to understand how an authentic project can gradually be formed. Let us watch its maturation in the life of Ojoy which I present as the *type* of an increasingly authentic existence.

At the beginning of his life, his act does not realize itself in a personal way. However, it is already pushing forward, tending towards its emancipation. Under its drive, Ojoy's organism develops, assimilating more and more substance. His personality and human culture are gradually formed through his contacts with his surroundings and the education which he receives. Little by little Ojoy takes his life in hand; his act emerges from the flux of situations which it traverses and begins to dominate them—in doing so, it realizes itself as a transcendental activity. This realization is identical with the awakening in him of moral sense. Discovering his life as a totality which is oriented, Ojoy is able to feel whether his actions take him in the right direction; he is able to make a certain distinction (first in a lived and non-reflective manner) between good and bad. In this light, Ojoy forms his first life-project: I must remain good.

We could hardly overemphasize the role played by education in the awakening of Ojoy's moral sense. Education has developed in him a religious mentality: he believes in God, prays to God and knows that he must "please" God. Education has also made him alive to a few imperatives: he must obey his parents, speak the truth, be kind to all. In fact, pleasing God and observing these few elementary precepts have become for him synonymous. These first discoveries point already to something very deep. Ojoy has realized, not in a theoretical but in a lived way, that remaining good (his life-project) means serving God and is connected with very concrete attitudes at home, at school and wherever he goes; he understands vaguely that God speaks to him in various ways and that there is a way of saying yes to God.

As years pass, Ojoy's experience and culture develop; his religion becomes more personal; he tries to answer with increasing fidelity the call of God, that call which is addressed to him through all the circumstances of his life, through the situations which he traverses and through the persons he meets. At the same time, Ojoy looks more and more attentively at the world about him; he realizes his solidarity with all the people who live with him on earth and feels his responsibility towards them. He shares in their joys and their sorrows, desires intensely to make them happy and to bring them closer to God. This attention to the world is accompanied by a deepening of his temporal horizon. Ojoy looks more keenly, more determinedly, into the future and decides with increasing maturity what his whole life will be.

We are here in the presence of an undoubtedly authentic life project.

Indeed:

(a) This life project is the fruit of Ojoy's unflinching fidelity. The present has become for him, as it were, the sacrament of the Divine Presence, a word spoken at the very core of his existence, a message to which he must give a concrete answer, which he has to translate into a living attitude.

This fidelity of Ojoy to the call of the present has given to every moment of his life a character of authenticity. He has not allowed himself to deviate from what he felt to be God's way—the way which his very fidelity and exacting sincerity had made him follow by a kind of instinct. As a result, he has formed a life project which is beyond doubt inspired by the Divine Will at work in him.

Let us note well the atmosphere of spiritual liberty which pervades the entire process. Ojoy's fidelity to the present, his surrender to the Divine Call, is the true liberating attitude which keeps him master of the influences which act upon him, which makes of all his decisions real personal initiatives—these decisions are intensely, inalienably *his* to the very extent that they refuse to be anything but God's. We understand this when we realize that our human liberty and personality are essentially participations in the Divine Liberty, in the Pure Act.

(b) Through daily prayer and reliance on God, Ojoy has understood that a human life is a process which develops not in an independent, autonomous way but in essential relation to God, that each authentic progress in spiritual life must always be acknowledged as God's gift. He knows that he works in vain if God himself does not build what he tries to construct. His life project has been matured in this atmosphere of trustful familiarity with God: it is a sacred vocation. At the same time, however, it is Ojoy's own invention: something which he has shaped with the very stuff of his daily life; it is Ojoy's own decision, a determination of his personal free will.

(c) Ojoy's project is without illusions; it is the fruit of authentic self-knowledge. Self-consciousness is, as we know, an essential property of human life. Therefore each mode of consciousness implies a certain way of living to which it is inseparably bound—*it is* a certain manner of living reflecting itself. Now Ojoy's life has been fidelity: he has allowed each situation of his life to be itself in him—that is, to be in him what God meant it to be, to be authentic. Therefore each moment of his life has been characterized by truthfulness, by conformity between his attitude and God's creative design.[41] This is the light in which his life project has taken shape.

(d) Ojoy's life project is characterized by concern for the others. His fidelity has developed in him a deep awareness of his relation to his fellow-men and of the social value of his personal existence. As a result, he has decided that his life will be a service. Concern for other persons is an essential characteristic of any authentic life-project. The end towards which our life is ordered is our self-realization not simply as individual persons but as members of the eschatological community. Therefore we cannot reach the end alone; we are so vitally related to one another that the perfection of each one of us is closely linked with the perfection of all. This means that the finality immanent in our individual natures has both a personal and a social dimension. If our existence is authentic, this finality will express itself in selfless service.

This enables us to understand the nature of authentic love. It is not enough to say that love is the urge which drives me towards others. This urge in fact may be instinct with morbidity and sel-

[41] We meet here Heidegger's famous assertion: "Das Wesen der Wahrheit ist die Freiheit", freedom is the essence of truth. Freedom is defined by Heidegger: "Das Seinlassen von Seienden", the letting-be of what is.

Our study has shown us the essence of freedom in our personal conformity with the Divine Intention at work in us, in our world—an attitude of life characterized by total dependence on God and at the same time by self-determination and spontaneity. Now, as consciousness is essentially life-conscious-of-itself, as truth is conformity of our consciousness with reality (reality being understood as things-as-they-are-meant-to-be), as reality is essentially life, as freedom resides in the conformity of our personal life with God's Creative Intention (the act by which we allow God's plan to realize itself in us and through us), it follows that freedom is the essence of truth.

We must be quite clear that this does not open the way to subjectivism or relativism. Freedom properly understood does not mean doing-as-one-likes (which implies as a rule a lack of self-determination, and, therefore, the negation of freedom), but in doing God's will—that is, allowing the world to be and to become what it is meant to be.

Heidegger feels impelled to oppose his notion of truth to the medieval view according to which the truth of the judgment resides in the conformity of intellect and thing, a conformity which is based on the ontological Truth of the thing—that is, its conformity with the Divine Intellect. Had Heidegger examined more profoundly the implications of his own position, he would have realized its fundamental "Uberreinstimmung" with the medieval view.

fishness. True love, as a participation in Divine Love, is essentially benevolence; it is the act by which I wish others to be truly themselves, to attain their full human stature and to realize their own personality not only on earth but finally as members of the eschatological community; therefore it is my desire for the supreme good of my fellow-men. True love makes other persons the centres of my preoccupations and, in a way, the poles of all my aspirations. I wish to live for them, to forget myself, to lose myself in them. I wish their lives to become really authentic, I wish them to know, love and serve God. Love of God and love of my fellow-men are one and the same reality. Loving obedience to the Creator is loving service of men, his creatures.

Self-sacrificing service is a liberating attitude. The more I forget myself in order to serve my fellow-men, the more also I weaken the seductive power of the influences which tend to carry me away; therefore the more self-determined I am, the freer I become. I grow in spiritual freedom to the very extent that I sacrifice myself for the salvation of those with whom I live on earth. Self-annihilation is the condition of authentic self-realization.

Thus we have seen that freedom—the essential characteristic of man—because it is a participation in the Divine Act—must, to remain itself, be obedience; we have seen how this fundamental obedience must express itself in a life-project; we have also studied the condition which this project must fulfil in order to be and remain authentic—that is, to be and remain supremely free (as free as a human act can be). We must now consider briefly freedom in its relation to evil.

I have pointed out that, from the very beginning, cosmic evolution is constituted by a struggle—the struggle which opposes the obedient cosmic persons who tend towards their authentic realization and build the whole according to God's will to the rebellious cosmic persons who refuse obedience to the Creator and fill the universe with their destructive desires. This struggle is at the heart of every object, of every event, of every historical development. This means that in any created reality there is both a vivifying power which works for our good and a deceptive or debilitating presence which seduces us in order to ruin us.

As human persons, we are members of a community in which various trends manifest themselves. Some persons direct their lives and lead their worlds towards the end in a more or less effective and constant way, other persons give little thought to the other world and are almost entirely concerned with earthly pursuits. These conflicting tendencies pervade the whole human world, constitute each part and each element of it, constitute the whole of human history—they are especially active in places of greater human concentration (because each man makes his influence felt especially in his immediate surroundings). These human agencies, let it be noted, must not be considered apart from the activities of the cosmic persons. The human conflict depends, as it were, on the cosmic conflict and reflects it, it translates it in human terms.

These facts show us the concrete setting in which our existences must actuate themselves. In each situation in which we find ourselves, there is both an urge-upwards and a pull-downwards—sometimes the former predominates, sometimes the latter has, as it were, the whole field to itself and operates in an arbitrary way. Our freedom perfects itself when we accept the situations which we traverse as God's gifts, when we allow what is vivifying in them to realize itself in us, when we integrate them in our life project, in our movement towards God, our Supreme End. This integration is not effected "by itself"; it entails an effort on our part and a fight. Therefore to be free and remain free, we must remain vigilant and strive hard. Because we are thrown into a world in which evil abounds, because we are members of a sinful community, we cannot live in an authentic way without making of our existence a contest. Authentic existence is a purposeful and persevering struggle, and the end is a prize to be won.

2. Inauthentic Existence

Authentic existence is existence in freedom. It implies a self-surrender because our existence *is* dependence—but a self-surrender which liberates and perfects us, which makes us win back, increased and strengthened, what we give away.

The whole field which our life-act constitutes and animates is traversed and agitated by personal influences which drive us in various directions. Our life is confluence or involvement.

There is a way of being influenced or involved which personalizes us and there is a way which dissolves and alienates our freedom. Inauthentic existence is alienated existence; it is an existence which is, to a great extent, moved, possessed, by alien intentionalities.

Who are those personal powers whose magic operates in us and tends to conquer us? It must be clearly understood that they cannot be persons who conform their will to the Creator's will. Such persons, even though they move us, do not act in us in an overpowering or debilitating way. Their action, instinct as it is with respect and love, is a personalizing action; it tends to elevate us, to make us what the Creator wishes us to be. Surrendering to their influence is surrendering to God. The persons who try to hypnotize, corrode, bedevil us, who act in us in a disturbing way, who empty us of ourselves, are necessarily persons whose will is perverted and malevolent, persons rebelling against the Creator.

In this section, I shall not attempt the impossible task of analysing all the various ways in which our existence may fall into inauthenticity. My aim is simply to indicate a few types of alienated existence and to study the problem of inauthenticity in connection with that of liberty. (Inauthentic existence cannot be grasped at a single glance. Different approaches must be made because the realm of inauthenticity is that of dispersion, instability, and aimlessness. There is no "Ariadne's Thread" to enable us to follow the "direction" of inauthenticity.)

i. *Inauthentic Existences*

The Illusion of Independence. I want to be autonomous, my own master in every field. I want my ideas to be "original", not everybody's views, but uninfluenced, "personal" views. I want to remain a "free" man, not the prisoner of moral, social and domestic imperatives, but an independent "individual" who decides for himself how he must live. I want all my actions to be out of the common, to be "spontaneous initiatives"; I want to do things my own way, to use things as I please. In short, I want my life to stand entirely by itself.

I am asking for the impossible. I cannot think and express myself without borrowing and making mine the language of everybody and, with it, everybody's ideas. I cannot act or work without taking up and carrying out the human intentions constitutive of things. I cannot live without letting everybody's life flow in me, feed and inspire me. The more I try to be "original", the more I fall into incoherence, inconsistence, insanity.

It is an illusion. The effort I make to be independent is not and cannot be a purely self-creative initiative. In the act of affirming myself as an autonomous individual, I allow an urge present in me to take possession of me and become the whole of my life. This urge is myself, no doubt—it is an evolution of my life—but it is also the expression in me of an alien presence which occupies my field of existence and endeavours to realize itself through me in a particular way. My act of affirming myself as an independent individual, while being the realization of a personal craving, is a surrendering of my will to this allurement (these two things are one and the same reality). I want to be my own master; in fact, I enslave myself.

In every form of pride, of autonomous self-affirmation, there is such a surrender, and it deprives me of my freedom and blinds me. In the modalities of its expressive centre in which it possesses itself integrally, my personal act, instead of acknowledging itself as an act transcendentally given to itself, instead of linking itself luminously, reverently, to its Creative Source, coils upon itself in independence and arrogance, posits itself as I-alone. Nevertheless, my act remains dependent. Its "autonomous" self-positing is in fact the taking up of itself-already-there, of all its potentialities, of a surge rising from the depths of itself-incarnate. As I affirm myself "independently", I surrender to this vital impulse, I allow it to possess me. In doing so, I allow certain types of alien "agencies" to realize themselves in me and through me. My self-affirming is a self-alienating.

Pursuing a "Worldly" End. My life-act expresses itself in a definite act-project through which the finality constitutive of my individuality actuates itself in a conscious and deliberate way. The greater the conformity between my life intention and the Creative Will, the greater also my freedom. While allowing myself to be led by God, to be inspired by the "good spirits", I possess myself in a truly self-determined manner and I lead an authentic human existence.

It may be that I do not give my life an orientation conformable to the Divine Intention: it may be that I pursue a worldly end which is not in harmony with the transcendent goal of my existence.

I am a businessman and live only to increase my wealth, to make my trade "successful". To this end, I use all possible means. In the various situations in which I find myself, my act incarnate, directing itself deliberately and lucidly towards its appointed goal, makes its expressive field an embodiment of this project, organizes it, fashions it into a prefigurement of the end which it pursues. This process requires great attention, vigilance, experience and discernment; it requires a certain amount of self-discipline, purpose and energy; it requires also insensibility and ruthlessness.

My life as an unscrupulous businessman is not mere dispersion; it is not a succession of situations each of which is lived for itself without reference to any goal; it is a meaningful unity constituted by a leading intention—an intention constitutive of a particular world. Let us try to characterize this system:

(1) The volitive drive which gives my life its concrete direction, its meaning and value, is undoubtedly mine. *I* want to be a successful businessman, *I* study the ways, *I* take the necessary steps, *I* use the means to realize this project.

Who is this *I*?

My project has taken gradual shape in my daily contacts with the personal environment in which I have moved, as the result of actions and decisions which were my own responses to influences, suggestions or allurements. As it stands today, it is a surrender of myself to the determining presence and action of a certain world; it is the realization of this world in me, in my world, it is its directedness through me towards new forms of existence. My act-realizing-itself-through-my-project is myself qua dominated by personal forces at work in me; it is myself qua actuating these influences in a particular way.

This yielding of my personal act to worldly enticements puts it in a state of servitude; all its energies are exercised in a climate of self-alienation; its purposiveness, with all its strength, is the determination of a "self" which is tied and, in a certain way, lost.

(2) My world is a twisted, monstrous reality. The persons with whom I live are not acknowledged as transcendent hypostases who must be respected, who must be listened to, loved and served. They are debased, reduced to the state of instruments which must be properly maintained if they are "efficient", but which must be put aside if they are "useless", and which must even be destroyed if they prove to be hindrances on my way. My existential attitude makes all events and situations into soulless realities; in them, I perceive no call, I do not feel any presence which drives me out of myself—or, if I do perceive and feel something, I stifle the voice that speaks, I shake off the hand which tries to lift me up.

(3) These facts do not imply that my life has become a mere third-person process. I am and remain an indestructible hypostasis; all my activities proceed from a distinctive personal centre, they are

actuations of *my* life-act. I am not simply a plaything in the hands of other persons who do with me what they like. There is a certain unity in my life: I direct things in a deliberate way towards my end; in the very process of making them live as modalities of my act-in-tension-towards-its-appointed-goal I possess the reflectiveness and, therefore, the freedom required to discern the way in which I must deal with them. However, at the very heart of my initiatives, there is a continual self-abasing surrender which prevents me from appreciating persons and events truthfully, which prevents me from being really the master of things (in the way appointed by the Creator), which, therefore, weakens, decentres, falsifies, my reflectiveness and my liberty. However self-determined I remain, I am internally alienated, I lead a radically inauthentic human existence.

Aimlessness. I have to a very large extent failed to give my life a personal direction; I have no definite life intention, no aim in view. What is the meaning of my life? This question has never concerned me. I do not know, and I do not care. I live each day as it comes, yielding to whims, to influences and enticements, to sudden inspirations. My life is a succession of unconnected moves, of fitful behaviours. . . .

I have never outgrown childhood. My life has never taken reflective possession of itself, it has never attained true self-consciousness and freedom. At the same time, the world and others have remained for me shallow entities. All is inconsistent, meaningless.

I am continually driven by the personal forces which influence me, which "occupy" me; I am their things, the fulfilment of their cravings. . . .

Nevertheless, I remain a distinctive human person. My life-act remains a basically transcendental reality. All my behaviours pertain to it in a radically unique and inalienable way.

They pertain to me as moved by others in many ways: my life is the life-in-me of the strange world which surrounds me and possesses me. . . .

ii. *Inauthenticity within Authenticity*

These examples show types of existence in which inauthenticity prevails. But pure inauthenticity is a lower limit which cannot be reached because it supposes *total* self-annihilation. There is no human existence which can be so debased as to be *completely* alienated, and become *purely and simply* the act of another person; therefore all human existence is characterized by a certain degree, however low, of authenticity—inauthenticity always develops within a basic authenticity; an inauthentic human existence is a *true* human existence which has fallen from the state in which it should be and towards which it remains positively ordained (this is precisely what constitutes its deformity, its tragedy).

As a rule, every human existence is characterized by some particular form of inauthenticity. In most human existences, there are fluctuations between a higher and a lower degree of authenticity.

I give my life a transcendental destination, I ordain it deliberately towards a temporal end which is, which I wish to be, in conformity with its higher goal; which is, which I wish to be, therefore, in conformity with the Divine Intention. As a rule, I act in accordance with my fundamental project, I realize this project through particular initiatives; I make my activities prefigurements of my end; I surrender myself to the action of the "good spirits". At the same time, I allow the world to find in me its true meaning; I allow other persons to tend through me towards their authentic realization.

However, at times, I allow myself to be carried away by forces which I feel in me—this happens, for instance, when I yield to impatience or anger, to laziness or jealousy. At such moments, I give away a part of my freedom, my act loses its usual reflectiveness, my way of living becomes narrower and less meaningful. There is in me a conflict between the general movement of my will which persists and its present involvement—a conflict which reflects and crystallizes in a particular way the great cosmic conflict.

As a result of my yielding, the fundamental authenticity of my life decreases, my determination is weakened and my vision of the end obscured. At the same time, there is in my world less harmony, less truth, less light, less "presence". Other persons are emptied of their own transcendental selfhood and become "functions" of my subjective state.

iii. *Inauthenticity and Freedom*

Our whole study has shown us that freedom is the essential attitude of man. This freedom perfects itself in the act of obedience by which he surrenders his will to God. In any other surrender, it destroys itself.

Let us consider an example which shows how, when I follow a

misdirected course of conduct, I am, at least radically, responsible for what I do.

I am working in my room. As I look through the window, my eyes fall on three goats grazing in the garden. This view incenses me. I interrupt my work and soon find myself chasing away the three animals. Am *I* responsible for this?

As I concentrate on my philosophical study, I actuate in a particular manner my life-project. This activity is free because it is mine, because I carry it out in a self-possessed, purposeful manner. Nevertheless I do not commit the whole of myself to it definitively. The fact that from time to time distractions take my mind away from its thinking indicates clearly that, however tense my effort may be, there remains in me a field of unactuated potentialities, an interplay of dissipating influences, of incipient actions which absorb a great part of my vital energies. Therefore my self-determination, my freedom, though real, is deficient. I possess myself in an imperfect way.

The sight of the three goats grazing in the garden is from the very first lived by me in a particularly "moving" manner: it is a call to a particular course of action; it is already the beginning of this determinate activity.

By whom am I determined? The impulse which I experience is the realization in me of an interplay of personal intentions which constitutes these goats-grazing-in-my-garden as parts of the world-existing-without-me. As soon as they penetrate into my psycho-physiological field, these intentions tend to realize themselves in me through a particular behaviour. Thus, while being distracted from my philosophical study and incited to a particular course of conduct by an urge which I feel in me (i.e., by a phenomenon taking place in my psycho-somatic apparatus), I am in a true sense "determined" by personal forces at work "around" me.

But these forces do not, strictly speaking, *compel* me to action. I feel impelled, but to the extent that it is my will which is impelled, *I* allow myself to be depersonalized, my freedom allows itself (freely, of course) to dissolve. This means that, however strongly I am moved to action, I am, at least radically, responsible for what I do.

According to the moralists, a transgression, to be a "mortal sin", must be committed in a serious matter with full knowledge and deliberation.

I perform an action in a fully conscious and deliberate manner when, realizing clearly the value of what I do, I do it wilfully, freely. From what has come to light in our study, it appears that these conditions are realized when I act in conformity with the Divine Will. As it actuates itself in accordance with the Creative Intention, my personal life-act is filled with light and dynamism: it sees itself and the world in relation to the end, it ordains itself and the world towards the end in a truly personal, self-determined way.

However, even then, my personal act does not determine itself fully. However intense the impetus of my will, in what I do, I do not attain the full realization of what I am meant to become, I do not reach my end. Thus I remain in a state of potentiality; I go on living in a plural world in which many courses of conduct are open to me. This is why, though I tend lucidly and deliberately towards my end, I still feel moved in many directions, I still experience myself as a field of possibilities and desires.

Suppose that, while actuating itself freely in accordance with the Creator's Will, my personal act feels the seduction of a certain possibility of action which is not in harmony with its fundamental project. In the light proceeding from its Creative Source, light which it possesses by the very fact of its being attuned to the Divine Act, my personal act sees clearly the misdirected character of the course of conduct which is proposed to it. It is not likely to surrender itself to this attraction, because it is moving firmly towards its authentic realization. If, in spite of all, it allows itself to err, this transgression will be committed in a fully conscious and deliberate manner.

It may be that my personal act incarnate, faced by obstacles, pulled in many directions, experiencing in itself various tendencies, allows its tension towards its end gradually to relax. As this slackening takes place, my vision of the end and my understanding of everything in relation to the end, are obscured. Darkness begins to invade my world because my act no longer links itself to the light-giving Creative Source with the same passion, because it has to some degree given away its reflectiveness and its liberty. In this situation, were I to adopt a wrong course of conduct, my transgression would no longer be committed in a thoroughly conscious and deliberate manner (though it may still constitute a "serious offence" because of the experience which I have acquired—that is, because of the persistence in my present existential set-up—in some modified form —of my past knowledge and determination).

When we look at the world, we can see that a great number of people have never realized clearly the meaning of their existence and have never formed in themselves a definite life-project. This is due to many factors: the education which they have received (or rather the fact that they have been deprived of an authentic education), the influence of the human environment in which they have grown up, their own indifference, maybe their refusal to let themselves be guided by persons who wanted their good.

These people have never attained a high degree of authentic reflectiveness and freedom. Their daily actions are, therefore, performed in a partly unconscious way, with a lack of *true* deliberation.

(Does this mean that they cannot commit what is technically called a "mortal sin"? Not necessarily; it may be enough for them to commit serious offences *as deliberately as they can* to make these transgressions into "mortal sins". However, it probably means that true mortal sins are *de facto* very rare, and that many persons are practically unable to sin mortally. Who can be the judge of his fellow-men?)

Conclusion

We must close our enquiry. In this study, we have tried to penetrate to the heart of things. This effort has given us a new vision of the universe. Broad vistas are open before us. This work is not an end, but a starting-point. Through its meanderings, it tries to show the central perspective in which the various aspects of our experience must be integrated in order to be properly valued and understood. The investigation must be carried on in all directions: new facets of reality must be brought out; we must specify more precisely the ways in which the human world must be built and a human life must be lived. The field to be explored is limitless.

This exploration cannot be the work of one man. It is my humble request to philosophers and to those who are interested in the sciences of man to make their own the experience which this work tries to express, so that this experience may be enriched and deepened, so that the facts which the various scientific disciplines bring to light may be understood in their proper perspective, and our enquiries may be better orientated. This assimilation requires a great amount of careful study and meditation. Many prevailing views and ways of thinking need to be corrected; a new mental attitude must be adopted and a new feeling acquired. Above all, an instinct which makes us appreciate the meaning of each particular fact within the multipersonal totality must be developed. Only protracted efforts, only a personal realization of things, can bring about such a revolution.

The universe has revealed itself as a system formed by a plurality of interpenetrating, mutually dependent personal acts-worlds. These acts-worlds are ordained by God towards their supreme actuation, towards the attainment of their authentic perfection. Their authentic existence is in the movement by which they realize this destiny. In so far as the human community is concerned, the end to be reached by each member is his own self-realization in the eschatological community.

The fact is that a great number of persons do not progress harmoniously towards their supreme end; many refuse to carry out in a personal self-determined way the intention by which they are constituted. As a result, there is aberrance, ugliness, disharmony in the universe; there are tensions, hostilities, contradictions; there is struggle.

Let us turn our attention to the human community.

While "on earth", I mould my personality according to the manner in which I live. The "I" which will die one day and live on in a new way will be the "I" which my daily actions have built; it will be the realization of whatever my earthly existence has been. If my daily existence is an inauthentic human existence, if the aim which I pursue is not in conformity with the Divine Intention, I actuate myself in a twisted way, I build within myself a disordered and decentred personality.

Can this be remedied? Human experience and reflection tell me that it cannot be. Continual inauthenticity in the way of living, continual surrender to evil influences, continual refusal to do God's will, provoke a mental distortion, a spiritual blindness, which are practically incurable. It does not seem that a death-bed "conversion" could rebuild a whole life. What is required is a recasting of the whole personality, a total regeneration of the whole man. But who on earth can create a man anew?

While living on earth, I build not only my future, but the future of the whole human family; I build the eschatological community. What will this community be?

What I see in the world, what I experience in myself seem to indicate that it will not be the eschatological community intended by the Creator, but the constitution of a strange world in which the inauthenticity of man's existence will assume a definitive shape. No doubt, I must assert that those persons who lead on earth an authentic human existence are progressing towards authentic self-realization and working for the uplift of the whole human family, but what can they do against the forces which lead mankind towards an eternal failure? What will the community of the elect be in the midst of the huge gathering of the reprobate—*with whom they will remain vitally related*?

As a man-made affair, what is history? Apparently, it is the progress of man, of the human world, towards a final disharmony. The whole issue seems to be decided. . . . Unless there be a force—a person—at work in the world to redeem, redress, rejuvenate it, to take in hand the whole of history and, in spite of all, lead it towards its authentic goal.

What force? And what man?

We should not despair. We have seen that each man is the object of a unique Divine Benevolence: God creates me as I am and desires my supreme realization in the eschatological community, God wishes history to reach its end.

How does God's Redemptive Love operate concretely. Philosophical reflection does not enable me to answer this question.

Raghabpur, December 1965

Index

Preliminary Remarks: (1) *The World of Persons* is the methodical unfolding of a single experience. This should be kept in mind by those who make use of this Index. Each particular point, to be rightly understood, must be seen within the totality of which it is an integral element.

(2) The Index of a book has to be a useful instrument. It must help the reader, never mislead him. The nature of the present work is such that the study of some of its "key-concepts" covers practically the whole book or, at least, very large sections of it. These notions are entered in the present Index in bold type without reference to any particular page save that on which they are first introduced. In most cases, by perusing the "Contents" (pp. xxiii-xxviii), the reader will be able to see the manner in which the study of these "concepts" develops in the present work.

Da... Due